Lecture Notes in Computer Science 2970

Edited by G. Goos, J. Hartmanis, and J. van Leeuwen

Springer
Berlin
Heidelberg
New York
Hong Kong
London
Milan
Paris
Tokyo

Francisco Fernández Rivera   Marian Bubak
Andrés Gómez Tato   Ramón Doallo (Eds.)

Grid Computing

First European Across Grids Conference
Santiago de Compostela, Spain, February 13-14, 2003
Revised Papers

 Springer

Series Editors

Gerhard Goos, Karlsruhe University, Germany
Juris Hartmanis, Cornell University, NY, USA
Jan van Leeuwen, Utrecht University, The Netherlands

Volume Editors

Francisco Fernández Rivera
Univ. Santiago de Compostela, Fac. Física, Dpto. Electrónica y Computación
15782 Santiago de Compostela, Spain
E-mail: fran@dec.usc.es

Marian Bubak
ACC CYFRONET/ICS UMM
al. Mickiewicza 30, 30-059 Kraków, Poland
E-mail: bubak@uci.agh.edu.pl

Andrés Gómez Tato
CESGA
Avda.de Vigo s/n, 15706 Santiago de Compostela, Spain
E-mail: agomez@cesga.es

Ramón Doallo
Univ. A Coruña, Fac. Informática, Dept. Electrónica y Sistemas
15071 Coruña, Spain
E-mail: doallo@udc.es

Cataloging-in-Publication Data applied for

A catalog record for this book is available from the Library of Congress.

Bibliographic information published by Die Deutsche Bibliothek
Die Deutsche Bibliothek lists this publication in the Deutsche Nationalbibliografie;
detailed bibliographic data is available in the Internet at <http://dnb.ddb.de>.

CR Subject Classification (1998): C.2.4, D.1.3, D.2.7, D.2.12, D.4, F.2.2, G.2.1

ISSN 0302-9743
ISBN 3-540-21048-2 Springer-Verlag Berlin Heidelberg New York

Springer-Verlag is a part of Springer Science+Business Media

springeronline.com

© Springer-Verlag Berlin Heidelberg 2004

Typesetting: Camera-ready by author, data conversion by Olgun Computergrafik
Printed on acid-free paper   SPIN: 10987209   06/3142   5 4 3 2 1 0

Preface

On behalf of the Program Committee, it is a pleasure for us to introduce the proceedings of the 1st European Across Grids Conference. This event was held in Santiago de Compostela, Spain, February 13–14, 2003. The conference, organized by the University of Santiago (USC), the University of A Coruna (UDC) and the Supercomputing Center of Galicia (CESGA), was promoted by the European CrossGrid project and supported by the GridStart Cluster.

The idea of organizing this event was born within the CrossGrid community. CrossGrid is developing its middleware, tools and applications in collaboration with DataGrid and GridLab and is open to collaboration with other Grid projects. USC, UDC and CESGA enthusiastically supported the conference idea. We consider the Across Grids Conference to be an important contribution to the objectives of the GridStart project.

The aim of this 1st European Across Grids Conference was to forge an annual forum in which researchers linked to European projects could present their research results in the field of Grid computing. This conference does not intend to replace the Global Grid Forum. However, we do find that research being conducted within European projects deserves a special meeting in which all researchers participating in the Grid development challenge can exchange ideas, experiences and, chiefly, results. We would like the effort of organizing this forum to find continuity in the following years in other European cities.

Our first interest was to bring together as many European Grid projects as possible. We believe we have been successful in attaining this aim. Papers and posters from DataGrid, CrossGrid, Damien, DataTAG, GridWay and GridLab were presented, as well as results of research funded by national Grid projects, including NORDUGRID and several Spanish Grid initiatives, such as RedeGrid. Our second interest was to show all topics being dealt with in Grid computing research. We believe that this objective was also achieved: research work on testbeds, QoS, network performance, resource brokers, input/output, databases, and security issues was presented.

Finally, we wanted authors and attendees to come from all over Europe. Many institutions from Spain, Poland, Cyprus, Greece, France, Germany, Slovakia, Austria, Ireland, Romania, Hungary, Sweden, Finland, Italy and the Netherlands were represented at the conference.

As a research forum, the quality of the contents is an extremely important issue. Due to the short period of time in which we had to organize this event (less than 6 months), we begun by requesting a short abstract (no more than 4 pages) about the work to be defended. Every abstract was reviewed by a panel of experts from several countries around Europe, as well as by local researchers in the field. Every abstract underwent at least 2 reviews, and many of the abstracts were reviewed by up to 5 experts. The Program Committee selected the 28 best abstracts to be presented in oral sessions, and 11 more abstracts for poster presentations. The contributed papers were divided into four oral sessions (A, B, C and D) plus a poster session.

Papers presented in session A addressed Grid middleware architecture, tools, evaluating possible migration to the OGSA model, authorization in VOs, and resource management. Resource management for Grids is an important topic as the Grid is a heterogeneous, geographically distributed, and inherently dynamic system, so efficient algorithms for resource discovery selection, and co-ordination, as well as job scheduling, monitoring and migration are of great practical importance.

Session B comprised experiences with Grid testbed deployment and operation, data management and optimization of data access, middleware for parallel I/O on Grids, and Grid-based distant e-learning. Most papers in this session present various aspects of data management such as secure ways of publishing metadata, stream-oriented database management, data stripping for access to and processing of large databases, optimizations to use local resources, and multiagent approaches to accessing data repositories.

Session C was devoted to the deployment of large applications on Grids; in particular to Grid services for interactive applications that were built on top of the HLA, Grid services for visualization of simulations, development of the Grid-enabled air quality parallel simulation with MPICH-G2, investigations of the implementation on a Grid of self-organizing maps for data mining, partitioning problems, and, finally, a migrating desktop for Grid-enabled applications.

The main topics of Session D dealt with performance and monitoring on the Grid. These papers present concepts and tools for the analysis and prediction of performance characteristics of applications running on Grid environments. This, in turn, requires an efficient infrastructure for monitoring the Grid and the applications. Two papers present experiments with network performance measurements.

Contributions presented as posters addressed the concept of the Grid, an overview of European Grid projects, Grid infrastructure and application monitoring, multimedia service management based on Grid middleware, a component model based on CORBA for Grid computing, a combination of the Mobile Internet and the Grid for large-scale computing, and resource sharing, as well as applications of Grid computing in bioinformatics and particle physics.

Last, but not least, we want to thank all of the members of the International Advisory Committee who encouraged us to go ahead with this conference project, the Program Committee, and all of the people at USC, UDC and CESGA who worked hard to make this conference a successful event. Of course, none of this would have been possible without support from our sponsors: HP Invent, GridSystems and RedeGrid.

December 2003

Marian Bubak
Ramón Doallo
Andrés Gómez
Francisco F. Rivera

Organization

The 1st European Across Grids Conference was organized by the Department of Electronics and Computing, University of Santiago de Compostela, the Department of Electronics and Systems, University of A Coruña, and CESGA (the Supercomputing Center of Galicia) in cooperation with the CrossGrid Project.

Organizing Committee

Francisco Fernández Rivera	University of Santiago, Spain
Ramón Doallo	University of A Coruña, Spain
Andrés Gómez	CESGA, Spain
Tomás Fernández Pena	University of Santiago, Spain
Fernando Bouzas	CESGA, Spain

Program Committee

Andrés Gómez	CESGA, Spain
Brian Coghlan	TCD, Ireland
Dick van Albada	UVA, The Netherlands
Holger Marten	FZK, Germany
Jorge Gomes	LIP, Portugal
Jesús Marco	CSIC, Spain
Marian Bubak	Cyfronet-UCI, Poland
Marios Dikaiakos	University of Cyprus, Cyprus
Michal Turala	INP Krakow, Poland
Norbert Meyer	PSNC, Poland
Peter Sloot	UVA, The Netherlands
Yannis Perros	Algosystems, Greece

Referees

S. Benkner	R. Doallo	A. Hoheisel
P. Brezany	D. Erwin	W. Hoschek
M. Bubak	T. Fahringer	K. Iskra
J.C. Cabaleiro	S. Fisher	R. Jones
F. Carminati	W. Funika	P. Kacsuk
B. Coghlan	M. Gerndt	J. Kitowski
E. Deelman	V. Getov	D. Kranzlmueller
U. Der	A. Gómez	P. Kunszt
M. Dikaiakos	L. Hluchy	D. Kurzyniec

Sponsoring Institutions

HP Invent
GridSystems
Galician Network for Parallel, Distributed and Grid Computing (RedeGrid)
University of Santiago de Compostela (USC)
University of A Coruña (UDC)
Ministry of Science and Technology
Xunta de Galicia
Supercomputing Center of Galicia (CESGA)
Fundación Pedro Barrié de la Maza

Table of Contents

Experiences on Grid Resource Selection Considering Resource Proximity*

Eduardo Huedo[1], Rubén S. Montero[2], and Ignacio M. Llorente[1,2]

[1] Laboratorio de Computación Avanzada, Centro de Astrobiología (CSIC-INTA),
28850 Torrejón de Ardoz, Spain
[2] Departamento de Arquitectura de Computadores y Automática,
Universidad Complutense, 28040 Madrid, Spain

Abstract. Grids are by nature highly dynamic and heterogeneous environments, and this is specially the case for the performance of the interconnection links between grid resources. Therefore, grid resource selection should take into account the proximity of the computational resources to the needed data in order to reduce the cost of file staging. This fact is specially relevant in the case of adaptive job execution, since job migration requires the transfer of large restart files between the compute hosts. In this paper, we discuss the extension of the Grid$W$ay framework to also consider dynamic resource proximity to select grid resources, and to decide if job migration is feasible and worthwhile. The benefits of the new resource selector will be demonstrated for the adaptive execution of a computational fluid dynamics (CFD) code.

1 Introduction

Grids bring together resources distributed among different administration domains to offer a dramatic increase in the number of available compute and storage resources that can be delivered to applications. The Globus middleware [1] provides the services and libraries needed to enable secure multiple domain operation with different resource management systems and access policies. It supports the submission of applications to remote hosts by providing resource discovery, resource monitoring, resource allocation, and job control services.

However, application execution on grids continues requiring a high level of expertise due to its complex nature. The user is responsible for manually performing all the job submission stages in order to achieve any functionality: resource discovery and selection; and job preparation, submission, monitoring, migration and termination [2]. We have presented in [3] a new Globus experimental framework that allows an easier and more efficient execution of jobs on a dynamic grid environment in a "submit and forget" fashion. Adaptation to changing conditions is achieved by implementing automatic application migration following performance degradation, "better" resource discovery, requirement change, owner decisions or remote resource failure.

---

* This research was supported by Ministerio de Ciencia y Tecnología (research grant TIC 2003-01321) and Instituto Nacional de Técnica Aeroespacial (INTA).

F. Fernández Rivera et al. (Eds.): Across Grids 2003, LNCS 2970, pp. 1–8, 2004.

The most important step in job scheduling is resource selection, which in turn relies completely in the information gathered from the grid. Resource selection usually takes into account the performance offered by the available resources, but it should also consider the proximity between them. The size of the files involved in some application domains, like Particle Physics or Bioinformatics, is very large. Hence the quality of the interconnection between resources, in terms of bandwidth and latency, is a key factor to be considered in resource selection [4]. This fact is specially relevant in the case of adaptive job execution, since job migration requires the transfer of large restart files between the compute hosts. In this case, the quality of the interconnection network has a decisive impact on the overhead induced by job migration.

The architecture of the Grid*W*ay framework and its main functionalities are briefly described in Section 2. In Sections 3 and 4 we discuss the extension of the Grid*W*ay framework to also consider dynamic resource proximity to select grid resources, and to decide if job migration is feasible and worthwhile. The benefits of the new resource selector will be demonstrated in Section 5 for the adaptive execution of a computational fluid dynamics (CFD) code on a research testbed. Finally, in Sections 6 and 7 we describe related and future work, and give some conclusions about the brokering strategy presented in this research.

2   The Grid*W*ay Framework

Probably, one of the most challenging problems that the grid community has to deal with is the fact that grids present unpredictable changing conditions, namely: high fault rate, and dynamic resource availability, load and cost. Consequently, in order to obtain a reasonable degree of both application performance and fault tolerance, a job must be able to migrate among the grid resources adapting itself according to their dynamic characteristics.

The core of the Grid*W*ay framework is a personal *submission agent* that performs all the steps involved in job submission [2]. Adaptation to changing conditions is achieved by supporting automatic job migration. Once a job is initially allocated, it is dynamically rescheduled when the following events occur:

- A "better" resource is discovered
- The remote host or its network connection fails
- The submitted job is cancelled or suspended
- A performance degradation is detected
- The requirements or preferences of the application changed (self-migration)

The architecture of the *submission agent* is depicted in figure 1. The user interacts with the framework through a *request manager*, which handles client requests and forwards them to the *dispatch manager*. The *dispatch manager* periodically wakes up and tries to submit pending jobs to grid resources, it is also responsible for deciding if the migration of rescheduled jobs is worthwhile or not. Once a job is allocated to a resource, a *submission manager* and a *performance monitor* are started to watch over its correct and efficient execution.

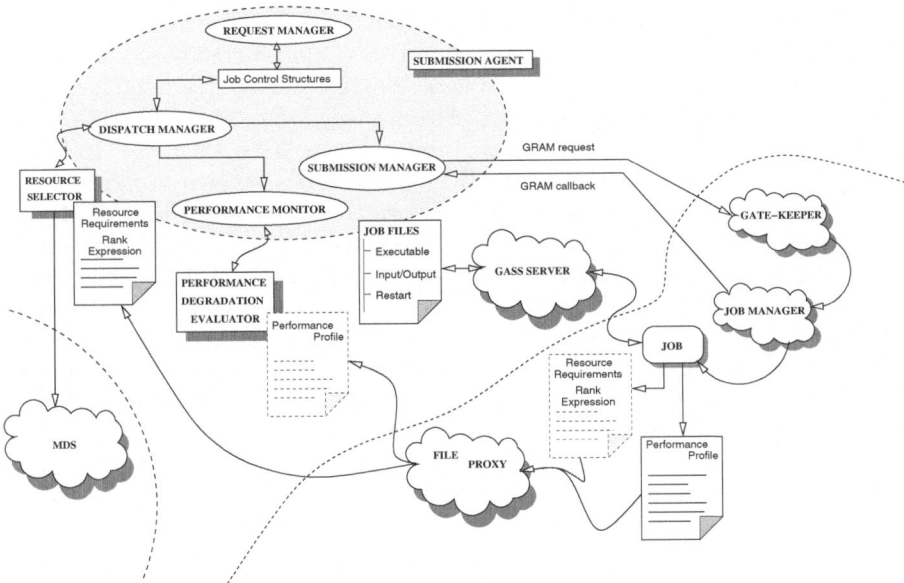

Fig. 1. The architecture of the Grid*W*ay framework.

The flexibility of the framework is guaranteed by a well-defined interface for each *submission agent* component. Moreover, the framework has been designed to be modular, to allow extensibility and improvement of its capabilities. The following modules can be set on a per job basis:

- *resource selector*, which builds a prioritized list of candidate resources
- *performance evaluator*, which is used to evaluate the application performance
- *prolog*, which prepares the remote system and performs input file staging
- *wrapper*, which executes the job and returns its exit code
- *epilog*, which performs output file staging and cleans up the remote system

3   Resource Selection Considering Proximity to Data

Due to the heterogeneous and dynamic nature of the grid, the end-user must establish the requirements that must be met by the target resources (discovery process) and a criteria to rank the matched resources (selection process). The attributes needed for resource discovery and selection must be collected from the information services in the grid testbed, typically Globus MDS. Resource discovery is usually based on static attributes (operating system, architecture, memory size...) taken from MDS GIIS (Grid Information Index Service), while resource selection is based on dynamic attributes (disk space, processor load, free memory...) taken from MDS GRIS (Grid Resource Information Service).

The dynamic network bandwidth and latency between resources will be also considered in the resource brokering scheme. Different strategies to obtain those network performance attributes can be adopted depending on the services available in the testbed. For example, Globus MDS could be configured to provide such information by accessing the Network Weather Service [5] or by activating the reporting of GridFTP statistics [6]. Alternatively, the end-user could provide its own network probe scripts or static tables.

The brokering process of the GridWay framework is shown in figure 2. Initially, available compute resources are discovered by accessing the MDS GIIS server and, those resources that do not meet the user-provided requirements are filtered out. At this step, an authorization test (via GRAM ping request) is also performed on each discovered host to guarantee user access to the remote resource. Then, the dynamic attributes of each host is gathered from its local MDS GRIS server. This information is used by an user-provided rank expression to assign a rank to each candidate resource. Finally, the resultant prioritized list of candidate resources is used to dispatch the job.

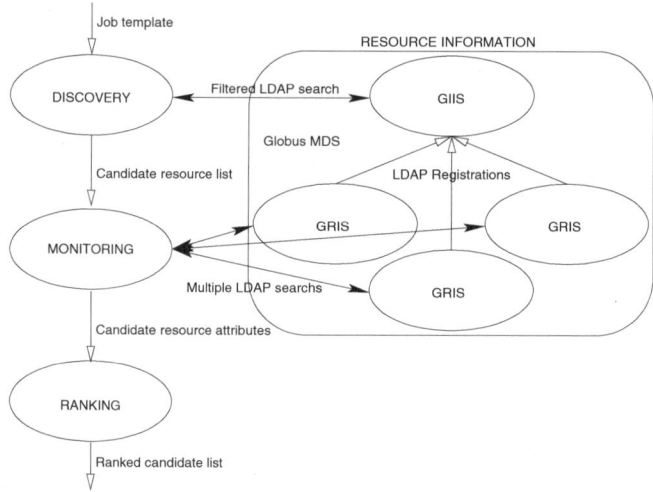

Fig. 2. The brokering process scheme of the GridWay framework.

The new selection process presented in this paper considers both dynamic performance and proximity to data of the computational resources. In particular, the following circumstances will be considered in the resource selection stage:

- The estimated computational time on the candidate host when the job is submitted from the *client* or migrated from other *execution host*.
- The proximity between the candidate host and the *client*, to reduce the cost of job submission, job monitoring and file staging.
- The proximity between the candidate host and a remote *file server*, to reduce the transfer costs of input or output files stored in such server.
- The proximity between the candidate host and the current or last *execution host*, to reduce the migration overhead.

4   Performance Model

In order to reflect all the circumstances described previously, each candidate host (h_n) will be ranked using the *total* submission time (lowest is best) when the job is submitted or migrated to that host at a given time (t_n). In this case, we can assume that the submission time can be split into:

$$T_{sub}(h_n, t_n) = T_{exe}(h_n, t_n) + T_{xfr}(h_n, t_n) \tag{1}$$

where $T_{exe}(h_n, t_n)$ is the estimated computational time and $T_{xfr}(h_n, t_n)$ is the estimated file transfer time.

Let us first consider a single-host execution, the computational time of a CPU-intensive serial application on host h at time t can be estimated by:

$$T_{cpu}(h, t) = \begin{cases} \frac{Op}{FLOPS} & \text{if } CPU(t) \geq 1; \\ \frac{Op}{FLOPS \cdot CPU(t)} & \text{if } CPU(t) < 1 \end{cases} \tag{2}$$

where $FLOPS$ is the peak performance achievable by the host CPU, $CPU(t)$ is the total free CPU at time t, as provided by the MDS default scheme, and Op is the number of floating point operations of the application.

However, the above expression is not accurate when the job has been executing on multiple hosts and then is migrated to a new one. In this situation the amount of computational work that have already been performed must be considered. Let us suppose an application that has been executing on hosts $h_0 \ldots h_{n-1}$ at times $t_0 \ldots t_{n-1}$ and then migrates to host h_n at time t_n, the overall computational time can be estimated by:

$$T_{exe}(h_n, t_n) = \sum_{i=0}^{n-1} t_{exe}^i + \left(1 - \sum_{i=0}^{n-1} \frac{t_{exe}^i}{T_{cpu}(h_i, t_i)}\right) T_{cpu}(h_n, t_n) \tag{3}$$

where $T_{cpu}(h, t)$ is calculated using expression 2, and t_{exe}^i is the time the job has been executing on host h_i, as measured by the framework. Note that, when n is 0, expressions 2 and 3 are equivalent.

Similarly, the following expression estimates the total file transfer time:

$$T_{xfr}(h_n, t_n) = \sum_{i=0}^{n-1} t_{xfr}^i + \sum_j \frac{Data_{h_n, j}}{bw(h_n, j, t_n)} \quad j = client, file\ server, exec\ host \tag{4}$$

where $bw(h_1, h_2, t)$ is the bandwidth between hosts h_1 and h_2 at time t, $Data_{h_1, h_2}$ is the file size to be transferred between them, and t_{xfr}^i is the file transfer time on host h_i, as measured by the framework.

When the job is rescheduled due to a resource discovery timeout, the *dispatch manager* chooses the lowest ranked (lowest estimated submission time) candidate host for a migration only if it has a lower rank than the rank of the current *execution host* when the job was submitted; otherwise the migration is rejected. Therefore, the job will be migrated only if migration is considered to be profitable. However, when the job is rescheduled due to a remote host failure or an user request, the *dispatch manager* always grants the migration to the lowest ranked host, even if it has a higher rank than the last *execution host*.

5   Experiments

The behavior of the resource selection strategy previously described is demonstrated in the execution of a CFD code in our heterogeneous research testbed, summarized on Table 1. The target application solves the 3D incompressible Navier-Stokes equations using an iterative multigrid method [7].

Table 1. Characteristics of the machines in the research testbed.

Name	Model	OS	Speed	Memory
ursa.dacya.ucm.es	Sun Blade 100	Solaris 8	500MHz	256MB
draco.dacya.ucm.es	Sun Ultra 1	Solaris 8	167MHz	128MB
columba.dacya.ucm.es	Intel Pentium MMX	Linux 2.4	233MHz	160MB
cepheus.dacya.ucm.es	Intel Pentium Pro	Linux 2.4	200MHz	64MB
solea.quim.ucm.es	Sun Enterprise 250	Solaris 8	296MHz	256MB

In the following experiments, the *client* is ursa, which holds an input file with the simulation parameters, and the *file server* is columba, which holds the executable and the computational mesh. The output file with the velocity and pressure fields is transferred back to the *client*, ursa, to perform post-processing. Table 2 shows the available machines in the testbed, their corresponding CPU performance (in MFLOPS), and the maximum bandwidth (in MB/s) between them and the hosts involved in the experiment.

Table 2. Candidate machines in the testbed along with their CPU performance and bandwidth between them and the machines involved in the experiment (*client*=ursa, *file server*=columba and *exec host*=draco).

h	CPU	$bw(h, client)$	$bw(h, file\ server)$	$bw(h, exec\ host)$
draco	175	0.4	0.4	∞
columba	225	0.4	∞	0.4
cepheus	325	0.4	0.4	0.4
solea	350	0.2	0.2	0.2

Table 3 shows the estimated submission time (1), computational time (3) and transfer time (4) for a single-host execution on each of the available hosts. Resource selection based only on the estimated computational time would allocate the application to solea (lowest T_{exe}). However, when the resource selection

Table 3. Estimated and measured times for a complete execution without migration.

h_0	$T_{exe}(h_0, t_0)$	$T_{xfr}(h_0, t_0)$	$T_{sub}(h_0, t_0)$	Measured time
draco	171	20	191	200
columba	133	10	143	146
cepheus	92	20	**112**	**120**
solea	**86**	40	126	134

Table 4. Estimated and measured times for a migrated execution from draco (h_0=draco, $T_{exe}(h_0, t_0)$=171, t_{exe}^0=65, t_{xfr}^0=10).

h_1	$T_{exe}(h_1, t_1)$	$T_{xfr}(h_1, t_1)$	$T_{sub}(h_1, t_1)$	Measured time
columba	148	30	178	184
cepheus	122	40	**162**	**170**
solea	**118**	70	188	196

strategy takes into account the file transfer time, the job is allocated to cepheus (lowest T_{sub}). The measured submission time presents a reduction of about 10% compared with the resource selection based only on CPU performance.

The influence of the file transfer size is even more relevant in case of an adaptive execution, as shown in Table 4. In this case a migration from draco to each of the available hosts in the testbed is evaluated. When only the CPU performance is considered in the resource selection process, the job is migrated to solea (lowest T_{exe}). However, if resource proximity is also considered, the application would migrate to cepheus (lowest T_{sub}) that implies a reduction of the submission time of about 14%, compared with the resource selection based only on CPU performance.

6   Related Work

The selection stage of computational resources has been widely studied in the literature. For example, the resource selection service presented in [8] uses an extension of the Condor matchmaking algorithm called set matching to provide selection of resource sets. However, it is focused on distributed HPC applications and it only takes into account the proximity between the resources within a resource set. Also, a framework capable to migrate applications based on load conditions is proposed in [9], although it considers the migration overhead as a constant. Finally, several mechanisms for storage resource selection [10] and data replication [11] based on proximity have been proposed. We apply some of these ideas to the selection of computational resources, taking into account the possibility of job migration to deal with the dynamic nature of the grid.

7   Conclusions and Future Work

In this work we have analyzed the relevance of resource proximity in the resource selection process, in order to reduce the cost of file staging. In the case of
adaptive job execution the quality of the interconnection network has also a decisive impact on the overhead induced by job migration. In this way, considering
resource proximity to the needed data is, at least, as important as considering
resource performance characteristics. We expect that resource proximity would
be even more relevant for greater file sizes and more heterogeneous networks.

We are currently applying the same ideas presented here to develop a *storage
resource selector* module. The storage resource selection process is equivalent to
the one presented in figure 2, although the discovery process is performed by
accessing the Globus Replica Catalog. The resource selection is based on the
bandwidth between the selected compute resource and the candidate storage
resources, along with the values gathered from the MDS GRIS.

References

1. Foster, I., Kesselman, C.: Globus: A Metacomputing Infrastructure Toolkit. Intl.
   J. of Supercomputer Applications **11** (1997) 115–128
2. Schopf, J.M.: Ten Actions when Superscheduling. Technical Report GFD-I.4, The
   Global Grid Forum: Scheduling Working Group (2001)
3. Huedo, E., Montero, R.S., Llorente, I.M.: A Framework for Adaptive Execution
   on Grids. Intl. J. of Software – Practice and Experience (2004) (in press).
4. Allcock, W., et al.: Globus Toolkit Support for Distributed Data-Intensive Science.
   In: Proc. of Computing in High Energy Physics. (2001)
5. Wolski, R., Spring, N., Hayes, J.: The Network Weather Service: A Distributed
   Resource Performance Forecasting Service for Metacomputing. J. of Future Generation Computing Systems **15** (1999) 757–768
6. Vazhkudai, S., Schopf, J., Foster, I.: Predicting the Performance of Wide-Area Data
   Transfers. In: Proc. of Intl. Parallel and Distributed Processing Symp. (2002)
7. Montero, R.S., Llorente, I.M., Salas, M.D.: Robust Multigrid Algorithms for the
   Navier-Stokes Equations. Journal of Computational Physics **173** (2001) 412–432
8. Liu, C., Yang, L., Foster, I., Angulo, D.: Design and Evaluation of a Resource Selection Framework for Grid Applications. In: Proc. of the Symp. on High-Performance
   Distributed Computing. (2002)
9. Vadhiyar, S., Dongarra, J.: A Performance Oriented Migration Framework for the
   Grid. In: Proc. of the Intl. Symp. on Cluster Computing and the Grid. (2003)
10. Vazhkudai, S., Tuecke, S., Foster, I.: Replica Selection in the Globus Data Grid. In:
    Intl. Workshop on Data Models and Databases on Clusters and the Grid. (2001)
11. Lamehamedi, H., Szymanski, B.K., Deelman, E.: Data Replication Strategies in
    Grid Environments. In: Proc. of 5th Intl. Conf. on Algorithms and Architectures
    for Parallel Processing. (2002)

Decentralized vs. Centralized Economic Coordination of Resource Allocation in Grids

T. Eymann[1], M. Reinicke[1], O. Ardaiz[2], P. Artigas[2], L. Díaz de Cerio[2],
F. Freitag[2], R. Messeguer[2], L. Navarro[2], D. Royo[2], and K. Sanjeevan[2]

[1] Institute for Computer Science and Social Studies,
Albert-Ludwigs-University, Freiburg, Germany
{eymann,reinicke}@iig.uni-freiburg.de
[2] Computer Architecture Department,
Polytechnic University of Catalonia, Barcelona, Spain
{oardaiz,partigas,ldiaz,felix,meseguer,leandro,dolors,sanji}@ac.upc.es

Abstract. Application layer networks are software architectures that allow the provisioning of services requiring a huge amount of resources by connecting large numbers of individual computers, like in Grid or Peer-to-Peer computing. Controlling the resource allocation in those networks is nearly impossible using a centralized arbitrator. The network simulation project CATNET will evaluate a decentralized mechanism for resource allocation, which is based on the economic paradigm of the Catallaxy, against a centralized mechanism using an arbitrator object. In both versions, software agents buy and sell network services and resources to and from each other. The economic model is based on self-interested maximization of utility and self-interested cooperation between agents. This article describes the setup of money and message flows both for centralized and decentralized coordination in comparison.

1 Decentralized Resource Allocation Mechanisms and the Grid

Private computer centers, shielded from public networks, provide computation and data storage as a closed, private resource, and are mostly controlled by central arbitrator objects. In contrast, the openly accessible Internet resource pool offers more than 150 million connected hosts, and the number is growing exponentially, without any visible control instance. Even if only a fraction of this processing and storage capacity could be allocated properly, the resulting computation power would exceed private networks by far.

Currently there exist some Internet-wide public resource infrastructures, which are called Grids and Peer-to-Peer systems. Grids are Internet accessible computational resources provided to grid users for execution of computational intensive parallel applications. Peer-to-Peer systems are end-users computer connected to the Internet which provide their computational and/or storage resources for other end-users usage.

F. Fernández Rivera et al. (Eds.): Across Grids 2003, LNCS 2970, pp. 9–16, 2004.

A Grid Application Network scenario would be the distributed provisioning of web services for Adobe's Acrobat (for creating PDF files) in an Akamai-like application layer network; word-processor client programs would transparently address the nearest/cheapest Acrobat service instance. The overall objective in the network would be (a) to always provide access to Acrobat service, such that a minimum number of service demands have to be rejected, and (b) to optimize network parameters such as provisioning costs and network communication.

In order to keep such a network operational, service control and resource allocation mechanisms are required. However, these mechanisms are realized in existing operational large-scale distributed systems by employing a centralized coordinator instance (like an auctioneer or an arbitrator). This centralized approach has several drawbacks.

A first prerequisite for a central coordination instance to work properly is that the environment does not change its state between the beginning and the end of the computation process. Grid application networks, however, are very dynamic and fast changing systems: service demands and nodes connectivity changes are very frequent, and new different services are created and composed continuously.

A second related property is that the coordinator should have global knowledge on the state of the network. This is mostly achieved by calculating the time steps such that actual status information from all nodes arrives safely at the coordination instance. However, if the diameter of the network grows, this approach leads to long latency times for the nodes.

Third, a centralized coordinator is part of the problem that decentralized grid application networks are trying to solve: As bids and offers have to route through the network to the single instance which collects global knowledge and computes the resource allocation, the distribution and deployment of services throughout the network is counteracted. This is currently not a problem as the control information is small compared to the allocation data itself, but may increase when the principle is applied to more and more application areas.

These drawbacks lead to the search for a truly decentralized coordination concept which is able to allocate services and resources in real-time without a dedicated and centralized coordinator instance. This concept should on one hand be able to cope with technical shortcomings like varying amounts of memory and disk space, internet connection speed and sporadic appearance and disappearance of the services. On the other hand, it is desirable that the network as a whole shows optimised behavior with regard to low overhead communication, short computation times, pareto-optimal resource allocation.

Recent research in Grid computing has also recognized the value of price generation and negotiation, and in general economic models for trading resources and services and the regulation of supply and demand of resources in an increasingly large-scale and complex Grid environment. Examples are the Nimrod/G Resource Broker and the GridBus project [4].

As a free-market economy is able to adjudicate and satisfy the conflicting needs of millions of human agents, it would be interesting to evaluate if this decentralized organizational principle could also be used for coordination of grid application networks. In the remainder of this article, we first introduce a decentralized economic concept for coordination, the Catallaxy, and describe the CATNET project. The following section describes money and message flows in the grid application network economic model, both with a centralized (baseline) and a decentralized implementation. The article closes with some preliminary results and an outlook on the applicability of the concept to various domains.

2   Decentralized Economic Coordination: The Catallaxy Paradigm and the CATNET Project

In grid application networks, different types of resources can be scarce such as storage, bandwidth, and CPU cycles. Optimization criterions for allocating these resources can be based on cost-efficiency, performance or a combination of parameters. In this work, our goal is to develop a simulator, which allows to experimentally compare two main resource allocation strategies: A centralized approach in which decisions are taken centrally and a decentralized approach, where local agents negotiate resources using economic models.

The Catallaxy coordination approach [6] is a coordination mechanism for systems consisting of autonomous decentralized hard- or software devices, which is based on constant negotiation and price signaling between the devices. The mechanism is based on efforts from both agent technology and economics, namely agent-based computational economics [13], to develop new technical possibilities of coordinating decentralized information systems consisting of autonomous software agents. The software agents are able to adapt their strategies using machine learning mechanisms, and this constant revision of strategies leads to a co-evolution of software agent strategies, a stabilization of prices throughout the system and self-regulating coordination patterns [6]. The resulting patterns are comparable to those witnessed in human market negotiation experiments.

Earlier work in computer science has used economic principles for resource allocation in operating systems, packet routing in computer networks, and load balancing in distributed computer systems [5]. Most of these approaches rely on using a centralized auctioneer and the explicit calculation of an equilibrium price as a valid implementation of the mechanism. A successful implementation of the Catallaxy paradigm for a distributed resource allocation mechanism promises the advantage of a more flexible structure and inherent parallel processing compared to a centralized, auctioneer- based approach.

The goal of the CATNET project is thus to evaluate the Catallaxy paradigm for decentralized operation of grid application networks in comparison to a baseline centralized system. For the evaluation of the overall success of the control mechanism, we will use the "maximum social welfare-criterion", which is the sum of all utilities of the participating nodes [11]. This criterion balances both costs and revenue incurred by the nodes and allows comparing different variants of the Catallaxy and baseline implementations.

Social welfare maximizing solutions are a subset of "Pareto-efficient" ones; once the sum of the payoffs is maximized, an agent's payoff can increase only if another agent's payoff decreases [14]. The resource allocation efficiency of an agent adds to the revenue, while communication cost, measured as the ratio of data to control bandwidth consumption, adds to the costs. Increasing performance and decreasing communication in the whole network thus directly computes to relatively maximize social welfare. As this property also holds for local optima of the solution space, "social welfare" is considered to be the main, but not the only evaluation parameter. Other evaluation parameters will be the network traffic and service access latency.

3   Money and Message Flows in the Grid and Application Network

The lifecycle of a grid application network can be divided in two phases, the deployment and the allocation phase.

The goal of the deployment phase is the initial positioning of new resources, services, and service copies [2]. We assume that the deployment phase has already been carried out and services are initially located in the network.

The allocation phase, which is in the main focus here, changes resource allocations during the runtime of the network, meaning a re-allocation of the initial positions found in the deployment phase. During the runtime of the network, software agents in the network nodes buy and sell access to network service copies using a heuristic and adaptive negotiation strategy. Changes in prices for certain services reflect changes in the supply and demand situation, which are propagated throughout the network. Both client and service provider agents will adapt their strategies about where to buy and sell based on the received information, and thus continuously change the state of the network.

3.1   The CATNET Network Simulator

CATNET is a simulator for a generic grid application network (GAN). This GAN simulator is implemented on top of the JavaSim network simulator. It can be configured to simulate a specific GAN, such as a content distribution network or Peer-to-Peer network. Different agent types can be instantiated, namely clients, resource agents, and service agents. Network resources to be allocated encompass service access, bandwidth and storage.

JavaSim is a component-based, compositional simulation environment [3], [8]. It is a discrete event simulator targeted at networking research that provides support for simulation of real network topologies and grid application services, i.e. data and control messages among application network instances.

For the purpose of network modeling and simulation, the model defines on top of the autonomous component architecture a generalized packet switched network model. It describes the generic structure of a node (either an end host or a router) and the generic network components, which can both be used as base classes to implement protocols across various layers.

The CATNET application simulates two main control mechanisms for network coordination: a "baseline" control mechanism and a "catallactic" control mechanism. The baseline control mechanism computes the resource allocation decision in a centralized service/resource provider. The catallactic control mechanism has the characteristic that its resource allocation decisions are carried out by self-interested agents with only local information about the environment. Each agent has a resource discovery facility and a negotiation strategy module. The following class types are defined:

- Client: a computer program on a certain host, which needs access to a web service to fulfill its design objectives. The Client (C) tries to access that "service" at an arbitrary location within the computer network, use it for a defined time period, and then continues with its own program sequence. Client programs run on a connected network "resource".
- Service: an instantiation of a general application function, embodied in a computer program.
- Service Copy: one instance of the "service". The service copy (SC) is hosted on a "resource" computer, which provides both storage space and bandwidth for the access of the service.
- Resource: a host computer, which provides a limited number of storage space and access bandwidth for service transmission. Resources (R) are connected to each other via dedicated network connections.
- Network Connections: These connections are intended to be of equal length and thus of equal transmission time and costs.

The trace collection of the simulation execution is done via a database for processing at a later stage after the simulation.

3.2   Message Flows in the Baseline Model

In order to simulate different control mechanisms we first consider the baseline system as a special case of the generic catallactic control mechanism. Through configuration in input scripts, different behavior of the simulator can be set up. As a consequence, the comparison of simulation results should become easier to control and the development efforts focus on a single, generic system.

As Fig. 1.a shows, the centralized baseline mechanism employs a dedicated service coordinator (the master service copy, MSC), which is known to the individual service copies.

The client broadcasts a "request_service" message on its network connections. Either the receiving resource (R) provides a service copy (SC) of the requested type or not. If a SC is available, the resource routes the request to that service copy, adding its costs for storage and bandwidth consumption. The SC directs the request to the Master Service Copy (MSC), provided with information about costs and the amount of the message's hop counter, i.e. the number of passed resources, indicating the distance to the requesting client.

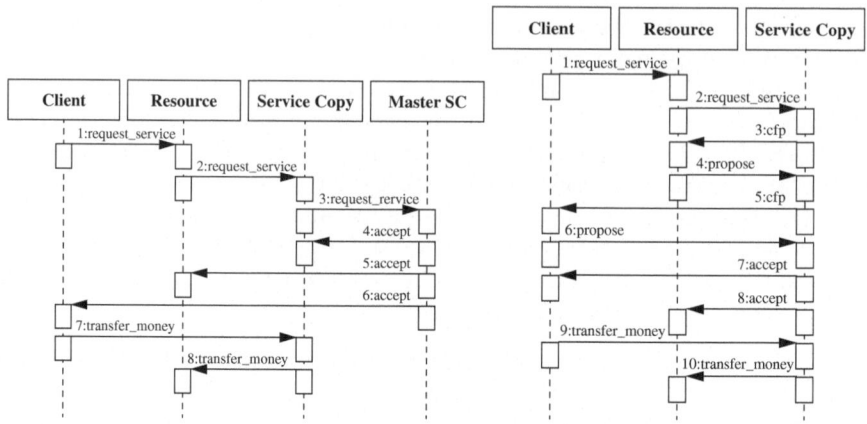

Fig. 1. Money and Message Flows. a) Baseline Approach; b)Catallactic Approach

Resource hosts (R) forward the received request – independent of the successful detection of the service – to their neighboring resource hosts, increasing the message's hop counter. Using this procedure, all adjacent resources will be inquired. If the hop counter exceeds a given number, the message is discarded.

The MSC receives all the information from the R/SC pairs, is able to compute the costs of providing a service and sends back an accept/propose message revealing the "cheapest" SC to the client. In addition, it informs the selected R/SC pair. The resource allocates a timeslot and the SC provides the service.

Contracts have to be fulfilled; a re-negotiation of allocations is out of the project's scope. Right after the service has been provided to the client, the client sends the formerly agreed reward to the SC, which redirects the payment share for bandwidth and storage to its R host.

3.3   Message Flows in the Catallactic Model

The Catallactic control mechanism has the characteristic that its resource allocation decisions are carried out by decentralized SCs with only local information about the environment; see Fig. 1.b.

Again, the clients send out a "service_request" message on its network connections in a Gnutella-like fashion [1]. The receiving resource forwards the message to the neighboring resource hosts. If the resource holds a SC of the requested type, the resource routes the request to it. In order to return a valid quote to the client, the SC has to inquire the resource about the provisioning costs by initiating a negotiation for bandwidth costs. A successful negotiation allows the SC then to negotiate for the price for the provision of the service with the client, like in a very shallow iterated contract net protocol [12].

The client orders all incoming proposals in its inbox and subsequently negotiates for service access. It is guided in its strategy by the subjective market price, which is computed from all price quotes the agent gets "from the market", regardless of the particular sender. If the initial offer price does not match within an interval around the market price, the negotiation will be discontinued. Otherwise, the agents will engage in a bilateral alternating offers protocol [10] until acceptance or final rejection of the offer.

An accept message from the client lets the SC confirm both negotiations (with the resource for bandwidth and with the client for service provision). The resource reserves bandwidth and the contracts are sealed. The service provision is mirrored by the according money flow. On the other hand, a reject message from the client immediately stops further negotiation and initiates a reject message from the SC to the resource.

To maximize utility, the agents will change their initial offer prices, starting with demand and supply prices given in an input data script, according to the following scheme: Rs and SCs as sellers will lower their offer price by one money unit if the negotiation was not successfully finished. They will raise their initial price by one money unit after an offer has been accepted. The clients and SCs as buyers will change their initial prices vice versa.

If a SC has been turned down several times (having sent propose messages but never received an "accept"), it will try to relocate to another resource. According to the major share of received request messages, measured by incoming connections, the SC will ask the neighboring resource host for a free storage slot. If that target resource is fully occupied, the SC will ask the second-often relay of request messages and so on. If successful, the SC initializes a new instance at the target resource host and deletes the old instance. The overall effect is that SCs move themselves around the network in the physical direction of the demand. In the baseline approach, the SC wanting to relocate sends a query message to the MSC, who will inform the SC about where to relocate to.

4   Conclusion and Outlook

One of the goals of the CATNET project is the setup for a network simulator which can simulate different coordination models. This article shows how centralized and decentralized coordination can be supported with a relatively simple addition to the negotiation protocol, so that comparable results are produced. The findings can be visualized using NAM [9];

The final evaluation whether the baseline or catallactic mechanism receives better results has not been made yet. This result will be achievable in the last project phase in spring 2003. For the time being, the CATNET simulator in itself already allows investigation into allocation and messaging behavior in grid application networks.

If CATNET is successful with regard to the Catallactic control mechanism, allocation and scheduling questions in other decentralized network domains like hospital logistics, factory logistics or adaptive supply chain management [7] could also be targeted.

In our view, CATNET stands at the very beginning of research into Catallactic Information Systems. Future research work can be divided into an agent technology layer and an application-specific layer. Both are linked in a feedback loop. On one hand, the technology has to constantly (and imperfectly) model an ever-changing state of the application world. On the other hand, technology's results and the behavior of its single elements directly influence the application state by means of self-organization.

Future research will address the design of control institutions for large, open, and heterogeneous agent societies. These institutions should influence the multi-agent systems to enable them to emergently develop towards a state of desirable global behavior where security, trust and welfare are provided to all participants.

References

1. Adar, E., Huberman B.A.: Free Riding on Gnutella. First Monday, 5, 10, 2000. http://www.firstmonday.dk/issues/issue5_10.
2. Ardaiz, O., Freitag, F., Navarro, L.: Multicast Injection for Application Network Deployment. 26nd IEEE Conference on Local Computer Networks.Tampa, Fla., 2001.
3. Breslau, L., Estrin, D., Fall, K., Floyd, S., Heidemann, J., Helmy, A., Huang, P., McCanne, S., Varadhan, K., Xu, Y., Yu H.: Advances in Network Simulation. IEEE Computer, 33, 5, 59-67, 2002. http://ceng.usc.edu/~helmy/vint-computer-mag-article.pdf.
4. Buyya, R., Abramson D., Giddy J.: A Case for Economy Grid Architecture for Service-Oriented Grid Computing. 10th IEEE International Heterogeneous Computing Workshop (HCW), 2001.
5. Clearwater, S.H.: Market-based control a paradigm for distributed resource allocation. World Scientific, Singapore, 1996.
6. Eymann, T.: Co-Evolution of Bargaining Strategies in a Decentralized Multi-Agent System. AAAI Fall 2001 Symposium on Negotiation Methods for Autonomous Cooperative Systems, 2001.
7. Eymann, T., Padovan, B.: The Catallaxy as a new Paradigm for the Design of Information Systems. Proceedings of The World Computer Congress of the International Federation for Information Processing, 2000.
8. JavaSim Project: JavaSim. Ohio State University, EEng Dept. http://www.javasim.org.
9. NS/NAM Project: NAM Network Animator. USC Information Sciences Institute, 2002. http://www.isi.edu/nsnam/nam/index.html
10. Rosenschein, J.S., Zlotkin, G.: Rules of encounter - designing conventions for automated negotiation among computers. MIT Press, Cambridge, 1994.
11. Sandholm, T.W.: Negotiation Among Self-Interested Computationally Limited Agents. University of Massachusetts, Amherst, 1996.
12. Smith, R.G.: The Contract Net Protocol: High-Level Communication and Control in a Distributed Problem Solver. IEEE Trans. on Computers, 29, 1104-1113, 1980.
13. Tesfatsion, L.: How economists can get alife. Arthur, W.B., Durlauf, S., and Lane, D.A. (eds.). The Economy as a Evolving Complex System II, 533-564. Addison Wesley, Redwood City, CA, 1997.
14. Varian, H.R.: Intermediate Microeconomics. W.W. Norton, New York, 1999.

The EU-CrossGrid Approach
for Grid Application Scheduling*

Elisa Heymann[1], Alvaro Fernández[2], Miquel A. Senar[1], and José Salt[2]

[1] Universitat Autónoma de Barcelona, Barcelona, Spain
{elisa.heymann,miquelangel.senar}@uab.es
[2] Instituto de Física Corpuscular, Valencia , Spain
{alvaro.fernandez,salt}@ific.uv.es

Abstract. This paper presents the approach being followed to implement scheduling components that are integrated as part of the EU Cross-
Grid project. The purpose of these components is to provide a basis for
supporting the efficient execution of distributed interactive applications
on Grid environments. When a user submits a job, the scheduling services search for the most suitable resources to run the application and
take subsequent steps to ensure a reliable launching of the application.
All these actions are carried out according to user-defined preferences.

1 Introduction

The Grid is an abstraction of distributed heterogeneous systems that has gained
much attention in recent years, as shown by current initiatives such as the Gri-
Phyn, iVDT, GrADS, EU-DataGrid, GridLab or EU-CrossGrid projects. The
middleware infrastructure provided by these projects will greatly simplify the
process of application deployment on computational grids.

In particular, the main objective of the EU CrossGrid project is to take advantage of a collection of machines distributed across Europe, and that constitute
a Grid, by making it available to execute user applications. The applications that
will use this Grid are mainly parallel and interactive. Although the project will
initially benefit from EU Datagrid middleware [1], specific components are currently under development in order to target the concrete requirements of Cross-
Grid applications. Specifically, new resource-management services will be needed
to control the execution of user applications written in MPI in an automatic,
reliable and efficient way.

Datagrid has developed a whole resource management system that was originally targeted to sequential applications. It is based on the Condor ClassAd [2]
library for carrying out resource selection and, in the near future, it plans to
support MPI applications running on a single cluster. In the CrossGrid resource
management, we have adopted the same formalism used in Datagrid to describe

---

* This work has been partially supported by the European Union through the IST-
2001-32243 project "CrossGrid" and partially supported by the Comisión Interministerial de Ciencia y Tecnología (CICYT) under contract TIC2001-2592.

F. Fernández Rivera et al. (Eds.): Across Grids 2003, LNCS 2970, pp. 17–24, 2004.

jobs [3]. Additionally, our first prototype has been built on the current Datagrid Resource Broker, in order to provide additional support for parallel applications.

There are a number of ongoing research efforts in Grid computing that are considering task allocation problems. Nimrod-G [4] is a tool for the automated modeling and execution of parameter sweep applications (parameter studies) over global computational grids. The AppLeS project [5] has been developing schedulers that were generally developed as prototypes to support research into application-level scheduling algorithms for specific applications. However, these schedulers were not general-purpose, to be used for any application. Recent efforts in the GrADS project [6] try to generalize this approach by decoupling the scheduler core that carries out the search procedure from the application-specific and platform-specific components. The GrADS approach, however, requires a performance model that is an analytical metric for predicting application execution times on a given set of resources.

Within this framework, this paper describes our resource-management approach designed for the CrossGrid project. The paper is organized as follows: Section 2 describes the overall architecture of our resource management services, Section 3 describes two of the main services and Section 4 contains the final conclusions of this work.

2 General Architecture of CrossGrid Resource Management

This section describes the global architecture of our scheduling approach. The scenario that we are targeting consists of a user who has a parallel application and wishes to execute it on grid resources. When users submit their application, our scheduling services will be responsible for optimizing scheduling and node allocation decisions on a user basis. Specifically, they will carry out three main functions:

1. Select the "best" resources that a submitted job can use. This selection will take into account the application requirements needed for its execution, as well as certain ranking criteria used to sort the available resources in order of preference.
2. Perform the necessary steps to guarantee the effective submission of the job onto the selected resources. The application is allowed to run to completion.
3. Monitor job execution and report on job termination.

Figure 1 presents the main components that constitute the CrossGrid resource-management services. A user submits a job to a Scheduling Agent (SA) through a web portal. The job is described by a JobAd (Job Advertisement) using the EU-Datagrid Job Description Language (JDL) [3], which has been conveniently extended with additional attributes to reflect the requirements of interactive and parallel applications. The main attributes added are the following:

- *JobType*: Type of executable: this attribute differentiates between sequential and MPI jobs. Two types of MPI jobs are supported: MPICH-P4, (MPI jobs prepared to run only on a single cluster) or MPICH-G2 (MPI jobs prepared to run over multiple sites).
- *NumCPU*: Number of CPUs required by the job (required for MPI applications).
- *Priority*: Value in the rank 0...20, describing the priority of the job (lower values imply higher priorities; high-priority interactive jobs should have value 0).

The SA selects candidate resources to run the application by sending the Resource Searcher the JobAd containing all the requirements and preferences that the job needs for its execution. The Resource Searcher returns a list with all the combinations of suitable resources available for running the job.

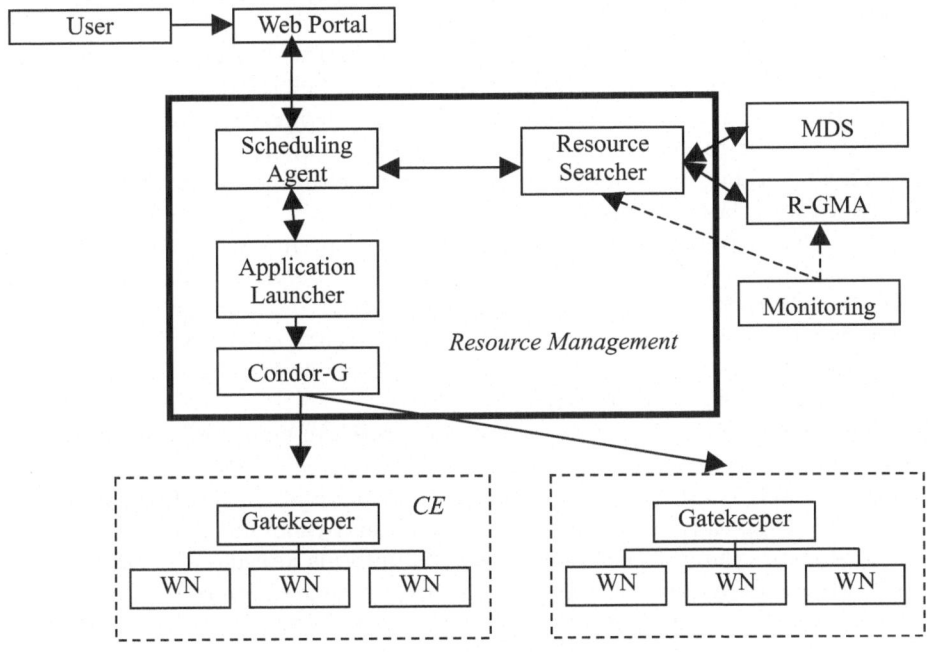

Fig. 1. Resource-Management Architecture.

Computing resources in the CrossGrid architecture are available as Computing Elements (CE), which provide the abstraction of a local farm of Working Nodes (WN). This local farm (or CE) is accessed through a Gatekeeper. Thus, the list of resources returned by the Resource Searcher consists of a Computing Elements list, which may eventually be grouped into sets, if the submitted job is an MPICH-G2 job and its requirements cannot be fulfilled by a single CE alone.

Subsequently, the Scheduling Agent selects a CE or a group of CEs on which to run the MPI job, according to the following criteria:

1. Groups of CEs with fewer numbers of different CEs will be selected first. This criterion tends to run MPI on a single cluster, which will avoid large message latencies between tasks allocated in different clusters.
2. If there is more than one group with the same number of CEs, the group having best global rank will be selected first. Ranks are assigned to each CE (or groups of CEs) according to certain performance metrics (e.g. overall MFLOPS, main memory, etc.).

The SA passes the job and the first-selected CE (or group of CEs) to the Application Launcher, who is responsible for the actual submission of the job on the specified CE. Due to the dynamic nature of the Grid, the job submission may fail on that particular CE. Therefore, the Scheduling Agent will try the other CEs from the list returned by the Resource Searcher until the job submission succeeds or fails. In the later case, the Scheduling Agent notifies the user of the failure.

Each SA will keep permanent information about all user jobs and it will ensure that all necessary resources are co-allocated before passing a parallel job to Condor-G [7]. It will also be responsible for managing the available resources in a way that guarantees that high priority jobs (i.e. interactive) are able to run as soon as possible, while lower priority jobs are either temporarily vacated or suspended for a latter resubmission.

Most CrossGrid applications are characterized by interaction with a person in a processing loop. Therefore, an important role to be played by the Scheduling Agent Management is that of taking responsibility for handling job priorities. In our first prototype, priorities will be used to sort the list of pending jobs. In future prototypes, we plan to include both pre-emption mechanisms and temporal-pause mechanisms of low-priority jobs.

The above-mentioned services will be integrated in an overall architecture in which multiple SAs and a single Resource Searcher will exist within a Virtual Organization. SAs (and their Application Launcher and Condor-G counterpart) control user applications on the users' behalf, and there could be one SA-AL-Condor-G set per user. The Resource Searcher informs SAs about the availability of grid resources and only a limited number of these are required. Although our current prototype still exhibits a centralized architecture in which SA and RS are merged in a single entity, by providing a more decentralized set of Scheduling Agents in future prototypes, we hope that EU-CrossGrid resource-management services will avoid both the single point of failure and the performance bottlenecks incurred in centralized solutions, and that they will therefore provide higher reliability.

3   Resource Management Components

We now describe certain details on the main components introduced in the previous section, namely, the Resource Searcher and the Application Launcher.

3.1   Resource Searcher

The main duty of the Resource Searcher is to perform the matchmaking between job needs and available resources. The RS receives a job description as input, and produces as output a list of possible resources in which to execute the job. Resources are grouped into sets. Each set is a combination of Computing Elements that provide the minimum amount of free resources, as specified by the JobAd. As we said before, JobAds are described using the Job Description Language (JDL) adopted in the EU-Datagrid project. This language is based on the Condor ClassAd library [2].

The matchmaking process carried out by the Resource Searcher is also implemented with the Condor ClassAd library. With this library, jobs and resources are expressed as ClassAds; two of these match if each of the ClassAd attributes evaluate to true in the context of the other ClassAd. Because the ClassAd language and the ClassAd matchmaker were designed for selecting a single machine on which to run a job, we have added several extensions to be applied when a job requires multiple resources (i.e. multiple CEs, in CrossGrid terminology).

With these extensions, a successful match is defined as occurring between a single ClassAd (the JobAd) and a ClassAd set (a group of CEs ClassAds). Firstly, the JobAd is used to place constraints on the collective properties of an entire group of CEs ClassAd (e.g., the total number of free CPUs has to be greater than the minimum number of CPUs required by the job). Secondly, other attributes of the JobAd are used to place constraints on the individual properties of each CE ClassAd (e.g., the OS version of each CE has to be Linux 2.4).

The selection of resources is carried out according to the following steps:

1. First step: a list is obtained of single CEs that fulfill all job requirements referring only to required individual characteristics. Currently, these are the requirements that are specified in the Requirements section of the file describing the job using JDL. This step constitutes a pre-selection phase that generates a reduced set of resources suitable for executing the job request in terms of several characteristics such as processor architecture, OS, etc.
2. Second step: from the list mentioned above, groups of CEs are made to fulfill collective requirements. For example, an attempt is made to fulfill the total number of CPUs required by a job by "aggregating" individual CEs. In the case of the number of CPUs required by the job, for instance, the Resource Searcher aggregates CEs to guarantee that the total number of free CPUs in the groups of CEs is larger than NumCPU, as described in the JobAd.

Figure 2 shows an example of the results obtained by the Resource Searcher for a job that requires 5 CPUs and wishes to use resource with a better performance in terms of the Average Spect Int benchmark (AverageSI in JDL).

Our current search procedure is not exhaustive, as it does not compute the power set of all CEs. This means that, in an example such as the one shown in 2a, for four suitable CEs CE1, CE2, CE3 and CE5, only two solutions are provided: CE2, CE1, CE3 CE1, CE5. Other possible solutions, such as CE1,

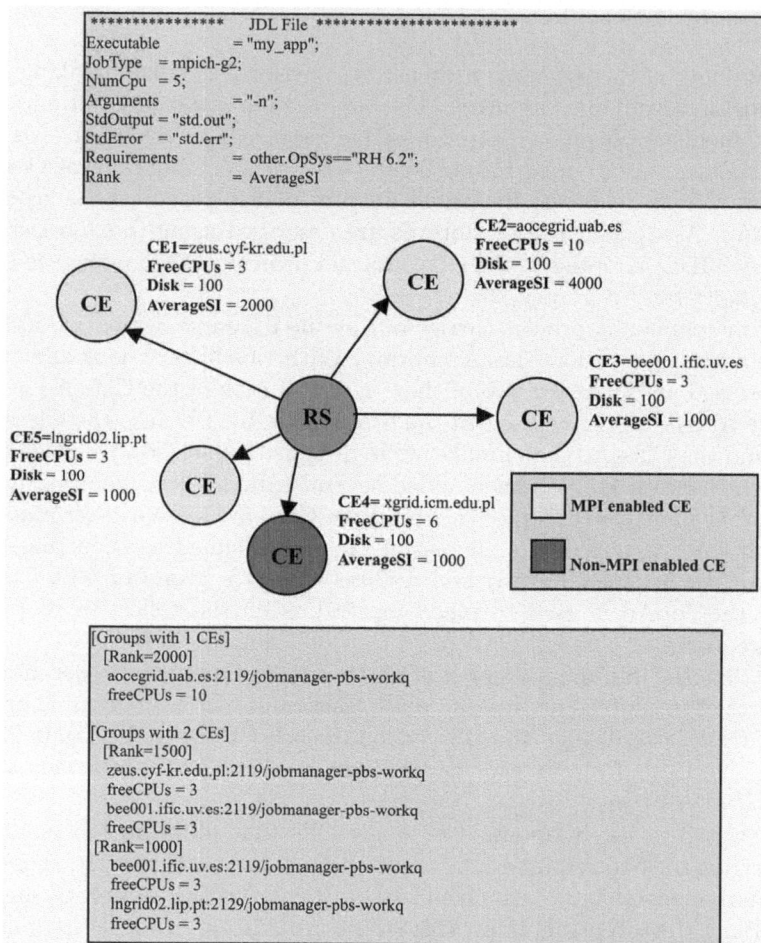

Fig. 2. Example of MPI application submission over CrossGrid sites and the result obtained by the Resource Selector.

CE3,CE5, are not considered because one subset of the CEs has already been included in a previous group.

In principle, this characteristic should not prevent our Resource Searcher from obtaining good selections. CEs are sorted according to a Rank expression provided by the user in the JobAd. According to the Rank expression (e.g., Average Spec Int benchmark in our example, as an indication of the computational power), the Resource Searcher sorts the suitable CEs in descending order. This means that the most desirable CEs or groups of CEs will be first. It is worth noting that selection of multiple resources has also been applied in [8]. In contrast to our approach, only the best resource or group of resources is selected. In our work, several choices are generated so that the final decision relies on the Scheduling Agent, which is able to try alternatives in the case of failing to actually submit the job in a given group of CEs.

The Resource Searcher currently supports information collection from the Globus Metacomputing Directory Service (MDS). It is also planned to add support for other resource-information systems, such as R-GMA, from the EU-DataGrid project, which will be also used to collect information obtained by different monitoring tools currently under development in the CrossGrid project.

3.2   Application Launcher

This service is responsible for providing a reliable submission service of parallel applications on the Grid. It spawns the job on the given machines using Condor-G [7] job management mechanisms. Currently, two different launchers are used for MPI applications.

The first one is used for MPI jobs compiled with the ch_p4 device. The launcher prepares a script that is sent to the remote cluster and is responsible for executing the job by issuing an mpirun command with the suitable arguments. The script also carries out transfers of input and output files and sets up all the necessary configuration files and directories in the remote cluster.

The second launcher is used for grid-enabled MPI jobs (namely, MPI applications compiled with the mpich-g2 device). This launcher coordinates the start-up of all MPI tasks in each remote cluster. The launcher takes advantage also of the services provided by the Condor-G system, which is a grid resource manager that provides an API and command line tools that allow the user to perform basic job submission and to obtain access to information about the execution of the job, providing a complete history of their jobs' execution. Condor-G has been designed primarily as a reliable front-end to a computational grid. Our MPICH-G2 launcher together with Condor-G guarantees error recovery and exactly-once execution semantics for MPICH-G2 jobs and constitutes a reliable submission service that substitutes the submission services provided by the Globus toolkit.

4   Conclusions

We have described the approach that is currently been followed in the EU-CrossGrid in order to provide automatic and reliable support of MPI job management over grid environments. The main components of our job management services are a Scheduling Agent, a Resource Searcher and an Application Launcher.

The Scheduling Agent is the central element that keeps the queue of jobs submitted by the user and carries out subsequent actions to effectively run the application on the suitable resources.

The Resource Searcher has the responsibility of providing groups of machines for any MPI job with both of the following qualities: (1) desirable individual machine characteristics, and (2) desirable characteristics as an aggregate. It is based on JobAds as a basic mechanism to represent both jobs and resources, and has been implemented by extending the Condor ClassAd library.

Finally, the Application Launcher is the module that, in the final stage, is responsible for ensuring a reliable starting of the application on the resources decided by the Scheduling Agent.

Our initial prototype has been built on an EU-DataGrid Resource Broker, which implies that it exhibits a highly centralized architecture. However, work is also in progress to provide an architecture in which multiple SA could connect to a common RS. Additionally, co-operation mechanisms will be also investigated at the level of Resource Searchers, so that queries to one RS could be forwarded to other RSs if insufficient resources were found by the original RS. This research also includes development of mechanisms that prevent potential deadlocks during the actual scheduling and submission of MPI applications over grid resources.

References

1. F. Giacomini, F. Prelz, "Definition of architecture, technical plan and evaluation criteria for scheduling, resource management, security and job description", DataGrid-01-D1.2-0112-0.
2. Rajesh Raman, Miron Livny, and Marvin Solomon, "Matchmaking: Distributed Resource Management for High Throughput Computing", Proc. of the Seventh IEEE International Symposium on High Performance Distributed Computing, July 28-31, 1998.
3. Fabricio Pazini, JDL Attributes - DataGrid-01-NOT-0101-0_4.pdf, http://www.infn.it/workload-grid/docs/DataGrid-01-NOT-0101-0_4-Note.pdf, December 17, 2001.
4. Rajkumar Buyya, David Abramson, and Jonathan Giddy, A Computational Economy for Grid Computing and its Implementation in the Nimrod-G Resource Broker, Future Generation Computer Systems (FGCS) Journal, Elsevier Science, The Netherlands, 2002.
5. H. Casanova, G. Obertelli, F. Berman and R. Wolski, "The AppLeS Parameter Sweep Template: User-level middleware for the Grid. In Proceedings of Supercomputing, November, 2000.
6. Holly Dail, Henri Casanova, and Fran Berman, "A Decoupled Scheduling Approach for Grid Application Development Environments", Proceedings of Supercomputing, November, 2002.
7. James Frey, Todd Tannenbaum, Ian Foster, Miron Livny, and Steven Tuecke, "Condor-G: A Computation Management Agent for Multi-Institutional Grids", Journal of Cluster Computing, vol. 5, pages 237-246, 2002.
8. Chuang Liu, Lingyun Yang, Ian Foster, Dave Angulo, "Design and Evaluation of a Resource Selection Framework for Grid Applications", Proceedings of IEEE International Symposium on High Performance Distributed Computing (HPDC-11), Edinburgh, Scotland, July, 2002.

Job Scheduling and Resource Management Techniques in Economic Grid Environments*

Rafael Moreno[1] and Ana B. Alonso-Conde[2]

[1] Departamento de Arquitectura de Computadores y Automática,
Universidad Complutense, 28040 - Madrid, Spain
`rmoreno@dacya.ucm.es`
[2] Dept. Economía Financiera, Contabilidad y Comercialización,
Univ. Rey Juan Carlos, 28032 - Madrid, Spain
`abac@fcjs.urjc.es`

Abstract. In this paper, we analyze the problem of grid resource broker-ing in the presence of economic information about the price of resources. We examine in detail the main tasks that a resource broker has to carry out in this particular context, like resource discovery and selection, job scheduling, job monitoring and migration, etc. Then, we propose an ex-tension of the grid resource information service schema to deal with this kind of economic information, and we evaluate different optimization criteria for job scheduling and migration, combining both performance and economic information. The experimental application benchmark has been taken from the finance field, in particular a Monte Carlo simulation for pricing European financial options.

1 Introduction

Computational Grids are emerging as a new computing paradigm for solving grand challenge applications in science, engineering, and economics [1]. Grid de-velopment involves the efficient management of heterogeneous, geographically distributed, and dynamically available resources. In this environment, the re-source broker (or scheduler) becomes one of the most critical components of the grid middleware. Following, we analyze in detail the main tasks that the resource broker has to carry out [2], and the most common approaches to perform these tasks, specially in case of the presence of economic information.

Resource Discovery and Selection. The first task of the scheduler is resource discovery. The main goal is to identify a list of authorized hosts that are available to a given user. Most resource discovery algorithms interact with some kind of grid information service (GIS), like MDS (Monitoring and Discovery Service) in Globus [3]. Once the list of possible target hosts is known, the second phase of the broker is selecting those resources that are expected to meet the time or cost

---

* This research was supported by Ministerio de Ciencia y Tecnología through the research grant TIC 2002-00334.

F. Fernández Rivera et al. (Eds.): Across Grids 2003, LNCS 2970, pp. 25–32, 2004.

constraints imposed by the user. In order to fulfill the user time restrictions the resource broker has to gather dynamic information about resource accessibility, system workload, network performance, etc. Moreover, if we contemplate an economic environment, the broker has to gather additional information about the price of the resources. Some environments like GRACE (Grid Architecture for Computational Economy) [4] provides a suite of trading protocols which enables resource consumers and providers to negotiate the cost of resources according to different criteria.

Job Scheduling. The next stage of resource brokering is job scheduling, i.e., the mapping of pending jobs to specific physical resources, trying to maximize some optimization criterion specified by the user. Most of the grid systems in the literature use performance-guided schedulers, since they try to find a job-to-resource mapping that minimizes the overall execution time (i.e. optimizes performance) [5] [6]. On the other hand, economy-guided schedulers include the cost of resources as optimization criterion [7] [8]. For example the Nimrod/G broker [7] allows users to specify a budget constraint (cost of resources), a deadline constraint (execution time), or both, and it incorporates different scheduling algorithms for cost optimization, and/or time optimization.

Job Migration. A grid is inherently a dynamic system where environmental conditions are subjected to unpredictable changes. In such a context, job migration is the only efficient way to guarantee that the submitted jobs are completed and the user restrictions are met. Most of the systems dealing with job migration face up to the problem from the point of view of performance [6] [9]. The main migration policies considered in these systems include, among others, performance slowdown, target system failure, job cancellation, detection of a better resource, etc. However, there are hardly a few works that manage job migration under economic conditions [8]. In this context, new job migration policies must be contemplated, like the discovery of a new cheaper resource, or variations in the resource prices during the job execution.

2   Resource Brokering in a Dynamic Economic Environment

In this work we investigate the influence of economic factors over dynamic resource brokering, in the context of the GridWay project [6]. We propose an extension of the MDS information service schema [3] in order to deal with economic information. Then, we evaluate different optimization criteria for job scheduling and migration, which combine both performance and cost information.

2.1   The GridWay Framework

The GridWay framework is a Globus compatible environment, which simplifies the user interfacing with the Grid, and provides the mechanisms for efficient execution of jobs on the Grid with dynamic adaptation to changing conditions. From the user point of view, the GridWay framework consists of two main components:

Command-Line User Interface. This interface significantly simplifies the user operation on the Grid by providing several user-friendly commands for submitting jobs to the Grid ("gwsubmit") along with their respective configuration files (job templates), stopping/resuming, killing or re-scheduling jobs ("gwkill"), and monitoring the state and the history of the jobs ("gwps" and "gwhistory"). For a given job, the template file must include the name of the executable file, its arguments, the name of the input and output files, the name of the restart files for checkpointing purposes in case of migration, and a per-job optimization criterion, which have to be maximized whenever is possible, when the job is scheduled on the Grid.

Personal Resource Broker. Each user interacts with its own personal resource broker, called Submission Agent. It is responsible for resource discovering, scheduling and submitting the user jobs, monitoring job performance, and migrating jobs when it is required. The scheduling policy is based on a greedy approach, so that the scheduler tries to maximize the optimization criterion specified by the user for each individual job, without considering the rest of pending, rescheduled or submitted applications. The migration of a job can be initiated by several events: (a) A rescheduling request sent by the user; (b) A failure in the target host; (c) A new better resource is discovered, which maximizes the optimization criterion selected for that job.

2.2 Extension of the MDS Schema and New Information Providers

To adapt the GridWay framework for dealing with economic information, it is necessary to extend the Globus MDS schema and design new information providers, which supply this kind of information to the Grid Resource Information Service (GRIS).

The extension of the MDS schema is achieved by adding to the LDAP directory a new structural object class called MdsEconomicInfo, and a new auxiliary object class called MdsCpuPrice. The attribute Mds-Cpu-Price-Per-Second of this object class contains the CPU price information generated by the resource provider, which uses an abstract monetary unit, called Grid Currency Unit (g.c.u.). In addition to these new object class and attributes, we have defined new auxiliary objects to manage the cost of other physical resources, like the cost of the memory space and disk space used by the program, or the cost of the network bandwidth consumed by the program. However, these elements are reserved for a future use, and they are not considered in this work.

The information provider for supplying the economic data is based on a simple implementation, since it reads the information about the cost of resources (CPU, memory, disk or network) from a file stored in each target host. In a future work, we plan to integrate the GridWay broker with the GRACE economic information providers [4] and GridBank [10], which include a suite of trading protocols for resource cost negotiation between resource consumers and resource providers.

3   Experimental Environment

3.1   The Benchmark: A Financial Application

The experimental benchmark used in this work is based on a financial application [11] [12] in particular, a Monte Carlo (MC) simulation for pricing European
Call options. We briefly describe this problem.

Using the assumption of no arbitrage, the price of a derivate security can be
computed as the expected value of its discounted payouts, where the expectation
is taken with respect to the risk-neutral measure. In the particular case of a
European call option, its price is the expected value of the payoff:

$$E\{e^{-r\Delta t}max(S(t+\Delta t) - X(t), 0)\} \qquad (1)$$

where t is the current time, r is the risk-free rate of interest, $X(t)$ is the exercise
price, Δt is the holding period, and $S(t + \Delta t)$ is the stock price at time $t + \Delta t$.

Although Black and Scholes [13] provide an exact analytic method for pricing European options, numerical solutions are also very attractive, since they
provide a general framework for solving this kind of problems, yet when an analytic model cannot be obtained. In particular, MC simulation exhibits significant
advantages relative to other numerical models: it is a flexible technique, easy to
implement, and inherently parallel, since random samples can be generated and
evaluated independently. Furthermore, the error convergence rate in MC simulation is independent of the dimension of the problem, since the standard deviation
of the MC estimation decreases at the order $O(1/\sqrt{N})$, where N is the number
of simulations.

The MC approach for pricing options is based on simulating the changes in
the values of the stock over the time horizon. The evolution of the asset, $S(t)$,
can be modelled as a random walk following a Geometric Brownian Motion:

$$dS(t) = \mu S(t)dt + \sigma S(t)dW(t) \qquad (2)$$

where $dW(t)$ is a Wiener process, μ the instantaneous drift, and σ the volatility
of the asset.

Assuming a lognormal distribution, using the It's Lemma, and integrating the
previous expression over a finite time interval, δt, we can reach an approximated
solution for estimating the price evolution of $S(t)$:

$$S(t + \delta t) = S(t)e^{(\mu-\sigma^2/2))\delta t + \sigma\eta\sqrt{\delta t}} \qquad (3)$$

where η is a standard normal random variable.

To simulate an individual price path for a given holding period Δt, using a
m-step simulation path, it is necessary to evaluate the price of the asset at each
time interval: $S(t+\delta t)$, $S(t+2\delta t)$,..., $S(t+\Delta t){=}S(t+m\delta t)$, $i = 1, 2, ..., n$, where
δt is the basic simulation time-step, i.e. $\delta t = \Delta t/m$.

To generate random numbers, we rely on the Scalable Parallel Random Number Generators (SPRNG) library, developed at the Florida State University [14].

This library includes different parallel random number generators, which can be used to develop a parameterized version of our Monte Carlo simulation algorithm. In our simulations, we have used the additive Fibonacci random number generator.

In particular, our experiment computes the expected price of a European Call Option over one year time horizon ($\Delta t = 1$), using a simulation time interval of one week ($\delta t = 1/52$), i.e., each simulation path is computed by a sequence of 52 time steps. The number of independent paths simulated is N=4 millions. The estimated price of the Call Option is given by the average value of the payoff computed for the 4 million simulations.

3.2 Results

In this section we investigate how the scheduling and migration decisions taken by the GridWay resource broker can change according to the optimization criterion specified by the user for a given job, and how these different decisions can affect to the overall execution time of the job, and the total CPU price.

Our Grid testbed consists of three Sun Workstations with Solaris 8, whose main characteristics are summarized in Table 1.

Table 1. Characteristics of the machines in the research testbed.

host	Model	Speed	Memory	Perform.(peak)
sunblade	Sun Blade 100	500MHz	256MB	1000 MFLOPS
ultra1	Sun Ultra 1	167MHz	128MB	334 MFLOPS
sun250	Sun Enterprise 250	296MHz	256MB	600 MFLOPS

In the subsequent experiments, we assume that the cost of different resources exhibits the following behavior (see Figure 1): When the program execution starts, all the three hosts on the grid charge the same CPU price per second (12 g.c.u.). Around two minutes later, the sun250 and ultra1 hosts reduce the CPU price to 6 g.c.u., and 5 g.c.u. per second respectively.

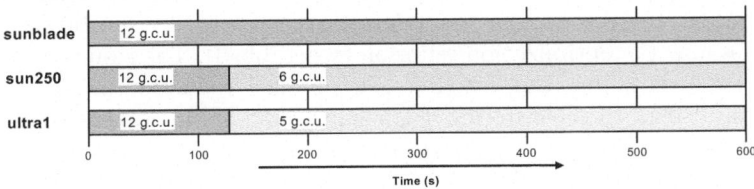

Fig. 1. Dynamic changes in the CPU prices of the testbed hosts.

Next, we analyze the different schedules generated by the resource broker under three different optimization criteria specified by the user:

Criterion #1: Performance * CPU-Free(%). This optimization criterion tries to minimize the overall execution time of the application. If the user establishes this criterion for the job, and assuming that all the machines are idle, the resource broker allocates the job to the host with highest performance, i.e., the sunblade host. Since changes in CPU prices have no effect on performance, the scheduler does not trigger any migration and the program is executed entirely on the initial host. Table 2 (#1) shows the time and the price of this schedule. Notice that the overall elapsed time includes de user and system CPU times, the I/O time, and also the overheads due to the transmission of the executable file, and the input and ouput files.

Criterion #2: 1 / CPU-Price-per-Second. This optimization criterion tries to minimize the total amount that the user pays for the CPU usage. To compute this amount only the user CPU time expended by the job is considered. Other times, like the system CPU time, the I/O time, or the CPU time expended by other processes are not considered. Using this optimization criterion, the resource broker will submit the job to the cheapest resource on the Grid. If two hosts are the same price, the broker selects that with maximum performance. Under this optimization criterion, the program execution starts on the sunblade host, which exhibits the highest performance at the same price. Two minutes later, when sun250 and ultra1 CPU prices change, the resource broker migrates the job to the new cheapest host, i.e., the ultra1 host. Table 2 (#2) displays the results for this schedule. As we can observe, this optimization criterion improves neither the price nor the time with respect to the first schedule. This is due to the low performance of the ultra1 host, which takes a long time to execute the program. Consequently, the total accumulated CPU price is higher than the previous case, despite the lower price per second of the ultra1 host.

Criterion #3: Performance / CPU-Price-per-Second. To avoid worthless migrations, we consider this third optimization criterion, which tries to minimize the performance to CPU price ratio. If the user specifies this criterion for the job, the program execution starts on the sunblade host, which exhibits the best trade-off between performance and price (see Table 3). When sun250 and ultra1 prices change, the resource broker migrates the job to the sun250 host, which maximizes now the optimization criterion (see Table 3). The results displayed in Table 2 (#3) show that this schedule gets an 8.2% reduction in the total CPU price with respect to the criterion #1, against a 32.4% increment in the overall elapsed time.

Figure 2 compares graphically the accumulated price and the overall elapsed time of the three schedules.

Table 2. Results for different schedules.

Criterion	CPU time (s)	Total Price (g.c.u.)	Elapsed time (s)
#1 Perf. * CPU-Free(%)	218.6	2,623.6	271.2
#2 1/CPU-price	103.2 + 348.6	2,981.7	553.3
#3 Perf./CPU-price	103.2 + 195.1	2,409.4	359.2

Table 3. Performance to CPU-price-per-second ratio for the testbed hosts.

Host	CPU-Price	(Perf./CPU-price)	CPU-Price	(Perf./CPU-price)
sunblade	12 g.c.u.	83.3	12 g.c.u.	83.3
sun250	12 g.c.u.	50.0	6 g.c.u.	100.0
ultra1	12 g.c.u.	27.8	5 g.c.u.	66.8

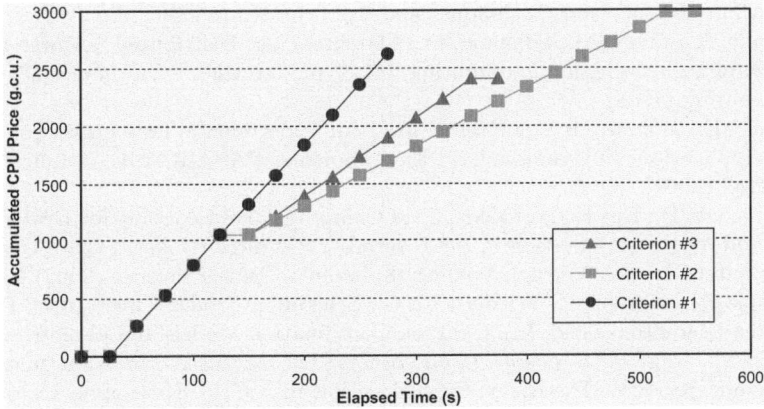

Fig. 2. Comparison of the schedules with different optimization criteria.

4   Conclusions and Future Work

This paper is focused on the problem of dynamic resource brokering in the presence of economic information. An extension of the MDS information service schema, in the context of the GridWay project has been proposed, in order to deal with this new kind of information. We have evaluated several optimization criteria for job scheduling and migration, and we conclude that, in order to reduce the overall CPU cost, it is important to use optimization criteria based on both performance and CPU price measures.

In a future work, we plan to incorporate to the brokering model the cost of other physical resources, like the cost of the memory and disk space used by the program, the cost of the network bandwidth consumed, etc. Other improvements contemplated include the evaluation of alternative optimization criteria, the development of new information providers, and the integration with the GRACE and GridBank environments, which supply a complete suite of economic information providers and trading protocols.

References

1. Foster, I., Kesselman, C.: The Grid: Blueprint for a New Computing Infrastructure. Morgan Kaufmann (1998)
2. Schopf, J.: A General Architecture for Scheduling on the Grid. Special issue of JPDC on Grid Computing (2002)
3. Czajkowski, K., Fitzgerald, S., Foster, I., Kesselman, C.: Grid Information Services for Distributed Resource Sharing. 10th IEEE Int. Symp. on High-Performance Distributed Computing (2001)
4. Buyya, R., Abramson, D., Giddy, J.: An Economy Driven Resource Management Architecture for Global Computational Power Grids. Int. Conf. on Parallel and Distributed Processing Techniques and Applications (2000)
5. Raman, R., Livny, M., Solomon, M.: Matchmaking: Distributed resource management for high throughput computing. Int. Symp. on High Performance Distributed Computing (1998)
6. Huedo, E., Montero, R.S., Llorente, I.M.: An Experimental Framework For Executing Applications in Dynamic Grid Environments. NASA-ICASE Technical Report 2002-43 (2002)
7. Abramson, D., Buyya, R., Giddy, J.: A Computational Economy for Grid Computing and its Implementation in the Nimrod-G Resource Broker. Future Generation Computer Systems Journal, Volume 18, Issue 8, Elsevier Science (2002) 1061-1074
8. Sample, N., Keyani, P., Wiederhold, G.: Scheduling Under Uncertainty: Planning for the Ubiquitous Grid. Int. Conf. on Coordination Models and Languages (2002)
9. Allen, G., Angulo, D., Foster, I., and others: The Cactus Worm: Experiments with Dynamic Resource Discovery and Allocation in a Grid Environment. Journal of High-Performance Computing Applications, Volume 15, no. 4 (2001)
10. Barmouta, A. and Buyya, R., GridBank: A Grid Accounting Services Architecture (GASA) for Distributed Systems Sharing and Integration. 17th Annual Int. Parallel and Distributed Processing Symposium (IPDPS 2003), Workshop on Internet Computing and E-Commerce (2003)
11. Moreno-Vozmediano, R., Alonso-Conde, A.B.: A High Throughput Solution for Portfolio VaR Simulation. 4th WSEAS Int. Conf. on Mathematics and Computers in Business and Economics (2003) in press.
12. Branson, K., Buyya, R., Moreno-Vozmediano, R., and others: Global Data-Intensive Grid Collaboration. Supercomputing Conf. (SC2003), HPC Challenge Awards (2003)
13. Dupire, B.: Monte Carlo Methodologies and Applications for Pricing and Risk Management. Risk Books, 1st edition (1998)
14. Mascagni, M., Srinivasan, A.: Algorithm 806: SPRNG: a scalable library for pseudorandom number generation. ACM Trans. on Mathematical Software (TOMS), Vol. 26, Issue 3, September (2000) 436-461

VOMS, an Authorization System for Virtual Organizations

R. Alfieri[1], R. Cecchini[2], V. Ciaschini[3], L. dell'Agnello[3], Á. Frohner[4],
A. Gianoli[5], K. Lõrentey[6], and F. Spataro[3]

[1] INFN and Department of Physics, Parma
[2] INFN, Firenze
[3] INFN, CNAF
[4] CERN, Geneva
[5] INFN, Ferrara
[6] ELTE, Budapest

Abstract. We briefly describe the authorization requirements, focusing on the framework of the DataGrid and DataTAG Projects and illustrate the architecture of a new service we have developed, the Virtual Organization Membership Service (VOMS), to manage authorization information in Virtual Organization scope.

1 Introduction

Authorization plays a key role in the process of gaining access to resources in a computational grid [1].

As for authentication, it is not feasible to administer authorization information on a local site basis, since users have normally direct administrative deals only with their own local site and with the collaborations they work in, but not, generally, with other entities.

It is convenient to introduce the following concepts:

- **Virtual Organization (VO)**: abstract entity grouping Users, Institutions and Resources (if any) in a same administrative domain [2];
- **Resource Provider (RP)**: facility offering resources (e.g. CPU, network, storage) to other parties (e.g. VO's), according to specific "Memorandum of Understanding".

From the authorization point of view, a grid is established by enforcing agreements between RP's and VO's, where, in general, resource access is controlled by both parties with different roles, and indeed the main difficulty is to clearly separate these two roles. To solve this apparent dualism, we can classify the authorization information into two categories:

1. general information regarding the relationship of the user with his VO: groups he belongs to, roles he is allowed to cover and capabilities he should present to RP's for special processing needs;

F. Fernández Rivera et al. (Eds.): Across Grids 2003, LNCS 2970, pp. 33–40, 2004.

2. information regarding what the user is allowed to do at a RP, owing to his membership of a particular VO.

We think that the first kind of information should be contained in a server managed by the VO itself, while the second is probably best kept at the local sites, near the resources involved and controlled by some kind of (extended) Access Control Lists (ACL).

In this note we briefly describe the authorization requirements, focusing on the framework of the DataGrid and DataTAG Projects [3,4,5], and illustrate the architecture of a new service we have developed, the Virtual Organization Membership Service (VOMS), to manage authorization information in VO scope.

The VOMS architecture uses the authentication and delegation mechanisms provided by the Globus Toolkit Grid Security Infrastructure (GSI) [6,7].

1.1 Authorization Requirements

Authorization, as stated before, is based on policies written by VO's and their agreements with RP's, that enforce local authorization. In general a user may be member of any number of VO's and his membership must be considered as a "reserved" information.

On the other hand, a VO can have a complex structure with groups and subgroups in order to clearly divide its users according to their tasks. Moreover, a user can be a member of any number of these groups.

A user, both at VO and group level, may be characterized by any number of roles and capabilities; moreover roles and capabilities may be granted to the user indefinitely or on a scheduled time basis (e.g. a certain user of the CMS collaboration is granted administrative role only when he is "on shift") or on a periodic basis (e.g. normal users have access to resources only during working hours).

The enforcement of these VO-managed policy attributes (group memberships, roles, capabilities) at local level descends from the agreements between the VO and the RP's, which, however, can always override the permissions granted by VO (e.g. to ban unwanted users). As a consequence, users must present their credential to RP's (and not just the authorization info).

1.2 VO Structure

Users of a VO are organized in groups which in general form a hierarchical structure with the VO itself as the root; the management of a group can be delegated. Excluding the root, each group may have, in general, several ancestors; note that we cannot have cycles in this structure (i.e. a group which is subgroup of itself). Thus we can represent the VO structure with a Direct Acyclic Graph (DAG)[1].

---

[1] The groups are the vertices of the graph and the subgroup-group relationships are the oriented edges.

Users are normally contained in subgroups: for a user being member of a particular group G implies that he is also contained in all ancestor groups, even if it not explicitly stated, up to the root (i.e. in all groups contained in the paths from G to the root).

Users are also characterized by roles they can cover in a group or at VO level (but in our model the VO is functionally equivalent to a group) and capabilities (properties to be interpreted by the local sites, e.g. ACL's). Roles are inherited by group members from ancestor groups (i.e. if a user as a role in a group and if he is member of one of its subgroups, he covers the same role in the subgroup), while the opposite is not generally true. The same inheritance rule applies for capabilities.

In conclusion, within this model, if a user U is member of the groups $\{\mathbf{G}_1, \ldots, \mathbf{G}_n\}$, noting with the triplet $(\mathbf{G}_k, \mathbf{R}_k, \mathbf{C}_k)$ the membership, roles and capabilities of U relatively to the group $\mathbf{G}_k$, the complete authorization information about U is formed from the set $(\mathbf{G}_1, \mathbf{R}_1, \mathbf{C}_1), \ldots, (\mathbf{G}_n, \mathbf{R}_n, \mathbf{C}_n)$.

1.3   Authorization Status in EDG

The Authentication and Authorization methods adopted by the EDG are based on the Globus Toolkit's Grid Security Infrastructure (GSI) [7].

In EDG, as originally in Globus, to access the Grid, the user first creates a proxy certificate (via grid-proxy-init procedure) that is then sent to the requested resources in order to access them.

In EDG Test-bed 1 each VO maintains information about its users in a LDAP server; each user is member of some groups of the VO. Note that, in the current implementation, subgroups, roles and capabilities are not supported; hence a differentiation among users is only manageable at the local sites. The RP's, periodically (e.g. daily) querying the LDAP servers, generate a list of VO users (in case banning unwanted entries or allowing non-VO users) and map them to local credentials (the so-called "grid-mapfile") granting users the Authorization to access local resources.

In EDG, the front-end of the farm (the *Gatekeeper*) has been modified and access these Authorization data via the Local Credential Authorization Service (LCAS) [10].

The main missing features of this architecture are flexibility and scalability. No roles, subgroups memberships and any other user peculiarity are supported. Moreover, the use of a RP-based database (i.e. the grid-mapfile), periodically updated, hardly scales in a production environment with a large number of users, each, potentially, with his groups, roles and capabilities, whereas in the test-bed the users situation is almost static, and user policy is very simple.

The solution, in our opinion, is to let users present the authorization data as they try to access the local resources (i.e. shifting from pull to push model); on the other hand we suspect that LDAP protocol is not the best choice to sustain the burden of a potentially high number of complex queries. To address these issues, we have developed, on a completely new basis, the VOMS system.

2   The VOMS System

The server is essentially a front-end to an RDBMS, where all the information about users is kept.

The VOMS System is composed by the following parts:

- **User Server:** receives requests from a client and returns information about the user.
- **User Client:** contacts the server presenting a user's certificate and obtains a list of groups, roles and capabilities of the user.
- **Administration Client:** used by the VO administrators (adding users, creating new groups, changing roles, etc...)
- **Administration Server:** accepts the requests from the clients and updates the Database.

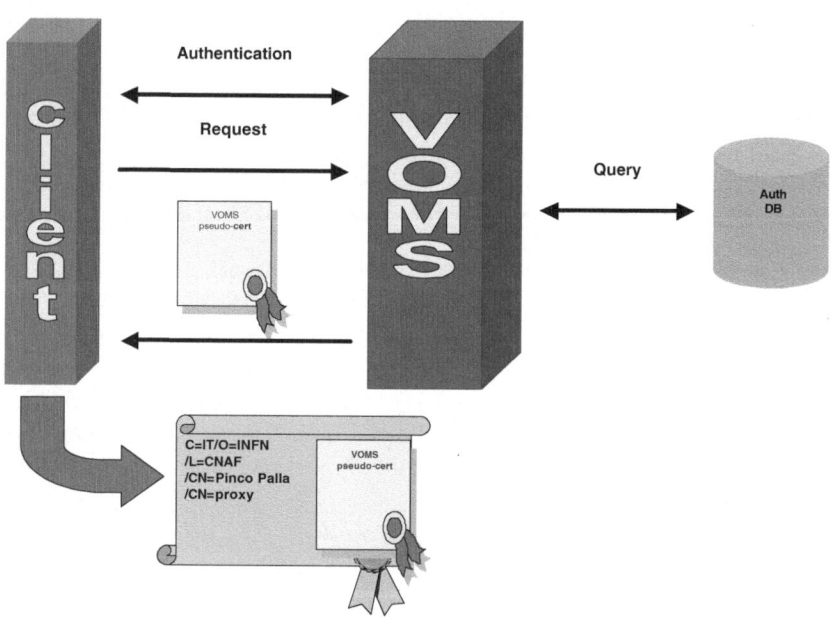

Fig. 1. The VOMS system

2.1   User Operations

One strong requirement we faced with, was to disrupt as little as possible – from the user's standpoint – the creation of the user proxy certificate [14]. To achieve this we have added a command (voms-proxy-init) to be used in place of grid-proxy-init. This new command produces a user's proxy certificate – like grid-proxy-init – but with the difference that it contains the user info from the VOMS server(s). This info is returned in a structure containing also the credentials both of the user and of the VOMS server and the time validity. All these data are signed by the VOMS server itself. We call this structure a "Pseudo-Certificate" (in the next release it will become an Attribute Certificate [8,9]).

The user may contact as many VOMS's as he needs.

In order to use the authorization information, the *Gatekeeper*, in addition to normal certificate checking, has to extract the additional information embedded in the proxy (the Pseudo-Certificate). This can be easily done with an appropriate LCAS plug-in [10]. However, as the VOMS info are included in a non critical extension of the certificate, this can be used even by "VOMS-unaware" *Gatekeepers*, thus maintaining compatibility with previous releases.

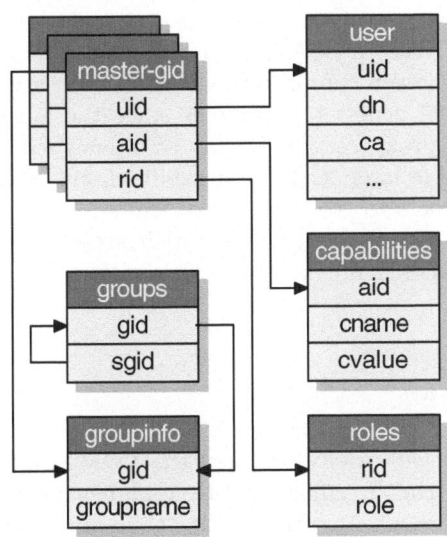

Fig. 2. The VO structure

2.2   Administration

The administrative clients (GUI and CLI) share a common server to modify the database. The server can be reached by the SOAP protocol, so that it can be easily converted into an OGSA service. The server consists in three sets of routines, grouped into services: the **Core**, which provides the basic functionality for the clients; the **Admin**, which provides the methods to administrate the VOMS database; the **History**, which provides the logging and accountability functionality.

All tables in the database have a `createdBy` and a `createdSerial` colums. The former contains the id of the requester of the operation that created this record. The latter contains a database-wide unique, ordered serial number – incremented for each modification on the database – that identifies the operation (it is a transaction id).

Copies of deleted and modified rows are kept in a corresponding archive table. Archive tables have the same scheme as data tables, except for two additional columns: `deletedBy`, the administrator who deleted the record, and `deletedSerial`, the transaction number of the operation.

By keeping all expired data in the database, we can conveniently, efficiently and accurately answer such questions as "Was user U in group G at time T?"

2.3   Security Considerations

The VOMS server does not add any security issues at user level since it performs the usual GSI security controls on the user's certificate before granting rights: it must be signed by a "trusted" CA, be valid and not revoked.

On the other hand, even compromising the VOMS server itself would be not enough to grant illegal access to resources since the authorization data must be inserted in a user proxy certificate (i.e. countersigned by the user himself). Hence the only possible large scale vulnerabilities are denial of service attacks (e.g. to prevent VO users to get their authorization credentials).

The main security issue about proxy certificates is the lack of a revocation mechanism; on the other hand these certificates have short lifetimes (12 hours, typically).

3   Related Works

In this paragraph, we will briefly compare the VOMS system with some analogous systems, namely the "Privilege and Role Management Infrastructure Standards Validation" (Permis), Akenti and the "Community Authorization Server" (CAS).

3.1   VOMS vs. PERMIS

PERMIS[11], implementing an RBAC (Role Based Access Control) mechanism, has been considered as an alternative to VOMS.

PERMIS has two modes of operation, push and pull. With push, the user sends his attribute certificates to PERMIS; with pull, PERMIS can be configured with any number of LDAP repositories, and it will search all of them for attributes of the user.

This second approach is clearly neither VOMS-oriented nor scalable.

Moreover VOMS, distributing the AC's to the users themselves, allows a much greater flexibility. For example, with VOMS a user who is a member of several groups and holds several roles can actually choose how much information about himself he may want to present to a site. It is also possible to obtain and present at the same time information on more VO's, a useful characteristic in case of collaborations between VO's.

The second major difference is the policy engine, where Permis is really powerful, because it can take a properly formatted policy file and make decisions based on the content of the file and the AC's it receives. On the contrary, VOMS does not focus on this problem, and it leave the interpretation of the AC's to other components (i.e. to local sites, namely to LCAS).

In conclusion VOMS and Permis are complementary: VOMS as a AC issuer, and Permis (slightly modified in its AC gathering) as an policy engine.

3.2   VOMS vs. CAS

CAS[12] has been developed by the Globus team to solve the same problem tackled by VOMS in EDG.

In our opinion, there are two major differences between CAS and VOMS.

The first is that CAS does not issue AC's, but whole new proxy certificates with the CAS server Distinguish Name as the subject; the authorization information is included in an extension.

As a consequence, when a service receives this certificate, it cannot effectively decide who the owner is without inspecting the extension. This means that existing services, in Globus-based grids, would need to be modified to use a CAS certificate; on the contrary using VOMS, since it adds the AC's in a non-critical extension of a standard proxy certificate, does not require this kind of modification to the services.

The second major difference is in the fact that CAS does not record groups or roles, but only permissions. This means that the ultimate decision about what happens in a farm is removed from the farm administrator and put in the hands of the CAS administrator, thus breaking one of the fundamental rules of the grid: the farm administrator has total control about what happens on his machines.

3.3   VOMS vs. Akenti

Akenti[13] is an AC-based authorization system.

In our opinion, there are three major differences between Akenti and VOMS.

The first is that Akenti does not use true AC's since their definition and description do not conform the standard[2].

The second is that Akenti is targeted on authorizing accesses on web resources, and particularly web-sites. This means that it is completely unfeasible to use it for other needs, for example in a VO.

The third is that Akenti does not link identities with groups or roles, but with permissions. This is done on the resource side, not removing the control from the resource itself, like CAS does; on the other hand, not having an intermediary like VOMS (or even CAS) will surely lead to fragmentation and inconsistencies between the permissions.

---

[2] At present nor VOMS uses standard AC's, but this will be changed in the next (production) release.

4 Future Developments

Future developments will include use of Attribute Certificates, replica mechanisms for the RDBMS, more sophisticate time validity for the VOMS certificates and subgroups.

References

1. Foster, I. and C. Kesselman (eds.), The Grid: Blueprint for a New Computing Infrastructure. Morgan Kaufmann (1999)
2. I. Foster, C. Kesselman and S. Tuecke, The Anatomy of the Grid, International Journal of High performance Computing Applications, **15**, 3 (2001)
3. The DataGrid Project: http://www.edg.org
4. The DataTAG Project: http://www.datatag.org
5. iVDGL - International Virtual Data Grid Laboratory: http://www.ivdgl.org
6. The Globus Project: http://www.globus.org
7. Grid Security Infrastructure: http://www.globus.org/security/
8. R. Housley, T. Polk, W. Ford and D. Solo, Internet X.509 Public Key Infrastructure Certificate and Certificate Revocation List (CRL) Profile, RFC3280 (2002)
9. S. Farrel and R. Housley, An Internet Attribute Certificate Profile for Authorization, RFC3281 (2002)
10. Architectural design and evaluation criteria: WP4 Fabric Management, DataGrid-04-D4.2-0119-2-1 (2001)
11. Privilege and Role Management Infrastructure Standards Validation: http://www.permis.org
12. L. Pearlman, V. Welch, I. Foster, K. Kesselman and S. Tuecke, A Community Authorization Service for Group Collaboration, IEEE Workshop on Policies for Distributed Systems and Networks (2002)
13. http://www-itg.lbl.gov/Akenti/
14. S. Tuecke, D. Engert, I. Foster, V. Welch, M. Thompson, L. Pearlman and C. Kesselman, Internet X.509 Public Key Infrastructure Proxy Certificate Profile, draft-ggf-gsi-proxy-04 (2002)

A Grid Framework
for Optimistic Resource Sharing

Norlaily Yaacob and Rahat Iqbal

School of Mathematical and Information Sciences
Coventry University, Coventry CV1 5FB
United Kingdom
{n.yaacob,r.iqbal}@coventry.ac.uk

Abstract. Grids are gaining more importance in this era of Internet technology to maximize the use of resources such as hardware and software infrastructure. The grid provides a platform to share information across the Net. Any application on the grid should be able to share available resources concurrently. In this paper, we present a grid framework for an optimistic resource sharing, which consists of different elements such as authentication, sharing, coordination and synchronization of resources. We discuss issues related to the resource sharing problem and propose a solution to it using reflective computation. Different classes of grid applications are also presented and some scenarios are used to elaborate each of them focusing on underlying issues related to the framework.

1   Introduction

The success of the Web for information sharing has promoted the idea of the Grid for computation [2]. In the last few years, a lot of time and resources have been spent for the exploration, classification and development of grid applications. Grids typically consist of a number of machines connected with each other through network infrastructure. Hardware, software, communication channels and security measures are its building blocks. The grids are used in concurrent and distributed computing, on-demand computing, data intensive computing and collaborative computing [1]. They support a wide range of users including grid developers, tool developers, application developers, system administrator and end users. An end user in grid environment should be able not only to invoke multiple existing systems and hardware devices but also to coordinate their interactions.

In this paper, we present a grid framework for an optimistic resource sharing, which consists of four elements such as authentication, sharing, coordination and synchronization of resources. We discuss issues related to the resource sharing problem and proposed a solution to it using reflective computation [5]. Benefits of the reflective system are highlighted in the concurrent object programming domains such as dynamic decision type system, message passing system, and simulation system [10]. In resource sharing, it can benefit areas such as monitoring the behavior of concurrently running objects, or distributed simulation.

F. Fernández Rivera et al. (Eds.): Across Grids 2003, LNCS 2970, pp. 41–48, 2004.

The rest of this paper is structured as follows. Section 2 presents grid properties and proposes a framework. Section 3 describes the reflective computational system. Section 4 presents different scenarios of grid applications. Finally, section 5 presents our conclusions. This section also outlines our future work.

2   Grid Framework

Computational grids evolve around sharing of networks, computers, and other resources. They provide support for services, which are distributed over multiple networked computers known as clusters. The proposed framework (see Figure 1) consists of elements such as authentication, sharing, coordination and synchronization. These elements reside on top of an Internet application. In order to propose a suitable framework, we need to understand the grid properties [6], which are as follows:

- Grids are **large** both in terms of the number of potentially available resources, and the geographical distances between them.
- Grids are **distributed**, that is the latencies involved in moving data between resources are substantial and may dominate applications.
- Grids are **dynamic**, that is the available resources change on the same time scale as the lifespan of a typical application.
- Grids are **heterogeneous**, that is the form and properties of sites differ in significant ways.
- Grids **cross the boundaries of human organizations**, so that policies for access to and use of resources differ at different sites.

2.1   Authentication

Authentication is a process of establishing the identity of the user. This will then establish the right of the user to share and use available resources on the grid. There is also a need to consider the integration with various local security constraints [2]. Once the user becomes a member of the grid environment, he or she can access all available resources for which he or she is authorized. The authorization protocol determines whether a user or a machine has the right to carry out a certain activity. There are three essential elements of information security: confidentiality, integrity and availability. For instance, if a user wants to access a certain object to perform action on it, he or she must be mapped in the local environment by means of his or her authorization, confidentiality, and integrity rights.

2.2   Sharing

Sharing involves accessing authorized resources. These resources include hardware such as RAM, disk space, communication channels and software such as programs, files and data. All machines on the Internet can share these resources in order to carry out their activities given that authentication and authorization have been granted. There is also a need to monitor available resources at any time. To do so, all the machines in grid environment need to register their available resources, which are then maintained and updated dynamically during computation.

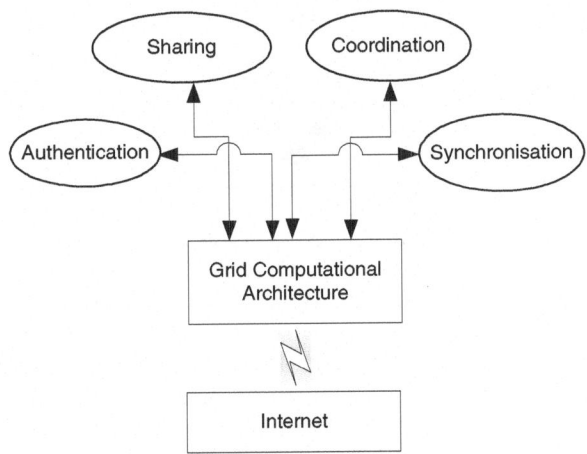

Fig. 1. A Framework of Grid

2.3   Coordination and Synchronization

Coordination manages dependencies between activities [8]. Interdependency is viewed as a temporal relationship between activities. For instance, a program which needs to run on multiple machines due to lack of resources on its own machine must be divided into independent sub-programs. These sub-programs need to be coordinated and synchronized to complete the task. Lets consider two cases of sub-programs running in parallel. The first case consists of three sub-programs with two available resources, while any two of the three sub-programs are executed until completion. The third one will have to wait until one of the two sub-programs releases its resources. The second case is where the third sub-program depends on the completion of first two sub-programs, i.e. the results of the two sub-programs enable the execution of the third one. Any delay in the completion of either of the program will effect the execution of the third one.

3   A Reflective Computational System

This section introduces a reflective computational system, which is a potential implementation solution for grid applications.

Computational systems based on a reflective architecture have the ability to change and control part or all of the system during execution. Computational

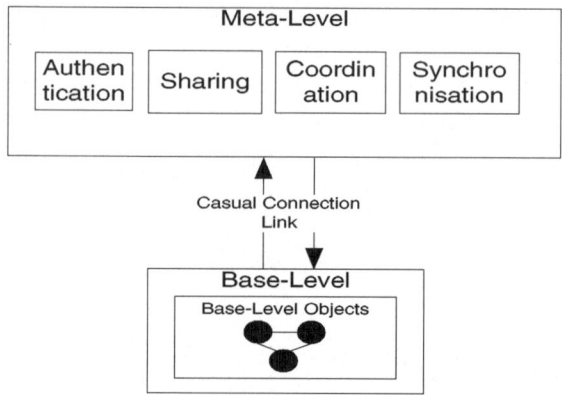

Fig. 2. Reflective Architecture

reflection is the process of reasoning about and acting upon the computational system itself [5]. Such a system must therefore contain some data, which represents the structural and computational aspects of that system. These data are modelled as meta-objects. In addition, there must be a causal connection link between this self-representation at the *meta-level* and the actual computation being performed at the *base-level*. As a result, any changes at the meta-level will be reflected at the base-level. The reflective architecture for the proposed grid framework is shown in Figure 2. The components of the framework which are authentication, sharing, coordination and synchronisation reside at the meta-level. In this architecture, each object involves in an application has its own meta-object which models both the structural and behavioral aspects of that object. Meta-object of each component reflects the computation of the base-level objects. These are shown by the causal connection link between objects at the base-level and the meta-level.

For applications which require sharing of resources there exist a controller at the meta-level that acts as a manager to maintain the available shared resources. During computation the manager constantly monitors the consumption of each resources, when it detects that a particular resource is available, the manager gives this message to objects at the base-level. Coordination and synchronization also exist between base-level objects and meta-level objects. This shows that the behaviour of an object in a system can be monitored from outside through its meta-objects. As a result, the representation of the base-level methods may be changed dynamically during computation.

4   Grid Applications

In this section, we present different scenarios of grid applications such as resource sharing, scheduling and simulation. Each of them differs in the number and type of participants, the types of activities, the duration and scale of the interaction, and the resources being shared.

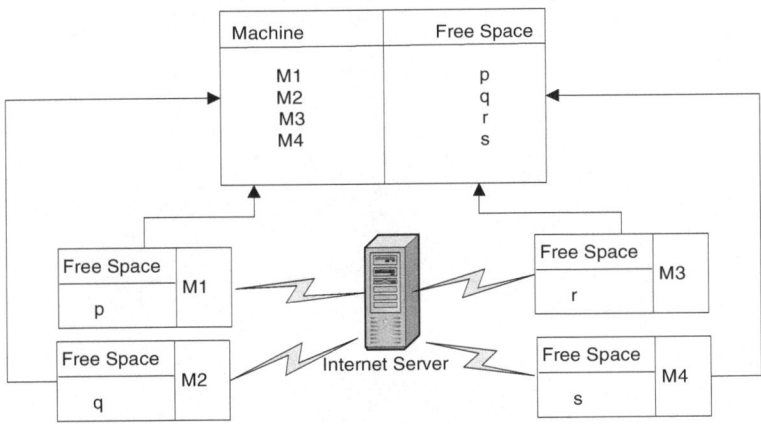

Fig. 3. Sharing Resources

Scenario 1: A computer linked to the Net needs to complete a task but faces difficulties due to its RAM limitation. Any idle computers on the Net should be integrated to complete this task.

A machine should be able to decide on how much of its resources such as function, operation, and data can be shared with other machines. At the user level, a table of available resources is created. This table acts as a reference, which is maintained and updated dynamically during computation. Figure 3 illustrates this scenario. If machine M1 is sharing a resource with machine M2, there is a possibility at a later stage that M2 does not give the authority to access its resources due to lack of resources.

Scenario 2: The timetable scheduling at the university is a complex task to perform manually. The person in-charge i.e. the timetable scheduler needs to gather relevant information on the chosen modules from various databases available on different machines.

In order to access information from different databases for timetable scheduling, it involves the heterogeneity issues [3,4]. Heterogeneity issues need to be resolved for sharing purposes. They are grouped under three categories: syntax, structure and semantic. They can be resolved by establishing mapping between heterogeneous databases and building a shared ontology. This is illustrated in Figure 4. The shared ontology also plays a pivotal role in multi-agent communication [7].

Scenario 3: A car manufacturer planned to develop a feasibility study for components of a new concept car. This simulation integrates software components developed by different suppliers, with each element operating on the suppliers' computers.

In simulation, authentication is required between different suppliers and manufacturer to share related databases. The coordination between suppliers and,

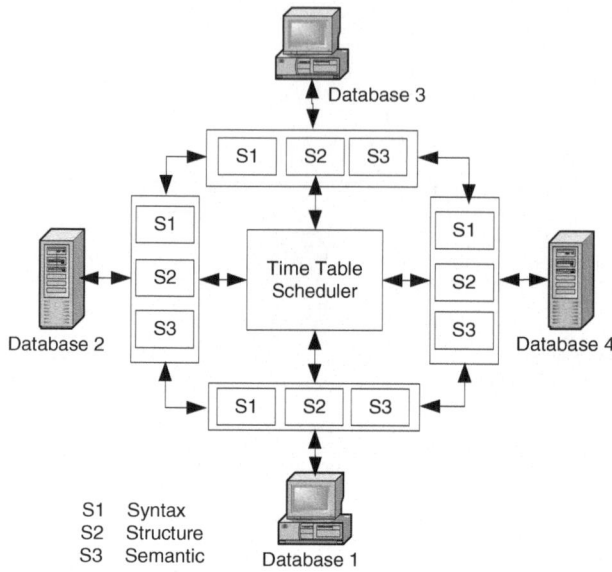

Fig. 4. Schedule Architecture

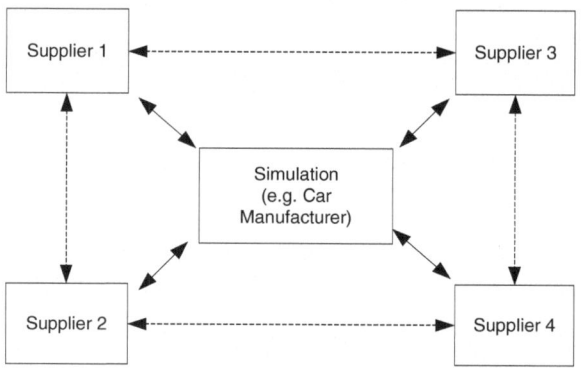

Fig. 5. Car Manufacturer Simulation

between suppliers and manufacturer is required in order to coordinate and co-operate activities with each other as shown in Figure 5. In this case, an efficient synchronization technique [10] needs to be introduced between suppliers' databases and between the suppliers' and manufacturer's databases.

The evaluation of the proposed framework is carried out based on grid properties (see Table 1).

Table 1. Comparison of Grid Applications

Class of Examples	Grid Properties	Framework Support
Sharing	Dynamic	Authentication of Internet server in order to locate available resources, sharing of available free spaces, coordination and synchronization between machines.
Scheduling	Heterogeneous	Authentication of scheduler, sharing of databases,coordination between database administrator and scheduler and synchronization of updated records.
Simulation	Distributed	Authentication of different suppliers and manufacturer,sharing of simulated databases, coordination between suppliers and between suppliers and manufacturer, synchronization between suppliers'databases and between the suppliers and manufacturer databases.

5   Conclusions

This paper has presented a framework of grid, which emphasizes on authentication, sharing of resources, coordination and synchronization. Reflective computation which consists of base-level and meta-level declarations has been discussed as a potential implementation technique to support grid applications. It enables sharing of resources in a system to be monitored from the outside through its meta-object. The results of such monitoring are used to modify methods used by an object for optimized computation during program execution.

Our future work will include the development of the framework and the design of toolset. This will involve building a library of meta-objects to support sharing, coordination and synchronization of resources. We will also focus on further evaluation of the framework.

References

1. Foster, I., and Kesselman, C., (eds). "The Grid: Blueprint for a New Computing Infrastructure", Morgan Kaufmann, San Francisco, 1999.
2. Foster, I, Kesselman, C, & Tuecke, S, "The Anatomy of the Grid: Enabling scalable virtual organizations", Int. J. High Performance Comp. Appl. 15(3), 2001.
3. Kashyap, V., and Sheth, A., "Semantic Similarities between objects in multiple databases", Management of Heterogenous and Autonomous Database Systems, 1999.
4. Kim, W. and Seo, J.: "Classifying schematic and data heterogeneity in multidatabses system", IEEE Computer, 1991.
5. Maes, P., "Concepts and Experiments in Computational Reflection", In Proceedings, OOPSLA 87 Conference, 1987.

6. Skillicorn, D., "Motivating Computational Grids", In Workshop on Global and Peer-to-Peer Computing on Large Scale Distributed Systems at CCGrid 2002.
7. Stuckenschmidt, H. and Timm, I. J. "Adaption Communication Vocabularies using Shared Ontologies", Proceedings of the Second International Workshop on Ontologies in Agent Systems (OAS), Bologna, Italy, 2002.
8. Thomas W. Malone, Kevin Crowston, "Interdisciplinary Study of Coordination", ACM Computing Survey, Vol. 26, No.1, March 1994.
9. Visser, U., Stuckenschmidt, H., Schlieder, C., Wache, H., & Timm, I., "Terminology Integration for the Management of distributed Information", 2002.
10. Yaacob, N., "Reflective Computation in Concurrent Object-Based Languages", PhD Thesis, University of Exeter, England, 1999.

Search Engines for the Grid: A Research Agenda

Marios Dikaiakos[1], Yannis Ioannidis[2], and Rizos Sakellariou[3]

[1] Department of Computer Science, University of Cyprus, Nicosia, Cyprus
mdd@ucy.ac.cy
[2] Department of Informatics and Telecommunications, Univ. of Athens, Greece
yannis@di.uoa.gr
[3] Department of Computer Science, University of Manchester, Manchester, UK
rizos@cs.man.ac.uk

Abstract. A preliminary study of the issues surrounding a seach engine for Grid environments, GRISEN, that would enable the provision of a variety of Grid information services, such as locating useful resources, learning about their capabilities, expected conditions of use and so on. GRISEN sits on the top of and interoperates with different underlying Grid middleware and their resource discovery mechanisms. The paper highlights the main requirements for the design of GRISEN and the research issues that need to be addressed, presenting a preliminary design.

1 Introduction

The Grid is emerging as a wide-scale, distributed computing infrastructure that promises to support resource sharing and coordinated problem solving in dynamic, multi-institutional Virtual Organisations [10]. In this dynamic and geographically dispersed setting, *Information Services* are regarded as a vital component of the Grid infrastructure [5,14]. Information Services address the challenging problems of the discovery and ongoing monitoring of the existence and characteristics of resources, services, computations and other entities of value to the Grid. Ongoing research and developments efforts within the Grid community are considering protocols, models and API's to provide an information services infrastructure that would allow efficient resource discovery and provision of information about them [5,12,6,14].

However, the identification of interesting and useful (in the user's context) resources can be a difficult task in the presence of too many, frequently changing, highly heterogeneous, distributed and geographically spread resources. The provision of information-services components, as currently envisaged by the Grid community [5], is a first step towards the efficient use of distributed resources. Nevertheless, the scale of the envisaged Grids, with thousands (or millions) of nodes, would also require well defined rules to classify the degree of relevance and interest of a given resource to a particular user. If one draws on the experience from the World Wide Web (arguably, the world's largest federated information system), efficient searching for information and services in such an environment will have to be based on advanced, sophisticated technologies that are automatic,

F. Fernández Rivera et al. (Eds.): Across Grids 2003, LNCS 2970, pp. 49–58, 2004.

continuous, can cope with dynamic changes, and embody a notion of relevance to a user's request. In the context of the WWW, this role is fulfilled by search engines [2].

The vision of this paper is that the technology developed as part of web search engine research, along with appropriate enhancements to cope with the increased complexity of the Grid, could be used to provide a powerful tool to Grid users in discovering the most relevant resources to requests that they formulate. Thus, our primary objective is to study issues pertaining to the development of search engines for the Grid. An additional objective is to design a search engine for Grid environments, named GRISEN, which can facilitate the provision of a wide range of information services to its users and can make this transparent from the particular characteristics of the underlying middleware. GRISEN is not intended to act as a substitute of existing systems for resource discovery, resource management or job submission on the Grid. Instead, GRISEN is expected to be a high-level entry point for the user for locating useful resources, learning about their capabilities, expected conditions of use, and so on, providing a unified view of resource information regardless of any possible different middlewares. This way, users can pinpoint an appropriate set of Grid resources that can be employed to achieve their goals, before proceeding with firing their application.

The remainder of the paper is structured as follows. Section 2 states the problem that motivated this research. Section 3 sets the requirements of GRISEN. Section 4 presents the initial design for GRISEN's architecture. Section 5 highlights the issues that need to be addressed. Finally, Section 6 concludes the paper.

2   Background and Problem Statement

Grid environments were first developed to enable resource sharing between remote scientific organisations. As the concept evolved, information services have become an increasingly important component of software toolkits that support Grids.

A *Grid Information Service* is a software component of the Grid middleware that maintains information about *Grid entities*, i.e., hardware, software, networks, services, policies, virtual organizations and people participating in a Grid [5,9]. This information, which is encoded according to some data model, can be made available upon request by the Grid information service that provides also support for binding, discovery, lookup, and data protection.

From the outset, *Directories* have been adopted as a framework for deploying Grid Information Services. Typically, directories contain descriptive attribute-based information and are optimized for frequent, high-volume search and lookup (read) operations and infrequent writes [1]. Access to directories is provided via Directory Services, which wrap directory-based repositories with protocols for network access and mechanisms for replication and data distribution. Globus information services, for instance, are provided by the Metacomputing Directory Service (MDS) [9,5], which is based on the Lightweight Directory Access Protocol

(LDAP) [20,17,15]. The goal of MDS is to allow users to query for resources by name and/or by attributes, such as type, availability or load. Such queries could be of the sort of "Find a set of Grid nodes that have a total memory of at least 1TB and are interconnected by networks providing a bandwidth of at least 1MB/sec" or "Find a set of nodes that provide access to a given software package, have a certain computational capacity, and cost no more than x," and so on. Along similar lines, the Unicore Grid middleware [7] publishes static information about resources. Users annotate their jobs with resource requirements; a resource broker, currently being developed for the EC-funded EuroGrid project will match user-specified requirements with available resources.

However, the means used for publishing resource information, in either Globus or Unicore, do not aim to support sophisticated, user-customized queries or allow the user to decide from a number of different options. Instead, they are rather tied to the job submission needs within the particular environment. As we move towards a fully deployed Grid — with a massive and ever-expanding base of computing and storage nodes, network resources, and a huge corpus of available programs, services, and data — providing an effective service related to the availability of resources can be expected to be a challenging task. If we draw from the WWW experience, the identification of interesting resources has proven to be very hard in the presence of too many dynamically changing resources without well-defined rules for classifying the degree of relevance and interest of a given resource for a particular user. Searching for information and services on the Web typically involves navigation from already known resources, browsing through Web directories that classify a part of the Web (like Yahoo), or submitting a query to search engines [2].

In the context of the Grid, one can easily envisage scenarios where users may have to 'shop around' for solutions that satisfy their requirements best, use simultaneously different middlewares (which employ different ways to publish resource information), or consider additional information (such as, historical or statistical information) in choosing an option. The vision of this paper is that search engine technology, as has been developed for the WWW, can be used as a starting point to create a high-level interface that would add value to the capabilities provided by the underlying middleware.

3   Requirements

A search engine for resource discovery on the Grid would need to address issues more complex and challenging than those dealt with on the Web. These issues are further elaborated below.

Resource Naming and Representation. The majority of searchable resources on the World-Wide Web are text-based entities (Web pages) encoded in HTML format. These entities can be identified and addressed under a common, universal naming scheme (URI). In contrast, there is a wide diversity of searcheable "entities" on the Grid with different functionalities, roles, semantics, representations: hardware resources, sensors, network links, services, data repositories, software components, patterns of software composition, descriptions of programs, best practices of problem solving, people, historical data of resource usage, virtual organizations. Currently, there is no common, universal naming scheme for Grid entities.

In MDS, Grid entities are represented as instances of "object classes" following the hierarchical information schemas defined by the Grid Object Specification Language (GOS) in line with LDAP information schemas [18,15]. Each MDS object class is assigned an *optional* object identifier (OID) that complies to specifications of the Internet Assigned Numbers Authority, a description clause, and a list of attributes [16,18]. The MDS data model, however, is not powerful enough to express the different kinds of information and metadata produced by a running Grid environment, the semantic relationships between various entities of the Grid, the dynamics of Virtual Organizations, etc. Therefore, relational schemas, XML and RDF are investigated as alternative approaches for the representation of Grid entities [6,19,11]. Moreover, the use of a universal naming scheme, along with appropriate mapping mechanisms to interpret the resource description convention used by different middlewares, would allow a search engine for the Grid to provide high-level information services regarding resources of different independent Grids that may be based on different middlewares.

Resource Discovery and Retrieval. Web search engines rely on Web crawlers for the retrieval of resources from the World-Wide Web. Collected resources are stored in repositories and processed to extract indices used for answering user queries [2]. Typically, crawlers start from a carefully selected set of Web pages (a seed list) and try to "visit" the largest possible subset of the World-Wide Web in a given time-frame crossing administrative domains, retrieving and indexing interesting/useful resources [2,21]. To this end, they traverse the directed graph of the World-Wide Web following edges of the graph, which correspond to hyperlinks that connect together its nodes, i.e., the Web pages. During such a traversal (crawl), a crawler employs the HTTP protocol to discover and retrieve Web resources and rudimentary metadata from Web-server hosts. Additionally, crawlers use the Domain Name Service (DNS) for domain-name resolution.

The situation is fundamentally different on the Grid: Grid entities are very diverse and can be accessed through different service protocols. Therefore, a Grid crawler following the analogy of its Web counterpart should be able to discover and lookup all Grid entities, "speaking" the corresponding protocols and transforming collected information under a common schema amenable to indexing. Clearly, an implementation of such an approach faces many complexities due to the large heterogeneity of Grid entities, the existence of many Grid platforms adopting different protocols, etc.

Globus seeks to address this complexity with its Metacomputing Directory Service [5]. Under the MDS approach, information about resources on the Grid is extracted by "information providers," i.e., software programs that collect and organize information from individual Grid entities. Information providers extract information either by executing local operations or contacting third-party information sources such as, the Network Weather Service or SNMP. Extracted information is organized according to the LDAP data model in LDIF format and uploaded into LDAP-based servers of the Grid Resource Information Service (GRIS) [16,17]. GRIS is a configurable framework provided by Globus for deploying core information providers and integrating new ones.

GRIS servers support the Grid Information Protocol (GRIP), an LDAP-based protocol for discovery, enquiry and communication [5]. GRIP specifies the exchange of queries and replies between GRIS servers and information consumers. It supports discovery of resources based on queries and information retrieval based on direct lookup of entity names. GRIS servers can register themselves to aggregate directories, the Grid Index Information Services (GIIS). To this end, they use a soft-state registration protocol called Grid Registration Protocol (GRRP). A GIIS can reply to queries issued in GRIP. Moreover, a GIIS can register with other GIIS's, thus creating a hierarchy of aggregate directory servers. End-users can address queries to GIIS's using the GRIP protocol.

Nevertheless, MDS does not specify how entities are associated with information providers and directories, what kinds of information must be extracted from complex entities, and how different directories can be combined into complex hierarchies. Another important issue is whether information regarding Grid entities that is stored in MDS directories is amenable to effective indexing. Finally, as the Grid scales to a large federation of numerous, dispersed resources, resource discovery and classification become a challenging problem [12]. In contrast to the Web, there is no global, distributed and simple view of the Grid's structure that could be employed to drive resource discovery and optimize replies to user queries.

Definition and Management of Relationships. Web-page links represent implicit semantic relationships between interlinked Web pages. Search engines employ these relationships to improve the accuracy and relevance of their replies, especially when keyword-based searching produces very large numbers of "relevant" Web pages. To this end, search engines maintain large indices capturing the graph structure of the Web and use them to mine semantic relationships between Web resources, drive large crawls, rate retrieved resources, etc. [4,2].

The nature of relationships between Grid entities and the representation thereof, are issues that have not been addressed in depth in the Grid literature. Organizing information about Grid resources information in hierarchical directories like MDS implies the existence of parent-child relationships. Limited extensions to these relationships are provided with cross-hierarchy links (references). However, traversing those links during query execution or indexing can be costly [14]. Alternatively, relationships can be represented through the relational models proposed to describe Grid monitoring data [6,8].

These approaches, however, do not provide the necessary generality, scalability and extensibility required in the context of a Grid search engine coping with user-queries upon a Grid-space with millions of diverse entities. For instance, a directory is not an ideal structure for capturing and representing the transient and dynamic relationships that arise in the Grid context. Furthermore, an MDS directory does not capture the composition patterns of software components employed in emerging Grid applications or the dependencies between software components and data-sets [3,13]. In such cases, a Search Engine must be able to "mine" interesting relationships from monitoring data and/or metadata stored in the Grid middleware. Given that a Grid search engine is expected to be used primarily to provide summary information and hints, it should also have additional support for collecting and mining historical data, identifying patterns of use, persistent relationships, etc.

The Complexity of Queries and Query Results. The basic paradigm supported by Search Engines to locate WWW resources is based on traditional information retrieval mechanisms, i.e., keyword-based search and simple boolean expressions. This functionality is supported by indices and dictionaries created and maintained at the back-end of a search engine with the help of information retrieval techniques. Querying for Grid resources must be more powerful and flexible. To this end, we need more expressive query languages, that support compositional queries over extensible schemas [6]. Moreover, we need to employ techniques combining information-retrieval and data-mining algorithms to build proper indexes that will enable the extrapolation of semantic relationships between resources and the effective execution of user queries.

Given that the expected difficulty of queries ranges from that of very small enquiries to requests requiring complicated joins, intelligent-agent interfaces are required to help users formulate queries and the search engine to compute efficiently those queries. Of equal importance is the presentation of query results within a representative conceptual context of the Grid, so that users can navigate within the complex space of query results via simple interfaces and mechanisms of low cognitive load.

4   GRISEN Architecture

The effort needed to provide adequate information services on the Grid can partly be leveraged by considering, as a starting point, existing search engine technologies, which are subsequently enhanced with appropriate models and mechanisms to address the problems discussed above. In our envisaged Grid Search Engine, GRISEN, crawlers crawl the Grid collecting meta-information for Grid resources and policies thereof. Collected information is organized by a number of constructed indexes representing semantic and policy information about each resource. Access to GRISEN is provided to users through an intelligent-agent interface enabling simple, keyword-based searches and more complicated queries that take as arguments user-needs and preferences.

The purpose of GRISEN is not to change the existing layered architecture of the Grid or to substitute systems at each layer. Instead, GRISEN provides a universal interface that sits on the top, exploits the information provided by the layers underneath, and can be used by users to pinpoint a set of Grid resources

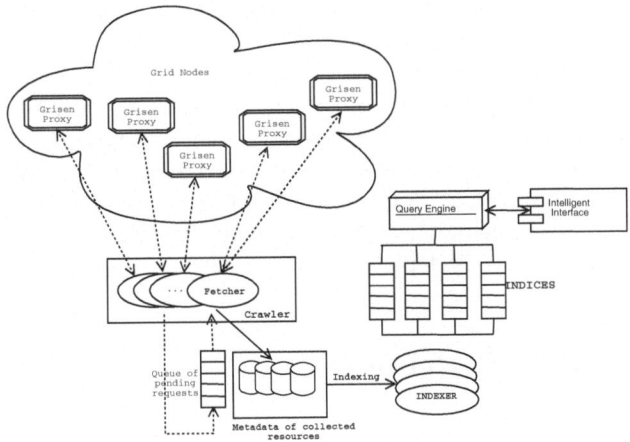

Fig. 1. Architecture of GRISEN.

that can be employed to achieve their goals, before proceeding with firing their application and invoking the necessary tools and services at the collective layer.

The architecture of GRISEN is established upon the notion of a Grid resource, which is represented by a complex data model, defined in the context of GRISEN. For the metadata of a Grid node to be retrievable by GRISEN, it has to become available at an information provider node or proxy, wherefrom it will be fetched by GRISEN.

Therefore, each Grid node is expected to have a corresponding proxy. Typically, the proxy is closely integrated with the node, in order to facilitate the efficient generation and publishing of the node's metadata. The proxy achieves this with the invocation of enquiry mechanisms provided at the fabric layer of the Grid. Some proxies, however, provide information about a wider range of resources belonging to different nodes under, for instance, the information directory service of a common administrative domain. Alternatively, proxies provide information regarding resources that span throughout different administrative domains but are perceived as a single subsystem or family of resources by application developers and users (e.g., a network connection, an index of CFD software, etc). Finally, a set of Grid resources can be represented by more than one proxy, each of which may provide complementary information.

Consequently, and due to the variety of existing and emerging Grid platforms, protocols and middleware, the specification of the proxy must comply with only a minimum set of requirements that enable the retrieval of metadata about the corresponding Grid resource from its proxy, via well defined, open protocols. Furthermore, each proxy should be uniquely identifiable via a universal naming scheme, possibly compliant to the naming schemes of the WWW (URL).

GRISEN consists of five basic modules: (i) **Proxies** distributed throughout the Grid, running query mechanisms at the fabric layer of the Grid to extract information about local resources. (ii) The multi-threaded, distributed **"crawler"** that discovers and accesses proxies to retrieve metadata for the underlying Grid resources, and transform them into the GRISEN data-model. (iii) The **indexer**, which processes collected metadata, using information retrieval and data mining techniques, to create indexes that can be used for resolving user queries. (iv) The **query engine**, which recognizes the query language of GRISEN and processes queries coming from the user-interface of the search engine. (v) The **intelligent-agent interface** that helps users issue complicated queries when looking for combined resources requiring the joining of many relations. The overview of the whole system architecture is depicted in Figure 1.

5   The Context of GRISEN

GRISEN is expected to function in the context of a Grid viewed as a constellation of resources represented by "heterogeneous" information providers-proxies, with unique addresses, encapsulating meta-information about these resources in a common data model, and enabling the retrieval of this meta-information from remote hosts via well-defined protocols. To implement GRISEN in this context, the following issues need to be addressed:

Exporting Local Metadata into the Proxies: This issue refers to the extraction to the proxy of metadata describing the resources of a Grid node. Metadata must comply with a common data model to be defined in GRISEN. A specification of the proxy structure and interface to the Grid node are required; this interface must be compliant with the enquiry protocols implemented by various Grid platforms, different types of nodes, etc. A proxy can be many things: a simple index of local resources created by the Grid node, published on a Web server and accessed via HTTP; a daemon running on a network port of the node, awaiting for requests complying to a platform-specific protocol; a mobile agent launched by GRISEN and parked at a node hosting a directory of resources and running periodic queries to extract meta-information. Besides supporting the protocols of acknowledged Grid platforms like Globus or Unicore, GRISEN would need to employ a minimalist approach for defining, naming, addressing, and implementing proxies.

Discovery of Proxies: GRISEN must implement efficient mechanisms for discovery of Grid-resource descriptions throughout Internet. As a first step to facilitate the discovery process, GRISEN can explore naming schemes that can be adopted to identify proxies and Grid resources. Different approaches need to be studied and compared. For example: (i) periodic "crawling" of the Grid for the discovery of "passive" proxies, or (ii) updates of GRISEN structures by "active" proxies whenever metadata change. For the effective discovery of proxies in the presence of hundreds of thousands of Grid nodes on Internet, it is important to define and exploit the semantic and administrative "relationships" that will be established between Grid resources, as users exploit the benefits of the Grid and form dynamic Virtual Organizations, using multiple Grid nodes to solve a problem, coupling different codes, etc.

Retrieval of Metadata: Upon discovery of a proxy, GRISEN must retrieve and store its metadata for further processing. This simple task must be highly efficient and scalable with respect to the size of the Grid. Moreover, it is critical to incorporate proper scheduling, replacement and garbage-collection mechanisms in order to monitor and follow the rate of change of resources, to maintain the freshness of collected metadata, to achieve the prompt disposal of obsolete resources, etc.

Organization and Management of Data, Query Mechanisms and Interface: Collected metadata must be analyzed with techniques combining information-retrieval and data-mining algorithms to build proper indexes that will enable the extrapolation of semantic relationships between resources and the effective execution of user queries. A query language will be developed. Given that the expected difficulty of queries ranges from that of very small enquiries to requests requiring complicated joins, an intelligent-agent interface is required to help users formulate queries to the GRISEN data model.

6   Summary and Conclusion

The motivation for the ideas described in this paper stems from the need to provide effective information services to the users of the envisaged massive Grids. The main contributions of GRISEN, as it is envisaged, are expected to revolve around the following issues: a) The provision of a high-level, platform-independent, user-oriented tool that can be used to retrieve a variety of Grid resource-related information in a large Grid setting, which may consist of a number of platforms possibly using different middlewares. b) The standardization of different approaches to view resources in the Grid and their relationships, thereby enhancing the understanding of Grids. c) The development of appropriate data management techniques to cope with a large diversity of information

Acknowledgement

The first author wishes to acknowledge the partial support of this work by the European Union through the CrossGrid project (contract IST-2001-32243).

References

1. R. Aiken, M. Carey, B. Carpenter, I. Foster, C. Lynch, J. Mambreti, R. Moore, J. Strasnner, and B. Teitelbaum.   Network Policy and Services: A Report of a Workshop on Middleware.   Technical Report RFC 2768, IETF, 2000. http://www.ietf.org/rfc/rfc2768.txt.
2. A. Arasu, J. Cho, H. Garcia-Molina, A. Paepcke, and S. Raghavan. Searching the Web. *ACM Transactions on Internet Technology*, 1(1):2–43, 2001.
3. R. Bramley, K. Chiu, S. Diwan, D. Gannon, M. Govindaraju, N. Mukhi, B. Temko, and M. Yechuri. A Component based Services Architecture for Building Distributed Applications. In *Proceedings of the 9th IEEE International Symposium on High Performance Distributed Computing*, pages 51–59, 2000.

4. S. Brin and L. Page. The Anatomy of a Large-Scale Hypertextual (Web) Search Engine. *Computer Networks and ISDN Systems*, 30(1–7):107–117, 1998.
5. K. Czajkowski, S. Fitzgerald, I. Foster, and C. Kesselman. Grid Information Services for Distributed Resource Sharing. In *Proceedings 10th IEEE International Symposium on High Performance Distributed Computing (HPDC-10'01)*, pages 181–194. IEEE Computer Society, 2001.
6. Peter Dinda and Beth Plale. A Unified Relational Approach to Grid Information Services. Global Grid Forum, GWD-GIS-012-1, February 2001.
7. D. W. Erwin and D. F. Snelling. UNICORE: A Grid Computing Environment. In *Lecture Notes in Computer Science*, volume 2150, pages 825–834. Springer, 2001.
8. Steve Fisher. Relational Model for Information and Monitoring. Technical Report, Global Grid Forum, 2001.
9. S. Fitzgerald, I. Foster, C. Kesselman, G. von Laszewski, W. Smith, and S. Tuecke. A Directory Service for Configuring High-Performance Distributed Computations. In *Proceedings of the 6th IEEE Symp. on High-Performance Distributed Computing*, pages 365–375. IEEE Computer Society, 1997.
10. I. Foster, C. Kesselman, and S. Tuecke. The Anatomy of the Grid: Enabling Scalable Virtual Organizations. *International J. Supercomputer Applications*, 15(3), 2001.
11. D. Gunter and K. Jackson. The Applicability of RDF-Schema as a Syntax for Describing Grid Resource Metadata. Global Grid Forum, GWD-GIS-020-1, June 2001.
12. Adriana Iamnitchi and Ian Foster. On Fully Decentralized Resource Discovery in Grid Environments. *Lecture Notes in Computer Science*, 2242:51–62, 2001.
13. C. Lee, S. Matsuoka, D. Talia, A. Sussman, M. Mueller, G. Allen, and J. Saltz. A Grid Programming Primer. Global Grid Forum, Advanced Programming Models Working Group, GWD-I, August 2001.
14. B. Plale, P. Dinda, and G. von Laszewski. Key Concepts and Services of a Grid Information Service. In *Proceedings of the 15th International Conference on Parallel and Distributed Computing Systems (PDCS 2002)*, 2002.
15. Warren Smith and Dan Gunter. Simple LDAP Schemas for Grid Monitoring. Global Grid Forum, GWD-Perf-13-1, June 2001.
16. USC/ISI. *MDS2.2: User Guide*, 2 2003.
17. G. von Laszewski and I. Foster. Usage of LDAP in Globus. http://www.globus.org/mds/globus_in_ldap.html, 2002.
18. G. von Laszewski, M. Helm, M. Fitzerald, P. Vanderbilt, B. Didier, P. Lane, and M. Swany. GOSv3: A Data Definition Language for Grid Information Services. http://www.mcs.anl.gov/gridforum/gis/reports/gos-v3/gos-v3.2.html.
19. G. von Laszewski and P. Lane. MDSMLv1: An XML Binding to the Grid Object Specification. Global Grid Forum, GWD-GIS-002. http://www-unix.mcs.anl.gov/gridforum/gis/reports/mdsml-v1/html/.
20. W. Yeong, T. Howes, and S. Kille. Lightweight Directory Access Protocol. IETF, RFC 1777, 1995. http://www.ietf.org/rfc/rfc1777.txt.
21. D. Zeinalipour-Yazti and M. Dikaiakos. Design and Implementation of a Distributed Crawler and Filtering Processor. In A. Halevy and A. Gal, editors, *Proceedings of the Fifth Workshop on Next Generation Information Technologies and Systems (NGITS 2002)*, volume 2382 of *Lecture Notes in Computer Science*, pages 58–74. Springer, June 2002.

Design and Implementation
of a Grid-Enabled Component Container
for *CORBA Lightweight Components**

Diego Sevilla[1], José M. García[1], and Antonio Gómez[2]

[1] Department of Computer Engineering
University of Murcia, Spain
{dsevilla,jmgarcia}@ditec.um.es
[2] Department of Information and Communications Engineering
University of Murcia, Spain
skarmeta@dif.um.es

Abstract. Although Grid technology appears as a promising infrastructure for global computation and effective resource sharing, the development of Grid Applications is still based in traditional programming models such as Message Passing Interface (MPI), making it difficult to provide a good level of software reuse and productivity. Moreover, the Grid offers an environment where the component technology can be applied to a greater extent than ever, due to the intrinsic security enforced by the Grid, allowing the creation of a successful component market. Component technology accelerates software development enforcing software reuse and sharing. In this article we present CORBA-$\mathcal{LC}$ and the design of its Container, that manage components and provides them with non-functional aspects such as security, concurrency, distribution, load balancing, fault tolerance, replication, data-parallelism, etc. Component implementors can thus focus only on the component functionality itself, independently of these aspects, provided by the Container. Furthermore, we identify these non-functional aspects in the Grid Computing domain and show the current status of the implementation.

1   Introduction and Related Work

Grid technology [4] has emerged as a new paradigm for reusing the computing power available in organizations worldwide. Particularly, Grid toolkits like Globus [7] and frameworks like *Open Grid Services Architecture* (OGSA) [11] help establishing a standard framework for integrating new developments, services, users, organizations, and resources.

Within these frameworks, which offer the foundation for the development of the Grid, distributed component models fit seamlessly to provide a higher level services for integrating and reusing components and applications.

---

* Partially supported by Spanish SENECA Foundation, Grant PB/32/FS/02.

F. Fernández Rivera et al. (Eds.): Across Grids 2003, LNCS 2970, pp. 59–66, 2004.

Component models allow developing parts of applications as independent components. These components can be connected together to build applications, and represent the unit of development, installation, deployment and reuse [16].

Taken together, the benefits of both the Grid and components raise the level of reuse and resource availability, allowing the development of a "component market", in which all the organization offer their components and services.

Traditional component models such as *Enterprise Java Beans* (EJB) and the *CORBA Component Model* (CCM) [10] are not suited for Grid computing because the enterprise services overhead. Thus, other component models oriented towards the Grid have appeared, such as the *Common Component Architecture* (CCA) [1], the work of Rana et al. [8] and Furmento et al. [5]. However, these works do not offer a complete component model, neither packaging nor deployment models, making it difficult to manage applications and services in the Grid environment.

In this article we present the *CORBA Lightweight Components* (CORBA–$\mathcal{LC}$) distributed component model and study the design and implementation strategies for its component container.

2   The CORBA–$\mathcal{LC}$ Component Model

CORBA Lightweight Components (CORBA–$\mathcal{LC}$) [14,15] is a lightweight component model based on CORBA, sharing many features with the CORBA Component Model (CCM)[10].

The following are the main conceptual blocks of CORBA–$\mathcal{LC}$:

- **Components.** Components are the most important abstraction in CORBA–$\mathcal{LC}$. They are both a *binary package* that can be installed and managed by the system and a *component type*, which defines the characteristics of component instances (interfaces offered and needed, events, etc.) Component characteristics are exposed by the **Reflection Architecture**.
- **Containers and Component Framework.** Component instances are run within a run-time environment called **container**. Containers become the instances view of the world. Instances ask the container for the required services and it in turn informs the instance of its environment (its *context*). Component/container dialog is based on agreed local interfaces, thus conforming a component framework. The design and implementation strategies for the CORBA–$\mathcal{LC}$ containers are described in Section 3.
- **Packaging Model.** The packaging allows to build self-contained binary units which can be installed and used independently. Components are packaged in ".ZIP" files containing the component itself and its description as IDL and XML files. The packaging allows storing different binaries of the same component to match different Hardware/Operating System/ORB.
- **Deployment and Network Model.** The deployment model describes the rules a set of components must follow to be installed and run in a set of network-interconnected machines in order to cooperate to perform

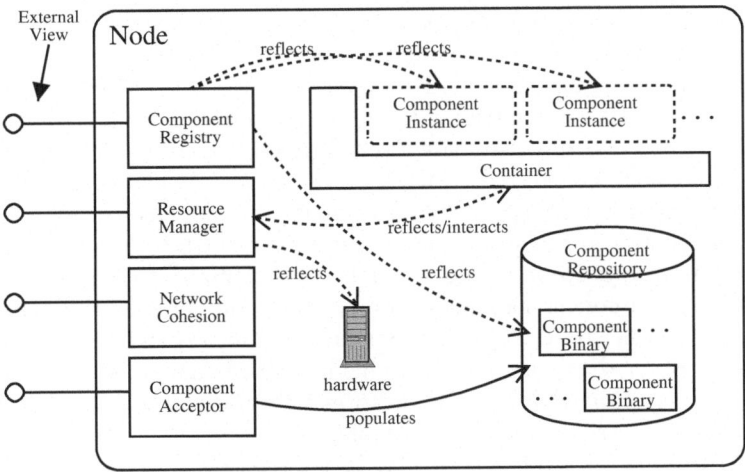

Fig. 1. Logical Node Structure.

a task. CORBA–$\mathcal{LC}$ deployment model is supported by a set of main concepts: **nodes**, the **reflection architecture**, the **network model**, the **distributed registry** and **applications**.

- **Nodes.** The CORBA–$\mathcal{LC}$ network model can be seen as a set of nodes (hosts) that collaborate in computations. Nodes maintain the logical network connection, encapsulate physical host information and constitute the external view of the internal properties of the host they are running on. Concretely, they offer (Fig. 1):
  * A way of obtaining both node static characteristics (such as CPU, Operating System type, ORB) and dynamic system information (such as CPU and memory load, available resources, etc.): *Resource Manager* interface.
  * A way of obtaining the external view of the local services: the *Component Registry* interface reflects the internal *Component Repository* and allows performing distributed component queries.
  * Hooks for accepting new components at run-time for local installation, instantiation and running [9] (*Component Acceptor* interface).
  * Operations supporting the protocol for logical *Network Cohesion*.
- **The Reflection Architecture.** Is composed of the meta-data given by the different node services:
  * The *Component Registry* provides information about (a) running components, (b) the set of component instances running in the node and the properties of each, and (c) how those instances are connected via ports (assemblies)[13]. This information is used when components, applications or visual builder tools need to obtain information about components.

* the **Resource Manager** in the node collaborates with the **Container** implementing initial placement of instances, migration/load balancing at run-time. Resource Manager also reflects the hardware static characteristics and dynamic resource usage and availability.

- **Network Model and the Distributed Registry.** The CORBA–$\mathcal{LC}$ deployment model is a network-centered model: The complete network is considered as a repository for resolving component requirements. Each host (node) in the system maintain a set of installed components in its **Component Repository**, which become available to the whole network. When component instances require other components, the network can decide either to fetch the component to be locally installed, instantiated and run or to use it remotely. This network behavior is implemented by the **Distributed Registry**. It stores information covering the resources available in the network as a whole.
- **Applications and Assembly.** In CORBA–$\mathcal{LC}$, *applications* are just special components. They are special because (1) they encapsulate the explicit rules to connect together certain components and their instances (*assembly*), and (2) they are created by users with the help of visual building tools. Thus, they can be considered as **bootstrap** components.

3   A Grid-Enabled Container for CORBA–$\mathcal{LC}$

Containers in CORBA–$\mathcal{LC}$ mediate between component instances and the infrastructure (both CORBA–$\mathcal{LC}$ runtime and the Grid middleware). Instances ask the container for needed resources (for instance, other components), and it, in turn, provides them with their *context* (the set of data associated with each component instance). The building blocks of a container are shown in Figure 2, as well as its responsibilities within a call by the component client. Concretely, container's responsibilities include [17]:

- **Manage Component Instances.** It interacts with the component factory to maintain the set of active component instances, as well as instance activation and deactivation.
- **Provide a Controlled Execution Environment for Instances.** They obtain all the network resources (their *view* or *context*) from the container, becoming their representative into the network. The communication between container and instances is made through agreed local interfaces.
- **Provide Transparent Fault Tolerance, Security, Migration, and Load Balancing.** The container intercepts all the calls made to the component instances it manages. This gives the container the chance to redirect the calls to the correct component or to group component instances to implement fault tolerance. There are two main strategies to implement this behavior:

  Interception. Using CORBA as a foundation, *Portable Interceptors* [10] can be used to intercept every call to the instance. This is more flexible and generic, but inefficient.

Code Generation. With this approach, an utility can take interface definitions and non-functional aspects of the component (described as XML files) and generate a customized container. The container becomes a wrapper for the component. This approach is more efficient because the container is made *for* the component. Moreover, the code generation can also convert the generated container into an *adapter* [6] to offer the component interfaces as Grid Services compliant with the OGSA specification [11].

3.1   Control Flow When Interacting with Component Instances

Figure 2 shows the flow that a client call follows within the Container. The client call in intercepted by the Container's POA[1] (1). The POA invokes the Servant Locator of the Container (2), who is in charge of locating the actual component instance for the call. If the instance is not already activated, it will activate it. Alternatively, the call may be redirected to another host depending on the requirements on the application (e.g. replication, etc.) (3). The Component Instance now takes the control, executing the required operation (4). During the operation, the instance may call the container to obtain services from the network (5), such as other components or resources. The instance then returns the results of the operation (6), and the Servant Locator takes the control again (7). At this point, it can decide whether to passivate the instance to save system resources or not. The POA finally returns the results to the caller. Points (3) to (7) represent interception points.

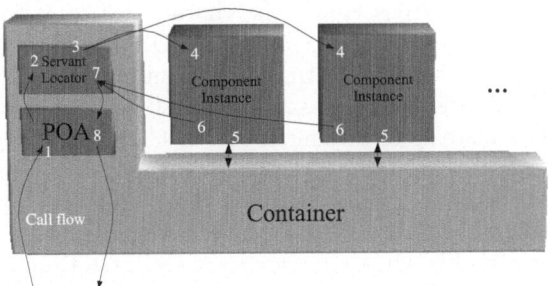

Fig. 2. Component instances and interception within a Container. The request comes from (and returns to) the client.

3.2   Aspect-Oriented Programming and the Grid

While traditional component models as EJB and CCM cover the needs of enterprise-oriented applications, we believe they are not suited for dealing with Grid or HPC applications, because of the burden of enterprise-oriented services, such

---

[1] Portable Object Adapter–Manages the set of CORBA objects hosted by a server.

as persistence or transactions. Moreover, they have a fixed set of aspects, making them difficult to adapt to those environments.

Following the Aspect-Oriented Programming (AOP) paradigm [2], we have identified a set of aspects that components can specify so that the container can manage them effectively in a Grid environment. This list is not exhaustive, and is a result of our ongoing research on this area:

- **Instance Lifetime and Service.** Defines the lifetime of instances. Helps the container to manage instances.
- **Integration with Grid Security.** Specifies the security restriction of this component. The container must ensure component security restrictions by leveraging the grid infrastructure.
- **Mobility.** If the component can travel or must be run remotely. The former allows physical component distribution. The latter is semantically equivalent to an OGSA service.
- **Fault Tolerance** and **Replication.** The container must ensure the level of fault tolerance required by the component (number of replicas, etc.)
- **Data Aggregation and Distribution.** This is interesting for data-parallel components, which can specify how many *workers* they need for the realization of their work, and know how to join partial results. The container is in charge of finding the workers, delivering the data and bringing back the results.

3.3   Aspect-Weaving Code Generator

Containers follow the AOP philosophy [3]. Components specify the non-functional requirements (*aspects*) they need from the environment. This specification is made through XML files describing the characteristics of the component in terms of the defined aspects. Figure 3 shows the CORBA–$\mathcal{LC}$ tool chain. The user provides both the IDL definitions for the component and the XML file describing the component characteristics. This separation allows using traditional ORBs and IDL2 compilers instead of forcing to use a CORBA 3 implementation as CCM does. The CORBA–$\mathcal{LC}$ Code Generator generates the code that interacts with the container for doing aspect weaving, and the IDL Compiler generates traditional CORBA stubs and skeletons. These, together with the Component Implementation provided by the user, are compiled into a Binary DLL (Dynamic Link Library). Finally, the CORBA–$\mathcal{LC}$ Component Packager gets the DLL and the metadata of the component (XML and IDL) and packages it for distribution.

Figure 4 shows the role of the generated weaving code. The component instance is composed of the generated code and the code supplied by the user. The weaving code interacts with the container to provide the required aspects. For instance, if the user (or the application) decides to log the calls to this instance, the generated code will do the logging before calling the actual instance implementation provided by the user. (The same can be applied for security, distribution, etc.) Just after applying desired aspects, it calls the user implementation. The implementation uses the container to obtain resources from the system, such as other components and so on.

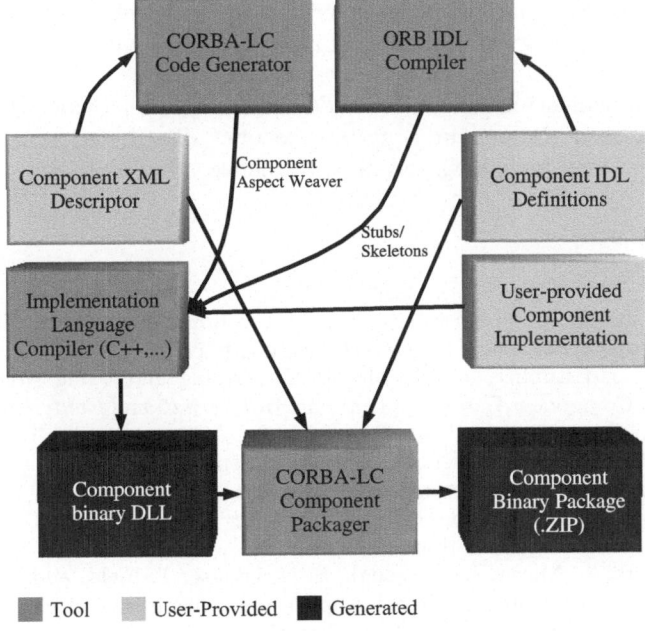

Fig. 3. CORBA–$\mathcal{LC}$ tool chain.

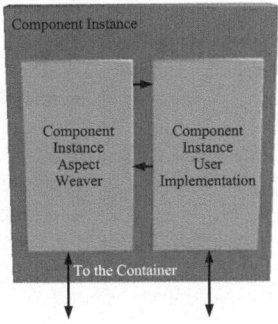

Fig. 4. Internal view of a component instance.

4   Status and Future Work

Current status of CORBA–$\mathcal{LC}$ allows building components and connect them. We are currently researching in the area of aspects suited for grid computing and the design and implementation of the CORBA–$\mathcal{LC}$ container. Concretely, we are working in the following fields:

- Identification of aspects suitable for Grid computing, and its application to CORBA–$\mathcal{LC}$ and the Container and Code Generator. [2].

 - The implementation of the Container and the different aspects such as Grid Security, leveraging the different Commodity Grid Kits (CoG) such as the CORBA CoG [12].
 - We are implementing the CORBA–$\mathcal{LC}$ distributed deployment, which interacts with each component container to offer distributed services such as replication, load balancing and fault tolreance.

References

1. CCA Forum. *The Common Component Architecture Technical Specification - Version 1.0.* http://z.ca.sandia.gov/~cca-forum/gport-spec/.
2. F. Duclos, J. Estublier, and P. Morat. Describing and Using Non Functional Aspects in Component Based Applications. In *International Conference on Aspect-Oriented Software Development, Enschede, The Netherlands*, April 2002.
3. J. Fabry. Distribution as a set of Cooperating Aspects. In *ECOOP'2000 Workshop on Distributed Objects Programming Paradigms*, June 2000.
4. I. Foster and C. Kesselman, editors. *The Grid: Blueprint for a New Computing Infrastructure*. Morgan Kaufmann, 1999.
5. N. Furmento, A. Mayer, S. McGough, S. Newhouse, T. Field, and J. Darlington. Optimisation of Component-based Applications within a Grid Environment. In *SuperComputing 2001, Denver*, November 2001.
6. E. Gamma, R. Helm, R. Johnson, and J. Vlissides. *Design Patterns: Elements of Reusable Object-Oriented Software*. Addison-Wesley, Reading, MA, 1995.
7. *The Globus Project Home Page.* http://www.globus.org/.
8. M. Li, O. F. Rana, M. S. Shields, and D. W. Walker. A Wrapper Generator for Wrapping High Performance Legacy Codes as Java/CORBA Components. In *Supercomputing'2000 Conference, Dallas, TX*, November 2000.
9. R. Marvie, P. Merle, and J-M. Geib. A Dynamic Platform for CORBA Component Based Applications. In *First Intl. Conf. on Software Engineering Applied to Networking and Parallel/Distributed Computing (SNPD'00), France*, May 2000.
10. Object Management Group. *CORBA: Common Object Request Broker Architecture Specification, revision 3.0.1*, 2002. OMG Document formal/02-11-01.
11. *Open Grid Services Architecture.* http://www.globus.org/ogsa.
12. M. Parashar, G. von Laszewski, S. Verma, J. Gawor, K. Keahey, and N. Rehn. A CORBA Comodity Grid Kit. *Concurrency and Computation: Practice and Experience*, 2002.
13. N. Parlavantzas, G. Coulson, M. Clarke, and G. Blair. Towards a Reflective Component-based Middleware Architecture. In *ECOOP'2000 Workshop on Reflection and Metalevel Architectures*, 2000.
14. D. Sevilla, J. M. García, and A. Gómez. CORBA Lightweight Components: A Model for Distributed Component-Based Heterogeneous Computation. In *EUROPAR'2001, Manchester, UK*, August 2001.
15. D. Sevilla, J. M. García, and A. Gómez. Design and Implementation Requirements for CORBA Lightweight Components. In *Metacomputing Systems and Applications Workshop (MSA'01), Valencia, Spain*, September 2001.
16. C. Szyperski. *Component Software: Beyond Object-Oriented Programming*. ACM Press, 1998.
17. M. Vadet and P. Merle. Les conteneurs ouverts dans les plates-formes composants. In *Journées Composants, Besançon, France*, October 2001.

First Prototype of the CrossGrid Testbed

J. Gomes[1], M. David[1], J. Martins[1], L. Bernardo[1], J. Marco[2], R. Marco[2],
D. Rodríguez[2], J. Salt[3], S. Gonzalez[3], J. Sánchez[3], A. Fuentes[4], M. Hardt[5],
A. García[5], P. Nyczyk[6], A. Ozieblo[6], P. Wolniewicz[7], M. Bluj[8], K. Nawrocki[9],
A. Padee[8,9,10], W. Wislicki[8,9], C. Fernández[11], J. Fontán[11], A. Gómez[11],
I. López[11], Y. Cotronis[12], E. Floros[12], G. Tsouloupas[13], W. Xing[13],
M. Dikaiakos[13], J. Astalos[14], B. Coghlan[15], E. Heymann[16], M.A. Senar[16],
G. Merino[17], C. Kanellopoulos[18], and G.D. van Albada[19]

[1] Laboratório de Instrumentação e Física de Partículas, Lisbon, Portugal
[2] Instituto de Física de Cantabria (CSIC), Santander, Spain
[3] Instituto de Física Corpuscular(CSIC), Valencia, Spain
[4] RedIris(CSIC), Madrid, Spain
[5] Forschungszentrum Karlsruhe GMBH, Germany
[6] Akademickie Centrum Komputerowe CYFRONET, Krakow, Poland
[7] Poznan Supercomputing and Networking Center, Poznan, Poland
[8] A.Soltan Institute for Nuclear Studies, Warsaw, Poland
[9] Interdisciplinary Centre for Mathematical and Computational Modelling,
University of Warsaw, Poland
[10] Instytut Radioelektroniki PW, Warsaw, Poland
[11] CESGA, Centro de Supercomputacion de Galicia, Santiago de Compostela, Spain
[12] National Center for Scientific Research "Demokritos", National and Kapodistrian
University of Athens, Dep. of Informatics and Telecommunications, Greece
[13] University of Cyprus, Cyprus
[14] Ustav Informatiky Slovenska Akademia Vied, Bratislava, Slovakia
[15] Trinity College Dublin, Ireland
[16] Universitat Autonoma de Barcelona, Spain
[17] Institut de Fisica d'Altes Energies, Barcelona, Spain
[18] Aristotle University of Thessaloniki, Greece
[19] Universiteit van Amsterdam, Netherlands

Abstract. The CrossGrid project is developing new grid middleware
components, tools and applications with a special focus on parallel and
interactive computing. In order to support the development effort and
provide a test infrastructure, an international grid testbed has been deployed across 9 countries. Through the deployment of the testbed and its
supporting services, CrossGrid is also contributing to another important
project objective, the expansion of the grid coverage in Europe. This
paper describes the status of the CrossGrid testbed.

1   Introduction

The CrossGrid international distributed testbed will share resources across sixteen European sites and this is one of the challenging points of the CrossGrid
project.

F. Fernández Rivera et al. (Eds.): Across Grids 2003, LNCS 2970, pp. 67–77, 2004.

The sites list range from relatively small computing facilities in universities, to large computing centers, offering an ideal mixture to test the possibilities of the Grid framework.

National research networks and the high-performance European network, Géant, will assure the interconnectivity between all sites. The network includes usually three steps: the local step (typically inside a University or Research Center, via Fast or Gigabit Ethernet), the jump via the national network provider (at speeds that will range from 34 Mbits/s to 622 Mbits/s or even Gigabit) to the national node, and finally the link to the Géant network (155 Mbits/s to 2.5 Gbits/s).

The figure 1 shows the geographical map for the different nodes, including the major "network" links.

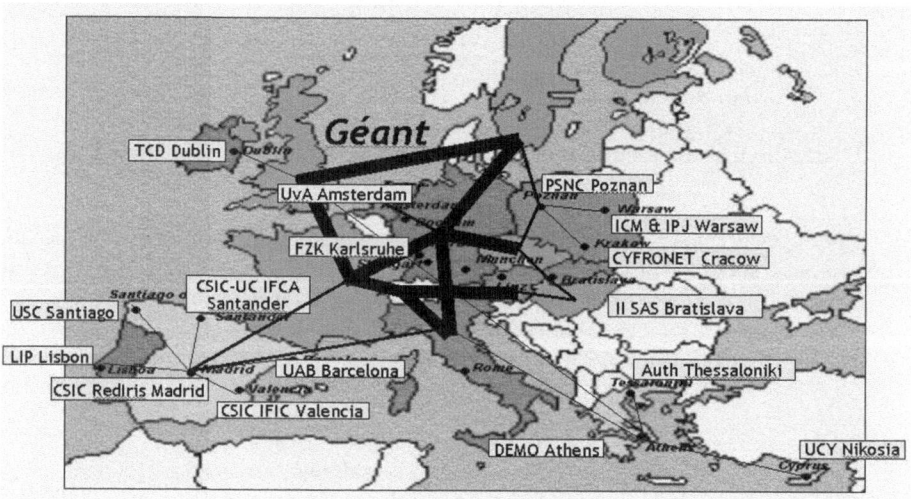

Fig. 1. CrossGrid testbed map.

The CrossGrid testbed largely benefits from the DataGrid [1] experience on testbed setup: since the CrossGrid middleware is being developed it was decided that initially the testbed middleware would have to be based entirely in Data-Grid (EDG) and Globus middleware distributions. The efforts to establish an integrated CrossGrid testbed started with the release of EDG 1.2.0, however several problems where found in the first deployed sites. The EDG release 1.2.2 with improved stability has allowed more sites to join in spite of some serious middleware limitations. Currently EDG 1.2.2 and 1.2.3 are deployed in the production testbed, while the version 1.4.3 is being tested at several validation sites; it is expected that it will overcome many of the major limitations of the previous versions allowing the interconnection of both CrossGrid and DataGrid testbeds.

2 Testbed Status

At least sixteen sites are foreseen to be included in the CrossGrid testbed[2], this number may be increased with the addition of more sites interested in the technologies and applications being developed by CrossGrid, and with the addition of more sites belonging to CrossGrid partners. These 16 sites are being deployed and registered into the CrossGrid Resource Broker (RB).

The table 1 shows the testbed deployment status in the end of February 2003.

Table 1. Testbed site status.

Site	Location	Version	RB registration
CYFRONET	Cracow	1.2.2	Production
ICM	Warsaw	1.2.2	Production
INS	Warsaw	1.2.2	Production
UvA	Amsterdam	1.2.2	NOT registered
FZK	Karlsruhe	1.4.3	Validation
IISAS	Bratislava	1.2.3	Production
PSNC	Poznan	1.2.2	Production
UCY	Nikosia	1.2.2	NOT registered
TCD	Dublin	1.2.3	Production
IFIC	Valencia	1.2.3	Production
IFCA	Santander	1.2.2	NOT registered
UAB	Barcelona	1.2.2	Production (under test)
USC/CESGA	Santiago	1.2.2	Production
Demokritos	Athens	1.4.3	Validation
AUTH	Thessaloniki	1.2.2	Production
LIP	Lisbon	1.2.3 1.4.3	Production, Validation (two clusters)

3 Testbeds

According with the CrossGrid testbed architecture and minimum hardware requirements [3] each site must have at least five system components:

Gatekeeper: is the system that provides the gateway through which Jobs are submitted to local farm nodes. The gatekeeper is the interface through which grid enabled systems can use the local resources.

Worker Node (WN): is a local farm computing node where jobs are actually executed. Jobs received by the Gatekeeper are sent to the WN through the local batch scheduling system. Many worker nodes can exist behind a single Gatekeeper. The combination of a Gatekeeper with their worker nodes is usually called a Computing Element (CE).

Storage Element (SE): is the generic name used for any storage resource that includes a Grid interface ranging from large Hierarchical Storage Management Systems to disk pools.

User Interface (UI): is the system used by end-users to submit jobs to the grid Computing Elements. The job submission is usually performed through a resource broker.

LCFG Installation Server: is used to install, configure and maintain the above systems from a single management system. The installation server is required for the proper installation and ease of maintenance of the EDG middleware.

Although we talk about a generic CrossGrid testbed, in fact several "testbeds" will co-exist to support different efforts, from pure development, to production after validation. The following testbeds are foreseen [4]:

Development Testbed: new middleware or application software development will require a dedicated small but well maintained testbed, allowing its test in a Grid aware framework. The testbed setup will include a dedicated minimal configuration, and the flexibility to adapt to the required changes in the external software packages (like for example migrating from Globus 2 to Globus 3, or from RedHat 6.2 to RedHat 7.3). The development testbed will also provide the environment to integrate the developed components into software releases.

Test and Validation Testbed: each new middleware release will require a complete validation process that will include extensive tests. These tests must be performed in a tight controlled environment without disturbing the production and development testbeds. The dedicated validation testbed supports this effort, and is being offered by LIP, FZK, CSIC(IFIC), USC(CESGA) and DEMO.

Finally the **Production testbed** will be used to run the applications, showing the Grid potential. It will be extended over all testbed sites: CYFRONET, ICM, INS, UvA, IISAS, FZK, PSNC, UCY, TCD, IFCA, UAB, USC, DEMO, AUTh, IFIC and LIP.

The first CrossGrid testbed prototype was born from the initial "test and validation" testbed, managed by the LIP group. This effort has been very successful: external site resources have been included in the corresponding Resource Broker and users joined the Virtual Organizations. Jobs have been successfully submitted through User Interface nodes at each testbed site.

Basic tests covering the Globus and EDG middleware functionalities have been performed using the testbed. These tests cover the job submission using Globus and the EDG RB, file transfer with GSI ftp, file replication with GDMP, file replication with the Replica Manager, the VO server and the MDS information system.

Currently the initial "test and validation" testbed running EDG 1.2.2 and 1.2.3 was moved into production, and a new "test and validation" testbed running EDG 1.4.3 is now deployed and running within a limited set of sites (LIP, FZK and Demokritos). This new "test and validation" testbed will be used to test the first CrossGrid software release that will include: monitoring tools, development tools, a remote access server, portals and a prototype of the parallel resource broker.

Tables 2 and 3 show the resources available in the production and validation testbeds respectively.

Table 2. "Production" testbed resources.

Computing Elements	15
Worker Nodes	69
CPUs	115
Storage Elements	14
Storage Capacity	2.7TB

Table 3. "Test and validation" testbed resources.

Computing Elements	3
Worker Nodes	4
CPUs	5
Storage Elements	3
Storage Capacity	1.2TB

The resource tables for the production testbed already show a considerable amount of computing and storage resources. The amount of resources will grow as the sites commit more nodes. Namely it is expected that once RedHat 7.3 is made available in the testbed several existing production cluster will be added to the grid. A method for adding existing clusters running different Linux flavours from the one supported by EDG, is being studied. If a suitable solution is found, then it will be possible to deploy existing Linux clusters as worker nodes without interfering with the installed software.

Although the "test and validation" testbed has fewer resources it has been very successful in testing the EDG releases 1.4.x. Their resources are currently providing the platform for the integration of the first CrossGrid software release.

4   Tests and Applications

Three CrossGrid sites (FZK, IFIC and LIP) have participated at the IST 2002 demonstration event showing the interoperation of the CrossGrid sites with other testbeds. During the demonstration several jobs have been successfully executed in the three participating CrossGrid sites.

In addition the first tests with MPI in the testbed have been performed. Since the EDG RB doesn't support parallel applications the program executions have been performed using the Globus job submission capabilities directly. The MPI package used for the tests was MPICH-G2 a variant of the MPICH implementation using Globus IO for inter-process communication and Globus DUROC for resource co-allocation. In the same context tests were performed on how to start the parallel applications. Although MPICH provides its own program start-up command named mpirun, the MPICH-G2 mpirun command has some limitations. Therefore other methods to submit jobs to selected resources have been tested.

At the same time, the first CrossGrid software prototypes are being developed. A prototype of the HEP application has been released, requiring MPI and very low latency. Tests aiming to validate the prototype architecture and the testbed middleware with a full CrossGrid application are being performed in the testbed. The tests of the HEP application have shown the feasibility of running full applications across testbed sites with MPICH-G2.

5   Collaborative Tools

The basic collaborative tools are the WP4 web pages (that can be found at http://grid.ifca.unican.es/crossgrid/wp4) and the videoconference system VRVS (http://vrvs.org): its usage allows that, coordination meetings take place regularly with the participation of all sites (14 meetings in 9 months). VRVS has proved to be both inexpensive and flexible since it uses the Internet as communications medium and supports a wide range of audio and video devices. Many operating systems are supported and most portable computers can be used with VRVS.

Web pages containing information about the central testbed services are available at the LIP web server. The main link for the pages related with the production testbed is http://www.lip.pt/computing/cg-services. These web pages also contain pointers to usage statistics and information on how to configure the testbed sites. Useful information on how to diagnose problems and a list of common configuration problems is also provided. The pages are both a central place to find updated information about the testbed and a first level user support tool where users can cross check their site configurations and obtain helpful hints on how to solve common problems. A second web page containing the same information for the test and validation testbed is available at http://www.lip.pt/computing/cg-tv-services.

6   Central Services

A set of central services[2] is required for proper testbed operation. These services are essential for user authentication, authorization, workload management, monitoring and location of file replicas.

One of the most important central services is the Virtual Organizations server that contains the CrossGrid VO. To use the CrossGrid VO for authentication, configuration changes have to be made in all testbed systems. The support for VO site configuration is provided through the central services web pages at http://www.lip.pt/computing/cg-services. CrossGrid users wishing to join the CrossGrid VO should send their request by Email with an explanation of their participation in the project and containing the X.509 user certificate. This procedure will be used until a web interface for VO enrollment,which is under development is made available.

The Resource Broker (RB) is the central service responsible for the management of the testbed workload. The RB receives user job requests submitted through User Interface nodes. Access control is performed using a local authorization file rebuilt from the CrossGrid VO server. Once a user is authenticated and authorized to access the RB the job description is transferred from the UI to the RB and a matchmaking operation is started to find computing resources matching the job requirements. In the matchmaking the RB uses information about the existing computing resources in the testbed obtained from the Globus MDS information system. For this purpose the RB consults a MDS Information Index (II) server containing pointers to the MDS information servers (published by every CE and SE). When the job description contains references to logical files the RB must also query the central Replica Catalogue to obtain the location of the corresponding physical replicas in order to select the CE that has a near SE containing replicas of the requested files. Finally the RB uses the central MyProxy server to renew the job credentials when needed.

The MyProxy server is an authentication credential proxy used by the RB to renew the proxy certificates of long-lived jobs. MyProxy stores certificates on behalf of other subjects and can issue or renew short-term proxy certificates based on stored certificates.

The system hosting the RB also hosts the Logging and Bookkeeping (LB) database. The LB is used to record information about job status and can be queried to obtain the status of a job or historic data about previously submitted jobs. The logging information is stored in a MySQL relational database.

Two RBs have been deployed, one for the production testbed and a second for the "test and validation" testbed. However in the production testbed the II server is hosted in the RB while in the "test and validation" it is hosted in a separate system.

The last central service is the Replica Catalogue (RC). Currently the RC is an LDAP server containing logical file names. For each logical file name the server contains the location of the physical file replicas. The physical file replicas can be stored in multiple testbed SEs. The replica catalogue is a key piece in the data access optimization since when combined with the RB it allows jobs to be executed at sites where the required data files are already present, hence minimizing data transfers and reducing data access time and network bandwidth usage. File replication software such as the Replica Manager and GDMP make use of the Replica Catalogue to register the location of the replicated files. Again two RCs have been deployed one for each testbed.

All CrossGrid central services are being hosted at the LIP Computer Centre in Lisbon.

7   Certification Authorities

The authentication of users and systems is performed through a public key infrastructure based on X.509 certificates. Since certificates must be issued by trusted certification authorities (CAs) CrossGrid choose to trust the national CAs already established by DataGrid, and to coordinate the deployment of new national CA's where necessary[2]. New grid certification authorities have been established in the countries where they were not previously available namely: Poland, Germany, Slovakia, Greece and Cyprus. A strong effort was made to make the new CAs recognized by DataGrid creating new opportunities for sharing resources between CrossGrid and DataGrid and therefore extending the grid coverage in Europe.

8   Testbed Monitoring

Users and site administrators can obtain information about the testbed status [2] from the mapcenter web pages available at http://mapcenter.lip.pt. Mapcenter is an important tool for testbed support since it provides a quick global view of the testbed status and historical data that can be used to identify the origin of problems occurred in the past. The mapcenter web pages are extremely important for site administrators since they allow them to check the site services connectivity. Mapcenter has been improved with the addition of links for usage statistics covering the RBs and CEs usage.

The statistics module for the RB collects information from the MySQL logging and bookkeeping database containing historical data about the job submissions performed through the RB. The current RB doesn't support parallel applications therefore all MPI application tests involving communication across clusters don't appear in the RB statistics. CrossGrid is working on extending the EDG RB to support MPI parallel applications. The tables 4 and 5 show the usage of both the production and validation RBs. The meaning of each table row is explained below:

- **Total users:** number of different user certificates that have been used to submit jobs through the RB.
- **Total jobs sent to the RB:** number of job submissions that have been attempted from user interfaces.
- **Total jobs accepted by the RB:** number of job submissions that have been authenticated and accepted by the RB.
- **Total jobs with good match:** number of jobs submitted for which the RB has found testbed resources matching the request. Matchmaking failures can be caused by jobs requesting unavailable or even inexistent resources.
- **Total jobs submitted by JSS:** jobs submitted by the RB to grid computing resources (Gatekeepers) using the Globus GRAM service.
- **Total jobs run:** number of jobs successfully submitted to grid resources.
- **Total jobs done:** number of jobs that have finished successfully.

The CE statistics module collects information from the gatekeeper log file in every testbed CE. The log file is first retrieved and then parsed to reconstruct the job submission records then web pages with a summary and statistics indexed per user and IP address are produced for each site.

Table 6 shows the total aggregated usage of the "production" CEs while table 7 shows the total aggregated usage of the "test and validation" CEs. The meaning of the CE statistics fields are the following:

- **Total job submissions attempted:** number of connections attempted to the gatekeeper TCP port. Unfortunately due to TCP scans this number can be higher than the actual real job submission attempts.

Table 4. Production RB usage.

Total users	35
Total jobs sent to the RB	2313
Total jobs accepted by the RB	2168
Total jobs with good match	2010
Total jobs submitted by JSS	1988
Total jobs run	1755
Total jobs done	1207

Table 5. Validation RB usage.

Total users	9
Total jobs sent to the RB	5407
Total jobs accepted by the RB	5396
Total jobs with good match	5178
Total jobs submitted by JSS	5167
Total jobs run	5022
Total jobs done	4976

- **Total ping jobs submitted:** number of globus GRAM pings submitted. These aren't real jobs, instead they are used to verify whether a specific globus job-manager is available.
- **Total jobs successfully submitted:** number of jobs submitted, accepted and for which a job-manager was started.

The failed jobs are divided into the following four fields:

- **LCAS failed jobs:** jobs submissions failed due to authorization issues.
- **GSS failed jobs:** jobs submissions failed the GSS authentication protocol. The port scans are included in this error type.
- **CRL failed jobs:** job submissions failed due to outdated CRLs.
- **Jobman failed jobs:** jobs submissions failed due to job-manager related problems such as an inexistent job-manager.

Another important source of information for site administrators is the "host check" web site at http://www.lip.pt/computing/cg-services/site_check. The "host check" web pages are produced by a diagnostics tool that verifies the installation and configuration of the CE and SE systems in the testbed by running several tests covering: file transfer, job submission, accuracy of the information published through MDS and the correctness of the relevant system configuration files. The "host check" web pages are being used to support the deployment of new sites by providing an automated site verification tool that covers the majority of the configuration issues. This tool has also proved to be extremely valuable in the testbed quality assurance helping on the monitoring and certification of new sites.

Table 6. "Production" CEs aggregated usage.

Total job submissions attempted	39168
Total ping jobs submitted	1496
Total jobs successfully submitted	14353
LCAS failed jobs	411
GSS failed jobs	22071
CRL failed jobs	254
Jobman failed jobs	583

Table 7. "Test and Validation" CEs aggregated usage.

Total job submissions attempted	86913
Total ping jobs submitted	2383
Total jobs successfully submitted	79836
LCAS failed jobs	63
GSS failed jobs	4557
CRL failed jobs	18
Jobman failed jobs	56

9   Software Repository

Regarding the software repository[5,6], the Savannah software package has been installed on http://gridportal.fzk.de. Savannah is a web-portal-application based on Sourceforge. It is based on a MySQL database and php/perl scripts and was adapted to the CrossGrid specific needs.

The portal provides the central software repository for CrossGrid. Furthermore Mailinglist-Forums, BugTrackers and CVS services are offered for developer and user communication. The software repository is the official site for the distribution of CrossGrid developed software. The repository also contains other user information such as the installation profiles for the several sites and documentation.

10   Helpdesk

The User Help Desk [5] is the main tool of the User Support Team, this specific development has been carried taking into account the guidelines for the unification of the DataGrid and the CrossGrid Helpdesk. The user Help Desk infrastructure allows all CrossGrid testbed users to get support for encountered problems or questions and access the CrossGrid user documentation. A user could be a scientist using the CrossGrid or a local system administrator of a CrossGrid testbed site. Users can ask all kind of questions related to the Cross-Grid Testbed, covering issues such as certificates usage, installation and configuration, job submission, network security, resource availability, etc. The Help

Desk Database administrator takes care of the utility and will control the efficiency of the method trying to improve it whenever possible. The CrossGrid HelpDesk is a Web based helpdesk system incorporating PHP, Javascript and MySQL, customized from the OneOrZero initiative. The help desk is oriented not only to end users but also to developers and system administrators.

Acknowledgements

We would like to thank the support from the following projects and institutions:

1. The CrossGrid project IST-2001-32243
2. The DataGrid project IST-2000-25182
3. A. Soltan Institute for Nuclear Studies, Warsaw, Poland, supported by EC IST-2002-32243 and KBN 621/E-78/SPB/5.PRUE/DZ208
4. Interdisciplinary Centre for Mathematical and Computational Modelling, University of Warsaw, supported by EC IST-2002-32243 and KBN 115/E-343/SPB/5.PRUE/DZ206
5. A. Soltan Institute for Nuclear Studies, Warsaw, Poland and Institute for Electronics and Information Technologies, Warsaw Technical University, supported by EC IST-2002-32243 and KBN 621/E-78/SPB/5.PRUE/DZ208
6. Interdisciplinary Centre for Mathematical and Computational Modelling, Univ of Warsaw and A. Soltan Institute for Nuclear Studies, Warsaw, Poland, supported by EC IST-2002-32243 and KBN 115/E-343/SPB/5.PRUE/DZ206

References

1. For a description of the European Data Grid project testbed see for example *Evaluation of Testbed Operation, EU-DataGrid IST-2000-25182, Feb 2002*, and references there in. Available as project deliverable D6.4 from Workpackage 6 at http://www.eu-datagrid.org
2. J.Gomes. *Testbed Extension and Site Status, EU-CrossGrid IST-2001-32243, Feb 2003*. Available as project deliverable D4.4 from Workpackage 4 at http://www.eu-crossgrid.org
3. J.Marco, R.Marco, J.Gomes, M.David, M.Hardt, J.Salt. *Detailed Planning for Testbed Setup, EU-CrossGrid IST-2001-32243, May 2002*. Available as project deliverable D4.1 from Workpackage 4 at http://www.eu-crossgrid.org
4. J.Gomes, M.David. *Test and Validation Testbed Architecture, EU-CrossGrid IST-2001-32243, Sep 2002* Available as project deliverable D4.2 from Workpackage 4 at http://www.eu-crossgrid.org
5. J.Marco, R.Marco, J.Gomes, M.David, M.Hardt, J.Salt. *Setup of First Testbed in Selected Sites, EU-CrossGrid IST-2001-32243, Sep 2002* Available as project deliverable D4.2 from Workpackage 4 at http://www.eu-crossgrid.org
6. J.Marco, R.Marco. *Testbed Prototype Release, EU-CrossGrid IST-2001-32243, Feb 2003* Available as project deliverable D4.4 from Workpackage 4 at http://www.eu-crossgrid.org

An Advanced Security Infrastructure
for Heterogeneous Relational Grid Data Sources[*]

Javier Jaén Martínez and José H. Canós

Departamento de Sistemas Informáticos y Computación
Universidad Politécnica de Valencia
{fjaen,jhcanos}@dsic.upv.es

Abstract. In this paper we deal with the problem of secure access to metadata information in Grid computing environments. The heterogeneity of the eventual data providers (with different local database management systems) and the enforcement of security policies for a vast number of potential data consumers are the two key problems to be solved. We present XSQL, a technology that solves the heterogeneity problem but lacks adequate security mechanisms for its use in grid like environments. As a consequence, we propose an advanced have security infrastructure with the necessary elements to be able to enforce complex policies based on identity and context information like roles and groups. The approach presented here results in authorization schemas that need no additional coding from data providers and, as a result, require little deployment efforts.

1 Introduction

The European Datagrid project [1] is one of the most ambitious initiatives in the field of Grid Computing. This project integrates a vast number of particle physics laboratories in search of new High Energy Physics by analyzing data that will be obtained from the Large Hadron Collider (the new accelerator under construction at the European Laboratory for Nuclear Research).

One of the main challenges of this project is the management of the huge amount of information that must be recorded, reconstructed and analyzed by physicist all over the world. Some preliminary estimations indicate that each major experiment will generate an average of 1 Petabyte of information per year that must be distributed seamlessly and on demand to all participants of a given collaboration in a grid like infrastructure. This infrastructure, in its current conception consists of regional centers organized hierarchically (Tiers), according to their computing and data storage facilities, so that tiers at a given level become data providers for lower level tiers.

Having in mind such an infrastructure, we have already considered in previous works [2,3,4] the main problems to be solved in the data management arena, namely: metadata management, efficient data transport, replication management, query optimization, and security. Particularly interesting is the problem of publishing metadata in a secure way. It is important to note that metadata publishing is a critical

---

[*] Work supported by Generalitat Valenciana ESCUT Project GV01-227.

F. Fernández Rivera et al. (Eds.): Across Grids 2003, LNCS 2970, pp. 78–85, 2004.
© Springer-Verlag Berlin Heidelberg 2004

issue because of the large volume of information to be processed. Searching for information would not be feasible by running queries on the original data but it is rather required that lower volume metadata is generated to achieve efficient information searching, location, and retrieval. Additionally, doing this in a secure way is mandatory because integrity and privacy of this type of information must be maintained in a distributed environment with thousands of users like the Data Grid.

Our paper argues that, given the heterogeneous nature of the Grid, technologies for integrating heterogeneous local publishing infrastructures are needed. We present XSQL [5] as a valid candidate for achieving such integration but highlight its security limitations for use in a grid-like environment. Consequently, we introduce a security infrastructure that has been designed and implemented to overcome the previous limitation and is now a key element of the test-bed infrastructure that is in place in the European Datagrid project. Section 2 describes XSQL as a valid technology for integrating heterogeneous Database Management Systems (DBMS). Section 3 details the security limitations of this technology and describes an advanced security infrastructure for integrating this technology in grid-like environments. Finally, Section 4 concludes and details some future work.

2   XSQL: A Technology to Integrate Heterogeneous DBMS

XSQL is a framework that allows any person familiar with SQL to create templates (XSQL pages) to produce XML documents from parametric SQL queries. Architecturally, this framework is implemented as a Java Servlet[8] running on a Web server which is compliant with the Java Servlets specification. One important aspect of this technology is that it is not bound to any specific vendor server-side infrastructure, e.g. the framework has successfully been tested with the following platforms: *Oracle9i Internet Application Server, Allaire JRun 2.3.3 y 3.0.0, Apache 1.3.9 or higher with JServ 1.0/1.1 or Tomcat 3.1/3.2 Servlet Engine, Apache Tomcat 3.1 o 3.2 Web Server + Servlet Engine, Caucho Resin 1.1, Java Web Server 2.0, Weblogic 5.1 Web Server, NewAtlanta ServletExec 2.2 and 3.0 for IIS/PWS 4.0, Oracle8i Lite Web-to-Go Server, Sun JavaServer Web Development Kit (JSWDK) 1.0.1 Web Server.*

A basic usage scenario of XSQL in a web server would be as follows (figure 1): a Web server receives a request of an XSQL page (.xsql extension). The server recognizes that an XSQL servlet is up and running and forwards the request. The servlet contains a processor of XSQL pages which is activated. The processor analyses the contents of the requested page, executes the SQL queries within it, transform the obtained results into a standard XML format and finally, if required, applies some XSLT transformations. Finally, the resulting document is returned to the requesting entity using HTPP as the underlying protocol.

This mechanism may be used in the context of our problem so that each regional center implements its metadata publishing mechanisms as a collection of XSQL pages stored on a local Web servers. By doing so, any lower level regional center may access such information with a standard protocol (HTTP) and obtain it in a standard format (XML) without having to access the specific services of the local DBMS.

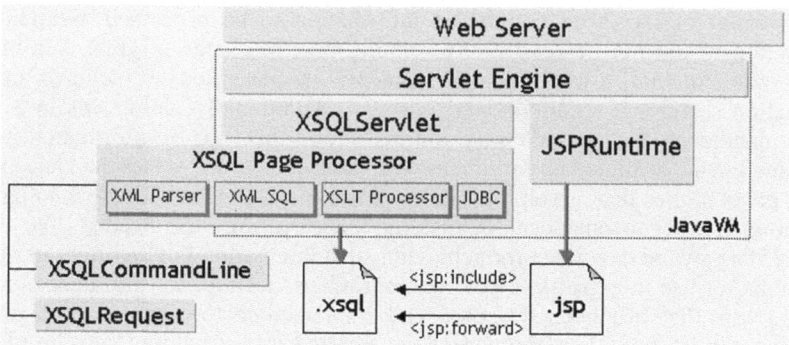

Fig. 1. Architectural view of the XSQL framework (Oracle9i XDK Release 2 9.2)

As a trivial but illustrating example of use of this approach in the context of the Data Grid project let us consider the following XSQL template:

```
<?xml version="1.0"?>
<RESULT connection="grid-demo" xmlns:xsql="urn:oracle-xsql">
 <xsql:query bind-params="key">
  SELECT DESCRIPTION, AUTHOR, TITLE, TO_CHAR(DATE,'DD/MON/YYYY') AS DATE,
ALGORITHM
    FROM DERIVED_DATA
   WHERE KEY = ?   /* ? is the variable bound to the "key" parameter */
 </xsql:query>
 <xsql:query bind-params="key">
   SELECT MIRROR
    FROM MIRROR_SITES
    WHERE KEY = ?
 </xsql:query>
 <!—More  xsql actions may follow here -->
</RESULT>
```

would give as a result the following XML document

```
<?xml version="1.0"?>
<RESULT>
<ROWSET>
 <ROW id="1">
    <DESCRIPTION> http://data_repository /derived_data.dat</DESCRIPTION>
    <AUTHOR> Javier Jaen</AUTHOR>
    <TITLE> Callibration derived data </TITLE>
    <DATE>08/May/1970</DATE>
    <ALGORITHM> http://algorithms_repository /Algorit1.class </ALGORITHM>
   </ROW>
   </ROWSET>
   <ROWSET>
 <ROW id="1">
   <MIRROR>http://mirrorsite.es/derived_data.dat </MIRROR>
```

```
    </ROW>
  <ROW id="2">
    <MIRROR>http://mirrorsite.fr/derived_data.dat </MIRROR>
    </ROW>
  <ROW id="3">
    <MIRROR>http://mirrorsite.de/derived_data.dat </MIRROR>
    </ROW>
    </ROWSET>
</RESULT>
```

and this result may be transformed by the server into a more convenient format by applying a XSLT transformation. For instance, if metadata are represented according to the Resource Description Framework (RDF) [6] the following XML document could be obtained :

```
<rdf:RDF>
<rdf:Description about="http://data_repository/derived_data.dat">
<s:Author>Javier Jaen</s:Author>
<s:Title> Callibration derived data </s:Title>
<s:Date>08/May/1970</s:Date>
<s:Algorithm>
<rdf:subject resource="http:// algorithms_repository /Algorit1.class"/>
</s:Algorithm>
<s:Mirror>
<rdf:Bag>
<rdf:li resource="http://mirrorsite.es/derived_data.dat"/>
<rdf:li resource="http://mirrorsite.fr/derived_data.dat"/>
<rdf:li resource="http://mirrorsite.de/derived_data.dat"/>
</rdf:Bag>
</s:Mirror>
</rdf:Description>
</rdf:RDF>
```

3   An Advanced Security Infrastructure

Security in XSQL pages is implemented by explicitly defining connection identifiers which are internally mapped into database connections. In our previous example, the presented XSQL page explicitly contained a database connection identifier: "grid-demo". However, this mechanism does not scale with the enormous number of users in a grid environment and is not flexible enough because connection names are bound statically to XSQL pages. For instance, if different types of users within a virtual organization would require different privileges or even different database instances one would need to define as many XSQL pages as groups or have parametric XSQL pages and force potential users to know in advance their database identifiers. Fortunately, a more flexible and scalable schema is possible that is based on existing security mechanisms already in place for Web applications.

3.1   HTTP over SSL

Since HTTP is the protocol used in our design to reach XSQL pages using standard URLs, it is easy to see that a straightforward access control mechanism can be implemented. One could use a secure extension of HTTP to restrict access to XSQL pages to authorized users only. Such a secure extension is already available and is widely known as HTTP over Secure Sockets Layer (SSL)[7]. The Secure Sockets Layer protocol is a protocol layer which may be placed between a reliable connection-oriented network layer protocol (e.g. TCP/IP) and the application protocol layer (in our case HTTP). SSL provides for secure communication between client and server by allowing mutual authentication, the use of digital signatures for integrity, and encryption for privacy. The protocol is designed to support a range of choices for specific algorithms used for cryptography, digests, and signatures.

3.2   Security Realms

Using HTTPS forces WEB servers to be modified to include SSL functionality and certificate management infrastructure in place to issue valid certificates to potential clients. Besides, it uses the URL scheme https rather than http and a different server port (by default 443). In those cases where such modifications are not possible, the use of security realms can be an alternative. A security realm is a mechanism used for protecting Web application resources. It gives the ability to protect a resource with a defined security constraint and then define the user roles that can access the protected resource. An example of a WEB server that has this type of realm functionality built in is Tomcat. It provides a mechanism so that a collection of usernames, passwords, and their associated roles can be integrated and used for access control. Tomcat provides two realm implementations called respectively memory and JDBC realms. Tomcat's MemoryRealm class uses an XML file as a repository for roles and user definitions. A sample memory realm XML file could be:

```
<tomcat-users>
          <user name="tomcat" password="tomcat" roles="tomcat" />
          <user name="role1" password="tomcat" roles="role1" />
          <user name="both" password="tomcat" roles="tomcat,role1" />
</tomcat-users>
```

3.3   An Advanced XSQL Access Control Mechanism

The access control mechanisms described above are definitely valid for implementing basic level security, however there are some unresolved issues. First, when using SSL, access control is enforced by inspecting the certificate that the client side presents during the handshake process. In this case access control policies are defined in terms of existing fields in the certificate (the validity period, the signing certificate authority, the distinguished name, etc). These fields can be even extended with X509 v3 extensions and most implementations of SSL provide mechanisms to access such extensions and implement complex policies. Though this is feasible, this access control mechanism is not bound to XSQL. This means that complex policies defined at the X509 certificate level cannot be propagated into database connections that are dependent on such policies. This also applies if security realms are used because information about roles and users defined in a JDBC realm is neither propagated. Second, even if this information could be propagated, data providers would need to write code in order to implement group level access policies.

To overcome these disadvantages we need a mechanism that allows for dynamic generation (not statically bound to XSQL pages) of different types of database connections and definition of group-level access policies, requires no additional coding by data providers and, finally, leverages on existing technologies like X509 certificates and Web servers.

These goals can only be achieved if XSQL provides de necessary flexibility and extensibility so that new authorization mechanisms can be defined. Fortunately, this is the case because every XSQL page is an XML document consisting of actions that are internally handled by specific software handlers implemented as Java classes.

Every time an action is found the page processor invokes the associated handler so that it performs the necessary operations and returns an XML fragment. At the very end, all the handlers have been invoked and the resulting XML fragments are glued in order to deliver a final XML document that contains the data obtained after executing all the actions contained in the XSQL page (see previous section).

Taking benefit of these extensibility feature and assuming X509 certificates as the mechanism to identify clients, our advanced XSQL access control mechanism would work as follows (see figure 2):

- The user enters a URL through a browser, which is interpreted and passed to the XSQL Servlet through a Java Web server. This is based on HTTPS and a client X509 certificate is requested (as part of the standard SSL handshake process)
- The XSQL page processor processes the requested XSQL page by looking for "Action Elements" from the XSQL namespace. The first action element to be processed being an authorization action element "<xsql:auth>"
- The page processor invokes the authorization action element handler class to process the element.
- The handler obtains all the client information from the SSL layer and uses this information to obtain group and role based information from the authorization repository.
- The handler also obtains information about security constraints (allowed database connection types) for the accessed XSQL page based on the group, role, and user information previously obtained.
- The handler decides whether SQL query execution is allowed or denied for the accessed XSQL page and dynamically embeds within the XSQL page the appropriate database connection information.
- The XSQL page processor continues the parsing of the remaining XSQL tags and the embedded SQL statements are executed with the database connection obtained from the previous steps.

It is important to note that not only X509 distinguished names but also roles and group based information is used when retrieving a database connection identifier. This allows a holder of a given X509 certificate to obtain different database connections according to this contextual information. Additionally, regular expressions over distinguished names are also allowed increasing this way the expressiveness of the enforced authorization policies and enabling scalable systems that enforce policies related to a great number of members within a virtual organization. As an example, one might define the following expression *"/C=CH/O=CERN/OU=Information Technologies/* "* to grant access to a given database instance to all the members belonging to the IT division at CERN. If these expressions are defined, certificates of requesting clients are matched against them using the Jakarta ORO matcher [9].

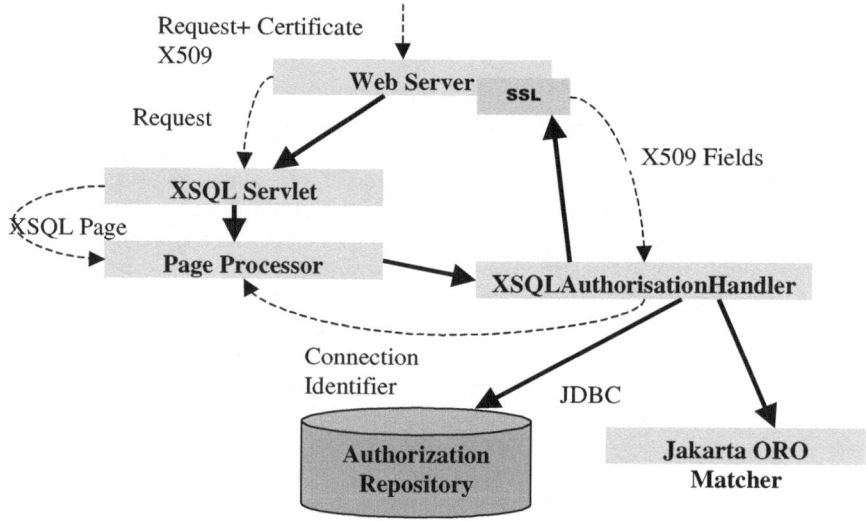

Fig. 2. Data flows and dependencies during authorization process

4   Conclusions and Future Work

In this paper we have dealt with the problem of secure access to metadata information in Grid computing environments. The heterogeneity of the eventual data providers (with different local database management systems) and the enforcement of security policies for a vast number of potential data consumers are the two key problems to be solved. We have presented a technology that solves the heterogeneity problem but lacks adequate security mechanisms for its use in grid like environments. As a consequence, we have designed and implemented the necessary elements to be able to enforce complex policies based on identity and context information like roles and groups. The approach presented here results in authorization schemas that need no additional coding from data providers and, as a result, require little deployment efforts. Besides, the use of standard protocols (HTTP+SSL) and data representation formats (XML) allows for further integration of these systems with future Web Services. We plan to add further functionality to our system like revocation lists and support additional context information. New standard protocols like SOAP will be also be supported so that integration of secure Grid metadata repositories with coming Web Services can be done. Our vision is that in the near future Data Grids will become efficient and secure data providers for Web Services and we believe that the work presented here is a step forward towards such integration.

References

1. The DataGrid Project. Accessible at http://eu-datagrid.web.cern.ch/eu-datagrid/
2. Wolfgang Hoschek, Javier Jaen-Martinez, Asad Samar, Heinz Stockinger, and Kurt Stockinger. Data Management in an International Data Grid Project. In 1st IEEE/ACM International Workshop on Grid Computing (Grid'2000), Bangalore, India, December 17-20 2000. Distinguished Paper Award.
3. Wolfgang Hoschek, Javier Jaen-Martinez, Peter Kunszt, Ben Segal, Heinz Stockinger, Kurt Stockinger, and Brian Tierney. Data Management in the European DataGrid Project. In The 2001 Globus Retreat, San Francisco, August 9-10 2001.
4. Dirk Düllmann, Wolfgang Hoschek, Javier Jaen-Martinez, Asad Samar, Ben Segal, Heinz Stockinger, and Kurt Stockinger. Models for Replica Synchronisation and Consistency in a Data Grid. In 10thIEEE Symposium on High Performance and Distributed Computing (HPDC-10), San Francisco, California, August 7-9 2001.
5. Oracle9i XML Developer's Kits Guide – XDK Release 2 (9.2) Part Number A96621-0. Accessible at http://otn.oracle.com/tech/xml/xdkhome.html
6. The Resource Description Framework http://www.w3.org/RDF/
7. Kipp E.B. Hickman, The SSL Protocol, 1995
   http://www.netscape.com/eng/security/SSL_2.html.
8. The Java Servlet Technology http://java.sun.com/products/servlet/
9. Jakarta ORO http://jakarta.apache.org/oro/

High-Performance GRID Stream Database Manager for Scientific Data*

Milena Gateva Koparanova and Tore Risch

Department of Information Technology, Uppsala University,
SE-75105 Uppsala, Sweden
{Milena.Koparanova,Tore.Risch}@it.uu.se

Abstract. In this work we describe a high-performance stream-oriented distributed database manager and query processor under development. It allows efficient execution of database queries to streamed numerical data from scientific applications. Very high performance is attained by utilizing many object-relational main-memory database engines connected through the GRID.

1 Introduction

We are developing a new kind of database manager utilizing the evolving GRID infrastructure [6] for distributed computations on large data streams. The *GRID Stream Database Manager (GSDM)* will have high performance and support for customizable representation of streamed data in distributed data and computational servers. The target application area is space physics, in particular the LOFAR/LOIS project [10,11,12], whose purpose is to develop a distributed software space telescope and radar utilizing the GRID. LOFAR/LOIS will produce extremely large raw data streams by sensor networks receiving signals from space. Various numerical selection and transformation algorithms are applied on these streams. The data is delivered to the client workstations for visualization and other processing in form of streams called *beams*, with rates of several gigabits per second [22].

Our approach to meet the demands of the LOFAR/LOIS online applications for very high performance and extensibility is to develop and utilize a distributed, main-memory, object-relational, and stream-oriented DBMS running on clusters of computers. We are extending an existing main-memory object-relational DBMS engine[17] with capabilities for processing distributed streams.

The remainder of the paper is organized as follows. In the next section we consider the need for and consequences from the stream orientation for the development of the system. Section 3 discusses GSDM as a new type of application for computational GRIDs. An overview of the GSDM system architecture is presented in section 4, and we summarize in section 5.

---

* This project has been supported by VINNOVA under contract #2001-06074.

F. Fernández Rivera et al. (Eds.): Across Grids 2003, LNCS 2970, pp. 86–92, 2004.

2   Stream Database Manager

Regular database management systems(DBMSs) store tables of limited sizes while stream database systems (SDBSs) also deal with on-line streams of unlimited size. The raw data and beams generated by LOFAR/LOIS sensor networks are typical examples of streams. A lot of research in stream data management has been done recently [1,2,4,5,9,13,14,20] and the area offers a number of open research questions. Several important characteristics of data streams make them different than other data: they are infinite, once a data element has arrived, it is processed and either archived or deleted, i.e. only a short history is stored in the database. It is also preferable to process stream data with order-preserving non-blocking algorithms.

The specifics of the data streams require to consider a data model that allows streamed data representations and operations over streams to be easily specified. Examples of stream-oriented data models and query languages are SEQ [19] and Tribeca [18].

The infinite size imposes a limitation in the stream representation in form of substreams of a limited size, called *windows*. Several operations that are specific for streams are introduced (e.g. resample and drop in [4]), while some traditional ones need new semantics in the context of stream windows (e.g. join of windows and moving window aggregates [20]).

Since stream data elements are arriving over time, a natural technique for querying such data are so called *continuous queries(CQs)* [21]. CQs are installed once and run continuously over incoming data elements until they are stopped explicitly. The presence of long-running CQs increases the importance of DBMS adaptability which motivates the work presented in [14]. Techniques as approximate query answering, data reduction, and multi-query optimization also gain greater importance and applicability in the context of stream data query processing.

SDBS architectures are proposed in [2,4]. A related area is distributed networks of sensors considered in [1,13], where a large numbers of small sensors, most likely power limited, generate relatively simple data at rates much slower than in our LOFAR/LOIS application. The scientific data streams in our application area have high generation rate and contain complex numerical data which suggest for non-relational stream representations by User-defined Data Types (UDTs). The continuous queries over LOFAR/LOIS streams contain application-dependant User-Defined Functions (UDFs) over UDTs.

Most of the SDBSs described in the literature have centralized query processing and scheduling where a central node has more or less global information about the system and makes optimization and scheduling decisions accordingly. The need for efficient execution of a number of CQs on clusters of GSDMs puts additional difficulties because of the distribution and parallelism. The architectural challenges in the design of a distributed stream processing system are discussed in [3]. In the GSDM system design we have faced and must address similar problems, e.g., how to distribute the work among the database nodes, what type of parallelism would give greater advantage for scientific data streams with UDFs applied, and how to coordinate the operations from a single pipeline running on different nodes or even clusters. Therefore algorithms for query optimization and scheduling have to be developed that take into account the specifics of the distributed GRID environment.

3   A Computational GRIDs Application

We can consider the GSDM project as a new kind of application for computational GRIDs. Utilization of parallel and distributed GRID environment is motivated by the following: i)The volume of data produced is too large to fit in a single main-memory, and therefore suggests data to be distributed among clusters of main-memories. ii) The very high data flow rate requires very high performance of insert, delete, and data processing operations.

Different kinds of parallelism can be utilized to achieve high performance. For very heavy computational operations data partitioning parallelism must be considered, while for cheaper operations a pipelined form of parallelism might be useful. The fragmentation strategies for data parallelism are well investigated for relational databases. Research has been done on data fragmentation problems in Object-Relational DBMSs that discusses how to achieve efficient parallel execution of UDFs while preserving their semantics [8,16].

Several projects as Globus [7] and Nordugrid [15] provide tools for building computational GRID infrastructures. We consider computational GRIDs as more appropriate for our GSDM than a regular parallel computer because of dynamics and scalability. Computational GRIDs are a natural extension of parallel computers allowing not only greater processing power, but also ability for dynamic resource allocation and incorporation of new nodes when necessary. For instance, if a new CQ with high cost UDFs is installed on the GSDM, this may require staging and starting the database manager on new nodes and scheduling some query operations on these. The dynamics can also be important characteristics in an environment where different numbers of data streams are used over time or the source streams have varying incoming rates. The efficient utilization of computing resources requires ability to dynamically incorporate new nodes to the system, and to free them for other users when not needed any more.

Utilization of the computational GRIDs for such a database management system opens several problems and research questions. Resource management of the computing nodes is performed typically by a batch system that takes care of job scheduling, queue placement, and prioritizing. Most of the applications for computational GRIDs run as batch jobs. The GSDM can be considered as a persistent job with dynamic resource requirements (increasing and decreasing over time) and interactive user interface. The DB managers and users must be provided with ability to install and stop different CQs during a user session without need to restart the system when some parameter has changed. Therefore, extensions of the job management systems of computers connected through the GRID are needed, such that interactive database query jobs are to be permitted. Working in a GRID environment also raises new security and accessibility issues.

For example, if a central scheduler is used for scheduling of the CQs, it must be accessible from all participating nodes, which limits its possible locations and creates a potential bottleneck. The GRID infrastructure should provide a new service by which database servers running on different clusters can communicate with very high performance.

4 GSDM System Overview

Figure 1 illustrates a scenario of applications interacting with the distributed GSDM system. There are three types of GSDM nodes. The *Metadata Manager* is a relatively light-weight server that stores the metadata of the system and interacts with users and applications. It receives GSDM commands and, depending on their kinds, might start or call other GSDM nodes. The GSDM commands can be, e.g., registration of a new CQ or a meta-query about the active CQs running currently in the system.

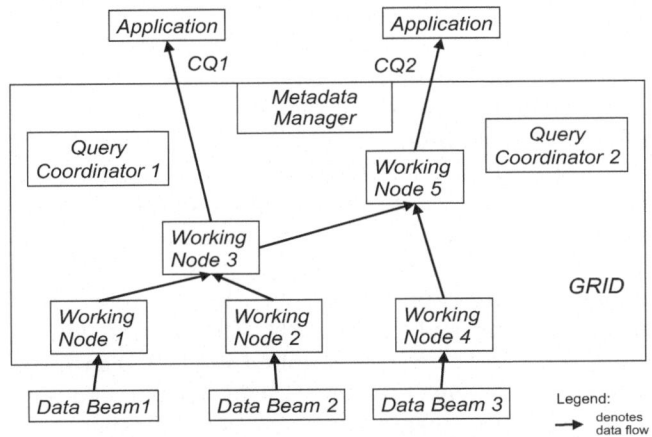

Fig. 1. GRID Stream Data Manager Scenario

In the figure there are two applications that have registered to the GSDM two different continuous queries, CQ1 and CQ2. A CQ can include regular set operators extended with user-defined application-dependent algorithms for stream filtering, transformation, and fusion. The queries in the example specify joining and filtering of data from three different data streams, called Data Beam 1,2, and 3. When the metadata manager receives command to register new CQ it starts a *GSDM Query Coordinator* node and delegates the service of the received continuous query to this node. For better scalability of the system there can be many coordinators as indicated in the picture where there is one coordinator node per CQ. The execution of CQs is performed by *GSDM Working Nodes*

(WNs). For a given CQ the query compiler of the query coordinator will construct a distributed execution plan to be executed on the working nodes. In the example, the query coordinator 1 has created an execution plan for CQ1 where the WN3 joins data streams from Data Beam 1 and 2 through the intermediate WN1 and WN2.

The arrows on the fig. 1 denote the data flow between stream sources, GSDM nodes and applications. The GSDM nodes also exchange control messages which are not shown to keep the scenario picture simpler.

In the scenario it is assumed that the source streams can access the IP addresses and deliver data directly to the working nodes 1, 2, and 4. This assumption is important since the target LOIS/LOFAR project produces very large streams that cannot be managed through a single node. Many computer resources accessible through the GRID infrastructure do not currently satisfy this requirement. It is desirable to consider such a requirement when new GRID-enabled computer resources are designed.

In the following we will describe in more details the software architecture of different GSDM nodes. The metadata manager interacts with the applications through the *application API* module. It provides primitives to register, start and stop monitoring a CQ. In its local database the metadata manager stores information about the registered and running CQs, coordinators, and working nodes. This allows the applications and users to ask meta-queries about, e.g., the status of CQs running currently in the system.

The query coordinator produces optimized distributed CQ execution plans by the module *CQ Decomposer and Optimizer*. When deciding how to assign the individual operations in the CQ execution plan to working nodes, the coordinator contacts the metadata manager in order to find out whether there are some other running CQs whose execution can be utilized by the new plan. In the example on fig. 1 the Query Coordinator 2 constructs the execution plan for CQ2 that combines three data beams and finds out that the working node 3 already joins the data beam 1 and 2 in the way as required in CQ2. The *Resource Manager* module in the coordinator can start new GSDM working nodes when necessary and stop the running ones when the user stops monitoring the correspondent CQs. In order to allocate new computer resources the resource manager module needs to cooperate with the resource manager of the cluster.

Figure 2 shows the architecture of a single GSDM working node. The *Continuous Query Manager* registers continuous queries sent by the coordinator and processes them continuously over incoming stream data. The CQs specification is based on regular database queries and the system internally uses a regular database *Query Executor* to execute them on the current stream windows. The stream data sources are received by the *Stream Consumer* module. It is a type of *wrapper* interface that takes care of data encoding into internal stream representation, builds windows of streamed data, controls the data flow, etc. In a data driven stream processing paradigm, the stream consumer must also open listening sockets in order to receive streamed data and have a policy to deal with stream overflow/ underflow. The stream consumer is instantiated for each accessed data stream of its kind. A particular stream consumer receives inter-GSDM streams. Stream consumer module is also needed by the application in order to receive streamed results. The *Continuous Query Producer* is a module that sends the resulting stream of a continuous (sub)query to the application or to the next working node in the CQ execution plan. The *Plug-ins* contain user-defined application-dependant algorithms for signal transformation, filtering, and combining, implemented as conventional programs and dynamically uploaded into the working nodes that need them.

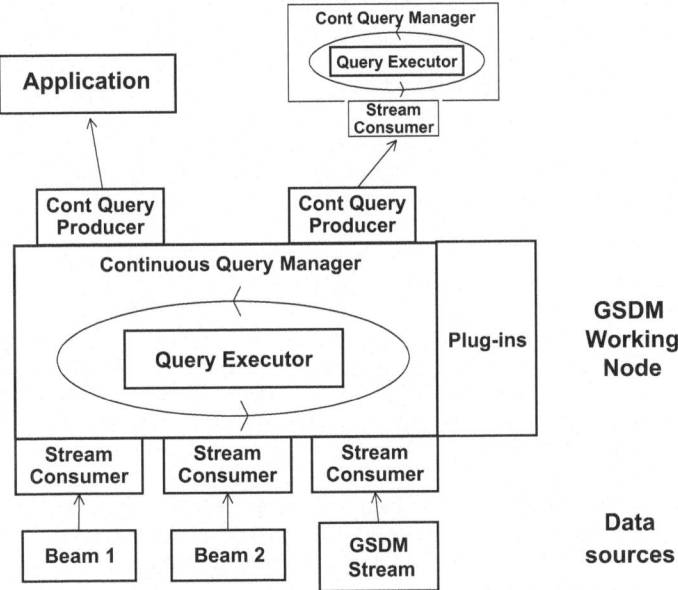

Fig. 2. GSDM Working Node Architecture

5   Summary

We described the GSDM project - a GRID-enabled, main-memory, object-relational and stream DBMS. Main-memory, distribution, and query processing provide high performance, while object-relational functionality provides extensibility capabilities. We utilize extensibility of an existing main-memory object-relational DBMS engine to add stream orientation and customized data representations of scientific data. This achieves flexible and high-performance processing of scientific streams in form of CQs with UDFs. We outlined the distributed architecture of the GSDM prototype system under development at Uppsala Database Lab and discussed some of the problems and open research questions that arose in the development process.

References

1. P. Bonnet, J. Gehrke, P. Seshadri: Towards Sensor Database Systems. In *Proc. of the 2nd Intl. Conf. on Mobile Data Management*, Hong Kong (2001)
2. B. Babcock, S. Babu, M. Datar, R. Motwani and J. Widom: Models and Issues in Data Stream Systems. *ACM PODS* (2002) 1-16
3. M. Cherniack, H. Balakrishnan, M. Balazinska, D. Carney, U. Cetintemel, Y. Xing, and S. Zdonik: Scalable Distributed Stream Processing. In *Proc. of the 2003 CIDR Conference* (2003)
4. D. Carney, U. Cetintemel, M. Cherniack, C. Convey, S. Lee, G. Seidman, M. Stonebraker, N. Tatbul and S. Zdonik: Monitoring Streams - a New Class of Data Management Applications. In *Proc. of the 28th VLDB Conference* (2002) 469-477
5. J. Chen, D.J. DeWitt, F. Tian, Y. Wang: NiagaraCQ: A Scalable Continuous Query System for Internet Databases. *SIGMOD Conference 2000* (2000) 379-390
6. I. Foster, C. Kesselman (eds.): *The Grid: Blueprint for a new Computing Infrastructure*. Morgan-Kaufmann (1999)
7. The Globus Project. http://www.globus.org
8. M. Jaedicke, B. Mitschang: On Parallel Processing of Aggregate and Scalar Functions in Object-Relational DBMS. *ACM SIGMOD Conference*, Seattle, USA, (1998)
9. L. Liu, C. Pu, and W. Tang: Continual Queries for Internet Scale Event-Driven Information Delivery. *IEEE Trans. on Knowledge and Data Engineering*, 11(14) (1999) 610-628
10. LOFAR: Low Frequency Array. http://www.lofar.org
11. LOIS - A LOFAR Outrigger in Scandinavia. http://www.physics.irfu.se/LOIS
12. Bo Thide (ed.): First LOFAR/LOIS Workshop, Sweden, June 17-19 (2001) http://www.physics.irfu.se/LOIS/Workshops/Vaxjo010617-19/index.shtml
13. S. Madden, M.J. Franklin: Fjording the Stream: An Architecture for Queries Over Streaming Sensor Data. *ICDE 2002* (2002) 555-566
14. S. Madden, M.A. Shah, J.M. Hellerstein, V. Raman: Continuously Adaptive Continuous Queries over Streams. *SIGMOD Conference 2002* (2002) 49-60
15. NORDUGRID: Nordic Testbed for Wide Area Computing and Data Handling. http://www.nordugrid.org/
16. K.W. Ng and R. Muntz: Parallelizing User-Defined Functions in Distributed Object-Relational DBMS. *IDEAS 1999* (1999) 442-445
17. T. Risch, V. Josifovski: Distributed Data Integration by Object-Oriented Mediator Servers. *Concurrency and Computation: Practice and Experience J.*, 13(11), John Wiley & Sons (2001)
18. M. Sullivan and A. Heybey. Tribeca: A system for managing large databases of network traffic. In *Proc. of the USENIX Annual Technical Conference*, New Orleans, LA, (1998)
19. P. Seshadri, M. Livny and R. Ramakrishnan: SEQ: A Model for Sequence Databases. In *Proc. of the 11th ICDE Conference* (1995) 232-239
20. P. Seshadri, M. Livny and R. Ramakrishnan: The Design and Implementation of a Sequence Database System. In *Proc. of the 22nd VLDB Conference* (1996) 99-110
21. D. Terry, D. Goldberg, D. Nichols, and B. Oki: Continuous Queries over Append-Only Databases. In *Proc. of the 1992 ACM SIGMOD Intl. Conf. on Management of Data* (1992) 321-330
22. C.M. De Vos, K. van der Schaaf, and J. Bregman: Cluster Computers and Grid Processing in the First Radio-Telescope of a New Generation. In *Proc. of the First IEEE/ACM International Symposium on Cluster Computing and the Grid-CCGrid'2001* (2001)

Optimization of Data Access
for Grid Environment

Lukasz Dutka[1,2], Renata Słota[1], Darin Nikolow[1], and Jacek Kitowski[1,2]

[1] Institute of Computer Science, AGH, al.Mickiewicza 30, 30-059, Cracow, Poland
[2] Academic Computer Centre CYFRONET AGH, Cracow, Poland
{dutka,rena,darin,kito}@uci.agh.edu.pl
Phone: (+48 12) 6173964, Fax: (+48 12) 6338054

Abstract. In the paper the architecture for accessing data in the grid environment, developed for EU CrossGrid Project, is presented. The local optimization problems for efficient data access and estimation of data access time are discussed mainly, while the overall architecture is proposed on the base of collaboration with European Data Grid.

1 Introduction

Existing grid technology can be separated into two major fields, the computational grids and the data intensive grids. Data grids are in particular interest at present, since they deal with data which cannot be kept and process locally due to their high volume and property issues. Separation of the program from the files it accesses, results in overheads in program development and execution. Therefore, one of the challenging problems for the grid is the optimization of the remote data access to the large datasets or databases.

The optimization of the remote data access can be defined as a global optimization and as a local optimization tasks. In the first case the main problem is to provide a mechanism for allocating the 'best replica' of the files that a job needs. In the second one the optimization of usage of local resources in storage nodes (i.e. storage elements) is implemented.

The global optimization of data access usually is being achieved by file replication, which is conceptually simple. However, maintaining an optimal distribution, with respect to files usage, needs optimization services, which allow constructing efficient replica manager and replica catalog tools [1,2,3,4]. Beside the global optimization, the local optimization of usage of storage node resources is useful, due to different kinds of data and different types of secondary/tertiary storage systems installed locally.

The purpose of the paper is to present the current state of system architecture for accessing data in the grid environment, developed for EU CrossGrid Project [5]. The local optimization problems for efficient data access and estimation of data access time are discussed mainly, while the overall architecture is proposed on the base of collaboration with WP2 European Data Grid.

The work is based largely on independent research lead by the authors on the field of large-scale system architectures aimed at development of an effective

F. Fernández Rivera et al. (Eds.): Across Grids 2003, LNCS 2970, pp. 93–102, 2004.

and easy to use system architecture for large-scale systems. Due to limitation of size, this paper does not define all aspects of Component-Expert Architecture, which were previously described and publicized [6,7,8]. But it describes specific implementation issues for grid storage.

Moreover this paper discusses implementation details about data access cost estimation for grid storage being implemented in EU CrossGrid Project together with Component-Expert Architecture (CEA). The implementation results are complement to the architecture and allowed us to verify practical impact of CEA for real environment.

2   Local Optimization of Data Access

Almost all grid elements, especially storage nodes, are very heterogenous. Each storage node can have different internal configuration. Among storage nodes there are secondary storage, like disk drives or disk arrays, and tertiary storage (like Hierarchical Storage Management, HSM) with automatic tape libraries, magnetooptical devices, etc. Moreover, the internal state of each Storage Node can be changed often. The goal of the local optimization is to provide data stored inside Storage Node in unified way and to estimate data access-factors. Furthermore, the provided solution have to be flexible, open to the future, and easy for modifications on demand. For this reason Component Expert Architecture (CEA) [6,7] has been chosen to develop internal architecture of Storage Elements. This architecture allows developing high flexible systems in easy way.

The concept of CEA is an extension of the classical component architectures. It operates on specially prepared components, which are independent modules realizing some functionality. However, each component in CEA has a description of its purpose, which is written using a component type and a component specialization. These elements are made up of a component header. The component type describes a general purpose of the component, while the component specialization, which constists of attributes list, provides detailed information about the most suitable component usage. The components are registered in Expert Component Management Subsystem (ECMS). For the application cooperating with CEA the components are accessible via ECMS. However, contrary to the classical architecture, the application does not know exactly which component should be used, but it requires selection of the best one from ECMS. The best component must fulfill two conditions: the same type as specified by the application and its specialization that matches to the passed call-environment. The matching is done by a rule-based expert system, which has built-in rules allowing it to decide which component fulfills the application requirements in the best way. During selection (deduction) external knowledge bases can be used to improve the quality of deduction. This multilevel processing of intelligent component selection makes applications independent from the components and development of software easier in very heterogeneous systems like grids.

2.1   CEA in CrossGrid Environment

In Fig. 1 complexity and different Storage Nodes configurations with variety of devices are shown. Storage Nodes function as the data providers and managers. To use data effectively, the environment requires estimations of data access latency and bandwidth, measured from the particular storage node internal point of view. In CrossGrid access factors estimation and data providing is organized using CEA. (To avoid confusion, the components, which are described in the previous section and are intended for CEA are called 'cecomponents' in the further part of this paper.) The main module realizing CEA is Component-Expert Subsystem (CEXS), which manages cecomponents and decides, using of built-in expert system, which cecomponent is the best. The decision is based on many factors but the most important one is similarity of a particular call-environment to cecomponent specialization. Rules process the call-environment form a request and try to match the closest cecomponent for the current context (call-env). It is worth to mention that attributes have different importance. Other components like GridFTP, Storage Element (STEL), and Data Access Estimator (DAES) work on each Storage Node and cooperate with CEXS.

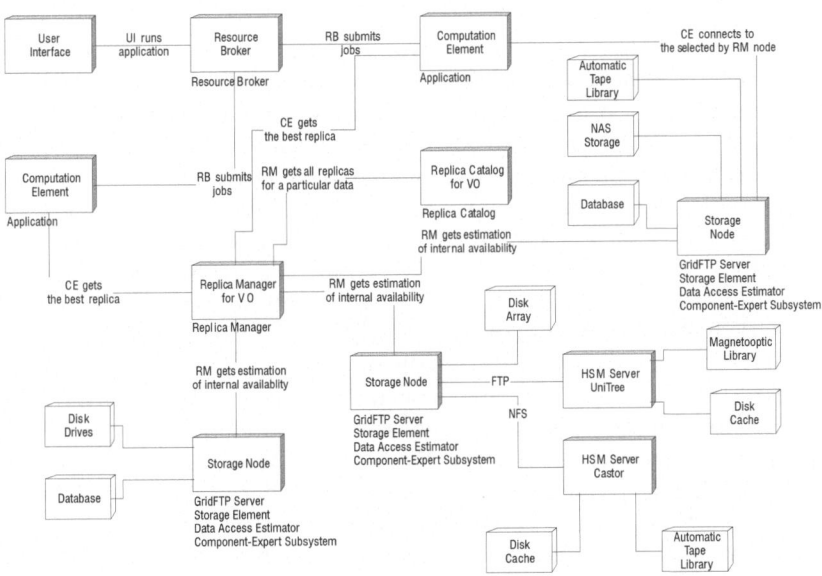

Fig. 1. Sample deployment diagram of access layer architecture.

The component diagram presented in Fig. 2 shows dependencies between components working on Storage Nodes and outside the environment.

Data Access Estimator provides interface estimating data-access-factors (bandwidth and latency) for a particular data object. Since it is constructed according Component-Expert Architecture, estimation is entrusted to one of

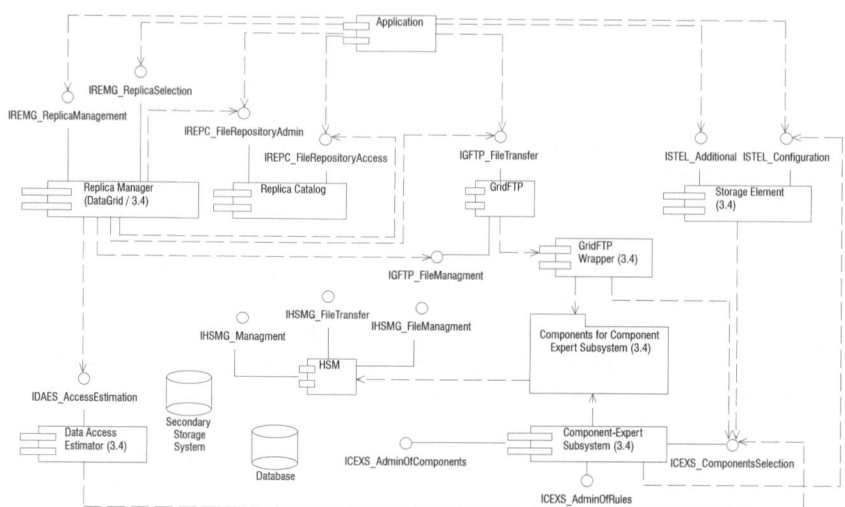

Fig. 2. Connections between access layer components.

the cecomponents with a determined type (in this case type = 'Estimate') and stored in the package 'Components for Component Expert System' (see Fig. 2). Selection of the best cecomponent is done by external module CEXS, which is equivalent of ECMS and Expert System described above. To make proper selection a call-environment has to be prepared by DAES.

Component-Expert Subsystem provides interface for selecting the best cecomponent on the call-environment base (ICEXS_ComponentSelection). Additionally, it provides interfaces allowing administration of rules' set (ICEXS_AdminOfComponents) and of cecomponents stored in Component Container (ICEXS_AdminOfComponents). CEXS has internally built-in the expert system, but the rules are stored externally and they can be reloaded on demand. The rules should be able to extend the call-environments passed by DAES, because they are usually very simple (consists of the global data object identifier only). The rules can use Storage Element, solely on the global data object identifier, to obtain: physical data location of the data object, type of storage keeping the particular data object, data object physical structure, way of communication with data object, etc. Found information is stored in the processed call-environment, and finally is returned to the caller together with a handle to the best cecomponent.

Storage Element, among other things, acts as the equivalent of External Knowledge Base. It keeps and provides all important information about internal configuration of the storage node. This information can be managed in easy manner by administrators of each Storage Node.

GridFTP server is used for data serving. In CrossGrid environment, all data access operations are caught by GridFTP Wrapper, which is CEA-oriented and it uses cecomponents selected by CEXS.

2.2   Implementation Issues

To make the discussion more precise, a set of attributes proposed for the first implementation of CEA is presented. The following set of attributes is used as a description of the component specialization as well as for the call-environment:

1. DataID,
2. DataPhysicalID,
3. StorageType,
4. ConnectionType,
5. RequiredThroughput,
6. DataType.

All components, briefly described in section 2.1, have been built using C++ language and had been designed using full object oriented architecture. All interfaces were developed using SOAP communication protocol, and were generated using gSOAP tool.

Using rule-based expert system CEXS component decides which cecomponent registered in Components Container is the best. Components Container is realized by the simple structure based on hash-tables. This structure could be roughly presented as a simple list of all available cecomponent headers. Virtual-Component class is used to register the cecomponent header.

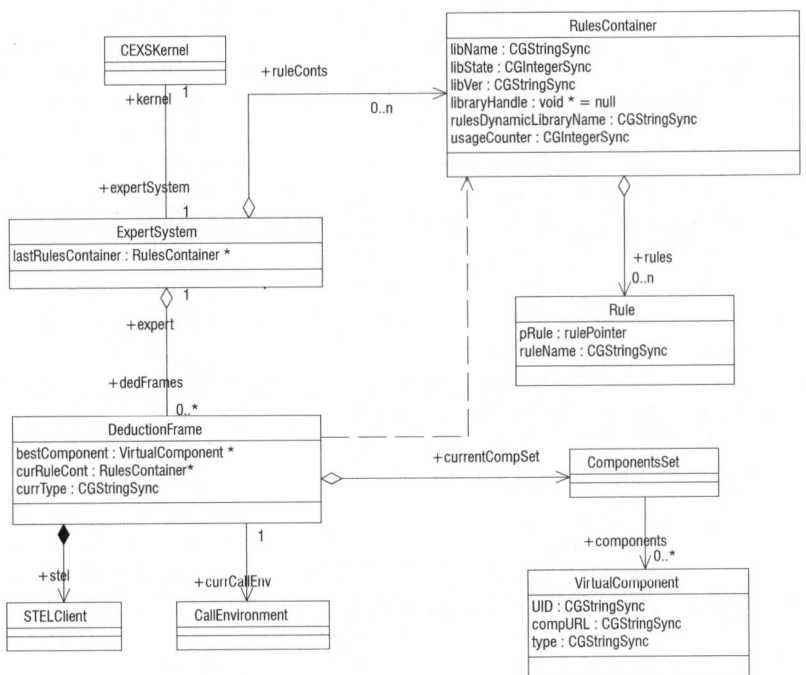

Fig. 3. Class Diagram of related to expert system part of CEXS.

However, effective realization of the expert system requires more sophisticated architecture (a diagram of classes related to the realization of the expert system is presented in Fig. 3). First of all, developed system should allow to interchange set of rules on the fly. Secondly, rules are developed independently from CEXS component. Thus, to fulfill these requirements, all rules are collected in the dynamic linking library, which contains a set of functions (see Fig. 4). Each of these functions realize one rule, which operates on data stored in the passed DeductionFrame object.

```
CGString Rule2(DeductionFrame* df)
{
  if( df->currCallEnv->has_attribute("DataID")
      && !(df->currCallEnv->has_attribute("DataPhysicalID") )) {
        action;
  }

  return "Rule03"; //name of the next rule in the deduction process
}
```

Fig. 4. Sample function being rule of the expert system.

All rules, written as the functions of the dynamic linking library, are registered as instances of the Rule class and are gathered by an instance of RulesContainer (see Fig. 3). This RuleContainer is aggregated by ExpertSystem, the object which has just one instance for the one CEXS component. Selected model using the dynamic linking library as the container of rules allows in easy way loading new set of rules on the fly. New loaded rules are registered as new instances of Rule and RulesContainer classes. The pointer to the last rule container keeping the newest rules is stored in the lastRuleContainer field of Expert System. The old instances of RulesContainer are kept until they are in use, and the new one is used for new deductions.

Each deduction carried by the ExpertSystem object has own data space realized by DeductionFrame class. Because CEXS is multithreaded, many deduction frames are allowed in the same time. The expert system carrying deductions passes to rules a pointer to an appropriate instance of DeductionFrame. Since in the proposed model rules do not have state, all data are stored in DeaductionFrame. The goal of deduction is to select the best cecomponent, thus the rules operate on the set of cecomponents, which in this model is realized by classes ComponentSet and VirtualComponent. The ComponentSet class at the beginning of deduction should get information about all registered cecomponents. During deduction rules eliminate not matching cecomponents until it is clear which one is the best or it is clear that no one fulfils requirements. These requirements are kept by CallEnvironment class related to DeductionFrame.

Very important fact is that CallEnvironment could be changed during deduction. It helps to increase the quality of cecomponent selection. In CrossGrid project interesting information could be obtained from STEL component, which manages whole configuration of the particular storage node. The rules using STELClient class can easy connect to STEL and get required data. All important data should be stored as the attributes of CallEnvironment, which finally is returned to the client of CEXS, which required cecomponent selection, together with a handle to the best cecomponent.

3 Data Access Estimation for HSM Systems

Large capacity Storage Nodes usually take advantage of an HSM (Hierarchical Storage Management) system to economically store their data. These systems are mainly based on some kind of tertiary storage like tape libraries and optical jukeboxes. The main idea of HSM systems is to use low-cost, slow media (tapes) to store less popular data and more expensive, fast access media (hard disk) for the most popular data. Data can be located on any level of the storage hierarchy. It causes that the data access time can vary significantly for HSM systems: from a few seconds to tens of minutes.

In the case of the optimization of data access, a priori knowledge of the access time to data is essential, i.e., for the Grid data replication system [1,5], which selects the data location to be used (since data are replicated into different storage systems located in different places). This will result in more efficient usage of the Grid resources and will decrease latency times.

The main focus of our study are HSM systems, thus the data access time in this study is considered as the sum of the startup latency time and the transfer time of the HSM itself, while the network overhead time is not taken into account.

3.1 Implementation for DiskXtender HSM System

The system is based on event driven simulation of the HSM system. It makes use of the gray-box approach [8] (see also the open approach [9]), in which the relevant HSM information is accessible via native tools of the HSM system. The events are generated using knowledge about the HSM system. Two modules, Monitor and Simulator, are introduced (see Fig.5). They make use of the HSM

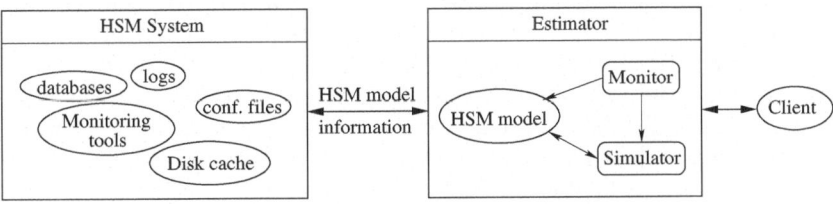

Fig. 5. Data access estimation for DiskXtender.

model data, which is a kind of data structure keeping current the HSM system state, defined by states and characteristics of both media changers and drives, number of slots and drives for the automated library, request and event queues, and other elements.

Monitor collects essential information about the current state of the HSM system for supplying it to Simulator, which – in turn – simulates future state changes in order to estimate time of arrival for the given file. The Monitor module also provides Simulator with information about the request queue; it measures and feedbacks the real access times as well.

In Table 1 the DiskXtender utilities, used to obtain the essential information about the configuration and the state of the HSM system, are shown.

Table 1. DiskXtender utilities used.

Utility	Information obtained
diskstats	request queue
tsedit	file location - on which tape, start block and size
tapestats	states of the drives
getfilediskstats	if the file is cached
readmap	type of the media

The following configuration files are also scanned at the beginning of the simulation: `DiskXtender.conf`, `tape.conf`, `ioctl.conf` and `tpdevs` [10].

3.2   Experimental Results

The experiments were performed in the ACC CYFRONET-AGH in Cracow. This site is equipped with the following tertiary storage hardware:

- ATL2640 – automated tape library with 3 DLT7000 drives and 264 Compact IV DLT tapes,
- ATL7100 – automated tape library with 4 DLT7000 drives and 100 Compact IV DLT tapes,
- HP660ex – magneto-optical jukebox with 4 Magneto-Optical Disc (MOD) drives and 128 plates.

The tertiary storage hardware is managed by the DiskXtender HSM software licensed for 5TB and running in distributed way on two HP9000 servers. The system is in production and is used by the scientific community in Cracow.

The testing of the system was performed by comparison of the estimated access time for some randomly chosen files residing on tapes with the real time of accessing those files. Both latency times are logged by the testing script. The HSM system was lightly loaded. The files sizes were between 10MB and 100MB.

The results are presented in Table 2). In this table the Estimated Time of Arrival, ETA, is compared with the Real Time of Arrival, RTA, for a given request. The relative error is significant for some cases.

Table 2. Single request tests results for tapes.

Nr	RTA [s]	ETA [s]	Absolute Error [s]	Relative Error [%]
0	180	264	84	47
1	365	203	162	44
2	253	234	19	8
3	181	203	22	12
4	283	279	4	1
5	256	204	52	20
6	286	203	83	29
7	237	238	1	0
8	278	254	24	9

During the tests we observed that there were high deviations of the mounting time values, which were supposed to be constant. This is probably because of the distributed configuration of the DiskXtender instalation in ACC CYFRONET AGH. The positioning time model also causes errors, because of the ideal tape model used in this prototype implementation, which does not take into account the localization of data blocks over a tape. This localization can differ significantly depending on the data compression rate and the positions of bad blocks along the tape. Another reason for the high errors could be the fact that the drives and robots parameters have been adopted from the vendor specification without taking into account the software overhead.

The results from the single request tests for files residing on MOD systems, for which the access time is much easier to predict, showed that the relative error was usually within the 10% limit.

4   Conclusions and Further Works

In this paper we have focused on "local" data access problems in grid environment. Described in this work implementation of the CEA resulted in simplification of internal structure of software developed for data access handling. The obtained solution was very flexible, well fitted to heterogenous environment and easy adaptable for new incoming technologies.

Further progress is based on European DataGrid (EDG) WP2's Replica Manager [1] and Replica Location Services [3]. Collaboration on specifying web service interfaces, cooperation on code development of EDG WP2's replication software (in particular Reptor) is also planned. Extensions of getAccessCosts() and getNetworkCosts(), as well as reuse of getBestFile() and getSECosts() are relevant examples.

Acknowledgements

The work described in this paper was supported in part by the European Union through the IST-2001-32243 project "CrossGrid" and by the Polish Committee for Scientific Research (KBN) 112/E-356/SPB/5.PR UE/DZ 224/2002-2004 project. AGH grant is also acknowledged. We are grateful to Ms. Marta Majewska for assistance during preparation of the paper.

References

1. Bell, W.H., Cameron D.G., Capozza, L., Millar, P., K. Stockinger, Zini, F., Design of a Replica Optimisation Framework, CERN Technical Report, 2002, WP2 - Data Management EU DataGrid Project, http://edms.cern.ch/document/337977.
2. Bell, W., Cameron, D., Capozza, L., Millar, P., Stockinger, K., and Zini, F., Simulation of Dynamic Grid Replication Strategies in OptorSim, in: Proc. of the 3rd Int'l. IEEE Workshop on Grid Computing (Grid'2002), Baltimore, USA, November 2002, Lect.Notes in Comput. Sci., Springer.
3. Chervenak, A.L., Deelman, E., Foster, I., Iamnitchi, A., Kesselman, C., Hoschek, W., Kunst, P., Ripeanu, M., Schwartzkopf, B., Stockinger, H., Stockinger, K., and Tierney, B., Giggle: A Framework for Constructing Scalable Replica Location Services, in: Proc. of the 3rd Int'l. IEEE Workshop on Grid Computing (Grid'2002), Baltimore, USA, November 2002, Lect.Notes in Comput. Sci., Springer.
4. W. Hoschek, J. J. Martinez, P. Kunszt, et al., "DataGrid - Data Management (WP2) Architecure Report" http://grid-data-management.web.cern.ch/grid-data-management/docs/DataGrid-02-D2.2-0103- 1_2.pdf.
5. CrossGrid - Development of Grid Environment for interactive Applications, EU Project, IST-2001-32243, Technical Annex.
6. Dutka, L., and Kitowski, J., Application of Component-Expert Technology for Selection of Data-Handlers in CrossGrid, in: D. Kranzlmüller, P. Kacsuk, J. Dongarra, J. Volkert (Eds.), Proc. 9th European PVM/MPI Users' Group Meeting, Sept. 29 - Oct. 2, 2002, Linz, Austria, Lect.Notes on Comput.Sci., vol.2474, Springer, 2002, pp. 25-32.
7. Dutka, L., and J. Kitowski, J., Expert technology in information systems development using component methodology, in: Proc. of Methods and Computer Systems in Science and Engng. Conf. Cracow, Nov.19-21, 2001, pp. 199-204, ONT, Cracow, 2001 (in Polish).
8. Nikolow, D., Słota, R., Kitowski, J., Data Access Time Estimation for HSM Systems in Grid Environment to appear in Proceedings of the Cracow Grid Workshop, December, 2002.
9. Nikolow, D., Słota, R., Dziewierz, M., Kitowski, J., Access Time Estimation for Tertiary Storage Systems, in: Monien, B., Feldman, R. (Eds.), Euro-Par 2002 Parallel Processing, 8th International Euro-Par Conference Paderborn, Germany, August 27-30, 2002 Proceedings , vol. 2400, Lect.Notes in Comput.Sci., Springer, 2002, pp. 873-880.
10. DiskXtender Manual; Legato Systems, Inc. - http://www.legato.com/products/diskxtenderunix.cfm.

ATLAS Data Challenges in GRID Environment on CYFRONET Cluster

Tomasz Bołd[1,2], Anna Kaczmarska[2], and Tadeusz Szymocha[2]

[1] University of Science and Technology, Mickiewicza 30, 30-059 Krakow, Poland
bold@ftj.agh.edu.pl,
[2] Institute of Nuclear Physics PAS, Radzikowskiego 152, 31-342 Krakow, Poland
{Anna.Kaczmarska,Tadeusz.Szymocha}@ifj.edu.pl

Abstract. The LHC ATLAS experiment at CERN will produce 1.6 PB of data per year. The High Energy Physics analysis techniques require that corresponding samples of at least 2 PB of Monte Carlo simulated data are also required. Currently the Monte Carlo test production is performed, in steps called Data Challenges. Such production and analysis can be performed in distributed sites. The computing model should allow for central brokering of jobs and management of huge amounts of data. The Grid environment is a possible solution. Data Challenges have to prove reliability and usability of the Grid. Main effort is to use Grid as 'yet another job submission system'. Some tentative solutions are presented and some weaknesses of existing software are pointed out. Additionally, perspectives of further development and improvements are indicated.

1   ATLAS Data Challenges

A Toroidal LHC Apparatus (ATLAS) on Large Hadron Collider (LHC) at European Organization for Nuclear Research (CERN) will collect data with 40 MHz rate, what may result in more then 66 PB of data per year. Neither physics interests nor capabilities of data storage allow for such production. The data reduction has to performed in real time of the data collection. The multi-level trigger system reduces output to interesting events only. This system is under development. In order to test the trigger algorithms Monte Carlo (MC) samples comparable in size to real data are required. There are four steps of MC data production chain (see Fig. 1):

- generation of events,
- simulation of a detector response,
- reconstruction,
- analysis of reconstructed data.

The event generation step of processing takes a theoretical model as input which generates events of various proton-proton interactions providing momenta and energies of outgoing particles. Programs used for this purpose are called MC

F. Fernández Rivera et al. (Eds.): Across Grids 2003, LNCS 2970, pp. 103–110, 2004.

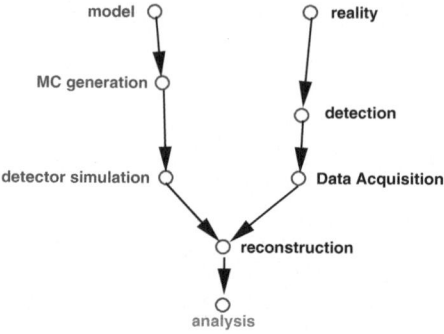

Fig. 1. Typical data flow in processing for HEP application.

generators (PYTHIA, JETSET [1], etc.). This generation step does not require large computing power and a typical output size of an event is several kBytes.

In the simulation of a detector response step the particles are tracked through the various detector components (particle interaction with matter and with electromagnetic fields is imitated). The GEANT [2] package is used for this purpose. As a result the responses from every channel of each sub-detector is given. The format of the output is identical to the format of data taken from readout electronics. As a consequence reconstruction and analysis of generated and experimental data are performed in the same way. This step is usually performed once. Typical output size of an event is 2-3 MB.

The goal of the reconstruction step is to derive parameters of particles trajectories from the detector readout signals. This trajectories extend over several sub-detectors. This information contains the multiplicity of the event, particles parameters like energies, momenta, positions etc. The same procedure concerns both, real detector events and simulated ones. Reconstruction process uses pattern recognition methods like histogramming, Hough transformations [3] and Kalman's filters [4]. They are adopted for the particular detector geometry. Reconstruction efficiency achieves more than 90% even in experiments with track multiplicity as high as several thousands (heavy ions collisions).

The analysis step is specific for particular physical process studied and usually results in creation of reasonably small data samples. Those are subject of iterative re-processing.

Presented paper is focused on the detector simulation step. The production of many (10^8) events samples of different physics processes overcomes CERN storage capacity and available CPU. For that reason the whole process is going to be distributed around the collaborating institutions. The ATLAS experiment initiated so called Data Challenges (DCs) for software check, validation of the computing model and data model as well as for production of data samples. There are several DC steps:

1. DC0 test phase. It was run during November - December 2001.
2. DC1 has started in May 2002 and it is divided into 3 phases:

- Phase 1 - major production run - April - August 2002 [5]
- Phase 2 - generation of data samples for high level trigger studies and production of the pile-up data
- Phase 3 - reconstruction and analysis of data collected in Phase 2 - the first half of 2003

3. DC2 -production of 10^8 samples mainly in OO-databases and large scale physics analysis using Grid tools, foreseen for 2004.

The data will provide useful information for physics understanding in the ATLAS detector. Studies of reconstruction algorithms are going to be performed using simulated data. All efforts are to prepare experimentalists for real data coming out of detector.

2   The ATLAS Data Processing within Grid Environment

The ATLAS experiment is going to solve its processing needs within the Grid environment. Before it happens, processing of MC samples can prove reliability and usability of the Grid for this purpose. Additionally all this exercises can provide real feedback to the Grid developers and gained experience should be fruitful for both communities.

First attempts to stress the Grid by ATLAS DC1 production and analyzes were performed within European Data Grid (EDG) testbed [6]. They proved the Grid usability but also pointed out weak points in EDG development. Certain number of fixes and redesign of some concepts were triggered by this activity. Also other LHC experiments performed similar tests [7]. In July and August 2002 NorduGrid and three US Grid testbeds participated in test production of DC1 phase 1 [8].

3   Processing at CYFRONET

3.1   The *ZEUS* Cluster at CYFRONET

The collaboration of the Henryk Niewodniczanski Institute of Nuclear Physics PAS in Krakow (INP) and the Academic Computer Center UST (CYFRONET) (within the CrossGrid project [9]) created cluster which was used for ATLAS DCs. Currently (February 2003) the cluster consist of homogeneous nodes of Intel Xeon processors ($\sim$ 30 kSI2k in total) and Network Attached Storage (NAS) of capability of $\sim$ 0.5 TB. Machines are running RedHat Linux and EDG Grid tools. The cluster configuration is a typical CrossGrid one:

- Computing Element (CE) gatekeeper node,
- Storage Element (SE) node,
- Worker Nodes (WN),
- User Interface (UI),
- SE disk space visible on each WN (NFS mounted).

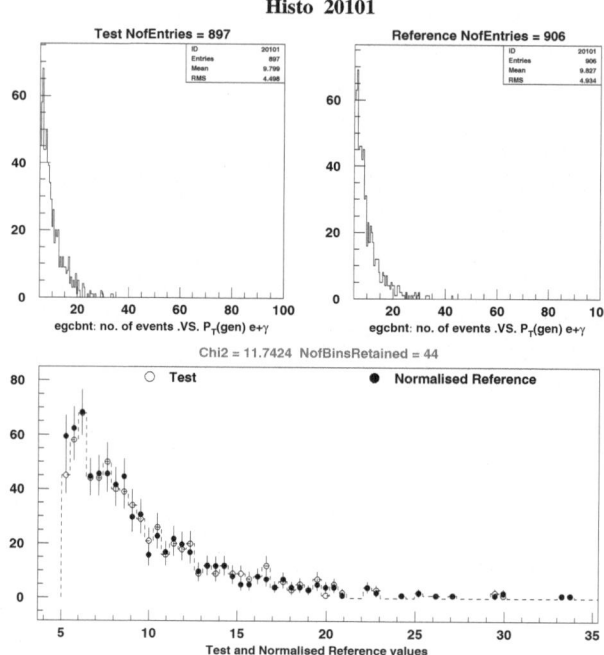

Fig. 2. One of 92 sample histograms compared during CYFRONET site validation. Top plots depict transverse momentum distribution of particles in reference (right side) and validated (left) samples. Plot at the bottom shows the above distributions normalized to the same number of events and superimposed.

3.2   Validation of CYFRONET Cluster

The first step of DC is validation of participating site. The procedure ensures that all computing environments are similar, so they produce exactly the same results on the same set of input data. Every site is supposed to take validation input data, produce detector response simulation data and return output to validation center at CERN. If produced data are statistically identical, site becomes valid ATLAS DC production site and can take data to process [10]. The validation procedure is slightly different for each DC phase as production software changes.

The CYFRONET cluster successfully passed the validation procedure for DC1 phase 1 and phase 2. The sample plots from validation data are presented in figure 2.

3.3   Preparing to the Production

The first step was to prepare set of shell scripts that facilitate jobs submission. This was based on experience from interactive validation processing. In scripts development process the main difficulty comes from principle uncertainty imposed by the Grid, namely from final CE location. At the beginning the simplest solution was chosen. Suite of shell scripts performing separated tasks was developed and tested separately. These tasks were:

- Job environment preparation. Job describing variables were set, necessary input files were enabled (copied or linked), and some system parameters were checked (like available disk space).
- Job execution. Software included in EDG ATLAS distribution was used.
- Job termination. Output files were copied to storage. Remaining files were removed. Log files were saved.

This scenario seemed to be reasonable solution but several weaknesses were pointed out. Indicated problems were solved before production was initialized (see section 3.5).

The final solution is following:

1. User selects samples to be processed by editing several fields in production script. This script will be running on destination computing element.
2. Subsequently user executes developed shell script called produce which uploads production script to the SE. Then using globus-job-submit starts processing by submission a number of jobs. Identifiers of sets to be produced are given as arguments to the produce command. Job IDs with corresponding identifiers are recorded in a file.
3. User queries CE for jobs execution statuses by running another script called check. The output provides insight in current production state in user friendly identification manner.
4. The check script allows also standard output and standard error retrieval after job termination.

The scripts produce and check prove to be quite universal tool.

3.4 Production

The input files to be processed were brought to storage element via FTP transfer to UI and then using Globus GSIFTP tool to SE. Files were transfered form CERN CASTOR tape storage [11].

Input files for simulation are quite small comparing to generated output. Size of input per one physical event is several tens of kBytes; output event size is about 3 MB.

A 3 files containing in total 15000 of $WH \rightarrow \nu\mu gg(m_H = 400$ GeV) events was retrieved. Production started using formerly prepared suite of scripts. The 125 output partitions of total size ~ 140 GB were simulated. The output was copied back to CASTOR.

The Globus has proved its reliability and the submission - inspection - retrieval sequence was 100 % operative. Certain obstacles were found. They are described in following sections and applied solutions are given.

3.5   Obstacles and Improvements

The difficulties met during DC1 on CYFRONET cluster are listed below together with tentative solutions allowing to finalize the production. Some suggestions for Grid sites configuration are also derived.

1. The Globus offers two ways of jobs execution: "submit" and "run" methods. The missing element in submission was execution script staging. Since this was very desired functionality the bypass was found. The submitter script first uploads execution script to SE. After completion Globus submits job which executes aforementioned script. This solution has obvious limitations and disallows for real distributed processing, though using `globus-url-copy` might remove this limitation.
2. Another limitation is mere execution progress monitoring. Namely the only `RUNNING` message is available in Globus during job execution. Required verbosity was achieved via log files generated directly on SE during execution. Inspection of them allowed progress monitoring, since the jobs could run even few days. Such treatment of logs appeared to be a remedy for crashing PBS when standard output and standard error were lost. The jobs with lost `stderr` and `stdout` were candidates for reprocessing since crucial informations were kept in logs.
3. The special care has to be taken in case of massive production in multiprocessor machines or systems sharing working disk space. Unsurprisingly, the interaction between jobs took place. Namely jobs cleaning disk space after execution are disturbing each other. The simplest way to avoid this kind of problems is to set separate working directories for each job.
4. The detector response simulation of 50k events requires about 1GB of input data. Data amount produced was 130GB (125 files ~1GB each). The transfer of large files is unreliable via slow network with the use of standard `ftp` client-server. Finally the use of `bbftp`[12] improved situation. The achieved speed-up was about 10 times and reliability was dramatically improved.
5. Two modes of input file access were investigated. Namely copying of input from SE before execution or using symbolic links (in consequence copying on fly during job execution). The observations are shown in figures 3 and 4.

4   Conclusion and Outlook

The first ATLAS data sets were processed on CYFRONET cluster successfully. Experience with Globus indicated its functionality and reliability. Several corrections and improvements were discussed. Perspectives are:

1. integration with ATLAS data bases,
2. automatization of output data transfer to CERN,
3. continuation of the production (massive simulation of MC events).

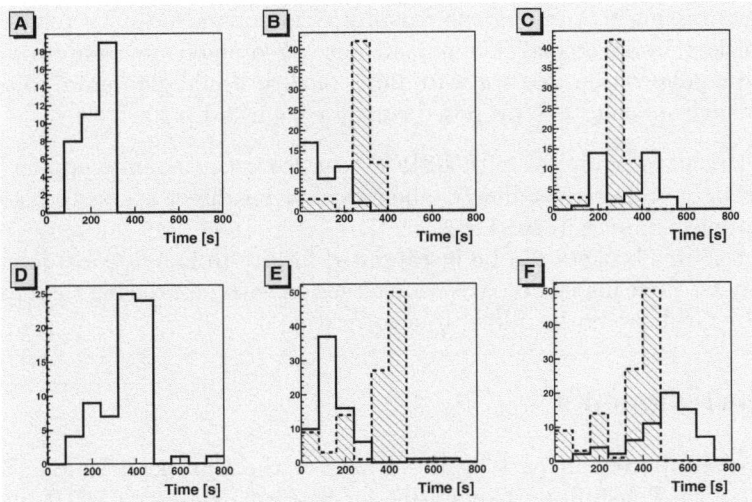

Fig. 3. Comparison of efficiency of job execution depending on the access mode of input file: pre-staging (hollow histograms) and on fly copying during execution (hatched histograms). The plots show number of jobs vs. consumed time per job. The top rows corresponds to cluster load by 20 simultaneous jobs. Bottom row - 32 jobs. First column shows time spent on copying, second - time spent on calculation, third - a cumulative time.

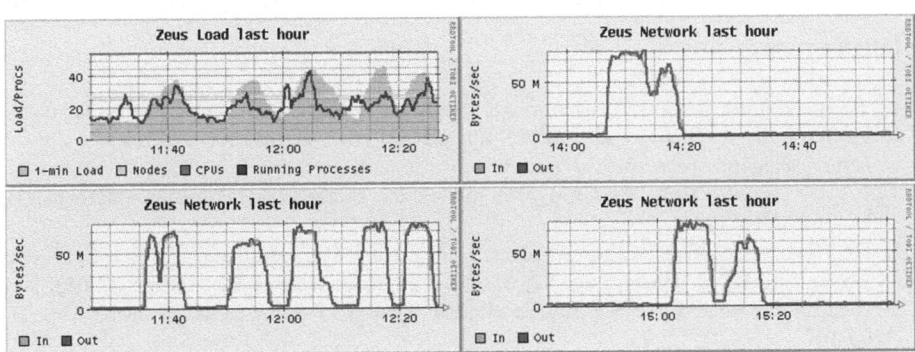

Fig. 4. Figures on the left are comparison of system load and network usage during input provisioning by pre-staging and on fly copying. The spikes from left to right side correspond to: cp, ln, cp, ln, ln exercises. A 20 of jobs were simultaneously submitted. Figures on the right show difference in network usage in copying (top) and in pre-staging (bottom). A 32 jobs were running in parallel.

In the further future the following activities are planed:

1. use of EDG brokering abilities,
2. coordination of the production within one ATLAS VO common for the EDG and the CrossGrid.

A few missing features in the existing Grid software can be relatively easily mimicked by scripting. Though, in authors opinion, few improvements in the Grid configuration and software functionality would give more reliable and efficient environment. The proposed changes are listed below:

- the UI can be equipped with GSIFTP service with custom mapping between user login and user certificate, allowing user for direct access to her/his files from jobs running in the Grid.
- the resource brokers can be instantiated locally to handle local jobs traffic,
- a way for some inspection or even interaction with jobs during their execution in the Grid should be added to a software.

Acknowledgments

Work was supported in part by the grants of the European Union IST-2001-32243 and the Polish State Committee for Scientific Research SPUB nr 620/E-77/SPB/5.PR UE/DZ 465/2002-2004.

Editorial help of P. Malecki in the preparation of this article is admitted.

The support of P. Nyczyk and A. Ozieblo the CYFRONET cluster administrators was of great value.

Encouragement by M. Turala and P. Malecki during the work is highly appreciated.

References

1. T. Sjoestrand. PYTHIA 5.7 and JETSET 7.4. CERN Program Library W5044
2. F. Bruyant, R. Brun et al., GEANT. CERN Program Library W5013
   http://wwwinfo.cern.ch/asd/geant/
3. P.V.C. Hough. 1962. Method and means for recognizing complex patterns, US Patent 3069654.
4. R.E.Kalman (1960), A New Approach to Linear Filtering and Prediction Problems. Trans. ASME, J. Basic Eng. 82, 35-45. R.E. Kalman and R.S. Bucy (1961), New Results in Linear Filtering and Prediction Theory, Trans. ASME, J. Basic Eng. 83, 95-107.
5. The ATLAS Data Challenge 1, The ATLAS DC1 Task Force
   http://atlas.web.cern.ch/Atlas/GROUPS/SOFTWARE/DC/DC1/
6. The EDG Testbed project page, *http://marianne.in2p3.fr/*
7. The Exabyte Challenge Databases for LHC experiments
   http://wwwinfo.cern.ch/asd/cernlib/rd45/papers/bulletin.html
8. The NorduGrid project page *http://www.nordugrid.org/documents/atlasdc1.html*
9. The CrossGrid project page, *http://www.crossgrid.org/*
10. The DC Physics Validation
    http://atlas.web.cern.ch/Atlas/GROUPS/SOFTWARE/DC/Validation/www/
11. J.P. Baud, J.D. Durand, B. Couturier, C. Curran, G. Lee, European Laboratory for Particle Physics (CERN)
    http://castor.web.cern.ch/castor/Welcome.html
12. The bbftp project page *http://doc.in2p3.fr/bbftp/*

MAPFS-Grid: A Flexible Architecture
for Data-Intensive Grid Applications

María S. Pérez[1], Jesús Carretero[2], Félix García[2], José M. Peña[1], and Víctor Robles[1]

[1] DATSI, FI, Universidad Politécnica de Madrid, Spain
[2] Departamento de Informática, Universidad Carlos III de Madrid, Spain

Abstract. Grid computing constitutes one of the most important computing paradigms appeared in the last decade. Data grids are grid system, whose main concern is the efficient and reliable management of data. These systems have had a growing interest due to the increasing number of applications using a huge amount of data, known as data-intensive applications. They present problems related to both grid systems and I/O systems. This paper describes MAPFS-Grid, a flexible and high-performance platform for data grid applications.

1 Introduction

I/O system constitutes a bottleneck in most of the current computing systems, due to its poor performance. The usage of parallel file systems is one of the most widely used alternative for avoiding this problem, traditionally known as *I/O crisis*.

Because of the improvements in hardware and, moreover, the decreasing prices of computer components, clusters have become an appropriate alternative in parallel and distributed computing. Nevertheless, the high demand of both computation and storage, needed by a great number of applications, which manage a huge amount of data, requires the usage of new technologies, such as grid computing.

Grid computing becomes one of the most important computing paradigms appeared in the last decade. This kind of computing allows applications to use low-load periods of all the nodes connected to a high-speed network. Unlike a conventional cluster, a high-performance grid infrastructure involves a heterogenous set of computing nodes, situated in different locations, and using different structures and policies. Grid technology allows hard-computing problems demanding huge storage facilities to be solved in an efficient way. In fact, one of the major goals of grid computing is to provide an efficient access to data, being data-intensive grid applications (or data grids, in short) one of the most relevant grid architectures [6]. Data-intensive applications usually make use of data management systems, by means of data mining and data warehousing techniques or other information management algorithms, which require efficient information retrieval capacities and a global and broad storage space. A data grid can fulfill the needs of these environments.

This paper presents MAPFS-Grid, a multiagent architecture, based on MAPFS [12], whose main goal is the deployment of MAPFS capabilities in a grid environment.

The outline of this paper is as follows. Section 2 describes the role of I/O access in grid computing. Section 3 presents MAPFS-Grid as a flexible infrastructure for data-intensive

F. Fernández Rivera et al. (Eds.): Across Grids 2003, LNCS 2970, pp. 111–118, 2004.
© Springer-Verlag Berlin Heidelberg 2004

grid applications. Section 4 describes MAPFS-Grid architecture. Section 5 describes how MAPFS-Grid can interact with other data grid infrastructures. Section 6 shows the results obtained for the evaluation of applications using MAPFS in a grid environment. Section 7 shows the related work. Finally, section 8 summarizes our conclusions and suggests further future work.

2   The Role of I/O Access in Grid Computing

Nowadays, there are a huge number of applications creating and operating on large amounts of data, e.g. data mining systems extracting knowledge from large volumes of data. Existing data-intensive applications have been used in several domains, such as physics, climate modeling, biology or visualization.

As we mentioned previously, data-intensive grid applications try to tackle the problems originated by the needs of a performance-full I/O system in a grid infrastructure. In these architectures, data sources are distributed among different nodes. Also, a typical data grid requires access to terabyte or higher sizes datasets. For example, high-energy physics may generate terabytes of data in a single experiment. Accesses to data repositories must be made in an efficient way, in order to increase the performance of the applications used in the grid. Furthermore, data-intensive grid applications have several functional requirements and access patterns.

Currently, there are different systems that offer services to access resources in a data grid. Accessing heterogeneous resources with interfaces and different functionalities is solved, in most of the cases, by means of new services that offer a uniform access to different types of systems. Examples of this kind of systems are Storage Resource Broker (SRB) [1], DataCutter [3], DPSS [16], and BLUNT [9]. All these systems use replication to improve the I/O performance and reliability.

In any case, the I/O system must be flexible enough to match data-intensive applications demands. The usage of hints, caching and prefetching policies or different data distribution configurations can reduce latency and increase I/O operations performance.

3   MAPFS-Grid Features

As we mentioned previously, a key feature of data grids infrastructures is the flexibility. MAPFS is a multiagent architecture, which provides this property mainly by means of three approaches:

1. System topology configuration: Ability to change system topology, setting the I/O nodes and their relationships. This feature is achieved by means of *storage groups*.
2. Access pattern specification: Although MAPFS is a general purpose I/O system, it can be configured in order to adapt to different I/O access patterns. The main configuration parameters of the MAPFS system are: (i) I/O caching and prefetching, approaches that increases the I/O operations efficiency, because of the optimal usage of disk caches, and (ii) usage of hints on future access patterns. MAPFS offers an independent API, different from the I/O operations API, which allows applications to configure the access patterns, which are translated to hints by the I/O system. All these features can be configured through the usage of *control user operations*.

3. There are different reasons to allow some functionalities (such as caching or prefetching) to run in parallel on different nodes and even in data servers. Moving executions to data servers may reduce network latency and traffic. The *agent* technology is a suitable framework for integrating these functions in the storage system, because of its adaptability to different domains and the agents autonomy.

MAPFS-Grid takes advantage of all these features with the aim of building a flexible and powerful infrastructure for data grids.

3.1 MAPFS-Grid Storage Groups

A storage group is defined in MAPFS as a set of servers clustered as groups. These groups take the role of data repositories. These groups can be built applying several policies, trying to optimize accesses to storage groups. Some significant policies are:

– Grouping by server proximity: Storage groups are built based on the physical distribution of data servers. Storage groups are composed of servers in close proximity to each other. This policy optimizes the queries addressed to a storage group because of the similar latency of messages sent to servers.
– Grouping by server similarity: Storage groups are composed of servers with similar processing capacity. This policy classifies storage groups in different categories, depending on their computational and I/O power.

The system topology can be changed dynamically. In this case, data must be reconstructed, degrading the performance of the I/O system. In order to avoid data reconstruction, MAPFS defines two types of storage groups, main storage groups and secondary groups, which form a lattice structure between them [14]. This approach postpones data reconstruction until the system schedules a defragmentation operation, which is used for deleting secondary groups and simplifying the storage system description.

3.2 Applications Access Pattern Specifications in MAPFS-Grid

Hints are structures known and built by the I/O system, which are used for improving the read and write operations performance. MAPFS uses these hints to access data. For example, storage systems using hints may provide greater performance since they use this information to decrease cache faults and to prefetch data most probably used in next executions. In other words, the more information it has been used, the less uncertainty in the future access guesses and, therefore, the better prefetching and caching results. In MAPFS, hints can be obtained in two ways: (i) given by the user, that is, the user application provides the necessary specifications to I/O system, and (ii) built by the multiagent subsystem. If this option is selected, the multiagent system must analyze the access pattern of the applications in order to build hints for improving data access. This feature can be achieved using statistical methods or historical logs.

If hints are provided by the user application, it is necessary for the system to provide syntactic rules for setting the system parameters, which configure the I/O system. On the other hand, if the multiagent subsystem creates the hints, it is also necessary to store them in a predefined way. In any case, lexical and syntactic rules must be introduced in the system.

The system is configured through several operations, which are independent of the I/O operations, although these last ones use the former operations. The configuration operations are divided into: (i) Hints Setting Operations, operations for establishing the hints of the system (they can set and get the values of the different fields of the hints), and (ii) Control User Operations, higher level operations that can be used directly by the user applications to manage system performance.

We refer the reader to [13] for a more detailed description of this interface.

3.3   MAPFS-Grid Agents Hierarchy

MAPFS uses an agent hierarchy, which solves the information retrieval problem in a transparent and efficient way. The taxonomy of agents used in MAPFS is composed of:

- Extractor agents: They are responsible for information retrieval, invoking parallel I/O operations.
- Distributor agents: They distribute the workload to the extractor agents. These agents are placed at the higher level of the agents hierarchy.
- Caching and prefetching agents: They are associated with one or more extractor agents, caching or prefetching their data.
- Hints agents: They must study applications access patterns to build hints for improving data access.

4   MAPFS-Grid Architecture

MAPFS file system uses as underlying hardware infrastructure a cluster of workstations [12]. Clusters are, in some sense, the predecessors of the grid technology.

Supercomputers have been replaced by clusters of workstations in a huge number of research projects. A relevant sample of this fact is the evolution of particle physics computation in CERN (European Organisation for Nuclear Research). Experiments over its previous LEP accelerator were made in IBM and CRAY supercomputers. In the early 1990's, the experimentation environment was replaced by tens of RISC processors. In the late 1900's, clusters of hundreds of Linux PCs were used in the accelerator. The new LHC accelerator will be used by 2007. This accelerator demands new solutions, since it has to manage several petabytes of data. 200,000 interconnected nodes are said to be necessary for the LHC accelerator, which arises both financial and technical difficulties. The solution involves resource sharing of a huge number of geographical distributed institutions, by means of grid computing. Analogously, MAPFS has modified its architecture aiming at the achievement of the grid computing advantages.

MAPFS is based on a client-server architecture using general purpose servers, providing all the MAPFS management tasks as specialized clients. In the first prototype, we use NFS servers. NFS has been ported to different operating systems and machine platforms and is widely used by many servers worldwide. Therefore, it is very easy to add new data repositories to the data grid infrastructure. The only requirement of these data servers is to use NFS and export a directory tree to data grid users. Data is distributed through the servers belonging to a storage group, using a stripe unit.

On the client-side, it is necessary to install MAPFS client, which provides a parallel I/O interface to the servers. This module is implemented with MPI (Message Passing Interface)[10], the standard message passing interface, widely used in parallel computing. MPI allows different processes to run in parallel over MAPFS. Nevertheless, this technique is not suitable for the dynamic interconnection of heterogeneous nodes, because MPI is a static solution, which must know a priori the IP address of all the nodes of the topology. Thus, MAPFS-Grid requires grid technology, interoperable with MPI, because MAPFS is based on this interface. In order to fulfill these requirements, MAPFS-Grid uses MPICH-G2 [4], such as described in next section.

5   Interoperability with Other Grid Architectures

One of the major goals of a data grid infrastructure is to provide access to a huge number of heterogeneous data sources. In this sense, it is important that MAPFS-Grid can interoperate with other grid architectures, giving access to their data repositories. Because MAPFS is implemented with MPI, its integration with other grid infrastructures is relatively simple, using MPICH-G2, a grid-enabled implementation of the MPI, which makes possible running MPI programs across multiple computers at different sites.

Applications can use MAPFS-Grid together with other grid architectures. In this case, it is possible to extend storage groups with other nodes accessible through the Globus services. Concretely, the Global Access Secondary Storage (GASS) service [2] is used in order to stage programs to remote machines and to support efficient communication in dynamic grid environments. The integration between MAPFS and GASS is not redundant, because GASS does not provide the full functionality of a parallel file system. MAPFS provides a rich parallel interface, which can be used in wide area computing with the aid of GASS and other Globus services.

6   MAPFS-Grid Evaluation

In our implementation, we need to evaluate the performance of: (i) storage groups, (ii) control user operations, and (iii) multiagent subsystem.

In order to measure the performance of the first aspect, experiments were run in two different storage groups, which use the server similarity grouping policy, because of the technical differences of both groups. The first storage group (G_1) is composed of four nodes Athlon 650MHz, with 256 MB of RAM memory, connected by a Gigabit network. The second storage group (G_2) has six nodes Intel Xeon 2.40GHz, with 1GB of RAM memory with a Gigabit network. The storage group G_2 provides better performance. However, the storage group G_1 offers bigger storage capacity. These two storage groups constitutes a possible topology of our data grid. Our experiment consists in a process per node running a multiplication of two matrices, where the matrices are stored in the grid, using MAPFS-Grid as underlying platform. The resultant matrix is also stored in a distributed fashion. A prefetching multiagent subsystem is used, which is responsible for prefetching rows and columns of the matrices. In this case, hints provided by the applications are the indexes of the matrix row and the matrix column of the element calculated in every iteration. It is possible to prefetch data to be used later in the executions, using this information. The multiagent subsystem obtains optimum values for the prefetching phase. In this way, we evaluate the usage of control user operations and the performance of the multiagent subsystem.

This experiment was compared to another one, which consists in multiplying the same matrices stored in the local disk through the usage of a traditional I/O system. The size of the matrices is 100 MB.

Figure 1 shows the speedup of the MAPFS solution for the group G_1 versus local solution, varying the access size used in the I/O operations. As can be seen, the speedup is very close to the maximum speedup. Figure 2 represents the execution time of the groups G_1 y G_2 for the matrix multiplication. As we previously mentioned, the storage group G_2 provides better results, although the storage group G_1 provides higher storage capacity. The usage of different policies in MAPFS-Grid allows applications to take advantage of the flexibility of this infrastructure, depending on their current needs.

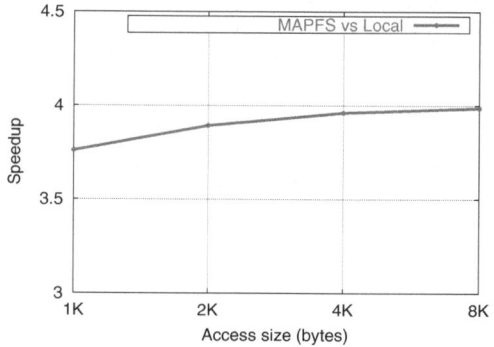

Fig. 1. Speedup of the MAPFS-Grid solution (group G_1) versus Local solution.

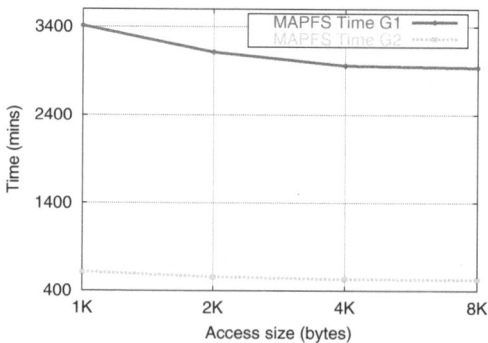

Fig. 2. Comparison between different storage groups.

7   Related Work

Grid technology provides a framework in which heterogeneous and distributed computing resources can be shared among several organizations and institutions, through high-speed networks, with the aim of solving high-cost and data-intensive problems. Foster et al. [5] compares grid technology to electrical power grid, in the sense that a user must be able to use computational resources in the same way than electrical power, that is, everywhere, with a reliable service, and having an acceptable cost.

Distributed scientific applications running in a high-speed network of 17 USA research centers were shown in SuperComputing'95 congress. This demonstration constituted the starting poing of several research projects related to the distributed resource-sharing. One of the first grid projects was the NASA Information Power Grid (IPG), which allows NASA resources to be integrated and managed.

Grid owns a *de facto* standard, knows as Globus. Globus [7] provides a software infrastructure, which includes basic protocols and services for grid applications.

Additionally, several researchers and commercial companies are investigating topics related to data-intensive grids and I/O systems used in computational grids. The problems tackled by these research lines are similar to those discussed in this paper. Armada [11] is a framework that allows grid applications to access datasets distributed across a computational grid. Applications combine modules called *ships* into graphs called *armadas*.

The Remote I/O (RIO) library [8] is a tool for accessing to files located on remote file systems. RIO follows the MPI-IO interface. MAPFS also provides this feature.

Kangaroo [15] belongs to the Condor grid project and it is a reliable data movement system that keep applications running. Kangaroo service continues to perform I/O operations even if the process that initiated these requests fails.

Legion is an object-oriented infrastructure used in distributed computing. LegionFS [17] provides UNIX-style I/O operations, using Legion services such as naming or security. Unlike LegionFS, MAPFS provides a rich parallel I/O interface.

MAPFS-Grid allows applications to access remote data in an efficient way, making possible access to storage groups belonging to other data grids, by means of the usage of MPICH-G. Furthermore, data access patterns configuration provides flexibility to applications using MAPFS-Grid. This last characteristic is different from the rest of the systems previously described.

8   Conclusions and Future Work

In this work we have presented MAPFS-Grid as an extension of the MAPFS I/O architecture for data-intensive grid applications. MAPFS-Grid constitutes a new data grid infrastructure, which provides flexibility and dynamic reconfiguration to applications mainly by means of three approaches: (i) storage groups, (ii) access patterns specifications, and (ii) a multiagent subsystem responsible of running specific functionalities. These features have been evaluated through the implementation of a scientific application, achieving a speedup very close to the maximum one.

As future work, it would be interesting to evaluate the performance of the system with other topologies and other kind of applications.

References

1. C. Baru, R. Moore, A. Rajasekar, and M. Wan. The SDSC storage resource broker. In *Proceedings of CASCON'98*, Toronto, Canada, 1998.
2. Joseph Bester, Ian Foster, Carl Kesselman, Jean Tedesco, and Steven Tuecke. GASS: A data movement and access service for wide area computing systems. In *Proceedings of the Sixth Workshop on Input/Output in Parallel and Distributed Systems*. ACM Press, 1999.
3. M. D. Beynon, R. Ferreira, T. Kurc, A. Sussman, and J. Saltz. DataCutter: Middleware for filtering very large scientific datasets of archival storage systems. In *Proceedings of the 2000 Mass Storage Systems Conference*. IEEE Computer Society Press, Mar 2000.
4. I. Foster and N. Karonis. A grid-enabled MPI: Message passing in heterogeneous distributed computing systems. In *Proceedings of SC'98*. ACM Press, 1998.
5. I. Foster and C. Kesselman, editors. *The Grid: Blueprint for a New Computing Infrastructure*. Morgan Kaufmann, 1999.
6. Ian Foster. *Computational Grids*. 1999. Chapter belonging to [5].
7. Ian Foster and Carl Kesselman. Globus: A metacomputing infrastructure toolkit. *The International Journal of Supercomputer Applications and High Performance Computing*, 11(2):115–128, Summer 1997.
8. Ian T. Foster, David Kohr, Rakesh Krishnaiyer, and Jace Mogill. Remote I/O fast access to distant storage. In *Proceedings of the IOPADS 1997*, pages 14–25, 1997.
9. M.R. Martinez and N. Roussopoulos. MOCHA: A self-extensible database middleware system for distributed data sources. In *Proceedings of the ACM SIGMOD International Conference on Management of Data*, Dallas, TX, May 2000.
10. The Message Passing Interface (MPI) standard. *http://www-unix.mcs.anl.gov/mpi*
11. Ron Oldfield and David Kotz. Armada: a parallel I/O framework for computational grids. *Future Generation Computer Systems*, 18(4):501–523, 2002.
12. María S. Pérez, Jesús Carretero, Félix García, José M. Peña, and Víctor Robles. A flexible multiagent parallel file system for clusters. *International Workshop on Parallel I/O Management Techniques (PIOMT'2003) (Lecture Notes in Computer Science)*, June 2003.
13. María S. Pérez, Ramón A. Pons, Félix García, Jesús Carretero, and Víctor Robles. A proposal for I/O access profiles in parallel data mining algorithms. In *3rd ACIS International Conference on SNPD*, June 2002.
14. María S. Pérez, Alberto Sánchez, José M. Peña, Víctor Robles, Jesús Carretero, and Félix García. Storage groups: A new approach for providing dynamic reconfiguration in databased clusters. In *2004 IASTED Conference on PDCN (To appear)*, February 2004.
15. Douglas Thain, Jim Basney, Se-Chang Son, and Miron Livny. The Kangaroo approach to data movement on the grid. In *Proceedings of the Tenth IEEE Symposium on High Performance Distributed Computing (HPDC10)*, August 2001.
16. B. Tierney, J. Lee, W. Johnston, B. Crowley, and M. Holding. A network-aware distributed storage cache for data-intensive environments. In *Proceedings of the Eighth IEEE International Symposium on High Performance Distributed Computing*, pages 185–193, Redondo Beach, CA, Aug 1999.
17. Brian S. White, Michael Walker, Marty Humphrey, and Andrew S. Grimshaw. LegionFS: A secure and scalable file system supporting cross-domain high-performance applications. In *Proceedings of the IEEE/ACM Supercomputing Conference (SC2001)*, November 2001.

RAID-1 and Data Stripping across the GRID

R. Marco[1], J. Marco[1], D. Rodríguez[1], D. Cano[1], and I. Cabrillo[1]

Instituto de Física de Cantabria (CSIC-Universidad de Cantabria),
Avda. Los Castros s/n, 39005 Santander, Spain

Abstract. Stripping techniques combined with an adequate replication policy across the Grid offer the possibility to improve significatively data access and processing times, while eliminating the need for local data mirroring, so saving significatively on storage costs. First results on a local cluster following a simple strategy are presented.

1   Introduction

Data Grids do demand new techniques for optimizing large distributed data volumes access and processing. At the same time, replication techniques should assure the absence of a single point of failure. Addressing the first point is possible employing complete true data-stripping techniques. An intelligent use in combination with the replica mechanism, resembling the RAID-1 scheme, and in fact replacing it for local redundancy, can solve the problem.

Large Data Volumes (with typical size of several Terabytes) will be processed in Data Grids. In general, the processing will require the definition of a filter, returning a given data subset. Data-mining techniques will usually operate on the result of this first filter, more or less complex, and could define additional filters [1].

Flexible software-only storage appliances designed to meet the storage needs in a Grid aware environment [3], can be integrated in the framework proposed, replacing the use of Resilient Server Facilities (like those based on RSF-1 [2]).

2   Data Stripping and Optimization of Data Access and Processing

As indicated before, optimization of data access requires distributed techniques, and one expects a distribution of a given dataset in a given number of subsets, to be stored and then accessed from a given number of storage nodes, and then processed at a given number of distributed working nodes. Optimization of Data Processing requires so a good data balancing, that, moreover, must be preserved in what possible after the application of filters.

Let's give an example based on our experience processing the data from the DELPHI experiment [4] in the LEP accelerator at the CERN laboratory based in Geneva. The data used in a physics analysis for the search of the Higgs boson (referred as the Hqq sample) corresponds to about 12 GB of real data, and

F. Fernández Rivera et al. (Eds.): Across Grids 2003, LNCS 2970, pp. 119–123, 2004.

132 GB of simulated events, these including 60 GB of *four-fermion* events, 60 GB of *qcd* background, and 12 GB of Higgs signal. Note that these different background sources are reflected in the so-called "topology" of the events: *qcd* background events have a cigar-like shape, in terms of energy distribution, while *four-fermion* events are more spherical.

After the pre-selection of generic four-jet events, the sample is divided in around 3000 files with similar size, where 1200 correspond to the simulation of *qcd* background, a similar number of files to the simulation of *four-fermion*, and only 300 to the Higss signal and a similar number for the real data.

Distributed across 20 node resources, each node would have to "process" about 6 GB of data,corresponding to 60 files of *qcd* background, a similar number for four-fermion background, and only 15 files for real data itself and the generated Higgs signal. Any division of the data across the nodes would make sense if all the data is used all the time. But this is not the usual case. If for example we decide to apply a first filter, the resulting sample could be distributed in a completely unbalanced way. For example just asking for high event sphericity, the *qcd* background could be reduced by 90%, while the four-fermion background could be reduced by 20% only: 6 nodes assigned for processing QCD would now handle only 6 GB in total, i.e., 1 GB each, while 6 nodes assigned to four-fermion MC will have to process more than 6 GB each. The total time for processing will be penalized by this unbalance, by a factor worse than 5.

The solution to this problem is the application of a total stripping technique: datasets should be uniformly spread across the available storage nodes. In our case, each node will have about 7 GB of data, but the composition will be the same for all: 3 GB qcd, 3 GB four-fermion, and less than 1 GB for signal, and real data.

3   Implementation: RAID-1 across the Grid

This stripping has to be defined in first instance by the corresponding Virtual Organization. To fulfil the request of no single point of failure, data has to be made redundant in the grid. Following the RAID model for local storage, we propose a RAID-1 like mechanism across the grid: each dataset in a local disk should have at least a mirror replica somewhere outside the local site. This means that, if the network is fast enough, no local redundancy is needed, and in particular the use of local disks can be optimized with no need for RAID-1 or higher , and fast and efficient RAID-0 can be used. When a local disk fails, the system should recover using the replica located not locally, but across the grid. This means a reduction of about 40% in local disk cost, but requires the development and maintenance of this "RAID" service at the grid infrastructure level.

A typical configuration is the "mirror" one. Assume two groups are collaborating in a given data analysis. After defining the dataset, they strip this volume to each local cluster. Following the previous example, the same dataset would be installed in stripped way at each of the two sites. If one of the sites fails, its information can be recovered from the other one, so the site doesn't need any RAID-1 configuration, but redundancy is preserved.

In this paper we describe the results using two clusters, each with 20 nodes, linked across a fast-ethernet connection, where a manual RAID service has been implemented. Also the experience regarding the manual recovery from the failure of a single RAID-0 IDE server is described, and compared to the alternative of a RAID-1 IDE data server.

The difference in processing time comparing the stripped and non-stripped option for the samples indicated above is reported.

The multi-site strategy should be optimized depending on the resources location and their availability, and will be the subject of future papers.

4   First Results

The Santander Grid Wall, a cluster with 80 nodes each one being an IBM X220 server dual PIII-1.26 GHz processor with 640 MB RAM and 36 GB SCSI and 60 GB IDE disks, connected via fast-ethernet to three 3Com 24-port gigabit stacked switches, has been used in the test. Figure 1 shows this setup.

Typical write speeds are 20 MB/s on the IDE disk, and around 50 MB/s for the SCSI one. These speeds should be compared to the single fast-ethernet speed, close to 10 MB/s.

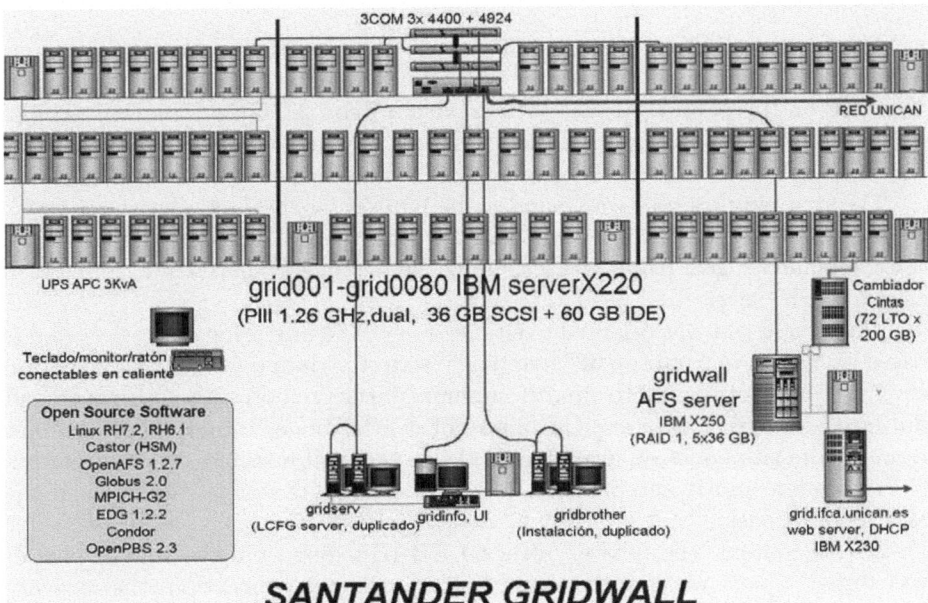

Fig. 1. The Santander GridWall cluster.

The test, using the data previously described, included the installation of this four-jet dataset, the recovery of the info in a node, and the recovery of the whole site data.

Figure 2 shows the different disk configurations used in these tests.

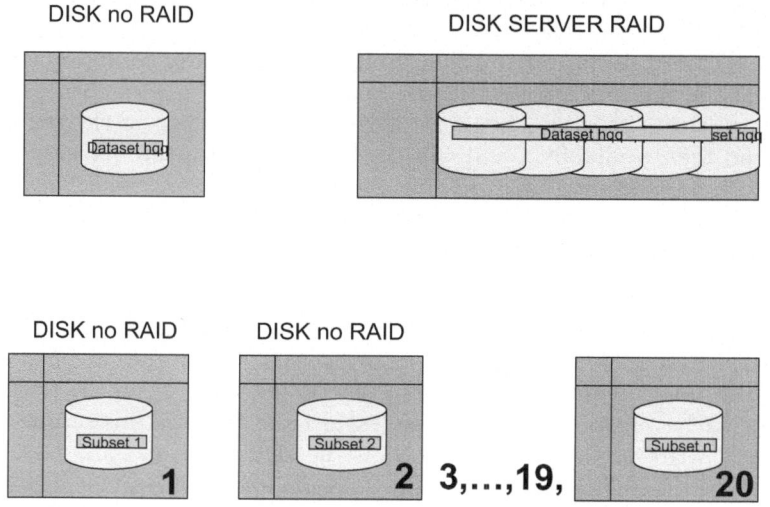

Fig. 2. Disk configurations used in the tests.

The first test involved the complete stripping process on the previous complete dataset, from a disk server into a set of 20 cluster nodes. The disk server was built on top of an IBM X235 server with a Xeon 2.0 GHz processor and 512 MB RAM, using a RAID-0 IDE configuration with a 3Ware-12-7500 controller and 8 x 120 GB IDE disks. It also includes a Gigabit network connection.

The stripping process was found to be limited by the fast ethernet network connection, and took 214 minutes. Similar results were obtained using either the scp command, or grid-ftp. It was also found that compression poses a significative charge on the sever.

The second test was oriented to site recovery. The mirroring strategy tested is based on "stripping" on top of "stripping": strip the data on each local node into several nodes in the remote site, to minimize future remote site nodes overhead during the recovery process. On failure of a local node, the idea is to recover from remote site nodes on available local site nodes, if possible, or keep/migrate to remote site use if not possible. Recovery can be completed later when the local node is back.

In this context, the recovery of a 60 GB IDE disk from the remote cluster was tested. Speed was limited again by fast-ethernet connection. the recovery took 104 minutes.

5   Conclusions and Future Work

Stripping techniques combined with an adequate replication policy across the Grid offers the possibility to improve significatively data access and processing times, while eliminating the need for local data mirroring, so saving significatively on storage costs.

Tests on a local cluster with fast ethernet network connections for each node show that recovery of an IDE lost disk was limited by the available network bandwidth. To overcome this limitation, tests with Gigabit ethernet connection will be conducted, expecting to push the limit to the actual disk write speed.

Future tests in a real distributed Grid environment will show if explicit QoS mechanisms are needed to make this technique fast and reliable enough, on top of the new Géant network infrastructure.

References

1. for an example see the contribution to this conference from D.Rodriguez et al.: *Interactive Distributed Data Access in a Grid Environment.*
2. See http://www.starfiretechnology.com/products/hac/rsf1.html *Testbed Extension and Site Status, EU-CrossGrid IST-2001-32243, Feb 2003*
3. John Bent, Venkateshwaran Venkataramani, Nick LeRoy, Alain Roy, Joseph Stanley, Andrea C. Arpaci Dusseau, Remzi H. Arpaci-Dusseau, Miron Livny *Flexibility, Manageability, and Performance in a Grid Storage Appliance Proceedings of the Eleventh IEEE Symposium on High Performance Distributed Computing Edinburgh, Scotland, July 2002.* Available from http://www.cs.wisc.edu/condor/nest/
4. For a short description of the DELPHI experiment, and in particular the search for the Higgs boson at LEP see: *Search for the standard model Higgs boson at LEP in the year 2000.* by DELPHI Collaboration, *Phys.Lett.B499:23-37,2001*

A Parallel I/O Middleware
to Integrate Heterogeneous Storage Resources on Grids

José M. Pérez Menor, Félix García, Jesús Carretero, Alejandro Calderón,
Javier Fernández, and José Daniel García

Computer Architecture Group, Computer Science Department,
Universidad Carlos III de Madrid, Leganes, Madrid, Spain
{jmperez,fgarcia}@arcos.inf.uc3m.es
http://www.arcos.inf.uc3m.es

Abstract. The philosophy behind grid is to use idle resources to achieve a higher
level of computational services (computation, storage, etc). Existing data grids
solutions are based in new servers, specific APIs and protocols, however this
approach is not a realistic solution for enterprises and universities, because this
supposes the deployment of new data servers across the company. This paper describes a new approach to data access in computational grids. This approach is
called GridExpand, a parallel I/O middleware that integrates heterogeneous data
storage resources in grids. The proposed grid solution integrates available data network solutions (NFS, CIFS, WebDAV) and makes possible the access to a global
grid file system. Our solution differs from others because it does not need the installation of new data servers with new protocols. Most of the data grid solutions
use replication as the way to obtain high performance. Replication, however, introduce consistency problem for many collaborative applications, and sometimes
requires the usage of lots of resources. To obtain high performance, we apply the
parallel I/O techniques used in parallel file systems.

Keywords: Data Grids, Parallel I/O, data declustering, High performance I/O.

1   Introduction

Currently there is a great interest in the grid computing concept. Usually this concept
denotes a distributed computational infrastructure in the field of the engineering and
advanced science [8]. A grid is composed by geographically sparse resources that join
to form a *virtual* computer. The resources (computers, networks, storage devices, etc)
that define the grid are heterogeneous and reside in differentiated domains. This kind of
systems differ from other distributed environments as clusters or local area networks in
several aspects:

1. They are located in several administration domains.
2. The communication network used is Internet. This feature allows to build a grid
   with resources placed, for example, in Europe, America or Asia.
3. The different resources of the grid have a high degree of heterogeneity and must be
   accessible from any other part of the grid.

F. Fernández Rivera et al. (Eds.): Across Grids 2003, LNCS 2970, pp. 124–131, 2004.
© Springer-Verlag Berlin Heidelberg 2004

4. The grid must be transparent to the users. They should not know where their programs are being executed or their data are being stored.

Most of the advances that have been developed in grid computing have been centered on exploiting grid computational resources from the process point of view, taking apart the storage point of view. Nevertheless, for many applications, the access to distributed information (DataGrid) is as important as the access to processing resources; since the majority of the scientific and engineering applications need the access to big volumes of data in a efficient way. Other times the information generated by the applications exceeds the capacity of local storage resources, and the data generated must be stored in remote storage devices. To accomplish this goals several systems have been developed, but usually they are difficult to use, require specific data servers and do not exploit all the storage resources in an efficient way. In this paper we present a parallel I/O middleware for grids, called GridExpand, that integrates existing servers using protocols like NFS, CIFS or WebDav[17], without need complex installations, and that facilitates the development of applications by integrating heterogeneous grid-resources under homogeneous and well known interfaces like POSIX and MPI-IO. This system apply the parallel I/O techniques used in most of parallel file systems to grids environments.

The rest of the paper is organized as follows: Section 2 describes the related work performed in the storage aspect on grids and other distributed systems. Section 3 presents the design of the data grid architecture proposed. Section 4 shows some evaluation results. Finally, Section 5 presents some conclusions and the future work.

2   Related Work

The efforts developed in the access to distributed data in grids are based on the creation of new services for the access to big volumes of information and specialized interfaces for grid. Examples of this systems are: Globus [16], Storage Resource Broker (SRB) [1], DataCutter [2], DPSS [15], and MOCHA [10]. These solutions are not suitable for the integration of the available storage data servers (NFS servers, CIFS, HTTP-WebDAV, etc), and they forces the users to learn new APIs, install new servers, and modify or adapt their applications. On the other hand, the solutions developed use the replication as the way to obtain high performance accesses to data, bringing data near the clients that use them. This solution supposes that applications do not modify the data that they use [6]. The use of replication originates two main problems: it supposes an intensive use of resources, not only in storage, but also in management. Furthermore, it is not appropriated for applications that modify the same set of information, because some resources must be used in collaborative environments. A way to improve the performance of I/O, specially in distributed systems is parallel I/O. The usage of parallel filesystems and parallel I/O libraries have been studied in a great number of systems and platforms: Vesta [7], PIOUS [11], ParFiSys [5], Galley [12], PVFS [4], Armada [13]. Most of those systems use a special file server, but in heterogeneous systems as grids this is not always possible. The work presented in this abstract uses the ideas proposed in the Expand parallel file system [9] [3] that relies on the usage of several NFS file servers in parallel.

3   GridExpand Design

To solve the problems previously addressed, the authors have defined a new data grid approach that integrates all available data storage servers and applies parallel I/O techniques to them. This architecture is called GridExpand and it is based on the effective integration of existing protocols, services and existing solutions.

The idea is to provide a parallel I/O middleware that allows to integrate the existing heterogeneous resources from the point of view of the client without needing to create or to install new servers, and using existing APIs, like POSIX or MPI-IO. Integrating multiple resources and using parallel I/O techniques allow to increase the performance and storage capacity of the system.

The GridExpand architecture is presented in Figure 1. This architecture allows the usage of several heterogeneous clusters to define parallel distributed partitions, where data are striped. The servers used to store the data are traditional storage servers as NFS, CIFS or WebDav. GridExpand uses the available protocols in a network to communicate with the data servers without needing specialized servers. Using the former approach offers several advantages:

1. No changes to the servers are required. All aspects of GridExpand operations are implemented on the clients. For example: for NFS we use RPC and the NFS protocol, for CIFS we use TCP/IP and the SMB protocol, and for HTTP-WebDav we use TCP/IP and the HTTP protocol with the WebDAV Distributed Authoring Protocol.
2. The parallel I/O middleware construction is greatly simplified, because all operations are implemented on the client side. This approach is completely different to that used in many current data grid systems, that implement both client and server sides.
3. It allows parallel access to both data of different files and data of the same file.
4. It allows the usage of servers with different architectures and operating systems.
5. It simplifies the configuration, because the protocols proposed are very familiar to users. For example, to use NFS the server only needs to export the appropriate directories.

To provide large storage capacity and to enhance flexibility and performance, GridExpand combines several data servers to provide a generic stripped partition which allows to create several types of file systems. The Figure 1 shows different partitions that can be defined in the grid: Intra-site partitions, as for example, the partition 4, and Inter-site partitions, as for example, the partition 1.

Furthermore, partition can be homogeneous, when all data servers in the partition use the same protocol, or heterogeneous, when different data servers protocols are used. This is an important feature because allows to integrate heterogeneous resources.

The files in GridExpand consists in several *subfiles*, one for each server in the distributed partition. All subfiles are fully transparent to the users. GridExpand hides those subfiles, offering to the clients a traditional view of the files. To exploit all the available storage resources, GridExpand provides several data allocation and load balancing algorithms that search for servers that are available to be used and to select several nodes to store the data of a file.

All file operations in GridExpand use a *virtual filehandle*. This virtual filehandle is the reference used in GridExpand to reference all operations. When Expand needs to

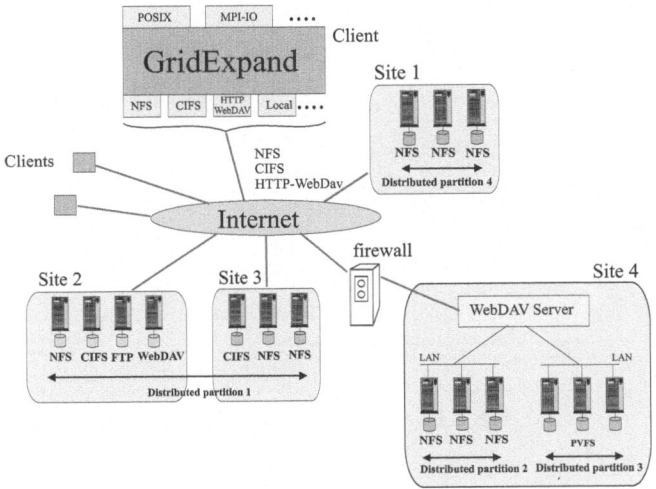

Fig. 1. GridExpand Architecture.

access to a subfile of the parallel partition, it uses the appropriated filehandle. A virtual filehandle in GridExpand is defined as follow:

$$\bigcup_{i=1}^{N} filehandle_i$$

where $filehandle_i$ is the filehandle (protocol dependant structure) used for the data server i to reference the subfile i belonging to the GridExpand file. These feature allows to use different data servers for the same distributed partition. To enhance I/O, user requests are split by GridExpand into parallel subrequests sent to the involved data servers. When a request involves k data servers, GridExpand issues k requests in parallel to the data servers, using threads to parallelize the operations (see Figure 2). The same criteria is used in all GridExpand operations. A parallel operation to k servers is divided in k individual operations that use the appropriate data server protocol to access the corresponding subfile.

3.1 User Interface

The access to the files is provided by standard interfaces like POSIX or MPI-IO. To accomplish this goal, GridExpand provides an Abstract File Interface (AFI) that allows the implementation of the typical interfaces (POSIX, Win32, MPI-IO) above it, and supports other advanced features as cache policy, prefetching, parallelism degree configuration and fault tolerance. The access to the servers and storage resources is provided by an Abstract I/O Adapter similar to the ADIO [14] used to develop portable implementations of MPI-IO. GridExpand, also provides an interface for Java applications. For Java applications we use the Extended Filesystem API provided by Sun for WebNFS. This API defines two means of access to files and file systems:

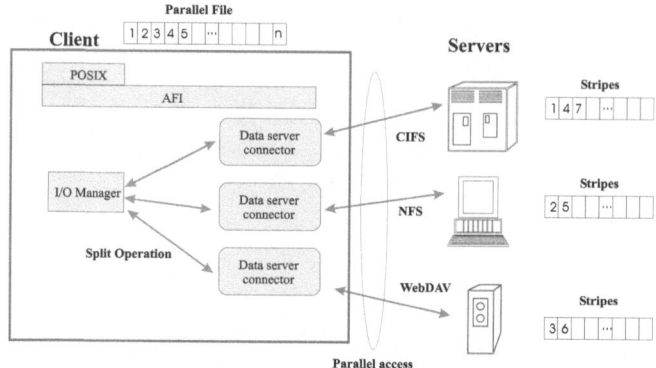

Fig. 2. Parallel Access in GridExpand.

- An XFile class that supports naming of files with URLs such as the type proposed in the NFS URL Scheme. Here users would specify URLs like "xpn://pato.arcos/file". The XFile class also provides a default "native" URL scheme using java.io.* which has a file naming syntax that varies according to the operating system that supports the Java Runtime Interface, such as Win95, UNIX, and VMS.
- Access to data through the XFileInputStream, XFileOutputStream, XRandomAccessFile, XFileReader and XFileWriter classes that are similar to classes that exists today in the JDK.

4   Performance Evaluation

In the evaluation we have used an image-processing application that processes a set of 128 images. All images have a size of 3 MB. On each image, the application returns a new image applying a fixed 64-pixel mask. The image processing process is decoupled, taking into account that we can analyze several images in parallel. This application has been executing on a grid configured using 8 workstations running Linux and connected through a Fast Ethernet switch. As data server we have used a NFS server on each node. Our experiments compare the performance of a single server using NFS and GridExpand with different intra-site partitions (NFS, 1, 2, 4, 8). The application used can be divided in several decoupled tasks (in the tests, from 1 to 32 clients). Fistly the tests have been performed using a linux platform (GridExpand and the test application implemented in C), and then the tests have been performed using a Java platform (with linux). Figure 3 shows the time needed to run the application, using POSIX interface and varying the number of subtasks (clients in Figure) and different distributed partitions (from 1 I/O node to 8 I/O nodes). The Figure also shows the performance obtained with NFS (NFS legend in Figure). Figure 4 shows the time needed to run the application using XFile Java Interface.

As can be seen in Figure 3, the performance achieved by the system is increased when GridExpand distributed partitions are used. The usage of distributed partitions on grids increases the total storage capacity. Furthermore, the usage of parallel I/O techniques

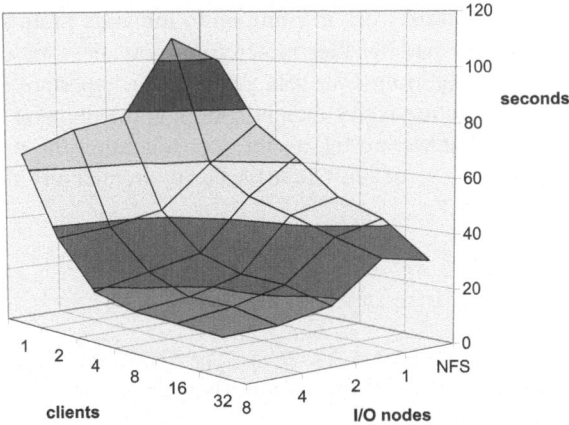

Fig. 3. Performance Results using POSIX interface.

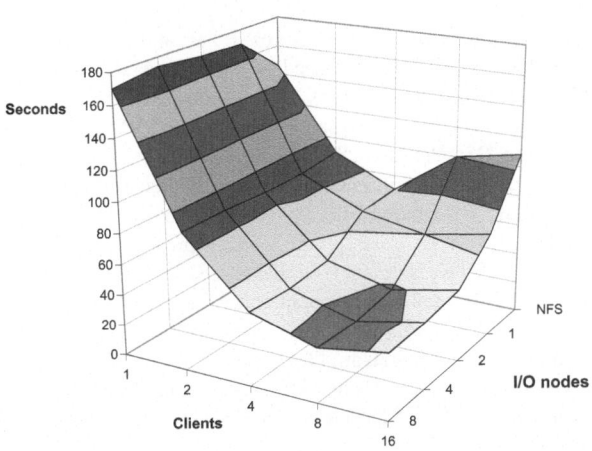

Fig. 4. Performance Results using the XFile Java Interface.

allows to obtain better performance results. For the Java version 4 we can observe that with 16 servers and 8 clients the performance is better than with 8 clients, this is due to the fact that we are overloading the clients machines with too much clients, that implies the execution of more Java virtual machines. In the future we hope to increase the scalability of the GridExpand Java version.

5 Conclusions and Future Work

In this abstract we have described the design of a parallel I/O middleware for grids, called GridExpand. This system provides a parallel I/O middleware that allows integrating the existing heterogeneous resources from the client's point of view without needing to create or to install new servers. Future work is going on to integrate more storage protocols, on to provide allocation for parallel files in heterogeneous network environments and on to develop prefetching algorithms for data grids. Other important aspect that we are considering to treat in the future is the authentication, at the moment the prototype use Unix integrated security but we are taking into consideration the use of Kerberos in the future for NFS and the use of the Globus security architecture through the use of GridFTP.

References

1. C. Baru, R. Moore, A. Rajasekar, M. Wan. The SDSC Storage Resource Broker. In Proceedings of the International Conference in High Energy and Nuclear Phisycs Teatro Antonianum, Padova (Italia). Feb. 2002.
2. M.D. Beynon, R. Ferreira, T. Kurc, A. Sussman, J. Saltz. DataCutter: Middleware for filtering very large scientific datasets of archival storage systems. In Proceedings of the 2000 Mass Storage Systems Conference, pages 119-133. College Park, MD,March 2000. IEEE Computer Society Press
3. A. Calderon, F. Garcia, J. Carretero, J.M. Perez, J. Fernandez. "An Implementation of MPI-IO on Expand: A Parallel File System Based on NFS Servers". In *9th PVM/MPI European User´s Group*, Johannes Kepler University Linz, Austria. sep 29-oct 2, 2002. Pp. 306-313
4. P.H. Carns, W.B. Ligon III, R.B. Ross, and R. Takhur, "PVFS: A Parallel File System for Linux Clusters," Tech. Rep. ANL/MCS-P804-0400, 2000.
5. J. Carretero, F. Perez, P. de Miguel, F. Garcia, and L. Alonso, "Performance Increase Mechanisms for Parallel and Distributed File Systems". *Parallel Computing: Special Issue on Parallel I/O Systems. Elsevier*, , no. 3, pp. 525–542, Apr. 1997.
6. A. Chervenak, I. Foster, C. Kesselman, C. Salisbury, S. Tuecke. "The Data Grid: Towards an Architecture for the Distributed Management and Analysis of Large Scientific". *Journal of Network and Computer Applications*. 23:187-200, 2001
7. P. Corbett, S. Johnson, and D. Feitelson, "Overview of the Vesta Parallel File System". *ACM Computer Architecture News*, vol. 21, no. 5, pp. 7–15, Dec. 1993.
8. I. Foster, C. Kesselman, editors. "The Grid: Blueprint for a New Computing Infrastructure." *Morgan Kaufmann*, 1999
9. F. Garcia, A. Calderon, J. Carretero, J.M. Perez, J. Fernandez "The Design of the Expand Parallel File System". *Accepted for publication in the International Journal of High Performance Computing Applications*, 2003
10. M.R. Martinez, N. Roussopoulos "MOCHA: A Self-extensible Database Middleware System for Distributed Data Sources". *In Proceedings of the ACM SIGMOD International Conference on Management of Data*, Dallas, TX. May 2000
11. S. A. Moyer and V. S. Sunderam, "PIOUS: A Scalable Parallel I/O System for Distributed Computing Environments," In *Proceedings of the Scalable High-Performance Computing Conferece*, 1994, pp. 71–78.
12. N. Nieuwejaar and D. Kotz, "The Galley Parallel File System". In *Proceedings of the 10th ACM International Conference on Supercomputing*, May 1996.
13. R. Olfield and D. Kotz, "The armada parallel file system", 1998. http://www.cs.dartmouth.edu/~dfk/armada/design.html.
14. W. Gropp R. Takhur and E. Lusk, "An Abstract-Device Interface for Implementing Portable Parallel-I/O Interfaces". In *Proceedings of the 6th Symposium on the Frontiers of Massively Parallel Computation*, Oct. 1996, pp. 180–187.

15. B. Tierney, J. Lee, W. Johnston, B. Crowley, M. Holding "Holding. A Network-aware Distributed Storage Cache for Data-intensive Environments". in *In Proceedings of the Eighth IEEE International Symposium on High Performance Distributed Computing*, pages 185-193. Redondo Beach, CA. Aug. 1999.
16. S. Vazhkuda, S. Tuecke, I. Foster "Replica Selection in the Globus Data Grid". *In proceedings of the International workshop on Data Models and Databases on Clusters and the Grid (DataGrid2001)*, IEEE Computer Society Press. 2001.
17. WebDav Resources. "Web-based Distributed Authoring and Versioning". 1998. http://www.webdav.org/

Mobile Work Environment for Grid Users

Mirosław Kupczyk[1], Rafał Lichwała[1], Norbert Meyer[1], Bartek Palak[1],
Marcin Płóciennik[1], and Paweł Wolniewicz[1]

Poznan Supercomputing and Networking Center
ul. Z. Noskowskiego 12/14, 61-704, Poznan, Poland
{miron,syriusz,meyer,bartek,marcinp,pawelw}@man.poznan.pl
http://www.man.poznan.pl

Abstract. In this paper we aim to describe the project developing the
Migrating Desktop infrastructure for the mobile users in a simple way.
Nowadays the easy access to the grid resources is the crucial to the users'
satisfaction. Using our framework the user achieves comfortable working
environment that could be customised, stored and recreated everywhere
where the Internet is present...

1   Introduction

In the paper we aim to describe the project developing the Migrating Desktop infrastructure for the mobile users in a simple way. We rather focus mainly
on the functionality than the technical details. This functionality refers to the
work environment of the users, which change their location very often. The mobility term refers to the users' activity. Users can move between workstations
and achieve the same desktop layout and all environment on every computer
connected to the Internet. The consideration of the mobile user with the active open connection to the Internet is a well-known problem and many other
projects respecting this functionality have been started. However this feature is
not the point of our project. This work is done under the EU CrossGrid project
IST-2001-32243 [1] and now it is in its starting point. What is needed for tomor-
row is the proper remote and individual access to the resources, independently
of the original location of the user. So far, the way of system usage has been
looking in the following way: the user sits at his workstation and works with his
favourite local applications. From time to time he launches a web browser and
plays with it. An advanced user wants to log in to the remote host and run his,
let us say, UNIX application. After computations, he somehow downloads output
files and accomplishes investigation of the results. Some of the experienced users
use protocols for emulating the remote environment in the graphical manner for
working with their files. The user is able to use many systems with different
resources and different security policies, sharing the resources among other people. The Migrating Desktop will create a transparent user work environment,
independently of the system version and hardware. In the paper we present the
functionality, the architecture and the main components of the core of developed
system. It consists of the Desktop Portal Server, the Roaming Access Server, and

F. Fernández Rivera et al. (Eds.): Across Grids 2003, LNCS 2970, pp. 132–138, 2004.

the Security component, the User Profile Manager and the Virtual Directory. For the grid enabled applications the new idea of application container framework has been investigated. The grid application is represented by a kind of wizard equipped with the demanded Application Plugin supported by the developers of the application.

2   The Overview of Architecture

The architecture of the entire CrossGrid project is much more complicated and we refer to the appropriate document [6]. However we introduce here some components and interfaces between them that correspond with the purposes of this paper. The main 'core' of the architecture is the Roaming Access Server. The name 'core' is chosen not by chance only but by its meaning in the entire framework. The Roaming Access Server is the module that is accessed every time when a user wants to execute any work within the grid. It could be very sophisticated sequence of activity, like: transfer of input files, preparation of the job parameters, submission of the job, etc. Every request passes through RAS component.

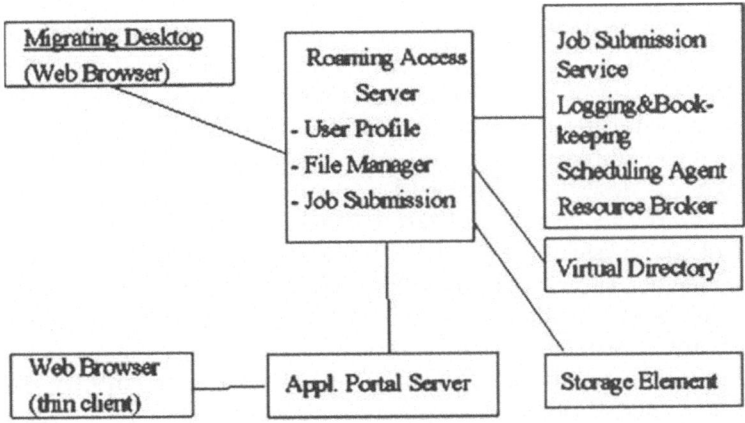

Fig. 1. The Architecture of the middleware (RAS).

From the functional point of view RAS is connected with the following modules[4]:
- The Application Portal Server,
- The Desktop Portal Server,
- The Profile Manager,
- The Job Submission Service,
- Logging and Bookkeeping Service,
- The Virtual Directory.

The schema of the functionality is shown on the fig 1. Now we describe briefly every aforementioned component. The Application Por-tal Server (APS) is a module, which resides on the server part of the client-server ar-chitecture. We would like to emphasize the difference between The Desktop Portal Server (DPS) and this one - DPS is located at the client side. Two kind of possible graphical user interfaces can be utilised by the user: thin client (any web browser) and a fat client - DPS that is developed in a java technology. The Migrating Desktop (MD) is the working name of DPS and this name will be used in this document. This name was introduced to avoid the mismatch between names Desktop and Application Portal Servers. APS is based on the Jetspeed technology. The interface to the RAS middleware uses the Web Service / SOAP technology. The Migrating Desktop will be discussed later on this work. During the initialisation of MD, the restore function of the Profile Manager (PM) is invoked and the MD is presented like it was saved before. The icons, windows lay-out, application settings are the same. However, there is a one exception regarding local references to the files and local applications. The authors designed the restore procedure of the local links on the same workstation that was used previously. The reason was that in many cases the IP or even DNS addresses of the same workstations are changed. That is why, we decided to store links to the local files locally. The most important element of the entire functionality is the one and consistent method of the job submission. The interfaces for performing this work are different and applications (interactive, batch) can be different too, but the submission mecha-nism is the only one. Nowadays the Job Submission Service (JSS) is represented by the set of modules integrated into one common module. JSS consists of the Resource Broker and the Scheduling Agent. In the future they will be separated due to the better performance. The interface between MD and JSS is described later on. During the definition stage of the project requirements we encountered the data management problem. How to handle the mapping of the physical and logical file names. There is no requirement for the user to remember all hosts and names of file stored there. The idea is to deliver the tool (the Grid Commander) that will compose the list of filenames without specifying any hostnames, transfer protocols and port numbers. All standard operations on the remote and local files can be executed. In case of job submission, the usage of the Grid Commander is unnecessary, because the transfer of input and output files is performed transparently and appropriate files are choosen in the Virtual Directory Browser. Virual directory is a SQL database that maintains the mapping between logical and phisical filenames.

3   Migrating Desktop

The user front-end is implemented as the fat client: advanced graphical java based application. The user interface called the Migrating Desktop, or grid desktop is a very useful environment that accomplishes an integrated set of services and real applica-tions, which could be run on the grid. The users can restore their environment in every place where the network access is possible. The authors are interested in the assimila-tion of the grid desktop with the operating system desktop as much as possible. One of the most visible feature of MD distinguishing from the APS is a very high similar-ity to the well-known environment like MS Windows or Linux KDE, GNOME, etc, see figure 2. This feature is not available through any Web Browser. Our aim is to replace the OS desktop with ours, which is more suitable for the grid working.

Fig. 2. The Migrating Desktop layout - example.

The Migrating Desktop will allow the user to access the grid resources from other computers like i.e. notebooks, or internet-coffee workstations. The Roaming Access and the Migrating Desktop features will not support "moving users". It means that no special mechanisms to access the grid resources via mobile phones, PDAs (such as palmtops, organisers, etc.) will be considered within the confines of the given project. The support of such hardware needs an extra environmental work respecting the bi-nary incompatibility with the widely used personal computers equipped with the J2RE 1.4.1 or higher. It will allow to run applications, manage data files, store per-sonal settings (configuration def-initions that characterise e.g. links to the user data files, links to applications, access to application portals and/or specialised infrastruc-ture, as well as windows settings), independently of the localisation or the terminal type. We want to emphasize that MD is designed for working with more than one grid. Nowadays, the only one is accepted, but in the future, every internal grid window will represent the different grid without loosing the functionality of the tools developed within the CrossGrid project.

4 Application Wizard

The Application Plugin and the Container is a tool located at MD side, in general view will suport the interface to the application specific inputs and output. This will allow preparing the portal framework, which is independent of the application, so that we could easily extend it and add the other applications. The Application Container is a framework for the Application Plugin. It is a frame in which the application plugin will appear. Giving the ApplicationContainer API that can be accessed from the plugin we support a very advanced tool for the general use. The Application Plugin is a content of the Application Container. It should pro-vide and implement two panels of the Job Submission wizard: arguments and job out-put. It should be able to visualise the output of the grid application. Application plugin must implement appropriate plugin interface. The Application Plugin can be a java applet and should implement all necessary interfaces to the Container. The Migrating Desktop provides the Wizard that user can use to specify the job details. This Wizard will simplify process of specifying parameters and limits, sug-gesting user defaults or last used parameters. It will consist of several panels. Two panels are reserved for the application specific plugin - the Argument Panel and the Job Output panels. The Wizard is responsible for the proper preparation of the user job. It automatically translates the parameters described in XML by the application programmers, layout, etc. to the JDL submission command. The JDL file is passed to JSS module and executed somewhere on the grid. Most complicated output - interac-tive, or semi-interactive should be supported by the Plugin.

5 Interactive Applications

We also focus on the work with interactive applications. The novelty of the devel-opment consists in the grid interactive application utilisation within the migrating users' environment. There are a lot of problems with the interaction in the grid envi-ronment. Some sort of solution has been proposed. When the user submits a Grid In-teractive Job (GIJ) he needs the allocation of grid resources throughout his "interactive session". During the whole session a bi-directional channel is opened between the user client and the application programme on remote machine. The entire job input and output streams are exchanged with the user client via this channel: the user sends input data to the job and receives output results and error messages. A very important feature in interactive environments is the ability to recovery from unexpected failures of e.g. workstation. There is no problem in case of batch jobs, but interactive applications need to be equipped with an extra functionality. It would be better not to rewrite the existing application codes respecting the new grid paradigm. However, it should be considered to build the additional linkable library for managing grid interactive session management.

6   Security

A lot of effort will be utilised in a Single Sign-On feature that has been widely spoken to be the most important feature in the upcoming grid technology. There are too many resources with an additional authorisation procedure; that is why we want to simplify the user access. Delegation of the credentials is the way we want to follow. The Globus Security Infrastructure (GSI) [3] will be used for our purposes. We de-cided not to store the private user keys on the remote hosts. This idea is convergent to the user privacy and the only one user is responsible for the key - the owner. As a bottom line of the middleware we use the Globus toolkit. These facilities give us an important functionality like security policy, simple remote operations, user account mapping, etc. The CrossGrid project is not the only star on the grid firma-ment but one of them and it cannot exist without any influence from the surroundings. Some elements used in this work come from the DataGrid project [2] like the idea of the grid interactive job submission and the Virtual Organisation (VO) paradigm.

7   Summary

In this paper we presented the overview of the functionality of developed system. It consists of several components, which are connected using the Web Service tech-nology. The most visible element for a human is so called Migrating Desktop. It gath-ers all facilities that make the grid resources available and useful. We noticed that this tool could connect several different grid frameworks. Our goal is to produce the gen-eral tool rather than specialised one, dedicated to the only one grid project. For the grid enabled applications the new idea of application container framework has been investigated. The mentioned functionality is developed within the CrossGrid project [5] and its first prototype has been ready since February 2003.

References

1. Annex 1 to the Development of Grid Environment for Interactive Applications - EU-CrossGrid Project, IST-2001-32243,
   http://www.eu-crossgrid.org/CrossGridAnnex1_v31.pdf
2. Annex to the Research and Technological Development for an International Data Grid - EU-DataGrid Project, IST-2000-25182,
   http://eu-datagrid.web.cern.ch/eudatagrid/1Y-EU-Review-Material/CD-1Y-EU-Review/3-DataGrid-TechnicalAnnex/DataGridAnnex1V5.3.pdf
3. Globus Toolkit 2.0, http://www.globus.org

4. Kupczyk, M., Lichwala, R., Meyer, N., et. al., Roaming Access and Portals: Software Requirements Specification, EU-CrossGrid Project, http://www.eurossgrid.org/Deliverables/M3pdf/SRS_TASK_3-1.pdf
5. EU CrossGrid project IST-2001-32243, http://www.eu-crossgrid.org
6. Lichwala, R., Palak. B., et al, Design Document: CG3.1-D3.2-v1.3-PSNC022-RoamingAccess&Portals.doc, http://www.eu-crossgrid.org

Grid-Enabled Visualization with GVK

Dieter Kranzlmüller, Paul Heinzlreiter, Herbert Rosmanith, and Jens Volkert

GUP, Joh. Kepler University Linz
Altenbergerstr. 69, A-4040 Linz, Austria/Europe
kranzlmueller@gup.jku.at
http://www.gup.uni-linz.ac.at

Abstract. The present status of visualization on the grid is not really satisfying. In contrast to other grid services, such as batch processing, data transfer, and resource scheduling, visualization is still utilized in the traditional point-to-point fashion, with applications integrating visualization as subroutine calls or even post-mortem. This situation is addressed by the Grid Visualization Kernel GVK[1], which proposes a fully grid-enabled approach to scientific visualization. The infrastructure of GVK features a portal for arbitrary simulation servers and visualization clients, while the actual processing of the visualization pipeline is transparently performed on the available grid resources.

1 Introduction

Grid Computing represents one of the most promising advancements for todays computational science and engineering [9, 10]. With the power of computational grids at hand, scientists are able to perform simulations at previously impossible and unexplored problem scales. Consequently, many research projects around the world are engaged in developing grid infrastructures and corresponding applications, the majority of them focusing on batch and throughput processing.

As an extension, the EU CrossGrid project (http://www.eu-crossgrid.org) intends to provide grid services for interactive applications. For this endeavor, the Cross-Grid project requires a series of novel grid services, which are not provided by existing grid middleware. An example is scientific visualization, which has previously been utilized with the following characteristics: Either the results of batch processing are downloaded to the users workstation and visualized locally, or the connection between simulation and visualization is established between static endpoints with traditional visualization toolkits. These two approaches are certainly not optimal for several reasons:

- They introduce a substantial delay when downloading the data from the simulation.
- They are limited by the processing power available at the user's location.
- They lack the flexibility offered by today's grid infrastructures.

The Grid Visualization Kernel (GVK) attempts to overcome these problems for scientific visualization on the grid. The visualization capabilities of GVK are provided

---

[1] The Grid Visualization Kernel (GVK) described in this paper is partially supported by the IST Programme of the European Commission under contract number IST-2001-32243.

F. Fernández Rivera et al. (Eds.): Across Grids 2003, LNCS 2970, pp. 139–146, 2004.

as flexible grid services via dedicated interfaces and protocols, while GVK itself relies on existing grid middleware to implement the functionality of the visualization pipeline. This paper describes the application of GVK within grid environments, and discusses how to provide a grid-enabled visualization service for arbitrary grid applications.

The paper is organized as follows: Section 2 provides an overview of visualization in general and GVK's approach in particular. Section 3 discusses the interfaces of GVK for providing input from simulations and for accessing output on visualization devices, while the construction of the visualization pipeline over available grid resources is described in Section 4. An overview of motivating and related work in this area is provided in Section 5, before a summary and an outlook on future work in this project concludes the paper.

2   Overview of Approach

Integrating visualization into an arbitrary application means to adapt some kind of visualization pipeline with appropriate transformations according to the provided data and the intended visual representations. The visualization pipeline is initiated by the application that provides the raw data. After performing the transformations of the visualization pipeline [12], such as filtering, visualization mapping, and rendering, the results of the visualization pipeline are forwarded to the visualization device. Figure 1 describes a typical visualization pipeline.

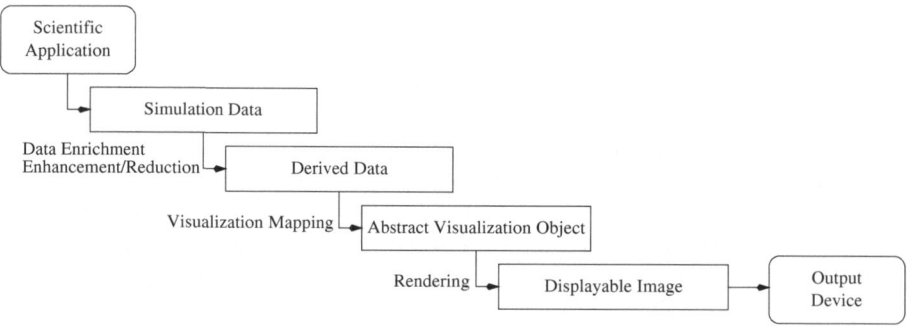

Fig. 1. Visualization Pipeline [12].

Based on this general view, the users' task when implementing visualization for a particular application can be divided into three steps:

(1) Definition of an input interface to extract the data to be visualized from the application
(2) Specification of the visualization pipeline to transform the raw data into the displayable image
(3) Definition of the connection to display the visualization results on the output device

These requirements represent the specifications of the Grid Visualization Kernel GVK. Instead of producing a visualization approach for one particular application, the intention of GVK is to provide universal visualization services for a wide range of applications. By providing visualization functionality as an extension of existing grid middleware approaches, GVK reflects some of the original ideas of grid computing itself. In concrete, the concept of GVK can be divided into two main parts with the following characteristics:

(a) The interface between the simulation and GVK on the one hand, and between GVK and the visualization device on the other hand, should be established transparently with well-known visualization techniques. The simulation and the visualization should be decoupled in time and space, and even multiple invocations of different visualization devices at the same time should be possible.
(b) The actual implementation of the visualization pipeline should be established according to the desired transformations of the input data, the minimum characteristics requested by the simulation and the maximum characteristics provided by the visualization device. The visualization itself should be as fast and as good as possible with the available grid resources.

3   Interface between Simulation and Visualization

The interface to GVK is established via available visualization toolkits. An example is the Open Visualization Data Explorer OpenDX[2], which has been utilized in our previous projects. Other examples include AVS[3] or VTK[4].

With such a visualization toolkit, the user specifies the visualization pipeline by constructing a data-flow graph from the simulation interface to the displayable image. In order to adapt the data-flow model to the application, the simulation interface must be defined according to the user's needs. The remainder of the visualization pipeline is then processed by the modules of the data-flow graph, which are arranged according to the desired output.

The difference between the traditional approach and the GVK visualization services is that some modules of the data-flow graph are replaced by corresponding GVK modules. Some possible examples for using GVK are as follows:

– To upload the simulation data onto the grid, the interface module must be a GVK interface module. The remainder of the visualization pipeline may then be processed within GVK itself or at the corresponding output device.
– To allow connections to the simulation data from arbitrary visualization clients, the last module of the data-flow graph must be replaced by a GVK output module. In this case, the transformations of the visualization pipeline may be partially performed by the simulation itself or within GVK.

---

[2] http://www.opendx.org/
[3] http://www.avs.com/
[4] http://public.kitware.com/vtk

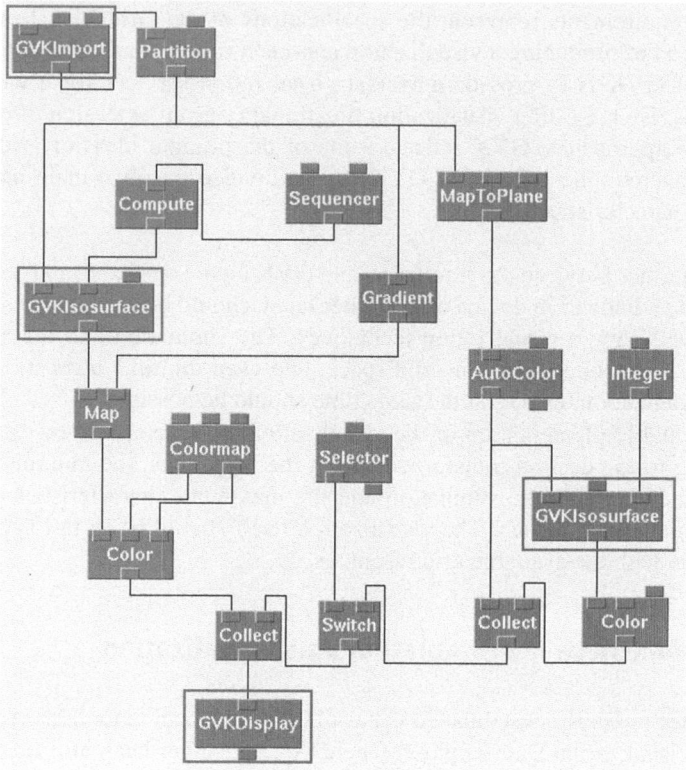

Fig. 2. Integrating GVK in the OpenDX visualization toolkit.

– It is also possible to replace intermediate nodes of the graph with corresponding
  GVK visualization modules, for example, if computationally intensive tasks should
  be distributed over the grid. An example is isosurface generation, which may be
  performed by a dedicated grid visualization service using available grid resources.

Figure 2 displays a screenshots of a data-flow model with the Open Visualization
Data Explorer OpenDX. The data-flow graph includes some modules that implement
the functionality of GVK as described above.

The advantage of this approach is that it enables the user to define arbitrary visualization pipeline configurations using the well-known data-flow approach. With GVK,
the pipeline can be split at any point, and the processing modules can be distributed
across the grid as desired.

4   Setting Up the Visualization Pipeline

During execution, the setup of the visualization pipeline has to be initiated by the simulation as shown in Figure 3. The procedure of the setup process is as follows:

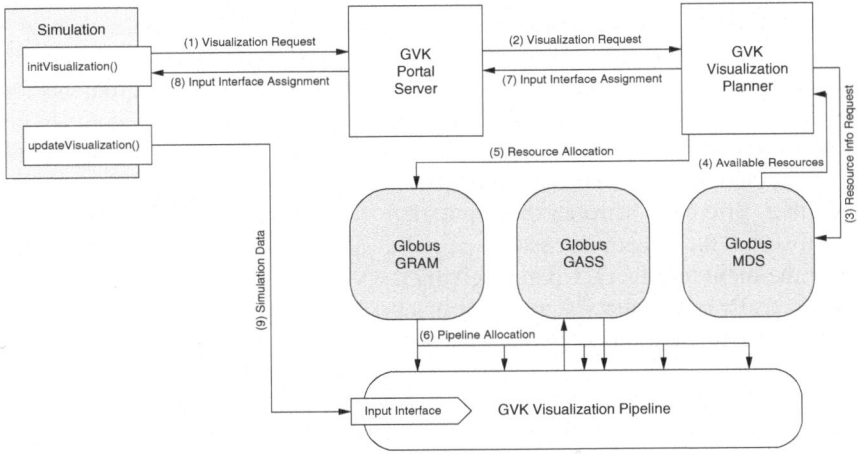

Fig. 3. Simulation Setup Process with GVK.

(1) During the initialization phase, the simulation sends a *visualization request* to the GVK portal server. The contents of this request are the minimal requirements to possible visualization clients.

(2) The portal server authorizes the simulation and forwards the *visualization request* to the GVK visualization planner.

(3) The visualization planner sends a *resource information request* to Globus Monitoring and Discovery Service MDS [6] in order to inquire about the available resources for the visualization pipeline.

(4) Globus MDS returns information about *available resources* to the GVK visualization planner.

(5) The visualization planner sends a *resource allocation* request to the Globus Resource Allocation Manager GRAM [5].

(6) Globus GRAM performs the visualization *pipeline allocation* and initializes all transformation modules as requested by the visualization planner.

(7) The visualization planner returns the *input interface assignment* to the GVK portal server about the newly initiated input interface of the GVK visualization pipeline.

(8) The portal server stores the new visualization service for future requests and forwards the *input interface assignment* to the simulation source.

(9) The simulation continues processing the data and updates the visualization (when appropriate) by sending *simulation data* to the input interface of the GVK visualization pipeline.

The diagram of Figure 3 describes only the simulation side of GVK's invocation. Please notice, that no output interface has been assigned to the visualization pipeline. In practice, the visualization planner has to decide about what to do with the received simulation data, and to configure the visualization pipeline accordingly. Depending on the available storage capacity, a certain amount of visualization data may automatically be stored at some place on the grid. Additional configuration options can be provided with the visualization request from the simulation.

The protocol for the visualization client is comparable to the simulation side with minor deviations. The registration of the visualization client is also initiated with a visualization request. However, instead of providing the minimum requirements for the visualization, the maximum capabilities available on the visualization client are given. With this information, that GVK portal server is already able to match corresponding pairs of simulation and visualization clients.

Another difference between the simulation side invocation and the client side invocation is that the client can assume partial availability of the visualization pipeline (at least the input interface). Upon receiving the visualization request and information about the grid's status, the visualization planner is able to complete the visualization pipeline setup. In addition, an output interface is initialized and connected to the visualization client.

Please note, that multiple clients may access GVK with visualization requests for one particular simulation. In this case, GVK is able to automatically multiplex the data streams in the visualization pipeline by setting up more than one output interface.

5 Related Work

The idea of GVK has been influenced by a number of related work in this area. The motivation of providing advanced services for grid applications is provided by a series of other approaches, e.g. the Open Grid Service Architecture OGSA [11] or NetSolve [3]. In this context, GVK represents a middleware extension for scientific visualization on the grid.

The field of distributed and high-performance visualization provides a series of other interesting work. We distinguish between

- grid-based visualization techniques,
- visualization on high-performance computing architectures, and
- support for distributed and remote visualization.

However, in contrast to GVK, these approaches apply a much tighter coupling between the simulation source and the visualization device.

Grid-based visualization techniques are presented in [1, 2, 7]. The goal of DV [1] is to distribute the visualization pipeline over various grid nodes while optimizing the locations of the different modules on the grid. DV's central concept is the active frame, a combination of the data to be rendered and a rendering program, which is sent from one node to another while passing through the visualization pipeline. The experimental science environment VLAM-G [2] provides visualization of scientific simulation results while hiding the complexity of the underlying grid middleware. However, it does not support dynamic adaptations to changes in resource availability. Similar to GVK and VLAM-G, the distance visualization system described in [7] is built on top of Globus [8]. It realizes a distance tomography system, that allows simultaneous connections of multiple display clients and support for data buffering and shared controls.

A different group of related work focuses on using high-performance computing architectures for visualization [14, 16]. The rendering system Chromium [14] exploits the computational power of a cluster to achieve high throughput of visualization data, while [16] describes real-time interactive volume visualization on a HPC shared-me-machine. Both approaches may be suitable candidates as part of the GVK visualization pipeline.

Support for distributed visualization is described in [4]. The WireGL system [4] enables remote rendering of OpenGL applications by encoding the commands into op-codes and sending these opcodes over the network to the visualization device. The amount of transferred data can be reduced by a mtehod of lazy state update. While WireGL does not provide a high level visualization toolkit, it may still be useful within GVK.

6 Conclusions and Future Work

The Grid Visualization Kernel as described in this paper is currently being imple-mented. Some modules are already available and demonstrate parts of the functionality of GVK. In [13], first experiments with GVK for volume visualization are presented, while [15] discusses possibilities to reduce the communication latency between the sim-ulation server and the visualization client. The latter uses well-known techniques from computer graphics to reduce the amount of data transferred from the simulation source to the visualization device.

While these existing examples represent a valid proof-of-concept, much more de-velopment work is required in this project. A missing issue of the current concept of GVK is support for interactivity, or rather returning feedback from the user to the sim-ulation. Nevertheless, we believe that the current protocol may easily be adapted to include the reverse path from the visualization client to the simulation server. Some initial investigations in this direction are currently being conducted.

The ambitious claim of universality is certainly a major benefit of GVK, yet it also means that much more work is required to provide the functionality of GVK to the grid computing community. A major test for GVK is provided within the EU CrossGrid project, which provides possible target applications for visualization on the grid. An integration of GVK is currently being conducted for bio-medical applications in coop-eration with the Universiteit van Amsterdam (UvA), Section on Computational Science (SCS) [17].

Acknowledgments

This work was supported by several of our colleagues, most notably Gerhard Kurka, Andreas Wasserbauer, Hans-Peter Baumgartner, and Peter Praxmarer.

References

1. M. Aeschlimann, P. Dinda, J. López, B. Lowekamp, L. Kallivokas, D. O'Halleron: *Prelimi-nary Report on the Design of a Framework for Distributed Visualization*, Proc. PDPTA '99, Las Vegas, Nevada, pp. 1833–1839 (1999).

2. H. Afsarmanesh, R. Belleman, A. Belloum, A. Benabdelkader, J.F.J. van den Brand, T.M. Breit, H. Bussemaker, G. Eijkel, A. Frenkel, C. Garita, D.L. Groep, A.W. van Halderen, R.M.A. Heeren, Z.W. Hendrikse, L.O. Hertzberger, J. Kaandorp, E.C. Kaletas, V. Klos, P. Sloot, R.D. Vis, A. Visser, H.H. Yakali: *VLAM-G: A Grid-Based Virtual Laboratory*, Scientific Programming Journal, Vol. 10, No. 2, pp. 173–181 (2002).

3. D. Arnold, S. Agrawal, S. Blackford, J. Dongarra, M. Miller, K. Seymour, K. Sagi, Z. Shi, and S. Vadhiyar: *Users' Guide to NetSolve V1.4.1*, Technical Report ICL-UT-02-05, Innovative Computing Laboratory, University of Tennessee, Knoxville, TN, USA (June 2002).

4. I. Buck, G. Humphreys, P. Hanrahan: *Tracking Graphics State for Networked Rendering*, Proc. of SIGGRAPH/Eurographics Workshop on Graphics Hardware, pp. 87–95 (2000).

5. K. Czajkowski, I. Foster, N. Karonis, C. Kesselman, S. Martin, W. Smith, and S. Tuecke: *A Resource Management Architecture for Metacomputing Systems*, Proc. IPPS/SPDP '98 Workshop on Job Scheduling Strategies for Parallel Processing, pp. 62–82 (1998).

6. K. Czajkowski, S. Fitzgerald, I. Foster, and C. Kesselman: *Grid Information Services for Distributed Resource Sharing*, Proc. Tenth IEEE International Symposium on High-Performance Distributed Computing (HPDC-10), IEEE Press, (August 2001).

7. I. Foster, J. Insley, G. von Laszewski, C. Kesselman, M. Thiebaux: *Distance Visualization: Data Exploration on the Grid*, IEEE Computer Magazine, Vol. 32, No. 12, pp. 36–43 (1999).

8. I. Foster, C. Kesselman: *Globus: A Metacomputing Infrastructure Toolkit*, Intl. Journal of Supercomputer Applications, Vol. 11, No. 2, pp. 4–18 (1997).

9. I. Foster and C. Kesselman: *The Grid. Blueprint for a New Computing Infrastructure*, Morgan Kaufmann Publishers, Inc. (1999).

10. I. Foster, C. Kesselman, S. Tuecke, *The Anatomy of the Grid: Enabling Scalable Virtual Organizations*, International Journal of Supercomputer Applications, Vol. 15, No. 3 (2001).

11. I. Foster, C. Kesselman, J. Nick, S. Tuecke: *The Physiology of the Grid: An Open Grid Services Architecture for Distributed Systems Integration*, Open Grid Service Infrastructure WG, Global Grid Forum (June 2002).

12. R.B. Haber and D.A. McNabb: *Visualization Idioms: A Conceptual Model for Scientific Visualization Systems*, In G.M. Nielson, B. Shriver, and L.J. Rosenblum, (Eds.): *Visualization in Scientific Computing*, IEEE Computer Society, Los Alamitos, NM, USA, pp. 74–93 (1990).

13. P. Heinzlreiter, A. Wasserbauer, H. Baumgartner, D. Kranzlmüller, G. Kurka, and J. Volkert: *Interactive Virtual Reality Volume Visualization on the Grid*, Proc. DAPSYS 2002, Linz, Austria, pp. 90–97 (Sept. 2002).

14. G. Humphreys, M. Houston, R. Ng, R. Frank, S. Ahern, P. D. Kirchner, and J. T. Klosowski: *Chromium: A Stream-Processing Framework for Interactive Rendering on Clusters*, Proc. SIGGRAPH 2002, San Antonio, Texas, pp. 693–702 (August 2002).

15. D. Kranzlmüller, G. Kurka, P. Heinzlreiter, and J. Volkert: *Optimizations in the Grid Visualization Kernel*, Proc. PDIVM 2002, Workshop on Parallel and Distributed Computing in Image Processing, Video Processing and Multimedia, IPDPS 2002, Ft. Lauderdale, Florida (April 2002).

16. S. Parker, M. Parker, Y. Livnat, P.-P. Sloan, C. Hansen, and P. Shirley: *Interactive Ray Tracing for Volume Visualization*, IEEE Transactions on Visualization and Computer Graphics, pp. 238-250 (July-September 1999).

17. P.M.A. Sloot, D. Kranzlmüller, G.D. van Albada, E. Zudilova, P. Heinzlreiter, abd J. Volkert: *Grid-Based Interactive Visualization of Medical Images*, Proc. HealthGRID, 1st European HealthGrid Conference, Lyon, France, p. 91 (January 2003).

Grid Services for HLA-Based Distributed Simulation Frameworks*

Katarzyna Zając[1,3], Alfredo Tirado-Ramos[2], Zhiming Zhao[2],
Peter Sloot[2], and Marian Bubak[1,3]

[1] Institute of Computer Science, AGH, al.Mickiewicza 30, 30-059 Kraków, Poland
{kzajac,bubak}@uci.agh.edu.pl
[2] Faculty of Sciences, Section Computational Science, University of Amsterdam
Kruislaan 403, 1098 SJ Amsterdam, The Netherlands
{alfredo,zhiming,sloot}@science.uva.nl
[3] Academic Computer Centre – CYFRONET, Nawojki 11, 30-950 Kraków, Poland

Abstract. Problem Solving Environments offer an integrating approach
for constructing and running complex systems and components, such as
distributed simulation and decision support systems. New distributed
infrastructures like the Grid support the access to a large variety of core
services and resources in a secure environment. In this paper we propose
an approach to Grid access for interactive Problem Solving Environments
built on top of the High Level Architecture (HLA), a mature distributed
simulation framework. This approach is based on a set of Grid Services
which allow the setup and interactive steering of complex Grid applications consisting of modules for simulation and visualization. We discuss
a three-level approach to the problem. In the first step we focus on discovery of HLA Runtime Infrastructure (RTI) processes that coordinate
distributed components of an interactive application. Next we investigate
efficient Grid-based data transfer protocols as a promising alternative for
current RTI communication. Finally, we will completely replace RTI by
Grid technology mechanisms. As a proof-of-concept example, we use the
CrossGrid biomedical simulation application, which requires near real
time steering of simulation parameters during runtime of the simulation
running on the Grid.

Keywords: interactive, problem solving environment, the grid, HLA,
CrossGrid.

1 Introduction

In the past few years, Grid computing has emerged as an important and rapidly
expanding approach to scientific distributed computing and distributed Problem
Solving Environments (PSEs), with examples like CONDOR-G [9]. Recently, Ian

---

* This research is partly funded by the European Commission the IST-2001-32243
Project "CrossGrid".

F. Fernández Rivera et al. (Eds.): Across Grids 2003, LNCS 2970, pp. 147–154, 2004.
© Springer-Verlag Berlin Heidelberg 2004

Foster [6] presented a checkpoint list defining a Grid as a system that coordinates resources that are not subject to centralized control, but where coordination should be done by means of standard, open, general-purpose protocols and should deliver nontrivial qualities of service.

Most of large-scale Grid deployments being undertaken, like the European DataGrid [5], are focusing on providing an infrastructure for batch systems, as opposed to interactive applications. Nevertheless, we believe that there is a clear need for the support of interative applications in near real time.

On one hand, there is currently a lot of effort going on to define standard "inter-Grid" protocols to create something more than a set of non-interoperable distributed systems, which may be used to build Grid-based PSEs. The Open Grid Services Architecture (OGSA) [7] is one of the results of this effort. In OGSA, the primary purposes are to extend the Web Services [16] terminology to include Grid concepts, and to manage the creation and termination of resources as services. The main focus is on the definition of abstract interfaces that allow services to cooperate without too much concern about the actual protocols being used. OGSA is a very general approach; it does not distinguish interactive services from batch services, and does not provide special support for near real time interactive systems. This is left to higher level services build on top of it.

On the other hand, there are existing solutions for distributed and interactive simulation systems that may be used as underlying frameworks for interactive PSEs. One of such frameworks is the High Level Architecture (HLA) [11], which existing implementations are based on Common Object Request Broker Architecture (CORBA) middleware [15]. HLA and CORBA do offer many features for developers of interactive and distributed applications. However, existing implementations lack the flexibility we believe essential for Grid-based interactive applications. In this position paper, we present an approach for extending existing HLA-based PSE frameworks for interactive simulations to the Grid.

The paper is organized as follows: Section 2 briefly introduces the U.S. Department of Defense's HLA implementation, and discusses its features in terms of Grid environment constraints. Section 3 describes our three-level approach for porting HLA concepts to the OGSA. We conclude in Section 4 with a brief discussion of current issues and future work.

2   HLA Basic Functionality

HLA Runtime Infrastructure (RTI) federations [11] are distributed systems that consist of multiple processes (Federates) communicating across computer nodes. HLA provides the application developers with a RTI that acts as a tuple space. In order to send messages, the applications that are plugged into the RTI have to publish well-defined objects in that space. The applications that want to receive messages have to subscribe to those objects. Each time an object is to be sent, the application must call a method that updates the attribute values of this object; RTI then notifies subscribed applications that the object has been updated.

Federates are controlled by the RTI Executive (RTIexec) process. The network address specified by the hostname or the Internet Protocol address of that machine plus the port number used, known as the endpoint of the process, is defined in a Federate configuration file. If the endpoint is not specified for the RTIexec, a multicast protocol is used for finding the RTI control process.

2.1   Current RTI Limitations

HLA provides application developers with a powerful framework for distributed simulation reuse and interoperability, however its design was not intended to support software applications that need to integrate instruments, displays, computational and information resources managed by diverse organizations. The Grid, however, was originally designed to address precisely those issues.

For instance, like other RTI implementations, the current RTI1.3-NG version 4.15 implementation is restricted in its communication protocol to the CORBA Internet Inter-Object Request Broker Protocol (IIOP), and requires common configuration files that specify the location of controlling components (endpoint of RTI control process), as well as a definition of the data to be exchanged, before runtime. Additionally, RTI does not provide security mechanisms similar to the ones provided by the Grid Security Infrastructure (GSI), and does not allow migration of distributed components.

2.2   Grid-Enhanced HLA RTI Infrastructure

We believe that Grid Services have the potential to bring remote and decentralized Federate service discovery and invocation to HLA. One may consider various levels of granularity while porting HLA concepts into the Grid.

We believe that the most coarse grain approach is to address the issue of the discovery of control Federate components. We call this RTI Layer migration. This discovery mechanism in HLA is one of our initial points of focus: HLA uses either a multicast discovery protocol, which does not scale well on large Wide Area Network (WAN) Grid distributed environments, or performs discovery via the specification of the RTIexec's endpoint through a naming service. We find this approach not very convenient, because the endpoint has be known in advance. As a first step, we plan to investigate the use of Grid services to address this issue.

As a finer grain approach, we intend to investigate the use of Grid core services for the transport of actual Federate data, once the RTIexec information has been made available via a Grid Service. We call this Federation Layer migration. We plan to experiment with Globus GridFTP and Globus I/O implementation extensions for interfacing with the RTI logical bus.

It is important to note that Grid communications are basically peer-to-peer (P2P). This has the consequence that the destination information, well encapsulated within HLA, has to be found on the application layer. As a third step and finest grain approach, we plan to reimplement HLA communications using Grid technologies. We call this Federate Layer migration.

3   Our Three Level Migration Approach to the Grid

3.1   RTI Layer Migration

For our first migration approach, we plan to publish the RTIexec as a Grid service in a Community Registry repository of services. This will allow remote services to publish their Grid Service Handles, so we can later compare data transfer between the two paradigms.

Initially, we are working on one well-known registry per Virtual Organization (VO), to bind the local Federate with the service and modify the RTI configuration file. We do not expect to migrate RTI execution at runtime at the moment. Nevertheless, we plan to investigate the use of OGSA discovery topologies and intelligent searching agents for dynamic Registry discovery. The Grid service information will initially be used for Federate and Federation initialization, in a simple pull mode. The information provided by the Grid service includes endpoint information of the RTIexec execution (i.e., machine address and port number), name of the executing VO for selecting the appropriate RTIexec to join, and RTIexec version number.

As mentioned before, we are also planning to use the Global Forum's Open Grid Services Infrastructure (OGSI) [14] to implement a higher level Community Registry service for VO and Federate registration and inspection of service data, based on the OGSA specification's Registry PortType. We expect this way to allow for the inspection of sites for available services and service data, via Web Services Inspection Language interfaces. It is noteworthy to mention, though, that the OGSI implementation of OGSA is expected to be available, at best, in the middle of 2003. In the meantime, we plan to work with OGSI alpha releases (known as technology previews) and develop our own Grid service infrastructure based on them.

3.2   Federation Layer Migration

One of the points in Ian Foster's checkpoints list is the requirement to use standard and open protocols to communicate services that form an infrastructure [6]. Within HLA two kinds of data can be exchanged between Federates, namely data objects and events. However, as mentioned before, current HLA implementations are generally restricted to the IIOP communication protocol.

We have decided to take a more scalable approach to communication between distributed simulation components or Federates, focusing initially on data object transfer. We are investigating Globus GridFTP and Globus I/O protocol extensions, since these protocols consider security issues and various techniques to increase bandwidth, like parallel data channels between hosts, and tuning Transport Control Protocol (TCP) window size. Although the GridFTP protocol is designed for file transfer [1], its extensions can be used for secure and efficient memory-to-memory transfer as well. This kind of extension is particularly important, for instance, for distributed biomedical applications, where large volumes of data may have to be transported to a visualization system.

Past experience with biomedical simulation systems shows us that a number of performance issues arise when dealing with throughput maximization of data transfers over the network, specially with large and distributed inter-domain WANs [2].

3.3   Federate Layer Migration and Related Issues

In the third step, we will redesign some of the functionalites of RTI components to build an event-based fully Grid functional service. We will support discovery and data transfer for interactive applications, and fulfill the requirements of high level Grid services [13].

Our approach for such an HLA event service to support this kind of functionality is shown in Figure 1.

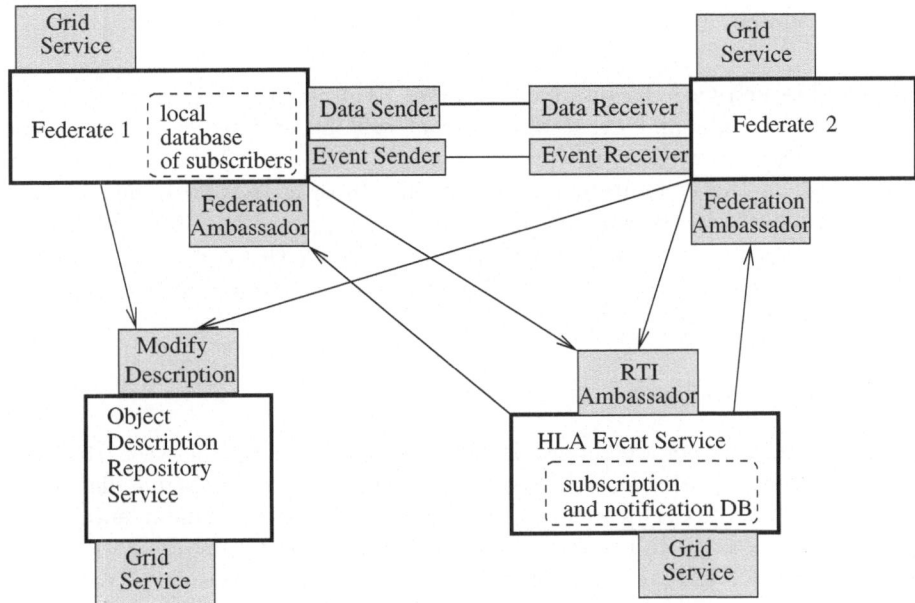

Fig. 1. Grid HLA Event Service basic components.

HLA Event Service. The interface of the service will be defined by translating existing HLA's RTIAmbasador Application Programming Interface into Web Services Description Language. The functionality of the RTI library will be encapsulated within the Grid Service, which can be itself a distributed high level service as shown in Figure 1. The internal design requires further investigation of data distribution management algorithms like effective matching subscriptions to publications as well as ownership and time management issues [12]. Up to now, we assume that the service manages a database of subscriptions and publications and performs matching each time the subscriptions or publications are changed.

Federate Interface. Application components that want to join the federation will have to provide a FederationAmbassador interface. The actual data and event sending will be performed directly. For instance, in Figure 1 the ports marked as "Data Sender" and "Data Receiver" will provide the GridFTP implementation features (parallel channels, negotiations of TCP buffer, security).

For events, we are looking into XEvents and Xmessages [10] and the OGSA notification service [7]. For instance, in the Figure 1 the ports responsible for event sending are marked as "Event Sender" and "Event Receiver" which have more or less symbolic meaning. After further elaboration they will be changed to something more specific, like OGSA "Notification Source" and "Notification Sink", or similar.

Object Description Repository Service. Currently, HLA requires explicit description of data and event objects that will be exchanged before the actual federation starts execution. This cannot be changed during runtime, and is specified in the Federate configuration file. In order to add dynamic modification capabilities, we will use an Object Description Repository Service. As can be seen in Figure 1, the we will provide a Modify Description PortType for actual altering of its contents. This PortType illustrates a general interface to the functionality provided by the service.

4   Discussion and Future Work

In this position paper we report on how to bridge the gap between HLA and the Grid, in order to support efficient and interactive near real-time distributed computing. This paper describes a roadmap to investigate fundamental issues and problems related to the bridging of this gap, by proposing a high level grid event service for interactive applications. Currently, we consider a three-level approach for migrating existing HLA-based distributed systems to access the Grid, for supporting interactive applications.

We have identified issues that we believe will have marked effects on the scalability of different approaches to migrating HLA into OGSA. Such issues include, for instance, the use of Web Service current bindings to the Simple Object Access Protocol, as well as the design and use of scalable approaches to dynamically discover community registries. We believe that public and private endpoint accessibility issues also need to be addressed.

As a proof-of-concept example, we will work with the European CrossGrid [4] biomedical application.

CrossGrid applications are characterized by the interaction with a person in a processing loop. Examples of these applications are interactive simulation and visualization for surgical procedures, flooding crisis team decision support systems, distributed data analysis in high-energy physics, and air pollution combined with weather forecasting [3].

The CrossGrid biomedical application, for instance, requires near real time steering of simulation parameters during runtime of the simulation via the Grid. We will interconnect the application components using an HLA-based middleware framework [17], built over an RTI communication bus.

Currently, we focus on the first two steps of this three layer approach; namely the RTI and Federation layers. We believe that experience gained during this work will eventually result in a full design and implementation of a service-oriented framework for distributed PSE Grid access.

We will investigate in the near future the use of Grid service patterns applied to build dynamic discovery services, one of the main issues that we have encountered in our investigations. A number of discovery topologies have been proposed by the Globus Project already [8], such as hierarchical with caching, hierarchical with forwarding, as well as topologies based on P2P meshes. These may include the use of soft-state registration and subscription to query registries and services in various ways.

Acknowledgments

We would like to thank Maciej Malawski for valuable discussions and useful remarks.

References

1. Allcock W., Bester J., Bresnahan J., Chervenak A., Liming L., Tuecke S.: GridFTP: Protocol Extensions to FTP for the Grid,
2. Belleman R.G., and Shulakov S.: High Performance Distributed Simulation for Interactive Simulated Vascular Reconstruction, International Conference on Computational Science (ICCS), Lecture Notes in Computer Science (LNCS) volume 2331, p. 265-274, 2002, Springer-Verlag, Berlin.
3. Bubak M., Malawski M., Zajac K.: Towards the CrossGrid Architecture. In: D. Kranzlmeller, P. Kacsuk, J. Dongarra, J. Volker (Eds.) Recent Advances in Parallel Virtual Machine and Message Passing Interface, Proc. 9th Eurpean PVM/MPI Users' Group Meeting, Linz, Austria, September/October 2002, LNCS 2474, pp. 16-24.
4. CrossGrid - Development of Grid Environment for interactive Applications, EU Project, IST-2001-32243, http://www.eu-crossgrid.org
5. Datagrid, http://www.eu-datagrid.org/
6. Foster I.: "What is the Grid? A three checkpoints list". GridToday Daily News And Information For The Global Grid Community July 22, 2002: VOL. 1 NO. 6
7. Foster I, Kesselman C., Nick J., Tuecke S.: The Physiology of the Grid: An Open Grid Services Architecture for Distributed Systems Integration. Open Grid Service Infrastructure WG, Global Grid Forum, June 22, 2002.
8. Foster I.,Kesselman C.: Introduction to Grid Computing, http://www.globus.org

9. Frey J., Tannenbaum T., Foster I., Livny M., and Tuecke S., "Condor-G: A Computation Management Agent for Multi-Institutional Grids", Journal of Cluster Computing volume 5, pages 237-246, 2002.
10. Slonimski A., Simmhan Y., Rossi A.L., Farrellee M., Gannon D.: XEvents/XMESSAGES: Application Events and Messaging Framework for Grid,
11. HLA specification, http://www.sisostds.org/stdsdev/hla/
12. High Level Architecture Run-Time Infrastructure RTI 1.3-Next Generation Programmer s Guide. https://www.dmso.mil/public/transition/hla/
13. OGSA work group draft, http://www.ggf.org/ogsa-wg/
14. OGSI, http://www.globus.org/ogsa/releases/TechPreview/index.html
15. Ryan C.O., and Levine D.L.: Applying a Scalable CORBA Events Service to Large-scale Distributed Interactive Simulations In: Proceedings of the 5 th Workshop on Object-oriented Real-time Dependable Systems. Monterey, CA.
16. Web services, http://www.w3.org/2002/ws/
17. Zhao Z., Belleman R.G.,van Albada G.D. and Sloot P.M.A.: AG-IVE: an Agent based solution to constructing Interactive Simulation Systems, in P.M.A. Sloot; C.J.K. Tan; J.J. Dongarra and A.G. Hoekstra, editors, Computational Science - ICCS 2002, Proceedings Part I, in series Lecture Notes in Computer Science, vol. 2329, pp. 693-703. Springer Verlag, April 2002. ISBN 3-54043591-3.

A Grid-Enabled Air Quality Simulation*

J. Carlos Mouriño[1], María J. Martín[1], Patricia González[1], Marcos Boullón[2],
José C. Cabaleiro[2], Tomás F. Pena[2], Francisco F. Rivera[2], and Ramón Doallo[1]

[1] Department of Electronics and Systems, University of A Coruña, Spain
jmourino@mail2.udc.es, {mariam,pglez,doallo}@udc.es
[2] Department of Electronics and Computer Science,
University of Santiago de Compostela, Spain
{marcos,caba,tomas,fran}@dec.usc.es

Abstract. The aim of this work, developed in the framework of the European CrossGrid Project, is to provide a high performance air quality simulation executing the STEM-II (Sulphur Transport Eulerian Model 2) program on a Grid platform. In order to test our proposal, an experimental Grid infrastructure made up of heterogeneous individual machines available in our work-center is used.

1 Introduction

STEM-II is an Eulerian air quality model which simulates transport, chemical transformations, emissions and depositions processes in an integrated framework. It is used to know in advance how the meteorological conditions (obtained from a meteorological prediction model) will affect the emissions effects of As Pontes Power Plant (A Coruña, Spain). The final aim is fulfilling, at all times, the European regulations referring to the emission of pollutants. The speedup in the simulation process is really important in order to save time when making decisions about modifications in the industrial process.

The model is computationally intensive because the governing equations are nonlinear, highly coupled and stiff. As with other computationally intensive problems, the ability to fully utilize these models remains severely limited by today's computer technology; thus, Grid computing will be applied to achieve an acceptable response time at a reasonable cost.

The structure of this paper is as follows: Section 2 explains the different sequential and parallel versions of the program, emphasizing on the Grid version. In Section 3 results obtained on an experimental Grid infrastructure are shown. Section 4 describes work in progress and future work. Finally, conclusions are discussed in Section 5.

2 High Performance Air Quality Simulations

Previously to the Grid-enabled version of the code, we developed different sequential and parallel versions of the program. First, a sequential optimization

* This work was supported in part by the CrossGrid European Project (Ref: IST-2001-32243) and by Xunta de Galicia under grant PGIDT01-PXI10501PR.

F. Fernández Rivera et al. (Eds.): Across Grids 2003, LNCS 2970, pp. 155–162, 2004.

of the code was carried out. The STEM-II program has large requirements of memory. A large number of variables are defined for each point of the simulated mesh and must be stored using large arrays. Thus, memory use and its access method influence directly on the efficiency of the code. The optimization of the sequential code was mainly focussed on the optimization of memory accesses. A reduction of 16.87% of the execution time was obtained [1]. Thus, we tried an automatic parallelization of the code using the automatic parallelizer available on the SGI platforms, PFA [2]. Unfortunately, the automatic parallelizer did not obtain any speedup since it was only able to detect trivially-parallel innermost loops. Then, we focus on the manual parallelization of the most time consuming stages of the program using OpenMP directives [3] for shared memory systems, and MPI [4] for distributed memory systems. Our parallel versions have been tested on different target architectures, specifically they were executed on a SGI O2000 multiprocessor [1], a Fujitsu AP3000 multicomputer [5], and a cluster of PC's [6].

The parallel versions of the code obtained important reductions in execution times. For instance, initially, using the original sequential code for a simulation of a complete day, we needed approximately 31 hours of execution time (more than a day) on a SGI O2000 system. Using 32 processors and the OpenMP parallel version of the code we were able to reduce a day simulation to only 1 hour of execution time in that system. Moreover, using only 4 processors we can simulate a complete day in only 5 hours. This improvement in the execution times is related both to the efficient use of multiple processors in the parallel code, and, to a large extent, to a better data locality exploitation.

2.1   Development of a Grid–Enabled Air Quality Simulation Program

There are several Grid middlewares to implement a parallel application over a Grid environment. The one used into the CrossGrid project is the Globus Toolkit. An existing MPI parallel application code can be migrated to a Grid environment fairly easily by introducing appropriate components from the Globus bag of services and using MPICH-G2, the Grid-enabled version of MPI.

MPICH–G2 [7] exploits the device architecture of the Argonne MPICH implementation. This way, the majority of MPI syntax and semantics are device–independent, and the hardware–specific details, such as those to support interprocessor communications in a heterogeneous platform, are provided by the "globus device" interface implemented in MPICH–G2.

The Globus Toolkit is an integrated set of tools and software that facilitates the deployment of applications that can exploit the advanced capabilities of the Grid and the design of production or prototype Grid infrastructures. Each component of the Globus Toolkit provides a basic service, such as authentication, resource allocation, information, communication, fault detection, and remote data access [8]. Using Globus Toolkit we can transparently benefit from uniform access to distributed resources.

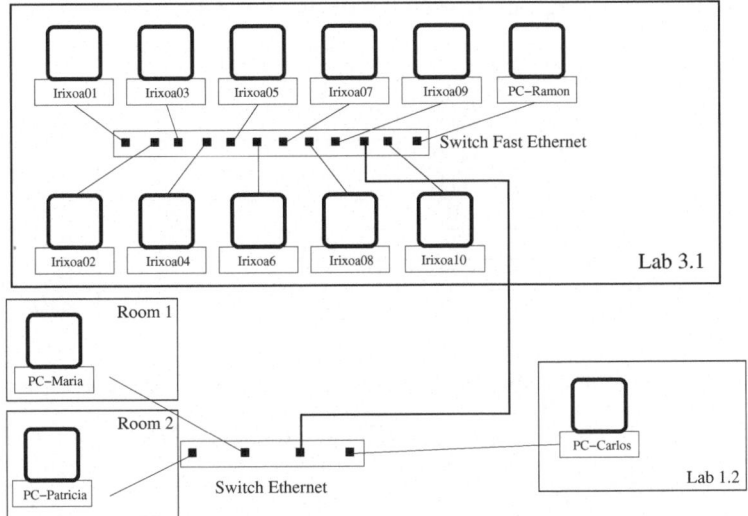

Fig. 1. Network configuration of the experimental Grid.

Since the goal of many Grid applications is to access remote data that are potentially geographically distributed, one of the primary challenges of building a Grid environment is providing an efficient I/O infrastructure. The Globus Access to Secondary Storage (GASS) from Globus is used to transfer the input files from the local machine to the remote nodes. In case the machines involved in the parallel execution of our application do not have the same architecture, the binary input files must be converted into a standard and architecture independent format, like for instance HDF5 [9].

3 Experimental Results

In order to test our application we have built an experimental Grid platform using the computational resources available in our laboratories. We have tried to avoid, as far as possible, putting restrictions on the heterogeneity of the nodes and network forming our experimental Grid. Each machine belongs to different users, and their disks are configured in a different way. Users have not free access to all the machines. The nodes have different processors and memory characteristics, although, all of them are based on the Intel architecture. The CPUs speed range from 450 MHz to 1.9 GHz, and the RAM memory from 128 MB to 1GB. The operating system is Linux Debian (with different kernel versions in different nodes), Globus v1.1.4 is used as middleware and MPICH-G2 is the message passing interface library available for parallel applications. With regard to the network characteristics, there are two different networks interconnecting the nodes, a Fast Ethernet network with a maximum bandwidth of 100 Mbps, and an Ethernet network with a bandwidth of 10 Mbps. Figure 1 shows the

Table 1. Times and speedup for 60 iterations using a Fast Ethernet network.

processors	total time	exec. time	comunic. time	startup time	speedup
Sequential	2344	2344	0	0	-
2	1479	1469	431	10	1.58
3	1121	1106	341	15	2.09
4	954	934	294	20	2.46
5	836	810	238	26	2.80
6	769	738	214	31	3.05
7	734	698	215	36	3.19
8	709	668	203	41	3.31

Table 2. Times and speedup for 60 iterations using an heterogeneous network.

processors	total time	exec. time	comunic. time	startup time	speedup
2	2479	2470	1015	9	0.94
3	1741	1724	635	17	1.35
4	1406	1386	496	20	1.67
5	1222	1194	409	28	1.92
6	1098	1067	354	31	2.13
7	1039	1000	344	39	2.25
8	969	916	344	53	2.42

network configuration. At this moment, our experimental Grid platform consists of 14 computing nodes, however, it can be easily extended by adding new PC systems.

Tables 1, 2, 3 and 4 show execution times in seconds consumed by our program and the speedup achieved with respect to the sequential version of the model. The total time represents the elapsed time from the program submission to the Grid (from the user local machine) to program conclusion. The execution time is the time consumed while the program is running, i.e., from the first sentence until the last one. The communication time is the time the root processor spends on distribution and gathering data among the processors. The difference between the execution time and the total time is the startup time.

Tables 1 and 3 show results for the situation where 60 (1 hour of real time) and 300 (5 hours) iterations, respectively, of the parallel code are running on nodes linked through the Fast Ethernet network, while Tables 2 and 4 show results when the nodes involved in a parallel execution are linked through the two different available networks (Fast Ethernet and 10Mbps Ethernet). Note that the communication time goes down in all the cases when the number of processors increases. This is because the more processors we have, the less data need to be sent to each processor. If the number of data to be communicated is larger than the maximum length provided by the system, the data has to be split, and several communications among the processors are needed. The number of communications will depend on the message size, which decreases as the number of processors increases.

Table 3. Times and speedup for 300 iterations using a Fast Ethernet network.

processors	total time	exec. time	comunic. time	startup time	speedup
Sequential	13495	13495	0	0	-
2	7750	7740	2061	10	1.74
3	5752	5737	1694	15	2.35
4	4737	4717	1544	20	2.85
5	4143	4117	1437	26	3.26
6	3772	3741	1395	31	3.58
7	3592	3556	1516	36	3.76
8	3410	3369	1504	41	3.96

Table 4. Times and speedup for 300 iterations using an heterogeneous network.

processors	total time	exec. time	comunic. time	startup time	speedup
2	12340	12331	6751	9	1.09
3	8946	8932	4817	14	1.51
4	7145	7125	3927	20	1.89
5	6066	6038	3370	28	2.22
6	5412	5381	3006	31	2.49
7	4978	4939	2904	39	2.71
8	5111	5060	2978	51	2.64

As it can be observed from these results the interconnection network in a MPI execution is a critical factor to obtain good performance results. The speedup using the heterogeneous network decreases due to the slower interprocessor communications. Moreover, our experimental platform uses a local network, so the performance will decrease even more if the nodes belong to different organizations and they are linked through a wide area network. This should be taken into account in the design of the scheduler tool in the CrossGrid project.

Note that the results, improve when the number of iterations increases. This is because the startup time depends linearly on the number of processors but it is independent of the number of iterations. Thus, its significance decreases when the number of hours simulated grows.

Figure 2 shows graphically the speedup achieved with these four configurations The relatively low speedup obtained is due to the characteristics of the used network. In our experimental platform the network is slow and it is shared by all the machines in our laboratory, approximately 70. The results are expected to be better if a dedicated network is available in the Grid for message-passing executions. Table 5 shows the results obtained in the execution of 300 iterations of the program in a cluster of PC's. The cluster consists of 16 Pentium III at 1 GHz interconnected through a Myrinet network with a maximum bandwidth of 200 Mbyte/sec.

Although better results are obtained in a Cluster, as was to be expected, the execution in a Grid is justified by its acceptable performance at a low cost. If the final CrossGrid Testbed offers a dedicated network this benefit will increase.

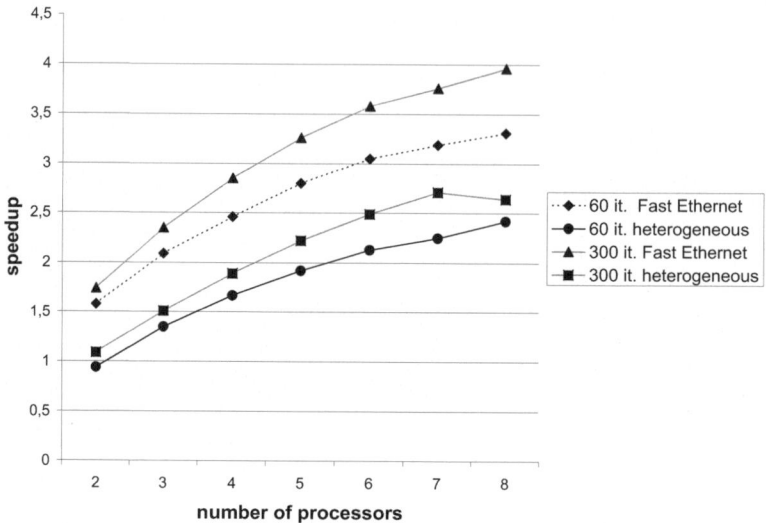

Fig. 2. Speedup obtained in different situations.

4   Work in Progress

As soon as the infrastructure of the CrossGrid project will be ready to perform MPI executions we will test the air quality simulation on the testbed platform. The Grid-enabled version described in this paper is portable to any Grid infrastructure, however, according to the new results we might develop new approaches to increase the performance taking into account the specific characteristics of the CrossGrid platform. Currently we are working about different data distribution in order to obtain a better load balancing.

On the other hand, in a Grid platform, made up of a large number of nodes, the probability of fault in any part of the system is high. Thus, it would be advisable to endow the application with any kind of fault tolerance mechanism. Currently we are studying fault tolerance options for the air quality simulation. The main idea is to save periodically the state of the application to a checkpointing file and to restart the application from the last checkpoint in case of fault.

Until now we have obtained good results using the Ckpt library [10] in the sequential simulation. However, the main inconvenience is the overhead of writing checkpointing files. One alternative we are testing is to use the libckpt library [11]. This library allows "user–directed checkpointing", i. e., user can supply directives to minimize the size of the checkpointing files.

The main problem we have found to design our application involving fault tolerance techniques is how to perform the checkpoint when dealing with the message–passing interface. Since the application is iterative, we plan, as future work, to checkpoint to a file the iteration in progress and the necessary variables to restart the program from that iteration. The main advantages of this approach

Table 5. Times and speedup for 300 iterations in a Cluster of PC's.

processors	exec. time	comunic. time	speedup
Sequential	10064	0	-
2	5712	418	1.76
3	4131	346	2.43
4	3285	302	3.06
5	2782	264	3.62
6	2447	233	4.11
7	2210	287	4.55
8	2027	269	4.96
9	1887	285	5.33
10	1789	188	5.62
11	1711	119	5.88
12	1624	165	6.20
13	1542	226	6.52
14	1538	221	6.54
15	1470	152	6.84
16	1388	216	7.25

are the portability and its easy extension to the parallel simulation, although it requires an exhaustive analysis of the variables from the programmer.

5   Conclusions

In this paper we have presented a Grid-enabled solution for the STEM-II air quality simulation model using the Globus Toolkit and the MPICH-G2 library. In order to test the application we have built our own Grid platform using resources available in our laboratories.

At the sight of the obtained results we can state that the interconnection network is a critical factor to obtain good performance results. In a real Grid the network load, its latency and its bandwidth will affect to the obtained speedup. The network characteristics will have to be taken into account by the CrossGrid scheduler tool when submitting a parallel job.

References

1. M. Parada, M.J. Martín, and R. Doallo. High Performance Air Pollution Simulation Using OpenMP. In *Workshop on High Performance Scientific and Engineering Computing with Applications, Proceedings of the 2002 ICPP Workshops*, pages 391–397, August 2002.
2. MIPSpro Power Fortran 77 Programmer's Guide. Silicon Graphics Inc., 1996.
3. Rohit Chandra, Ramesh Menon, Leo Dagum, Dror Maydan David Kohr, and Jeff McDonald. *Parallel Programming in OpenMP*. Morgan Kaufmann Publishers, 2000.

4. P.S. Pacheco. *Parallel Programming with MPI*. Morgan Kaufman Publishers, Inc., 1997.
5. J.C. Mouriño, M.J. Martín, R. Doallo, D.E. Singh, F.F. Rivera, and J.D. Bruguera. The STEM-II Air Quality Model on a Distributed Memory System. In *Workshop on High Performance Scientific and Engineering Computing with Applications, Proceedings of the 2001 ICPP Workshops*, pages 85–92, September 2001.
6. J.C. Mouriño, P. González, M.J. Martín, and R. Doallo. A cluster-based solution for a high performance air quality simulation. *Lecture Notes in Computer Science*, 2367:476–483, 2001.
7. Ian Foster and Nicholas T. Karonis. A Grid-Enabled MPI: Message passing in heterogeneous distributed computing systems. In ACM, editor, *SC'98: High Performance Networking and Computing: Proceedings of the 1998 ACM/IEEE SC98 Conference*. ACM Press and IEEE Computer Society Press, 1998.
8. I. Foster and C. Kesselman. GLOBUS: a metacomputing infrastructure toolkit. *International Journal Supercomputing Applications*, pages 115–128, 1997.
9. Robert Ross, Albert Cheng, Daniel Nurmi, and Michael Zingale. A Case Study in Application I/O on Linux Clusters. In ACM, editor, *SC2001, Denver*, November 2001.
10. Ckpt library. http://www.cs.wisc.edu/~zandy/ckpt.
11. James S. Plank, Micah Beck, Gerry Kingsley, and Kai Li. Libckpt: Transparent Checkpointing under Unix. In *Conference Proceedings Usenix Technical conference*, pages 213–223, 1995.

GRID Oriented Implementation
of Self-organizing Maps
for Data Mining in Meteorology

F. Luengo[1], A.S. Cofiño[2], and J.M. Gutiérrez[2]

[1] Dept. of Computer Science
Universidad del Zulia, Maracaibo, Venezuela
[2] Dept. of Applied Mathematics and Computational Sciences,
Universidad de Cantabria, Spain
http://grupos.unican.es/ai/meteo

Abstract. We study the efficiency of different alternatives for a scalable parallel implementation of the self-organizing map (SOM) in the GRID environment of variable resources and communications. In particular, we consider an application of data mining in Meteorology, which involves databases of high-dimensional atmospheric patterns. In this work, we focus in network partitioning alternatives, analyzing their advantages and shortcomings in this framework. As a conclusion we obtain that there is no optimal alternative, and a combination (hybridization) of algorithms is required for a GRID application.

1 Introduction

The CrossGrid project is one of the ongoing research projects involving GRID technology (http://www.cyfronet.krakow.pl/crossgrid/). One of the main tasks in the Meteorological applications package is the implementation of data mining systems for the analysis of operational and reanalysis databases of atmospheric circulation patterns. An important problem for many meteorological applications is clustering (or partitioning) the databases to find a set of representative prototypes of the atmospheric patterns in a region of interest. In this paper we analyze an unsupervised data mining clustering technique known as Self-Organizing Map (SOM), and study the suitability of different scalable parallel implementations for the GRID environment. Previous SOM parallel algorithms have focused on parallel computers with predetermined resources (processing units) and high-performance communications (see [1] and references therein). The main goal in this projects is designing an adaptive scheme for distributing data and computational load according to the changing resources available for each GRID job submitted. To this aim, some preliminary work is needed to understand the limitations and requirements of different parallel implementations of the SOM algorithm. In this paper, we analyze two different implementations for distributing computational resources, showing that none of these methods is the most efficient for all situations, but a hybrid strategy is needed.

F. Fernández Rivera et al. (Eds.): Across Grids 2003, LNCS 2970, pp. 163–170, 2004.

2   Meteorological Databases

Meteorological data mining applications work with huge meteorological databases created by reanalysis projects such as NCEP/NCAR and ERA/ECMWF. The NCEP reanalysis project covers the period from 1958 to present integrating a T62L28 model with 1.875° resolution. On the other hand ECMWF ERA reanalysis project extends from December-1978 to February-1994 (ERA-15) using a T106L31 model with 1.125° resolution; an extension of this reanalysis from mid-1957 to 2001 (ERA-40) is still under development (0.675° resolution). In both cases the total information volume is on the order of Terabytes, since data from approx. 20 variables (such as temperature, humidity, pressure, etc.) at 30 pressure levels of a 360×180 nodes grid is stored. For instance, Fig. 1(a) shows the grid covering Europe used for these models.

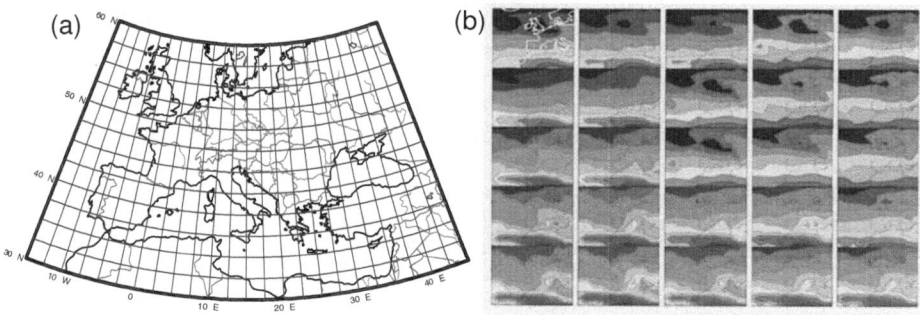

Fig. 1. (a) European region of ERA reanalysis grid (separation is 2.5° in meridians and parallels). (b) Surface temperature fields corresponding to 25 prototypes obtained with the SOM algorithm. For instance the upper-left prototype shows a isolated cold mass of air over Britain.

The above meteorological information is stored in databases world-wide using different formats (CDF, GRIB, etc.). The final goal of this work is developing a web service for SOM clustering meteorological information for user-selected geographical regions. Therefore, all the information (input and output) is formatted using XML schemas.

In particular, the above meteorological information is handled using the simple XML schema shown in Fig. 2. A particular instance is shown below:

```
<?xml version="1.0" encoding="UTF-8"?> <Class
xmlns:xsi="http://www.w3.org/2001/XMLSchema-instance"
   xsi:noNamespaceSchemaLocation="meteo.xsd">
 <Stream model="Wave model">
   <Version value="4096">
     <Type type="Forecast">
       <Date>1967-08-13</Date>
       <Time>12:00</Time>
```

```
        <Step>24</Step>
        <Number>0</Number>
        <Level type="Pressure level">1000</Level>
        <Parameter table="ECMWF">Z</Parameter>
      </Type>
    </Version>
  </Stream>
</Class>
```

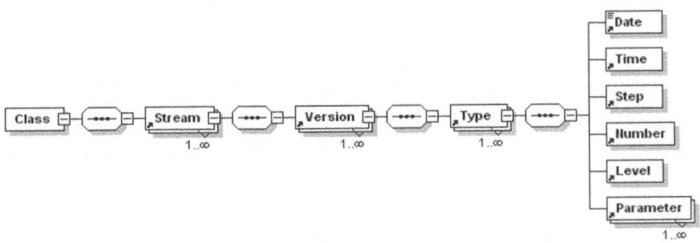

Fig. 2. XML schema for meteorological information of atmospheric circulation models.

3   Self-organizing Maps

Self-Organizing Maps (SOM) is one of the most popular data mining techniques, which is especially suitable for high dimensional data visualization, clustering and modeling (see [2] for an introduction). It uses an unsupervised learning algorithm (no domain knowledge is needed and no human intervention is required) for creating a set of prototype vectors (cluster centers) representing the data. Moreover, a topology preserving projection of the prototypes from the original input space onto a low-dimensional lattice (usually a 2D lattice) is carried out; for instance Fig. 1(b) shows a 5×5 SOM obtained from the ERA database for the temperature fields of the European region. Thus, the resulting ordered lattice can be efficiently used for extracting data features (like the situation of a isolated cold mass of air over Britain shown as a blue circle in the upper-right prototype of Fig. 1), clustering the data (such as the 25 clusters represented by the prototypes shown in Fig. 1), etc. Self-Organized maps have been recently applied in several meteorological problems, such as classifying climate modes and anomalies in the area of Balkans [3].

As shown in Fig. 3, a SOM is formed by an arbitrary number of clusters $C_1, \ldots, C_m$, located on a regular low-dimensional grid, usually a 2D lattice for visualization purposes (in this case $m = s \times s$). The vector $p_k = (i, j)$ represents the position of cluster C_k on the lattice, where $1 \leq i, j \leq r$. Moreover, each of the clusters C_k has also associated a prototype vector $c_k = (c_{k1}, \ldots, c_{kd})$, which describes the position of the cluster's center on the d-dimensional data space (some thousands of real numbers, for characterizing atmospheric patterns). For instance, if we define daily surface temperature patterns using the information provided by the reanalysis ERA-15 at 12 UTC, then the resulting data vectors $(v_1^k, \ldots, v_d^k)$, $k = 1, \ldots, n$, with $n = 15 \times 365 = 5500$ and dimension $d = 60 \times 30 = 1800$, would characterize the evolution of surface temperature over Europe the period 1979-1993. Therefore, a SOM trained to this data would find some representative configurations (prototypes) displayed on a 2D lattice which preserve original distances, hence self-organizing the obtained prototypes.

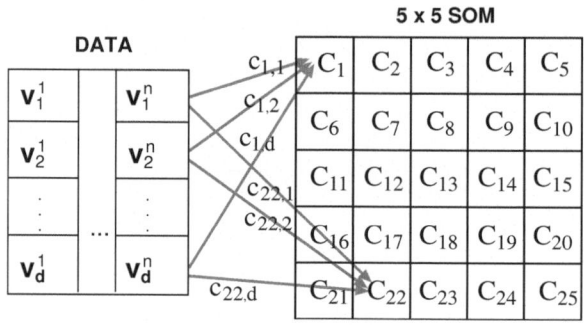

Fig. 3. Structure of a self-organizing map.

The vectors of the SOM are first initialized to random values. The goal of the training algorithm is iteratively adapting the prototype vectors, so the final prototypes become to represent a cluster of data vectors (those which are closer to the prototype). What makes SOM different from other clustering algorithms is that the training process includes a neighborhood adaptation mechanism so neighboring clusters in the 2D lattice space are quite similar, while more distant clusters become increasingly diverse. Therefore, SOM provides us with a neighborhood preserving mapping from a high dimensional space to the 2D lattice which quantizes the original data by means of m prototypes (the final prototype vectors of the SOM).

The batch implementation of the training proceeds in cycles; on each cycle, all data vectors are considered iteratively, one at a time (v_i), and the best-matching (or "wining") prototype c_{k_i} is obtained as the one minimizing the Euclidean distance to the data vector:

$$||v_i - c_{k_i}|| = min_k ||v_i - c_k||, k = 1, \ldots, m. \tag{1}$$

After each cycle the prototypes are moved according to the wined data vectors and also to its neighbors:

$$c_j = \frac{\sum_{i=1}^{n} v_i \, h(||p_j - p_{k_i}||)}{\sum_{i=1}^{n} h(||p_j - p_{k_i}||)}, j = 1, \ldots, m. \tag{2}$$

where the function $h(||p_1 - p_2||)$ is a neighborhood kernel which measures distances of clusters on the 2D lattice and determines the rate of change of cluster centers close to the winner unit in the lattice (usually a Gaussian function is considered: $h(x) = exp(-x/s(t)))$. The variance of the Gaussian neighborhood kerned $s(t)$ decrease monotonically with time, softening the topologic constrains – a linear decay to zero is usually chosen for these functions. – For a detailed description of different implementations of the method, the reader is referred to Oja et al. [2].

4   Parallelization in the GRID Environment

In this work we focus on the performance of different parallel implementations of the SOM training algorithm (2). To this aim we have used a cluster of 80 x220 IBM servers, Pentium III, 1.26 Ghz with 512 MB RAM, and 90 GB hard disks, connected with 100 Mbps Ethernet LAN (see http://grid.ifca.unican.es/ for details); each one of these servers constitutes a computing unit of the network. All the programs have been developed in C language using the MPICH-p4 implementation of Message Passing Interface (in the future, experiments in a GRID environment will be carried out using Globus Toolkit). Due to the inhomogeneous cluster communications in the GRID environment, one of the main problems is the size and amount of messages sent and received during the algorithm. Thus, a centralized master-slave architecture is chosen to avoid intensive message passing among computing units. Moreover, in the GRID environment the master should also check the computing units during the algorithm, and take decisions if any of them is not working properly. This point of view is different from other parallel implementations of SOM which use massive message passing on parallel machines [1].

The simplest form for parallelizing the SOM algorithm is splitting up the data, and hence the sum in (2), between different processors, as shown in Fig. 4(a). However, in this case, after each complete cycle the slaves must send the prototypes to the master, which computes them up, sending the final centers back to the slaves. This is not an efficient implementation for the GRID environment, since it requires intensive message passing of high-dimensional data.

Figures 4(b) and (c) show two different alternatives called SOM_R and SOM_C, respectively, for distributing computational resources with replicated (and centralized) prototype vectors (a pseudocode of these algorithms is given in Fig. 5). The different messages required for each of the schemes are shown in the figure using dashed lines, which may correspond to either an iteration of the algorithm, or a whole cycle. In Fig. 4(b), messages are minimized in size, but the prototypes should be replicated and updated in each computing element (SOM_R). On the other hand, in Fig. 4(c) calculations are only performed at the master, but messages to update the centers are sent to the slaves after each cycle (SOM_C). In both cases, the calculation of distances in (1) is equally distributed among the slaves. Therefore, a SOM with m clusters would be split up on the P slave processors, each of them computing m/p distances. Both point-to-point (MPI_Send and MPI_Recv) and collective (MPI_Bcast and MPI_Gather) communications have been used between the master and the slaves in different points of the algorithm.

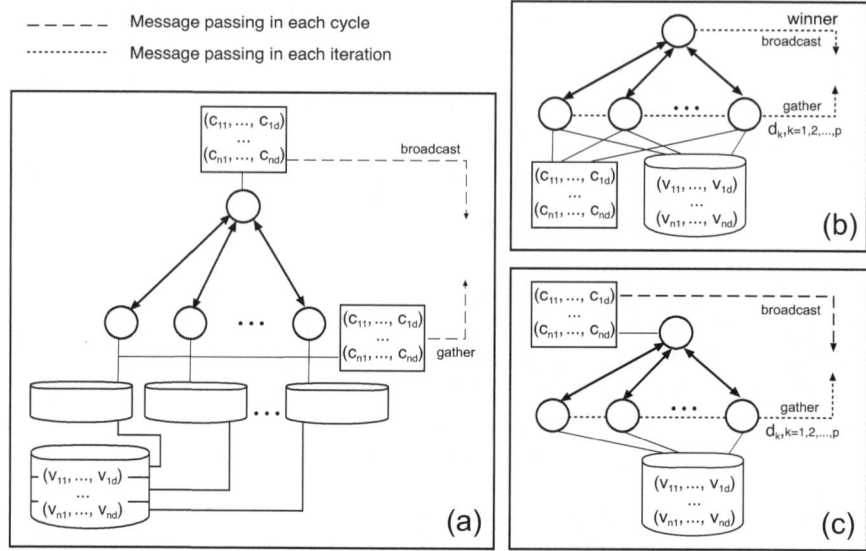

Fig. 4. Three different parallel schemes for the SOM training algorithm: (a) distributing data (b), SOM_R distributing computational resources with replicated prototype vectors, (c) SOM_C distributing computational resources with centralized prototype vectors.

To check the efficiency of these algorithms, we performed several experiments varying the number of clusters m, the dimension of data d, the size of the database n, and the number of cycles. Figure 6 shows the speedup curves obtained for $d = 500$, $n = 5500$ and variable SOM size (from $10 \times 5 = 50$ to $40 \times 40 = 1600$ clusters, or prototypes); the cluster prototypes are distributed in two, four, up to twenty processing units, obtaining the speedup curves for SOM_R and SOM_C schemes. In Fig. 6(a) we can see how the speedup of the SOM_R algorithm highly depends on the size of the SOM. This is not surprising, since in each iteration of the algorithm the master computes the winner and send it back to the slaves. This communication process ruins the parallel performance when the number of clusters is too small, since the computation of distances is done quick. On the other hand, Fig. 6(b) shows the speedup of the SOM_C algorithm. It achieves better speedup curves for small and medium network sizes, up to a given number of processing units. When the balance between message passing and slave computation is lost (e.g., by increasing the number of processor and, hence, decreasing the work done by each of them) the algorithm suddenly becomes inefficient, because of the expensive high-dimensional messages.

These results indicate that none of the schemes is the most efficient for all situations. Therefore, a hybrid strategy for distributing first data and, then, computational load is needed. This adaptive hybrid scheme is suitable for GRID environment, since the distribution of data and computing resources can be done according the changing resources available for each GRID job submitted.

- A $m = r \times r$ SOM is considered; c_k and $w_k \in I\!R^d$ represent the center of cluster C_k before and after applying topological constraints, respectively.
- $P + 1$ processors are used (1 master and P slaves).
- $T_i \subset \{1, \ldots, m\}, i = 1, \cdots, P$, indices of the prototypes assigned to processor i.

(code slave)
```
Initialize prototype vectors in all processors
```
for $(epoch = 1, \cdots, N_{epoch})$
```
        Initialize center vectors to 0
```
        for $(pattern = 1, \cdots, N_{pattern})$
                for (each $j \in T_i$)
```
                        compute distance  dⱼ
```
                end for
```
                compute winning node  gᵢ in Tᵢ
```
                MPI_Gather to communicate g_i to master
                $\{*_1\}$
        end for
        $\{*_2\}$
        for (each $j \in T_i$)
```
                update prototype vector  wⱼ
```
        end for
end for

(code master)
for $(epoch = 1, \cdots, N_{epoch})$
        for $(pattern = 1, \cdots, N_{pattern})$
                MPI_Gather to receive g_i from each slave
```
                compute winning node  g
```
                $\{*_3\}$
        end for
        $\{*_4\}$
end for

PARSOM R
$\{*_1\}$ **MPI_Recv** to receive winner node g from Master
$\{*_2\}$ **Nill**
$\{*_3\}$ **MPI_Bcast** to communicate the winner node g to Slaves
$\{*_4\}$ **Nill**

PARSOM C
$\{*_1\}$ **Nill**
$\{*_2\}$ **MPI_Recv** to receive the center vectors from Master
$\{*_3\}$ update center vectors
$\{*_4\}$ **MPI_Bcast** to communicate center vectors to Slaves

Fig. 5. Pseudocode of the SOM_R and SOM_C parallel algorithms.

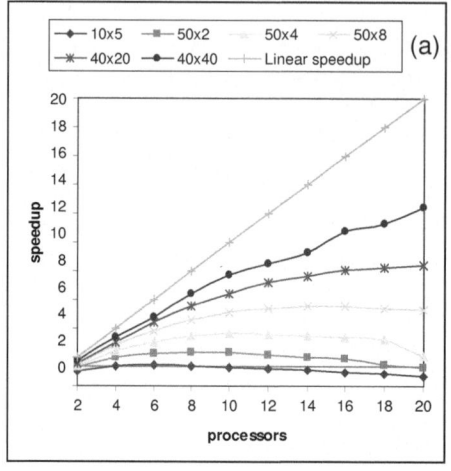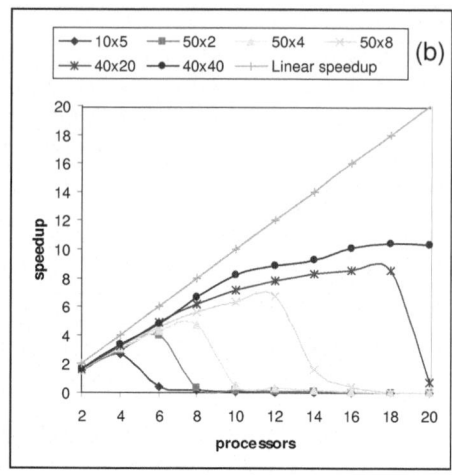

Fig. 6. Speedup for (a) SOM_R (b) SOM_C.

Acknowledgements

The work described in this paper is supported in part by the European Union through the IST-2001-32243 project "CrossGrid". The authors are also grateful to the Instituto Nacional de Meteorología INM, and the Comisión Interministerial de Ciencia y Tecnología (CICYT Project REN2000-1572) for partial financial support.

References

1. Lawrence, R.D., Almasi, G.S., and Rushmeier, H.E.: A scalable parallel algorithm for self-organizing maps with applications to sparse data mining problems, Data Mining and Knowledge Discovery **3** (1999) 171–195.
2. Oja, E., and Kaski, S.: Kohonen Maps. Amsterdam, Elsevier, 1999.
3. Cavazos, T.: Using self-organization maps to investigate extreme climate event, Journal of Climate **13** (2000) 1718–1732.

Grid Computing in Structure Determination of Biological Specimens by Electron Microscope Tomography

J.J. Fernández[1], J.R. Bilbao-Castro[2], R. Marabini[3],
J.M. Carazo[2], and I. García[1]

[1] Dpt. Arquitectura de Computadores, Universidad Almería, 04120 Almería, Spain
{jose,inma}@ace.ual.es
[2] Centro Nacional Biotecnología, Universidad Autónoma, 28049 Madrid, Spain
carazo@cnb.uam.es
[3] Escuela Técnica Superior, Universidad Autónoma, 28049 Madrid, Spain

Abstract. The present contribution describes a potential application of Grid Computing in Bioinformatics. High resolution structure determination of biological specimens is critical in BioSciences to understanding the biological function. The problem is computational intensive and distributed computing and Grid Computing are thus becoming essential. This contribution analyzes the use of Grid Computing and its potential benefits in the field of electron microscope tomography of biological specimens.

1 Introduction

Electron Microscopy (EM) is central to the study of many structural problems in BioSciences. Electron Microscope Tomography allows the 3D investigation of structure of biological specimens over a wide range of sizes, from cellular structures to single macromolecules. Knowledge of 3D structure is critical to understanding biological functions at all levels of detail.

Depending upon the nature of the specimen and the type of structural information being sought, different approaches of data collection and 3D reconstruction are used. For complex specimens, such as subcellular structures, the so-called "Electron Tomography" (ET) [1,2] approach is used, in which a set of large images is acquired at different orientations from a single specimen, via tilting it around one axis. For specimens in the macromolecular domain the so-called "3D Electron Microscopy" (3DEM) [3,4] is used, which involves processing thousands EM projection images, taken at very different orientations, to derive the 3D structure at resolution typically in the range of 6–20 Angstroms.

Rigorous structural analyses require that image acquisition and reconstruction be robust and introduce as little noise and artifact as possible at the spatial scales of interest, for a proper interpretation and measurement of the structural features. As a consequence, sophisticated tomographic algorithms have to be used to reconstruct biological specimens.

F. Fernández Rivera et al. (Eds.): Across Grids 2003, LNCS 2970, pp. 171–181, 2004.

Currently, the standard tomographic reconstruction method in the field is Weighted Backprojection (WBP) [5]. The method simply distributes the known specimen mass present in projection images evenly over computed backprojection rays. In this way, specimen mass is projected back into a reconstruction volume (i.e., backprojected). When this process is repeated for a series of projection images recorded from different tilt angles, backprojection rays from the different images intersect and reinforce each other at the points where mass is found in the original structure. Therefore, the 3D mass of the specimen is reconstructed (Figure 1). The relevance of WBP in ET mainly stems from its linearity and its computational simplicity. However, its main disadvantages are (i) the results may be strongly affected by limited tilt angle data obtained with the microcope, and (ii) WBP does not implicitly take into account the noise conditions.

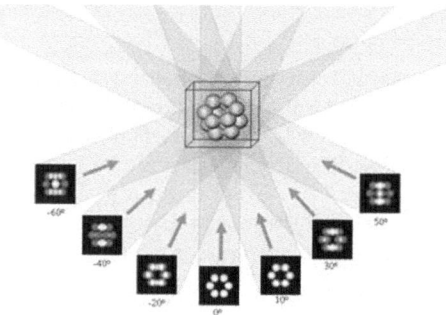

Fig. 1. Three-dimensional reconstruction from projections by backprojection. The projection images are projected back into the volume to be reconstructed.

The combination of iterative reconstruction methods with smooth basis functions (the so-called blobs, see Fig. 2) –as opposite to the well-known voxels– has been proven to be well suited for structural analysis under the extreme noise conditions in electron microscopy [6,7]. Conceptually, iterative methods proceed in the following way (Fig. 3). First, they start from an initial model. The model is progressively refined as iterations evolve. In every iteration, (1) projections

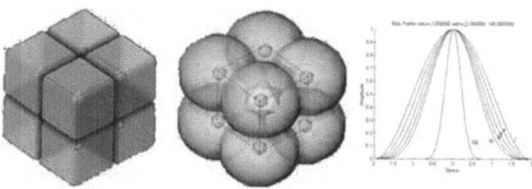

Fig. 2. Blobs. Right: profile of a blob: continuous function with smooth transition to zero. Center: Arrangement of overlapping blobs on a simple cubic grid. Left: For comparison purposes, arrangement of voxels on the same grid.

Iterative Reconstruction Algorithms
Conceptual scheme

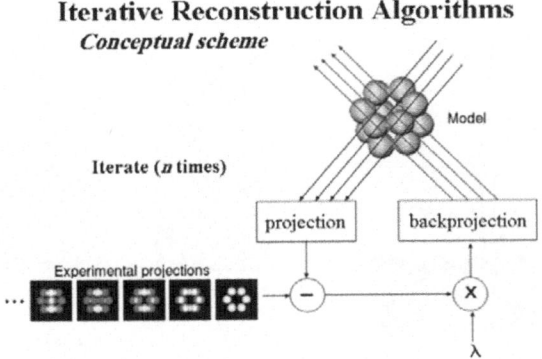

Fig. 3. Conceptual scheme of iterative methods for 3D reconstruction from projections.

are computed from the current model; (2) the error between the experimental projections and the computed ones is calculated; (3) the model is refined so that the error is minimized through "error backprojection").

These 3D reconstruction algorithms are characterized for their huge computational demands which come from (a) large memory requirements and (b) long computation times. The specimens subject of structural analysis rank from the subcellular level up to macromolecular level. In practice, this implies that the 3D reconstruction processes must deal with huge data volumes. In ET, hundreds of large projection images are combined to yield reconstructed volumes in the order of 2^{30} float-point numbers. In 3DEM, thousands of projection images (hundreds of thousands are expected for a near future) are combined to yield reconstructed volumes in the order of 2^{20} float-point numbers. Therefore, it is clear that 3D reconstruction is by itself a really heavy computational task.

On the other hand, reconstruction methods are also characterized by a relatively large set of free parameters. In order to fully exploit the capabilities of the algorithms, these parameters have to be optimized. The optimization aims at tuning the reconstruction algorithm for the specimen under analysis. This optimization may involve launching thousands of 3D reconstructions by following a certain optimization algorithm (brute force, gradient-driven, random-search, etc) to determine the optimal parameters. So, the optimization process is definitely much more computational resources consuming than the own reconstruction.

In summary, we are dealing with a grand-challenge application: the 3D reconstruction of biological specimens at medium/high resolution, which involves (a) a previous really-heavy procedure of parameter optimization to tune the algorithm and prepare it for its production stage, and (b) the structure determination of the biological structures by using the previously tuned algorithm.

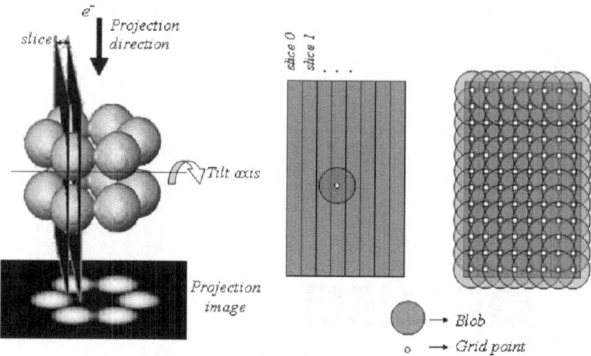

Fig. 4. Left: Single-tilt axis acquisition geometry. The slices are those one-voxel-thick planes orthogonal to the tilt axis. Center: The slices are depicted with columns, and the circle represents a generic blob which extends beyond the slice where it is located. Right: Blobs create a pseudo-continuous 3D density distribution representing the structure.

2   Parallel Strategies for 3D Reconstruction

Our group works in the development and application of strategies of distributed computing to structure determination of biological specimens by means of regularized iterative reconstruction methods. So far, we have developed an efficient strategy for tomographic reconstruction of subcellular structures [8] to work on clusters of workstations. Currently, our group also works in distributed strategies for 3DEM of macromolecules and viruses and for parameter optimization [9].

The parallel strategies that have been developed are based on *domain decomposition* and the SPMD model (*Single Program, Multiple Data*) in which every node in the system carries out, essentially, the same task over its own data domain. However, the concrete strategy finally adopted depends on whether the structural analysis is based on ET or on 3DEM.

In ET, the single-tilt axis data acquisition geometry (Fig. 4) allows a data decomposition consisting of dividing the whole volume to be reconstructed into slabs of slices orthogonal to the tilt axis (Fig. 5). The SPMD model then involves that the task to be carried out by every node is to reconstruct its own slab. Those slabs of slices would be independent if voxel basis functions were used. However, due to their overlapping nature, the use of blobs as basis functions makes the slices, and consequently the slabs, inter-dependent (see Fig. 4). Therefore, several times per iteration during the reconstruction process, there is a need for data communication among the nodes. We have developed an efficient Latency Hiding strategy [8] to minimize the penalty due to communication (Fig. 6).

In 3DEM, the SPMD model consists of splitting the set of projection images into groups, and distribute the groups across the computing nodes (Fig. 7). The nodes then process the particles in parallel, and once per iteration, they communicate the results to obtain the solution. This strategy proves to be interesting to analyze due to the implications in the convergence of the algorithm. The parallel

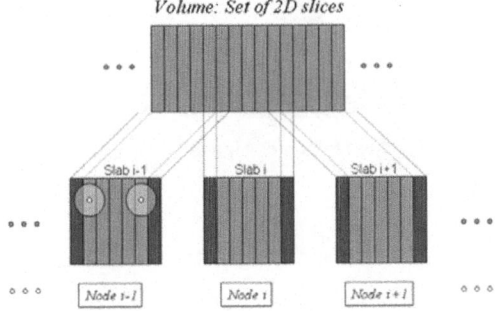

Fig. 5. Data decomposition in ET. Every node in the parallel system receives a slab including unique slices (light-gray), and additional redundant slices (dark-gray).

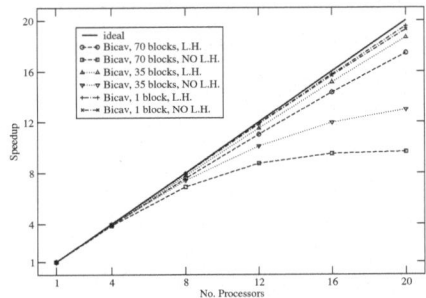

Fig. 6. Speedup for the efficient parallel strategy described for ET using different iterative reconstruction methods. These curves were measured in a cluster of PC-workstations connected via Fast-Ethernet. L.H. stands for "Latency Hiding" [8].

strategies allow to reduce the computation time per iteration but, however, may reduce the convergence rate of the algorithm [9].

The use of WBP instead of these sophisticated regularized iterative methods would make the parallelization straightforward. In ET, the reconstruction of each of the one-voxel-thick slices orthogonal to the tilt axis of the volume would be assigned to an individual node on the parallel system. In 3DEM, the strategy would be exactly the same as described above for iterative methods, except that no iterations would be needed. In ET of large specimens, parallel computing has already been applied to large-scale reconstructions by means of WBP [10].

3   Grid Computing in 3D Reconstruction

Our group is now interested in heterogeneous distributed and grid environments for these sort of grand-challenge applications. So far, the only Grid Computing approach in the field of tomography of biological specimens is being developed by

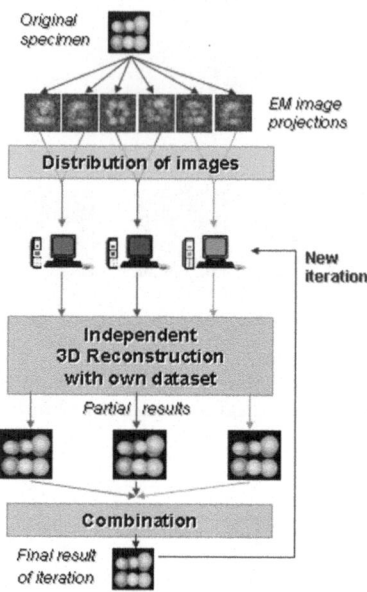

Fig. 7. Data decomposition in 3DEM. The whole set of images is distributed across the nodes. Every node carries out a 3D reconstruction with its own dataset. The final result of the iteration is obtained as a combination of the partial reconstructions.

our collaborators at the National Center for Microscopy and Imaging Research and the San Diego Supercomputing Center [11]. This approach is focused on ET of subcellular structures and is based on the simple WBP method, whose grid implementation is straightforward. One slice of work is assigned to a node at a time until all slices have been processed. The approach has a co-allocation strategy implemented so that available information from the batch scheduler is used to deploy the application in a grid environment. That sort of application-level scheduler is well suited to deal with the space-shared resources on the grid.

As stated above, our group develops regularized iterative tomographic reconstruction methods that yield better solutions under the conditions found in electron microscope tomography. Due to the computational complexity of these sophisticated methods, computational grids are being considered very attractive enviroments for high resolution structure determination of biological specimens. From the description in the sections above, two types of potential applications for grids can be distinguished: The optimization of the parameters for the problem at hand and the tomographic reconstruction itself.

– The parameter optimization. This is a class of application of "high-through-put computing": The grid should schedule large numbers of "independent tasks" with the goal of putting unused processor cycles (from idle, for example, computers in the grid) to work. Here, the "independent tasks" would be the different reconstruction processes with different parameters values involved in the optimization procedure. In a "high-throughput computing" approach, the user expects to get as many commited tasks as possible in a time interval or, in other words, the grid manages all its resources efficiently so that the maximum amount of his/her work is done.

– The final 3D reconstruction process. This is a class of application of "distributed supercomputing", in the sense that the grid should aggregate substantial computational resources in order to tackle the problem that could not be solved (or could take a really huge computation time) on a single system. So far, this type of procedures has been dealt with by means of "parallelization" techniques, using supercomputers or clusters of workstations, that alleviate the high computational demands. The grid then arises as a further step in this parallelization approach. The grid should provide the capabilities to use its hundreds or thousands of nodes as a large heterogeneous system. In a "distributed supercomputing" approach, the user expects to get the results as soon as possible. Thus the grid should allocate a set of its nodes to execute user's application in a "dedicate" way.

4 First Steps towards Implementation

4.1 Grid Software

The very first step to get a grid system working is to choose the software which will manage the capabilities that such an environment offers [12]. Some options are easily available through the Internet and many of them are open source so we must know which of those packages suites our requirements:

– Availability and productivity: Grid technologies aim at making all the systems inside an organization accesible to every member who may need it. The process of accessing those systems should be transparent and easy for the user. The system usage must be optimized so systems should not be overcrowded while others remain idle. The grid must provide information and scheduling mechanisms which will work together to make the best possible use of the resources. Making a good use of those mechanisms will increase productivity within an organization.
– Security: Authentication and authorization must be guaranteed within a grid system in order to avoid that privileged information could be compromised and that wrong people use non-authorized resources. Therefore the grid software must provide such mechanisms as well as encryption tools for secure communication.
– Data management: Due to the big amounts of data we are dealing with, the grid must provide tools for data management as secure and reliable file transfer, staging of executables, access to storage resources, use of remote data, etc..
– Scalability: Once the grid is running, it should not be affected by additions of new machines and other facilities to the grid structure. Therefore non servercentralized strategies are advisable. It is desirable that all the systems within

an organization are homogeneous but it is often impossible. Therefore the grid must provide ways to deal with heterogeneity problems mainly in terms of inter-process comunication.

Taking into account those requirements, and the features offered by the available packages, we have decided to use Globus Toolkit [13] as our grid middleware. Globus provides us with:

- The Grid Secure Infraestructure: also called GSI, it provides all the security management of the grid using public encryption for sensitive data, certificates for the authentication and authorisation, and SSL for the communication protocols.
- Information Services: The Globus Metacomputing Directory Service (MDS) provides mechanisms to build information systems so that we can query the grid about available resources. This can be a hierarchical information system so that adding new resources should not represent a big problem as it is updated automatically.
- Resource Management: The Globus Resource Allocation Manager (GRAM) is used for resource allocation and jobs submission. Using Resource Specification Language (RSL) we can query for multiple resources at a time, and GRAM will manage to allocate all of them if available.
- Data Management: GridFTP implements a data transfer protocol. GridFTP provides a secure, fast and reliable way to transfer files from one resource to another. There are more data management tools like the Global Access to Secondary Storage (GASS). These services make the access to remote filesystems transparent and are very useful to reduce data management problems such as incoherent or redundant information.

On the clusters belonging to the grid, scheduling policies like batch system queues have been implemented. In our case we are using OpenPBS (Portable Batch System) but we are testing different alternatives like Condor-G, which has the ability to make use of the idle CPU cycles of all the computers it is installed in. Condor-G is compatible with Globus, implying a big advantage in terms of integration.

Information services are vital in grid applications as they provide dynamic monitoring of the system allowing us to choose which systems perform better and their capabilities. Therefore, we can make predictions about the performance in our applications using specific systems across the grid and dinamically modifying the used resources in order to obtain better results. It should be desirable to build an automatic fully-adaptable execution system. We can find an important example of adaptative system in [14].

4.2   Parameters Optimization

The first application we are developing focuses on the task of parameters optimization. As described before, this is a "high-throughput computing" application which will take a great advantage of grid strategies. We are working with the Parallel Constrained Biased Random Search (PCBRS) [15] algorithm, an iterative algorithm for global optimization. Figure 8 shows the scheme of a global optimization application on a grid. The resources will be interconnected using grid tools like job submission, data transfer, scheduling policies, etc. The user will pass some parameters to the optimization process like number of iterations, number of systems to use and memory required so that the grid will look for the optimal group of available systems. Then, using an application-Globus interface, the optimization algorithm will send properly formed Globus job requests to Globus-enabled hosts so that they will carry out their own reconstruction using their own parameters. Once the different reconstructions are finished, the results are collected and evaluated using PCBRS. Then new reconstructions will be launched. This is an iterative process and it will finish when the solution reaches the accuracy requested by the user.

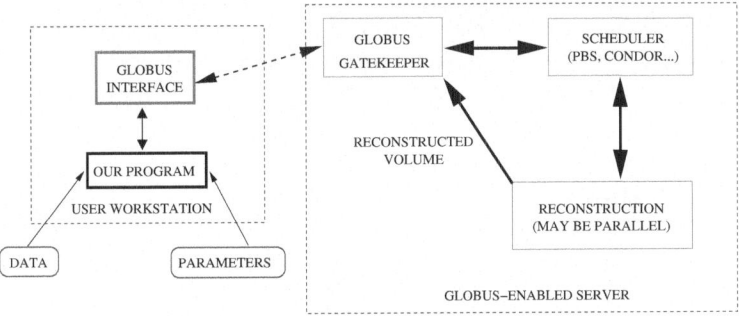

Fig. 8. Logical schema of globus usage for parameters optimization process using grid technologies.

4.3   Reconstruction

Once the parameters are optimized, the optimal parameters will be used for the "production stage" of the 3D reconstruction algorithm. The optimal parameters will tune the reconstruction for the specimens under study. 3D reconstruction by itself is a highly computational resources demanding process, and hence it is of a great interest to improve its efficiency by using parallel computing. As stated above, some efficient strategies have been developed to parallelize those reconstruction algorithms focused on clusters of workstations. Similar parallel strategies could be used for the grid implementation of the reconstruction algorithms. However, for an efficient execution, homogeneity of the systems would be highly desirable. Once more, Globus provides us with the tools to select a subset of homogeneous systems using the Globus Information System. Another alternative to explore is the development of the parallel reconstruction algorithms to be executed in heterogeneous environments. This alternative would exploit more efficiently the distributed capabilities of the grid.

5 Conclusion

This article has described a potential application of Grid Computing in Bioinformatics. High resolution structure determination of biological specimens is critical in BioSciences, but is computational intensive. Distributed computing and Grid Computing are thus becoming essential.

This contribution has analyzed the use of Grid Computing and its potential benefits in the field of electron microscope tomography of biological specimens. The benefits that Grid Computing could provide in the field of electron microscope tomography of biological specimens come into manifest: there are potential applications to exploit the "high-throughput" and the "distributed supercomputing" capabilities of the grid.

Furthermore, in this field, the grid may act as a powerful tool to afford problems that have not been dared so far. An example of this is the structure determination of large viruses at high resolution using these sophisticated iterative methods. Another example is the current challenge in the field of electron tomography, which is the reconstruction of whole cells with sufficient resolution for visualizing their molecular architecture. Distributed and Grid Computing will make it possible to afford those "grand challenge" applications currently unapproachable.

Acknowledgments

This work is partially supported by Spanish CICYT through grants TIC2002-00228 and BIO2001-1237.

References

1. Baumeister, W.: Electron tomography: towards visualizing the molecular organization of the cytoplasm. Cur.Opi.Struct.Biol. **12** (2002) 679–684
2. Medalia, O., Weber, I., Frangakis, A., Nicastro, D., Gerisch, G., Baumeister, W.: Macromolecular architecture in eukaryotic cells visualized by cryoelectron tomography. Science **298** (2002) 1209–1213
3. Frank, J.: Three Dimensional Electron Microscopy of Macromolecular Assemblies. Academic Press (1996)
4. Frank, J.: Single-particle imaging of macromolecules by cryo-electron microscopy. Annu. Rev. Biophys. Biomol. Struct. **31** (2002) 303–319
5. Rademacher, M.: Weighted Back-Projection Methods. In: Electron Tomography. Three-Dimensional Imaging with the Transmission Electron Microscope, J. Frank (Ed.). Plenum Press (1992) 91–115
6. Marabini, R., Herman, G., Carazo, J.: 3D reconstruction in electron microscopy using ART with blobs. Ultramicroscopy **72** (1998) 53–56
7. Fernandez, J., Lawrence, Roca, Garcia, I., Ellisman, Carazo, J.: High performance electron tomography of complex specimens. J. Struct. Biol. **138** (2002) 6–20
8. Fernandez, J., Carazo, J., Garcia, I.: Three-dimensional reconstruction of cellular structures by electron microscope tomography and parallel computing. J. Parallel and Distributed Computing (*submitted*) (2003)

9. Bilbao-Castro, J., Carazo, J., Garcia, I., Fernandez, J.: Parallel iterative reconstruction methods for structure determination of biological specimens by electron microscopy. IEEE Intl. Congress on Image Processing (*submitted*) (2003)
10. Perkins, G., Renken, C., Song, J., Frey, T., Young, S., Lamont, S., Martone, M., Lindsey, S., Ellisman, M.: Electron tomography of large, multicomponent biological structures. J. Struc. Biol. **120** (1997) 219–227
11. Peltier, S., Lin, A., Lee, D., Mock, S., Lamont, S., Molina, T., Wong, M., Dai, L., Martone, M., Ellisman, M.: The telescience portal for tomography applications. J. Parallel Distributed Computing (*in press*) (2003)
12. Foster, I., Kesselman, C., Nick, J., Tuecke, S.: Grid services for distributed system integration. Computer **35** (2002) 37–46
13. I. Foster, C.K.: Globus: A metacomputing infrastructure toolkit. Intl. J. Supercomputer Applications **11** (1997) 115–128
14. Wolski, R., Spring, N.T., Hayes, J.: The network weather service: A distributed resource performance forecasting service for metacomputing. Future Generation Computer Systems **15** (1999) 757–768
15. Garcia, I., Herman, G.: Global optimization by PCBRS. In: State of art in global optimization: Computational Methods and Applications. Kluwer (1996) 433–455

A Grid Representation
for Distributed Virtual Environments

P. Morillo, M. Fernández, and N. Pelechano

Instituto de Robótica, Universidad de Valencia
Polígono de la Coma, S/N, Paterna, Valencia (Spain)
Pedro.Morillo@uv.es

Abstract. Fast Internet connections and the widespread use of high performance graphic cards are making Distributed Virtual Environments (DVE) very common nowadays. The architecture and behavior of these systems are very similar to new grid computing applications where concepts such as sharing and high scalability are extremely exploited. However, there are several key issues in these systems that should still be improved in order to design a scalable and cost-effective DVE system. One of these key issues is the partitioning problem. This problem consists of efficiently assigning clients (3-D avatars) to the arbiters (servers) in the system. As an alternative to the ad-hoc heuristic proposed in the literature, this paper presents a comparison study of two evolutionary heuristics for solving the partitioning problem in DVE systems. Performance evaluation results show that heuristic methods can greatly improve the performance of the partitioning method, particularly for large DVE systems. In this way, efficiency and scalability of DVE systems can be significantly improved.

1 Introduction

Grid Computing and *Distributed Virtual Environments* (DVE) have evolved together in the development of high performance 3D real-time applications. A grid system ([5]), composed of a network of heterogeneous computers, is the logical framework to simulate a virtual world that is shared by thousands of users.

In a DVE system a collection of users are working on different computers connected to the Internet running an interactive 3D graphic program that simulates a virtual scene. Each user is represented in the virtual environment by a humanoid called *avatar*. Since this kind of systems supports visual interactions among multiple users in the shared 3D virtual environment, every change in the simulation have to be propagated to other participants. These participants are located in another computers within the grid system.

In order to handle an important number of avatars in the simulation, traditional architectures for these applications are based on a *central server* [15] or a *replicated* model [10]. Although both systems can manage more than a hundred of avatars simultaneously these systems become unfeasible when the number of avatars significantly increases.

Nowadays, parallel to the appearance of Grid computing applications, the way of developing these systems has changed. Instead of maintaining the whole simulation within a set of central computers, this is distributed among all the avatars that are currently running. Each of them controls and simulates its surrounding part of the scene and sends

F. Fernández Rivera et al. (Eds.): Across Grids 2003, LNCS 2970, pp. 182–189, 2004.

data to an arbiter node. This new methodology, called *server-network* architecture, has let to develop DVE systems with a large number of avatars geographically distanced. This architecture offers low latency performance and allocates more than three thousand avatars over Internet in real time. With this scheme, each avatar is sharing the same resources in the 3D virtual scene and the bottlenecks within the central simulators are avoided. In this sense, DVE systems can be seen as a large data Grid environment because of two main reasons. Firstly, the total amount of data within a simulation is segmented among their members, and secondly the reconfiguration methods for failure tolerance guarantee the correct working of the entire system.

As figure 1 shows, modern DVE systems contain a large set of clients (avatars) and servers (data arbiters). In order to manage all the simulation these clients have to be properly assigned to the arbiters. When an avatar moves in the virtual space it has to propagate a message through its associated server to the rest of clients within a certain area of interest (AOI). Depending on origin and destination avatars, two kinds of communication messages are defined. Fast intra-server communications when both the sender and receiver are assigned to the same server, and long inter-server otherwise.

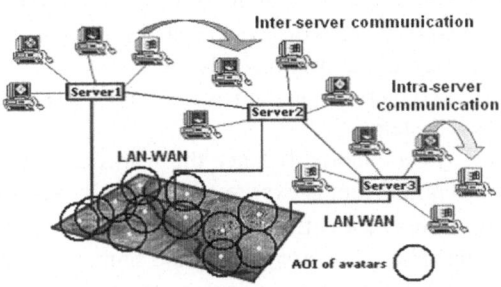

Fig. 1. Basic DVE communication model.

Nowadays DVE systems are used in a wide variety of applications such as collaborative design [14], civil and military distributed training simulations [12], distributed and interactive e-learning [13] and multi-player games [9].

DVE applications achieve to simulate large-scale virtual worlds through dispersed and heterogeneous computational resources. However, there are several key issues in these systems that should still be improved in order to design a scalable and cost-effective DVE. One of these key issues is the *partitioning problem*. Defined in [10] for DVE systems, this hot research problem consists in efficiently assigning the clients (3-D avatars) to the server nodes in the grid of computers. Effective solutions to this grid task provide low latency and high scalability to the DVE system.

This paper shows the behavior of DVE in grid systems and proposes two methods to solve the partitioning problem. These methods are based on evolutionary computation where a heuristic search scheme using Genetic Algorithms and Simulated Annealing are used to obtain good partitioning solutions.

2   The Partitioning Problem. State of the Art

Although a large set of communication models has been proposed in order to support large DVE systems ([2,15,16]), network-server architectures are becoming a de-facto standard. In these architectures, interconnected servers, that perform as data arbiters, organize the simulation control. Multi-platform clients are assigned to one of these servers, so that, for each avatar movement, a client only sends one update message to a server, and then the server propagates the message to other server and clients of the system.

In order to avoid a message outburst when the number of clients increases, areas of interest (*AOI* in [10], *locales* in [1] and *auras* in [15]) are defined for each one of the avatars. In this way, messages are only propagated from one avatar to the avatars that fall into its AOI. Depending on which is the destination avatar, intra-server and inter-server are messages are defined in a DVE scheme (see figure 1). This strategy allows DVE systems to complete very little workload, storage or messaging in order to maintain a consistent state among many avatars in a large simulation.

Lui and Chan have modelled the problem of efficiently assigning the clients of the simulations to the servers of the DVE system, called *partitioning problem*, as a quality function. This function estimates how the avatars can be assigned to the servers in order to ensure a high interactivity and to minimize the network traffic [10].

To achieve this goal, two factors (labelled as C_p^W and C_p^L) must be considered in an optimal design of a DVE system:

On one hand, DVE system should balance the workload generated by the avatars among the servers. This equilibrium is expressed by the C_p^W term and, logically, it can be properly adjusted if servers have different hardware features. On the other hand (C_p^L term), neighboring avatars should be assigned to the same server in order to minimize the overall inter-server traffic. Because topological reasons, it is not possible to satisfy this condition for the majority of the avatars. Therefore, it is necessary to find a suitable topological grouping.

According to these two parameters a cost evaluation function is offered to estimate the efficiency of a partitioning solution:

$$C_p = W_1 \, C_p^W + W_2 \, C_p^L, \text{ such as } W_1 + W_2 = 1.0 \tag{1}$$

In this equation, W_1 and W_2 denote the relative importance of the computational workload and the inter-server communication cost mentioned above. In the general formal case W_1 is equal to W_2 and equal to 0.5. It is evident that, when a DVE is working on a high performance network, the quotient W_1/W_2 may be much greater than one. Quite the opposite for a DVE working in a slow-shared network or Internet, where large messages latencies make the quotient to be close to zero.

In [10] authors demonstrate that the partitioning problem is NP-hard and offer a platform test to scientific community where every approximations to the problem can be checked and compared. Moreover, a refinement of their initial algorithm is proposed and a parallelization based on the amount of avatar criteria is presented in [11].

Other approaches have been published, with different denominations, in order to address the partitioning problem in DVE systems [2,16]. [16] describes an approach that groups the avatars following a regular distribution. In order to ensure a high interactivity to the users, this algorithm generates a number of grouped avatars equal to the number of servers in the DVE system. This solution does not obtain efficient results when avatars are located in a non-uniform distribution. [2] rejects dynamic concepts associated to avatars such as aura, AOI or locale. This technique divides the 3D virtual scene in a regular grid. For each cell, a multicast group is created. Therefore, avatars which are sharing a cell are assigned to the same server. This technique is performed by sharing multicast packets and saves a lot of inter-server messages to the DVE system. Despite it was a quick and determinist solution, this static classification performs badly when avatars are distributed in a non-uniform way within the 3D virtual scene. This technique does not take into account situations where avatars are massively located close to the frontiers of the cells. In this case it obtains inefficient partitioning solution, in terms of C_p quality function.

3   A New Approach

Solutions mentioned above for the partitioning problem share the same feature: they are custom techniques that are defined as ad-hoc heuristics to solve the problem.

As other researchers implement for another kind of problems [3], the solutions presented in this paper are based on evolutionary computation. In various domains of applications these heuristics search methods imitate principles of the nature in order to solve complex problems. Although simplistic from a biologist's viewpoint, these algorithms are sufficiently complex to provide robust and powerful search mechanisms. Although a variety of evolutionary algorithms had been proposed, this paper focuses on design and development of a solution for the partitioning problem based on genetic algorithms and simulated annealing.

Genetic Algorithms (GA), by using biological concepts, provide a learning method based on the idea of evolution by natural selection. Detailed in [7], GA start creating a population of pre-solution that will evolve generation by generation until it achieves a good quality population of post-solutions.

In order to solve the partitioning problem, the method proposed in this paper starts from a initial population of chromosomes. For each iteration, the number of chromosomes is equal to the number of partial solutions that the GA needs. For a given time step, each chromosome will be defined by a descriptor vector giving a possible configuration for the partitioning of the DVE. Therefore, each element of this vector will have assigned a range of values equal to the number of servers within the DVE.

The Genetic solution to the partitioning task follows four steps. Each of them has been adapted to the specifications of the particular problem:

Initial Solutions. To avoid the algorithm spending some of its initial iterations trying unsatisfactory combinations, good initial values need to be found in order to obtain low initial C_p costs. A method from pattern recognition, based on Graph-Theoretic [4], has been adapted to achieve fast initial solutions.

Number of Generations. It is necessary to set a maximum value for the number of generation in order to reduce the cost of the algorithm without increasing the computational time needed to obtain the solutions.

Inheritance Mechanism Based on Derivation. Starting with the initial solution new generations will be found by iteratively applying crossover between elements of the population. This crossover is represented by a derivative or inheritance scheme. Therefore, during each iteration a new child will be created for each of the N elements of the current population. Among the 2N chromosomes of the new population, the N elements with lower C_p will be chosen to be used for the next iteration. In order to create a child solution from a parent, two boarder avatars (BA) assigned to different servers will be randomly chosen from the current N chromosomes. BA is an avatar that although it lies within the AOI of another avatar, it is not assigned to the same server. These kinds of avatars will be the ones offering a higher probability of giving a successful permutation since they minimize inter-server communication.

The Mutation Process. Mutation is needed to escape from local minima. Once the child-vector has been obtained, mutation involves changing at random the server assigned to one of the elements of the population. Some other mutations such as the modification of several elements or the crossover between the characteristics of pairs of chromosomes have also been tested. But after several tests it has been found that the mutation of just one "bit" is the one offering the best results. It is important to mention that the mutation is a random process controlled by a parameter which needs to be carefully chosen for each specific experiment in order to achieve solutions with low C_p System Cost.

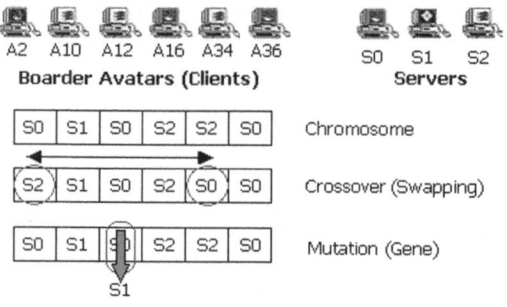

Fig. 2. Example of iteration: crossover operator and mutation.

In the above figure it is represented how six BA, obtained from the full set of avatars, are selected and defined as a chromosome. Then a crossover and a mutation are applied in order to obtain the breeding for the next generation.

The second solution is based on *Simulated Annealing* (SA). SA is a Monte Carlo approach for minimizing multivariate functions. Described in [8], this heuristic search method is based on a thermodynamic theory establishing that the minimum energy state in a system can be found if the temperature decreasing is performed slowly enough. SA is a heuristic search method that always accepts better solutions than the current solution, and also accepts worse solutions according to a probability system based on the system temperature. This method starts with a high system temperature (a high probability of accepting a worsening movement), and in each iteration system temperature is decreased.

Thus, SA can leave local minima by accepting worsening movements at intermediate stages. The search method ends when the system temperature is so low that worsening movements are practically impossible or when N iterations are performed without finding better solutions.

Each iteration consists of randomly select two different critical avatars assigned to different servers. Then, the servers that two critical avatars are assigned to are exchanged. If the resulting value of the quality function C_p is higher than the previous one plus a threshold T, that change is rejected. Otherwise, it is accepted and the search method decreases the value of the quality function C_p associated with each assignment. The threshold T used in each iteration of the search depends on the rate of temperature decreasing R, and it is defined as

$$T \quad = \quad R - \left(\frac{R \times i}{N} \right) \tag{2}$$

where N determines the finishing condition of the search.

As literature shows [3,8], the two key issues for properly tuning this heuristic search method are the number of iterations N and the temperature decreasing rate R. Although they are not shown here for the sake of shortness, we obtained the best results for SA method with N=3000 iterations and R=1.25. This procedure allows the system to move consistently towards lower energy states, yet still avoids local minima due to the probabilistic acceptance of some upward moves. Number of iterations and cooling schedule were characterized in the process to obtain high-quality clustering solutions.

4 Performance Evaluation

Following the evaluation methodology formulated in [11], it has been empirically tested adapted evolutionary heuristics in two examples of a DVE system: a SMALL world, composed by 13 avatars and 3 servers, and a LARGE world, composed by 2500 avatars and 8 servers. Two parameters has been considered: the value of the quality function for the obtained partition and also the computational cost, in terms of execution time, required by the search method in order to provide that partition.

Since the performance of the heuristic search methods may heavily depend on the location of the avatars, it has been considered three different distributions of avatars: uniform, skewed, and clustered distribution.

Table 1 and table 2 show the values corresponding to the final partitions calculated by each heuristic search method for both worlds, as well as the execution times required for each heuristic search method to obtain that final partition.

For the case of SMALL worlds, since a full solution tree scanning requires only to explore 3^{13} (1.594.323) different solutions, it is also possible to apply an exhaustive algorithm in order to compare the different computational times obtained. However it is not feasible to apply an exhaustive algorithm for the case of LARGE worlds where the solution tree has a dimension of 8^{2500} different results.

From obtained results, it can be seen that both proposed heuristics provide better (lower) C_p values than the Lui-Chan search method for skewed and clustered distribution of avatars. Also for all the distributions in SMALL worlds, these achieved C_p values are

Table 1. Results for SMALL DVE systems.

	Uniform distribution		Skewed distribution		Clustered distribution	
	Time (s.)	C_p	Time (s.)	C_p	Time (s.)	C_p
Exhaustive	3.411	6.54	3.843	7.04	4.783	7.91
Lui and Chan	0.0009	6.56	0.001	8.47	0.0011	8.76
Genetic	0.002	6.54	0.003	7.04	0.005	7.92
S.Annealing	0.004	6.54	0.005	7.46	0.004	7.91

Table 2. Results for LARGE DVE systems.

	Uniform distribution		Skewed distribution		Clustered distribution	
	Time (s.)	C_p	Time (s.)	C_p	Time (s.)	C_p
Lui and Chan	30.939	1637.04	32.176	3460.52	43.314	5903.80
Genetic	6.598	1779.76	14.593	2825.64	29.198	4905.93
S.Annealing	6.35	1707.62	13.789	262846	29.620	4697.61

very close to the obtained by an exhaustive search. The efficiency of proposed algorithms becomes important when the virtual world size increases to LARGE worlds. Execution times are significantly reduced for all the distributions of avatars and obtained solutions provide solutions where the load balancing and the amount of inter-server messages are improved.

These results have been obtained using a grid system composed of a network of PC-based computers. Nowadays, this grid system is installed at the University of Valencia. Although having a heterogeneous network, all the nodes satisfy some basic graphics requirements which are being Pentium IV processors with an nVidia graphic card.

5   Conclusions and Future Work

In this paper, a correlation between modern DVE architectures, based on network-server models, and the behavior of the last grid computing applications has been established. Because of the segmented information and all developed mechanisms to handle it, modern DVE perform as any other grid applications with a specific set of problems.

In this paper, a new method for solving the problem of efficient allocation of clients to servers of the DVE system is presented. This aspect is a key issue that allows to design scalable and cost-effective DVE systems. Instead of developing an ad-hoc technique for this NP-complete problem, as other research groups, two methods based on genetic algorithms and simulated annealing have been properly adapted and tuned to the problem specifications.

The experiments performed in the proof-of-concept system demonstrate that the proposed approaches obtain better quality solutions than the main reference in this topic for the same test patterns. Moreover, it achieves better scalability in large-scale DVE systems since it presents lower execution time as the virtual world sized is increased.

As future work, the development of an efficient parallelization of the proposed algorithm based on a master-slave scheme is planned. The obtained results in current research are currently being applied in the development of a collaborative driving simulator. In this system, future drivers will share a 3D virtual town where hundreds of drivers will be connected through a low bandwidth network such as the Internet.

References

1. D.B.Anderson, J.W.Barrus, J.H.Howard, "Building multi-user interactive multimedia environments at MERL", in *IEEE Multimedia*, 2(4), pp.77-82, Winter 1995.
2. P. Barham, T.Paul, "Exploiting Reality with Multicast Groups", in *IEEE Computer Graphics & Applications*, pp.38-45, September 1995.
3. H. Delmaire, J.A. Díaz, E. Fernández, and M. Ortega, "Comparing new heuristics for the pure integer capacitated plant location problem", Technical Report DR97/10, Department of Statistics and Operations Research, Universitat Politecnica de Catalunya, Spain, 1997.
4. R.Duda, P.Hart, D.Stork, "Pattern Classification", *Ed.Wiley Intescience, 2000*, pp. 567-580.
5. I. Foster and C.Kesselman, eds. "The Grid: Blueprint for a New Computing Infrastructure", *Mor-gan Kaufmann*, San Francisco, California. 1999.
6. I.Foster, C.Kesselman and S.Tuecke. "The Anatomy of the Grid: Enabling Scalable Virtual Organizations", *International Journal of Supercomputer Applications*, Vol. 15, No.3, 2001.
7. Randy L. Haupt, Sue Ellen Haupt, "Practical Genetic Algorithms", *Ed. Willey*, 1997.
8. P.V. Laarhoven and E. Aarts, "Simulated annealing: Theory and applications", *Reidel Publishers*, Dordrecht, Holland, 1987.
9. M. Lewis and J. Jacboson, "Game Engines in Scientific Research", in *Communications of the ACM*, Vol 45. No.1, January 2002.
10. John C.S. Lui, M.F.Chan and Oldfield K.Y, "Dynamic Partitioning for a Distributed Virtual Environment", *Department of Computer Science*, Chinese University of Hong Kong, 1998.
11. Jonh C.S. Lui and M.F. Chan, "An Efficient Partitioning Algorithm for Distributed Virtual Environment Systems", *IEEE Trans. Parallel and Distributed Systems*, Vol. 13, No.3, pp. 193-211. March 2002.
12. D.C.Miller and J.A. Thorpe, "SIMNET: The advent of simulator networking", in *Proceedings of the IEEE*, Vol. 83, No.8, pp. 1114-1123. August, 1995.
13. T. Nitta, K. Fujita and S. Cono, "An Application Of Distributed Virtual Environment To Foreign Language", in *Proceedings of FIE'2000. IEEE Education Society.* Kansas City, Missouri, October 2000.
14. J.M. Salles, Ricardo Galli, A. C. Almeida et al, "mWorld: A Multiuser 3D Virtual Environment", in *IEEE Computer Graphics*, Vol. 17, No. 2. March-April 1997.
15. S. Singhal and M. Zyda, *Networked Virtual Environments* (ACM Press, New York, 1999).
16. P.T.Tam,"Communication Cost Optimization and Analysis in Distributed Virtual Environment", *M. Phil second term paper, Technical report RM1026-TR98-0412*. Department of Computer Science & Engineering.The Chinese University of Hong Kong. 1998.

Interactive Distributed Data Access in a GRID Environment

D. Rodríguez, J. Marco, R. Marco, and C. Martínez-Rivero

Instituto de Física de Cantabria (CSIC-UC),
Avda. Los Castros s/n, 39005 Santander, Spain

Abstract. New interactive applications for the GRID environment will profit from the use of distributed computing techniques like the Message Passing Interface (MPI). The data these applications access should also be distributed for the sake of performance. We describe a method implemented in the European CrossGrid Project for enabling access to distributed data sources, for use in High Energy Physics and Meteorology data mining applications.

1 Introduction

GRID [1] technologies provide access to large shared computing resources distributed across different facilities. Interactive application like the ones included in the CrossGrid project profit from the use of distributed computing techniques like MPI [2]. For example, it has been shown that data mining applications, in particular the distributed training of a neural network, can speed up well with the number of computing nodes using MPI (see [3]).

The problem to be addressed in this paper is the access to the heterogeneous distributed data sources that these applications require. We describe the method implemented in the Task 1.3 of the European CrossGrid project [4].

We will consider the example of the data collected by the DELPHI [5] experiment at the LEP accelerator at CERN. For physics analysis, the information is prepared for a given channel. For this paper we have choose the search for the Higgs boson in the four jets channel (hqq).

2 Datasets and Catalogs

Datasets are the basic information units from a logical point of view. A Dataset contains data grouped by some characteristic features. These features should be meaningful for users, so they can choose between different Datasets for their jobs.

For example, for DELPHI data we define Datasets based in properties like: energy, processing, flavour... A Dataset can be composed of several files or be distributed along several databases. We will generically call these components of the Datasets subsets. Going back to the DELPHI example, for this prototype we will use our own Monte Carlo background sample generated as a set of files

F. Fernández Rivera et al. (Eds.): Across Grids 2003, LNCS 2970, pp. 190–197, 2004.

in a proprietary format, in this case PAW [6] ntuples, corresponding to a given coherent data taking period and processing version. In our example the data corresponds to the years 1999 and 2000, and the fourth processing (referred as *e1*). This collection of Datasets, that we will label as hqq-e1, contains several Datasets distinguished by the flavour and energy of the data. We have a total of 16 Datasets in the collection. Each of the Datasets we have used for this work contains between 20 and 200 ntuples.

We have defined and implemented a Datasets Catalog, as part of our future Metadata Catalog. The Datasets Catalog contains a list of the Datasets present in the system, and relates these Datasets with their subsets. These subsets are identified by a logical file name (*lfn*); which is a unique identifier. On a future step, these identifiers will be linked with the actual copies of the data by a Replica Catalog (see [7] and [8] for Grid Replica Management topics). Each copy of a subset is also uniquely identified by a physical file name (*pfn*). The Dataset Catalog also includes the Dataset metadata, i.e., the information that could be relevant for the users to make a decision on which Datasets their jobs will use.

Information modeling is the basic point when trying to access heterogeneous distributed data sources. In our case, an XML[1] model, compatible with the database structure, provides a good foundation to the variables description. We have this in XML Schema format in a web accessible repository for each Dataset. This completes our MetaData Catalog now, but in the future this information might also be moved to a relational database.

3 Distributed Data Access Services

Distributed data access and pre-processing proceeds in the High energy Physics (HEP) interactive analysis application design, through *Interactive Service DataBase servers, ISDB* (see [9]). Requests are expressed as XML documents, including the Dataset to access, the filter to be applied, and the description of the desired Resultset. This is returned in XML format if the requested data volume is small, otherwise as a handle to cache data or even a query handle for virtual data.

4 Data Sources

We are using two different kinds of data sources at the present time: PAW [6] files repositories and relational databases. In both cases the data correspond to the same Datasets: DELPHI background Monte Carlo simulated data of several energies.

In the first case, we have implemented for our prototype a service capable of executing simple queries on our PAW ntuples. The XML document containing the query is transformed by an XSL[2] transformation stylesheet in a script

---

[1] Extensible Markup Language.

[2] The Extensible Stylesheet Language.

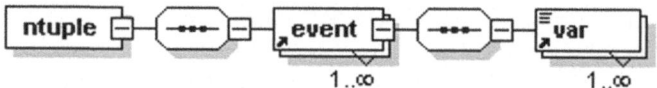

Fig. 1. Diagram of the XML Schema for the data input of the Artificial Neural Network Application.

containing the query parameters, and then used to perform a search for events matching the given criteria in the PAW ntuple. The query processing mechanism is a batch session of the PAW program fed by the previously generated script. The results are transformed back into XML format.

In the second case, we use a typical three-tier application approach for our prototype. The backend is a RDBMS, and the access to the data is done through several servlets ([10]) that translate the XML query to SQL, send it through JDBC to the RDBMS, and transform the Resultset back to XML format.

5   Prototype Implementation

Our prototype implementation is focused on serving data to our parallel ANN application (see [3]). So the output formats are such that can be directly read by that application, i.e., the produced XML complies with the XML Schema defined for the target application data sources. This XML Schema is shown in Fig. 1.

A PAW Data server has been developed as part of the project (see Fig. 2), while the IBM IDS[3] 9.20 is used for the O/R DBMS, following the scheme shown in Fig. 3. In both cases we use servlets as middleware to process and transform the XML queries to a format that can be understand by the respective program.

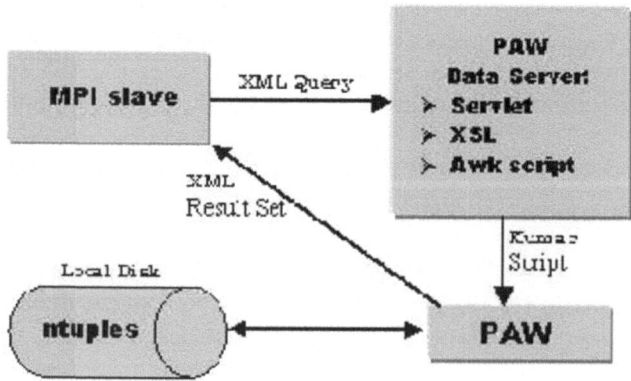

Fig. 2. Schema of PAW Data server.

---

[3] IBM Informix Dynamic Server.

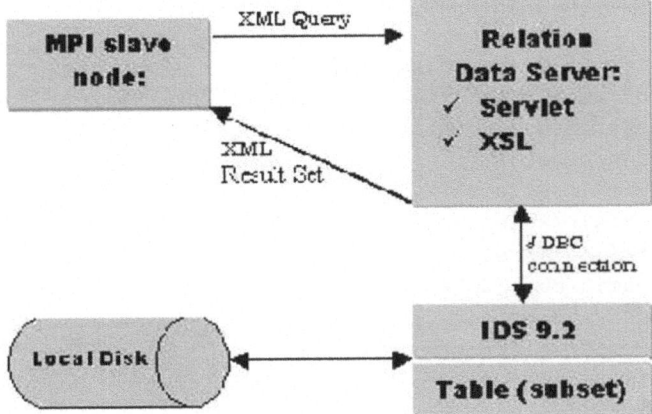

Fig. 3. Schema with a Relational Database as Data Source.

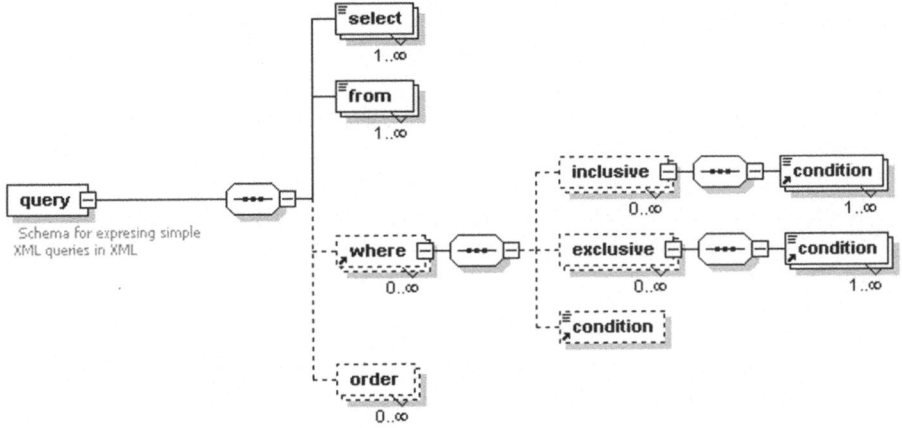

Fig. 4. Diagram of the XML Schema for the queries.

We have prepared a direct XML query format (see Fig. 4) such that we can process it for both the PAW ntuples and the RDBMS. This XML format is also used for the queries to the Dataset Catalog. The Dataset Catalog is also in a IBM IDS 9.20 server. It has two tables (Dataset and Ntuple), and a view (Catalog) which is a join of the two tables. The XML queries are parsed by a servlet that then makes a JDBC connection to the DBMS and returns the list of ntuples, i.e., their logical file names, in an XML document.

We also have several XSL stylesheets to transform these XML queries into a format that can be understand by the data source, i.e., SQL in the case of the RDB and in a "kumac" script in the PAW case.

For example, the following query in XML format:

```
<?xml version="1.0" encoding="UTF-8"?>
<query xmlns:xsi="http://www.w3.org/2001/XMLSchema-instance"
xsi:noNamespaceSchemaLocation="query.xsd">
 <select>y34</select>
 <select>hfx(2)</select>
 <select>hfx(4)</select>
 <select>thr(1,4)</select>
 <select>xeamin/80.</select>
 <select>aqcd</select>
 <select>piww4</select>
 <select>piww5</select>
 <select>pizz4</select>
 <select>pizz5</select>
 <select>xdijm/80.</select>
 <select>xe1e4/100.</select>
 <select>pbeq4(1)/8.+0.5</select>
 <select>pbeq4(2)/8.+0.5</select>
 <select>pbeq4(3)/8.+0.5</select>
 <select>pbeq4(4)/8.+0.5</select>
 <from>hqqana128_wphact20cc_e206.5_m80.4_lia0_1l_u1</from>
 <where>
  <inclusive>
   <condition field="Y34" type="bigger">0.003</condition>
   <condition field="xh2h4" type="smaller">0.9</condition>
  </inclusive>
 </where>
</query>
```

will be translated into the following SQL query:

```
SELECT y34, hfx_2, hfx_4, thr_1_4, xeamin/80, aqcd,
piww4, piww5, pizz4, pizz5, xdijm/80, xe1e4/100,
pbeq4_1/8+0.5, pbeq4_2/8+0.5, pbeq4_3/8+0.5, pbeq4_4/8+0.5,
FROM hqqana128_wphact20cc_e206.5_m80.4_lia0_1l_u1
WHERE Y34>0.003 AND xh2h4<0.9;
```

or into the following "kumac" script in the PAW case:

```
exe chain_ww208
cut $5 Y34>0.003.and.xh2h4<0.9
output = 0.
*
 1d 100 ' ' 10 -1 2
 n/pro 100 //ww/1000.xnn $5
 ini = $HINFO(100,'ENTRIES')
```

```
sh awk -f varlis2.awk queryvars >! genxml.f
n/loop  //ww/1000 $5.and.genxml.f([ini],[output])>1
*
```

A file with the list of the selected variables "queryvars" is also generated in the PAW case.

The distributed application itself uses the MPICH [11] MPI implementation: the request on a Dataset is translated into a set of n sub-requests corresponding to the n subsets of the selected Dataset; these are processed by n nodes, each one addressing a data server. The actual data servers are selected with the help of the *Replica Catalog*. A data server translates the query from its XML description into a suitable native form, which is processed. The query result is transformed back into an XML Resultset.

The *Interactive Service Database server* machine acts as MPI master, broadcasting the XML query in string format to n slave nodes, who then make this request explicit to a data server, that can be physically resident in the same hardware resource or not, depending on the optimization proposed by the *Replica Catalog* and the *Data Access Optimization* service.

In order to use the Globus authorization mechanism we have compiled MPICH with the Globus libraries, this grid enabled version of MPICH is called MPICH-G2.

6   Preliminary Results

The first results presented correspond to the test in a local cluster environment (see [12]). The data used corresponds to a HEP application: the distributed training of a Neural Network in the Higgs Boson search at LEP. The Dataset "*DELPHI-hqq-00-e*" including all relevant variables for the four-jet channel analysis, amounts to about 64 GB in its native form: PAW ntuples. They have been also transformed and stored in O/RDBMS, IBM-Informix Dynamic Server 2000 for comparative purposes.

All the Datasets have been stripped across 20 cluster nodes (each one being an IBM X220 server dual PIII-1.26 GHz processor with 640 MB RAM and 36 GB SCSI and 60 GB IDE disks). The query applied is a simple filter, reducing from near 1M events to about 300K, and the Resultset includes 16 variables, later used in the training of the Neural Network with 16-10-10-1 architecture. A PAW Data server has been developed, while the IDS 9.3 is used for the O/R DBMS.

Using the PAW based server we have send a query to get from the *ww208* Dataset with a total of 944101 events divided in 189 ntuples. We filter the Dataset to get the events with *xh2h4* smaller than 0.9 and *Y34* greater than 0.003, and choose 16 variables to get their values returned: y34, hfx(2), hfx(4), thr(1,4), xeamin/80, aqcd, piww4, piww5, pizz4, pizz5, xdijm/80, xe1e4/100, pbeq4(1)/8+0.5, pbeq4(2)/8+0.5, pbeq4(3)/8+0.5, pbeq4(4)/8+0.5. As you can see, some of them are derived quantities, and have to be calculated before returning the result.

The filter applied returns 323358 events (around one third part of the total) in an XML file. The time consumed with the data stripped as told before is 39 seconds.

To compare with we put the complete ww208 Dataset in another machine of the cluster. The time needed for the same operation was 184 seconds.

Note that processing time alone for the complete Dataset in one machine, i.e., the time needed to process the "kumac", previously generated, with PAW, is 166 seconds. So the actual speedup factor has not been evaluated yet.

7   Conclusions

We have developed a PAW data server that accepts queries in an XML format, and produces a Resultset file also in XML. The middleware needed to access both this PAW data server and the RDBMS has been developed using Java servlets and XSL stylesheets. We have also developed a client MPI application. The master consults the Datasets Catalog and the slaves access the data servers. The tests made up to now show a time reduction of a factor near 5. Anyway, we will need further tests.

8   Future Plans

We will complete the Metadata catalog, inserting in a database the XML Schema information about the Datasets. We will also study the compatibility of our solution with the software developed by DataGrid WP2 for Metadata management, namely Spitfire [13]. The plain servlets are planned to be converted into web applications.

The main objective, anyway, is to integrate this software with the ANN application of the CrossGrid WP 1.3 (High Energy Physics), and with the SOM application of the CrossGrid WP 1.4 (Meteorology).

Acknowledgements

This work has been mainly supported by the European project CrossGrid (IST-2001-32243).

References

1. I. Foster and C. Kesselman, editors. *The Grid: Blueprint for a Future Computing Infraestucture.* Morgan Kaufmann Publishers, 1999.
2. MPI standard. http://www-unix.mcs.anl.gov/mpi/standard.html
3. O. Ponce et al. *Training of Neural Networks: Interactive Possibilities in a Distributed Framework.* In D. Kranzlmüller et al. (Eds.) 9th European PVM/MPI, Springer-Verlag, LNCS Vol. 2474, pp. 33-40, Linz, Austria, September 29-October 2, 2002.

4. CrossGrid European Project (IST-2001-32243). http://www.eu-crossgrid.org
5. DELPHI collaboration. http://delphiwww.cern.ch/
6. Physics Analysis Worstation. http://paw.web.cern.ch/paw/
7. B. Allcock et al. Secure, Efficient Data Transport and Replica Management for High-Performance Data-Intensive Computing. Mass Storage Conference, 2001.
8. H. Stockinger et al. File and Object Replication in Data Grids. Journal of Cluster Computing, 5(3)305-314,2002.
9. CrossGrid Deliverable D1.3.1 *Application description, including use cases, for Task 1.3.*
10. Java Servlet Technology http://java.sun.com/products/servlet/
11. MPICH. http://www-unix.mcs.anl.gov/mpi/mpich
12. Santander GRID Wall. http://grid.ifca.unican.es/sgw
13. Spitfire. European Data Grid Project, WP 2. http://spitfire.web.cern.ch/Spitfire/

Dynamic Grid Catalog Information Service

Giovanni Aloisio, Euro Blasi, Massimo Cafaro, Italo Epicoco,
Sandro Fiore, and Maria Mirto

CACT/ISUFI, University of Lecce, 73100 Italy
{giovanni.aloisio,euro.blasi,massimo.cafaro,italo.epicoco,
sandro.fiore,maria.mirto}@unile.it

Abstract. Infomation is one of the main resources of a grid environment. Discovering and monitoring resources are challenging problems
due to the dynamic behaviour, geographic distribution and heterogeneity
of the grid resources. So, Information Services are fundamental in a grid
infrastructure and in this paper we present an information service based
on the relational data model. We propose a complementary approach to
the existing Globus Monitoring and Discovery Service based on LDAP.
We also describe the design of our DGC information service highlighting
its extensibility, flexibility, security, scalability and efficiency.

1 Introduction

Computational grids are heterogeneous, dynamic and distributed environments
that enable large-scale sharing of resources within groups of individuals and/or
institutions. A grid environment collects a lot of information, and information
itself is a critical resource in computational grids so it is necessary to manage
it properly. A fundamental element in a grid infrastructure is the Information
Service that provides some basic mechanisms for discovering and monitoring
distributed resources.

In the Globus Toolkit, a well known grid middleware that has been used
in many grid projects, the Monitoring and Discovery Service (MDS) [1],[2],[3]
provides directory services for grids. It allows managing static and dynamic information about the status of a computational grid and all its components and it
is based on the Lightweight Directory Access Protocol (LDAP) [4]. In particular,
many grid projects have been providing extensions to the MDS; we recall here
as an example the GridLab project [5] in which the CACT/ISUFI is involved
as the lead partner for WP10 that aims to provide far more advanced Grid information services [6] than those already existing, and a set of generic APIs for
accessing and publishing information to and from many different sources, including resource brokers, portals, workstations, mobile devices, etc. Another good
example is the DataGrid project [7], that implemented information providers for
the GLUE schema [8].

In this paper we propose a Dynamic Grid Catalog Information Service (DGC),
a complementary approach based on the relational data model [9].

The paper is organized as follows. Section 2 recalls differences between LDAP
and the Relational Data Model, Section 3 presents the challenges for our DGC

F. Fernández Rivera et al. (Eds.): Across Grids 2003, LNCS 2970, pp. 198–205, 2004.

Information Service. Section 4 describes the Infrastructure of the system we envision and finally Section 5 introduces possible scenarios in which we can integrate our DGC Information Service.

2   Differences between LDAP and the Relational Data Model

Flexible, secure and coordinated resource sharing between Virtual Organizations [10], requires the availability of an information rich environment to support resource discovery, decision making processes and to satisfy users. The Globus Toolkit exploits these functionalities through a LDAP directory structure. LDAP is a standard data model that, through an extensible directory access protocol, defines a method for accessing and updating information in a directory. A directory is often described as database, but it is actually a specialized database with features that set it apart from general purpose relational databases. Indeed, while directories are designed for information retrieval rather than for storing and updating information (they are meant to store relatively static information), a relational database needs to support applications with *high update volumes* (e.g., airline reservation and banking).

As pointed out by GGF Relational GIS Working Group [11],[12] and previous works [13],[14],[15] a key difference is that directories may not support *transaction*. These are all-or-nothing operations (atomic) that must be completed in total or not at all.

Another important difference between a directory and a general-purpose database is in the way information can be accessed. The directory service query language is both limited and restricted because it is essentially a *procedural* language, not a *declarative* one. This forces the user to know in advance explicitly the tree structure. Most databases support a standardized, very powerful access method called *Structured Query Language* (SQL). SQL allows *complex updates* and queries involving *joins* and including support for *data streams* as relations, through the SQL queries over data streams functionality.

Yet another difference between LDAP and the relational model is the possibility for the relational approach to store *historical information* related to a grid resource (e.g. CPU load in the last five days) in order to:

1. make statistics;
2. monitoring;
3. forecasting.

3   Challenges for the DGC Information Service

To design a good grid Information Service architecture there are many issues that must be taken into account and solved. We present them as follows talking about our proposed solutions:

- *Centralized/Decentralized approaches*: a centralized approach is very easy to manage but it introduces a lot of inherent problems such as:
  1) performance: indeed if many resources deliver their data to a unique centralized information server there is a performance bottleneck;
  2) scalability: when the number of client grows this centralized approach does not scale;
  3) fault tolerance: when the centralized server is not active the whole system temporarily can not work.
  A decentralized approach is difficult to manage but it is more reliable than the previous one.
- *Heterogeneity*: a grid environment often is highly heterogeneous so this element introduces additional complexity. We solve it designing a cross-platform or platform independent Grid Information Service.
- *Security*: in a distributed environment security is an extremely complex and multi-faceted problem. In order to address robust authentication and communication protection requirements, we adopt the Globus Security Infrastructure (GSI) protocols [16]. Resource owners must be able to control which principals can access the resources and under what conditions (authorization requirement and access policies).
- *Distributed Search*: in a distributed search the target of the queries is the grid. In a grid environment a lot of information can be published, so it is very important to retrieve these information and to combine them to infer new knowledge quickly.
  A White Pages search must also be provided, since the users usually want to know all/some information related to a specified resource. Obviously in this case the target of the queries is not the grid but a single resource.

4   Infrastructure of the DGC Information Service

In our infrastructure every Virtual Organization has one or more Global DGC relational information service (GDGC) where all grid resources can deliver their own data (dynamic collections related to individuals, institutions and computational resources). Every resource also store these informations in a Local DGC relational information service (LDGC). So a GDGC provides a means of combining arbitrary LDGC services in order to provide a coherent system image that can be explored or searched by grid applications.

GDGCs are then connected among them, in a connected graph, in order to:

1. promote flexible, secure and coordinated resource information sharing;
2. support information discovery and decision making processes.

Figure 1 depicts the structure of the DGC Information Service that we envision.

A LDGC can answer queries coming from other systems on the grid asking for information about a local machine; this service is called a White Page service. But it can also be configured to register itself with aggregate LDGCs such as a GDGC, providing a Yellow Page service.

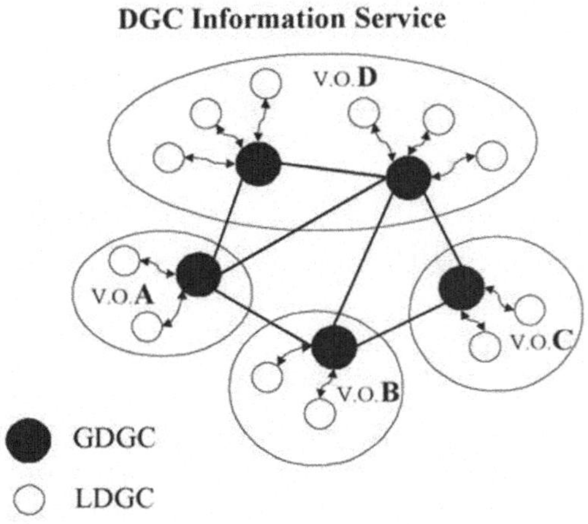

DGC Information Service

Fig. 1. DGC Information Service.

In our implementation we will design the following protocols:

1. local-global DGC Protocol in order to allow flexible and secure exchange of information between local and global DGC;
2. inquiry protocol in order to get information from LDGC;
3. global-global DGC Protocol in order to allow fast, reliable and secure distributed query among Global DGC Information Service.

In the first case the protocol is based on a mix of sinchronous push and asinchronous pull models. Sinchronous push is used when a local resource delivers its own data to a GDGC (e.g., every 5 minutes). On the contrary, asinchronous pull is used when a GDGC wants to recover data related to a specific resource (information recovery) or a client makes a request for certain information and the cache has expired (expired data). So a GDGC provides a caching service very similar to a web search engine. XML is used as a standard language for data transport.

In the second case the protocol is designed for inquirying a LDGC Relational Information Service. SQL is the standard language used for queries submitted to a DGC Information Service.

In the third case the protocol is designed for distributed query on the DGC Information Service, in particular for querying a GDGC Relational Information Service.

In order to avoid cycles, every query will be unambigously identified by a *Unique Query Identifier* (UQI). The UQI is composed by two parts separated by a @.

For instance, a generic UQI can be represented as follows:

IPADDRess@SerialHostIDentifier (IPADDR@SHID)

The first field (IPADDR) represents the IP address of the GDGC from which the query is generated. The second (SHID) is a serial number associated to the query. For instance the third query generated by the host *gandalf.unile.it* (193.204.78.207) will have the following UQI:

193.204.78.207@3

What happens when a query get across the DGC Information Service?
We can identify two cases:
1. node X generates the query
2. node X receives a query coming from node Y

In the former case, node X sends the query to all neighbours (that is, all nodes that are directly connected with X), then it keeps track of this operation storing (in its local UQI queue) the UQI and IP address of the neighbours that received the query. All neighbours that received the query store (in their local UQI queue), the UQI and the IP address of node X (in this way, they keep track of all incoming queries).

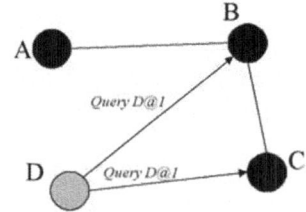

Local UQI Queues			
A	*B*	*C*	*D*
Host - UQI	*Host - UQI*	*Host - UQI*	*Host - UQI*
	D D@1	D D@1	B D@1
			C D@1

Fig. 2. Global-Global DGC Protocol: Case 1.

For instance, referring to Figure 2, node D sends the query with UQI equal to D@1 to nodes B and C.

In the latter case when node X receives an incoming query from node Y with a certain UQI, it controls immediately if all pairs (UQI,neighbour) are present (or not) in its local UQI queue.

We identify 2 sub-cases:
a) at least one pair (UQI,neighbour) exists that is not present in the local UQI queue;

b) all pairs (UQI,neighbour) are in the local UQI queue

In sub-case *a* the query is forwarded to all neighbours such that the pair (UQI, neighbour) is not present in the local UQI queue. After this operation the local UQI queue will be updated with this new entry.

In subcase *b* the query is discarded.

For instance, continuing the previous example (referring to Figure 3) after B receives from D the query with UQI equal to D@1, it forwards the query to A and C (sub-case *a*).

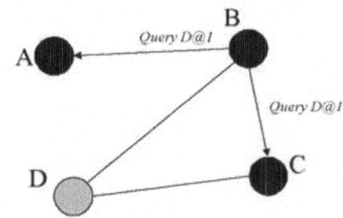

Local UQI Queues			
A	*B*	*C*	*D*
Host - UQI	Host - UQI	Host - UQI	Host - UQI
B D@1	D D@1	D D@1	B D@1
	C D@1	B D@1	C D@1

Fig. 3. Global-Global DGC Protocol: Case 2.

A and C update their local UQI queues with the new entry (B,D@1) but C discards the query (sub-case *b*) because all pairs (UQI, neighbor) are already available in its local UQI queue. Thus, we grant the entire coverage of the graph (obviously the graph must be connected). Once every GDGC receives the query, only the nodes that have a query result will answer directly to the node that originated the query (in our case nodes A, B, C answer directly to node D if they have a query result).

In order to avoid flooding, the protocol will also provide dynamic mechanisms that suspend temporarily links from which only duplicate queries come, but this feature is beyond the scope of this paper.

Finally, security is a fundamental requirement of our system .The security mechanism used in our DGC Information Service is the GSI, which enables the use of X509v3 certificates in order to provide authentication and authorization services (the proposed protocol grants secure mutual autentication among GDGC nodes).

5   Scenarios

The design of the GDC Information Service can support several scenarios.
Among the most important and relevant ones:

· automatic grid user profile discovery;
· resource grid discovery;
· application grid discovery.

In the first scenario any user can automatically obtain her grid user profile just
submitting a query to a DGC Information Service. For instance, this kind of
search can be particularly useful in Grid Portal applications because it allows
discovering all of the resources related to a certain user.

The second scenario occurs frequently and it is related to the need to discover
all of the resources that satisfy specific criteria.

The DGC Information service stores a lot of information such as architecture
type, operating system, network bandwidth and latency, memory (Ram and
Swap, free, used, total), active processes and so on, describing the structure and
the state of the grid so that any user can ask for instance:

· how many processors are available now?
· what are the resources with lowest CPU usage?
· where are the resources with required architecture, installed software, total
  ram, etc?

and she can both locate and determine the features of resources.
The third scenario can be very useful in order to discover:

· if an application related to some keywords exists;
· where are located some specific applications;
· what version of a particular application is installed on the grid resources.

It would be very useful to have a Grid Application Engine Search in order to
discover information related to the previous points via the web.

6   Conclusions

Due to dynamic behaviour, geographic distribution and heterogeneity of the
resources, information is a critical element in a grid environment. In this paper
we presented our DGC Information service architecture.

Our approach is based on a relational information service. It can be viewed as
a complementary approach designed according to the standards emerging from
Global Grid Forum working groups. We introduced the two main entities LDGC
and GDGC (Local and Global DGC Information Service) and the main protocols
that we envision.

Moreover, the DGC information service meets important requirements such
as security, extensibility, robustness and flexibility, in order to achieve better
results in terms of performance, scalability, decentralized maintenance etc.

Finally we also proposed three possible scenarios related to our information
service: automatic grid user profile discovery, resource grid discovery and application grid discovery.

References

1. Monitoring Discovery Service. http://www.globus.org/mds/
2. The Globus Project. http://www.globus.org
3. Aloisio, G., Cafaro, M., Epicoco, I., Fiore, S.: Analysis of the Globus Toolkit Grid Information Service. Technical Report GridLab-10-D.1-0001-1.0, 2002. http://www.gridlab.org/Resources/Deliverables/D10.1.pdf
4. Johner, H., Brown, L., Hinner, F., Reis, W., Westman, J.: Understanding LDAP. http://www.redbooks.ibm.com/pubs/pdfs/redbooks/sg244986.pdf
5. GridLab Project. http://www.gridlab.org/
6. Aloisio, G., Cafaro, M., Epicoco, I., Lezzi, D., Mirto, M., Mocavero, S.: The Design and Implementation of the GridLab Information Service. To appear in Proceedings of The Second International Workshop on Grid and Cooperative Computing (GCC 2003), 7-10 December 2003, Shanghai (China), Lecture Notes in Computer Science, Springer-Verlag, 2003
7. Data Grid Project. http://eu-datagrid.web.cern.ch/eu-datagrid/
8. The Glue Schema. http://www.cnaf.infn.it/~sergio/datatag/glue/index.htm
9. Eric K. Clemons. Principles of Database Design, Vol 1. Prentice Hall, 1985.
10. Foster, I., Kesselman, C., Tuecke, S.: The anatomy of the grid: Enabling scalable virtual organizations. International Journal of Supercomputer Applications, 2001.
11. Relational Grid Information Services (RGIS-RG). http://www.gridforum.org/1_GIS/RDIS.htm
12. Grid Forum. Information Systems and Performance area. http://www.gridforum.org/
13. Dinda, P., Plale, B.: A unified relational approach to grid information services. Technical Report GWD-GIS-012-1,GGF, 2001. http://www.cs.northwestern.edu/~urgis/gis012.pdf
14. Plale, B., Dinda, P., Von Laszewski, G.: Key Concepts and Services of a Grid Information Service. Proceedings of the 15th International Conference on Parallel and Distributed Computing Systems (PDCS 2002)
15. Hoschek, W., McCance, G.: Grid Enabled Relational Database Middleware, Informational Draft, 2001. http://www.cs.northwestern.edu/~pdinda/relational-gis/hoschek_mccance_ggf3.pdf
16. Tuecke, S.: Grid Security Infrastructure (GSI) Roadmap. Internet Draft 2001. www.gridforum.org/security/ggf1_2001-03/drafts/draft-ggf-gsi-roadmap-02.pdf

Network Performance Measurements as Part of Feasibility Studies on Moving an ATLAS Event Filter to Off-Site Institutes

Krzysztof Korcyl[1], Razvan Beuran[2,3], Bob Dobinson[2], Mihail Ivanovici[2,3],
Marcia Losada Maia[2,4], Catalin Meirosu[2,3], and Grzegorz Sladowski[5]

[1] Institute of Nuclear Physics, Radzikowskiego 152, 31-342 Krakow, Poland
Krzysztof.Korcyl@ifj.edu.pl
[2] CERN - European Laboratory for Nuclear Research
CH- 1211 Geneve 23, Switzerland
{Razvan.Beuran,Bob.Dobinson,Mihail.Ivanovici,Marcia.Losada.Maia,
Catalin.Meirosu}@cern.ch
[3] "Politehnica" University of Bucureşti, Faculty of Electronics and
Telecommunications, B-dul Iuliu Maniu 1-3, sector 6, Bucureşti, România
[4] Federal University of Rio de Janeiro, Cidade Universitaria, Rio de Janeiro, Brazil
[5] Cracow University of Technology, Warszawska 24, 31-155 Krakow, Poland
gregs@plusnet.pl

Abstract. In this paper we present a system for measuring network performance as part of the feasibility studies for locating the ATLAS third level trigger, the Event Filter (EF), in remote locations[1]. Part of the processing power required to run the EF algorithms, the current estimate is 2000 state off the art processors, can be provided in remote, CERN-affiliated institutes, if a suitable network connection between CERN and the remote site could be achieved. The system is composed of two PCs equipped with GPS systems, CERN-designed clock cards and Alteon Gigabit programmable network interface cards. In the first set of measurements we plan to quantify connection in terms of end-to-end latency, throughput, jitter and packet loss. This will be followed by running streaming tests and study throughput, IP QoS, routing testing and traffic shaping. Finally, we plan to install the event filter software in a remote location and feed it with data from test beams at CERN. Each of these tests should be preformed with the test traffic treated in the network on the "best effort" basis and also when the traffic is sent via a 'dedicated' channel. The description of the system initially deployed in CERN-Geneva/Switzerland and Cracow/Poland is followed by results from the first measurements.

[1] Work supported in part by the grants of the European Union IST-2001-32243 and the Polish State Committee for Scientific research, SPUB nr 620/E-77/SPUB-M/CERN/P-03/DZ/295/2000-2002 and SPUB-M nr 620/E-77/SPB/5.PR UE/DZ 465/2002-2004.

F. Fernández Rivera et al. (Eds.): Across Grids 2003, LNCS 2970, pp. 206–213, 2004.

1   Introduction

ATLAS is one of four experiments planned at the Large Hadron Collider at CERN from 2007 onward. The primary proton-proton interaction rate will reach 10^9 interactions per second, this has to be reduced by seven orders of magnitude prior to data recording. To achieve such a reduction a three-level trigger system is being designed. The first, fully synchronous with the LHC collider reduces the initial rate of 10^9 interactions per second to 100 kHz. The second level, asynchronous, based on farms of commodity processors, executes sequences of trigger algorithms on selected data from the detector's buffers and reduces the rate of accepted events by an additional two orders of magnitude. Events classified as interesting by the second level trigger are sent to the Event Builder (EB), where the detector data scattered over thousands of buffers are combined together. The event data aggregated in the EB are sent to the third level trigger - the Event Filter (EF) - where the simplified off-line reconstruction algorithms, running on farms of processors, will reduce further the trigger rate by another order of magnitude. The final 100 Hz rate of events with average size of 2 MB/event will be sent to permanent storage. The task of the EB is to decouple further processing from detector buffer's occupancy. It alleviates requirements for event processing latency. The events do not need to be processed fast, however they need to be processed with the same rate as they arrive: 2 kHz. With an optimistic assumption of 1 second processing time, this requires access to at least 2000 processors.

A large processing farm will be built at CERN, where the experiment will take place, however using distributed resources would reduce the necessary local investments. Such option could be considered as there will be substantial computing power installed in many national centers for off-line analysis. Some of these resources should become accessible via the Grid technology - the Crossgrid project investigates this possibility.

To use home based computing equipment efficiently will require very high performance networking at an affordable price. Assuming an average event size of 2 MB moving half of the EF events to the remote sites will require 2 GB/s bandwidth. The GEANT network (Gigabit European Academic Network) and it's successors will be good candidates to carry such traffic. We need to estimate the impact on event latency of moving the Event Filter to remote locations and on the performance of the whole trigger system.

We plan to make measurements to investigate asymmetry in the QoS parameters of the network in both directions. The routes may not be the same but also the traffic competing for services may experience more congestion in one direction than in the other. We plan to measure the one-way latency (as opposed to taking a half of the Round Trip Time (RTT)), packet loss and packets reordering. The assessment of the asymmetry in the QoS parameters is important for our feasibility studies because the Event Filter traffic is highly asymmetric with the bulk of data sent from CERN to outside institutes.

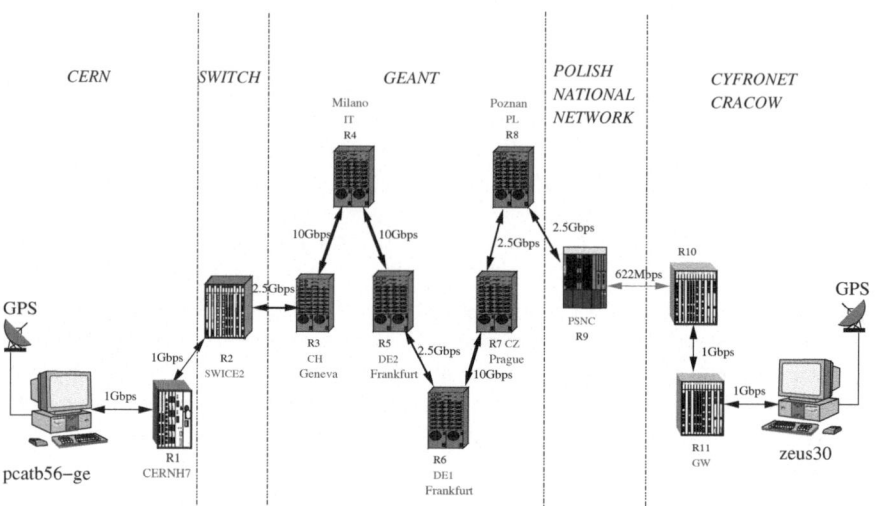

Fig. 1. Network path between CERN-Geneva-Switzerland and Cyfronet-Cracow-Poland.

2 Setup for Measurements

The setup to perform the network performance measurements is presented in Fig.1. Currently the system is installed at CERN-Geneva and in Cyfronet-Cracow. The system is composed of two PCs equipped with GPS systems [1], CERN-designed clock cards and Gigabit Ethernet Alteon programmable network interface cards [2]. The GPS system is used to synchronize time between the two PCs located more than 1000 km apart. The clock card is used to produce precise time stamps used to tag packets traversing the network. The programmable NIC is used to generate traffic according to traffic pattern descriptors as well as receive the time tagged packets and to make an on-line computation of latency and packet loss and throughput.

GPS System and Clock Cards. The usual way to measure network latency and avoid synchronization problems between two nodes is to measure the Round Trip Time (RTT) of packets sent from one node and returned back by a partner node. The network latency is assumed to be half of the RTT value on assumption that the time from sender and receiver and from receiver back to sender contribute equally to the RTT. This may not be true for two nodes separated by more than 1000 km and connected to the Internet.

To overcome problems with synchronization of geographically separated nodes we use a Global Positioning System (GPS) to provide a universal time reference. The GPS signal is freely available everywhere on Earth and a GPS receiver unit that has enough satellites in view, is able to give the Coordinated Universal Time (UTC) with accuracy in order of 100 ns. We are using off-the-shelf GPS receivers with the satellite signal received via exterior aerials and connected to the PCI bus of the computer. Each GPS card produces two output signals: 10 MHz clock and the PPS (Pulse-Per-Second) issued at every change of the UTC second with accuracy of 250 ns. These two signals are used by the CERN-designed clock card. The 10 MHz clock is multiplied on the clock card by 4 and used to update an internal counter. The 1 Hz PPS signal is used to reset the counter to a known value at each occurrence of the PPS signal (40 * 10^6 is added to the value of the counter at the previous PPS). Thus the clock synchronization system is based on two key points: the ability to reset counter at the same time (common start of the counters) and the ability to count exactly at the same rate (keep the counters synchronized). In this way the time difference between two synchronized systems is negligible (less than 500 ns) even after several days of running. This synchronization was verified for 2 systems on CERN site seeing the same satellites.

Programmable NIC. The Alteon programmable network interface card gives us the possibility to create a flexible network traffic generator and measurement tool. We have developed a set of software routines together with a GUI [3], [4] which we use to prepare descriptor files with traffic pattern we want to apply to the network.

Prior to starting any tests, each card receives a traffic description table containing the full IP and Ethernet headers of the packets to be generated, the size of the Ethernet packets and the time between two consecutively sent packets. We thus have full control over all the fields in the IP and Ethernet headers (including Type of Service at the IP level and Priority from the VLAN field of the Ethernet packet). TCP and UDP were not implemented due to the increased overhead associated with these protocols. UDP requires the computation of a control sum on the data being transmitted and this would be too expensive for the processor on-board the NIC. The TCP requires the maintaining of a full history (sliding window) of packets being transmitted and received and the on-board memory is limited to 1MB. Also, TCP would be too computationally intensive to achieve Gigabit speed with the current on-board processors. Our traffic generator generates streaming traffic at the raw IP level. The content of the packets can be considered as being random.

The outgoing packets are time stamped with time values synchronized to the clock card. The NIC communicates with the clock card 128 times per second over the PCI to get its current value of the time. These readings are used to adjust the NIC's on-board counter which is used to mark outgoing packets. The packets are also marked with sequence numbers to allow packet loss calculation and out-of-order packet detection.

The NIC receiving traffic from the network keeps synchronization with its associated clock card. The on-board counter is used to calculate the latency of incoming packets. The on-board processor builds a real time latency distribution. The histogram is transferred to the PC's host processor after the completion of the tests. This avoids sending individual packets to the host processor.

3   Measurements

For our tests we use the existing network infra-structure with two exceptions (see Fig.1). The PC at CERN has been attached directly to the CERN router connected to SWITCH (bypassing the CERN internal network). The PC in Cyfronet has been attached to the router connected to the Polish national network (bypassing the Cracow metropolitan network). The tests were performed with the test traffic treated in the network on "best effort" basis and also when the traffic was sent via an allocated channel of 100 Mbps on the Polish network (between Poznan and Cracow). In the tests aimed at latency and packet loss measurements we transmitted IP packets generated by the Alteon cards between the two test sites. The payload used in these tests varied between 48 and 1500 bytes. The traffic pattern was with either constant bit rate (CBR) or having Poisson inter-packet time distribution.

The list of network QoS parameters we measure is presented below:

- one-way average latency
- jitter
- packet loss
- average throughput
- latency histogram
- inter packet arrival time histograms
- IP packets re-ordering detection and quantification

4   Results

A summary of the results from our measurements is presented in Table 1.

Table 1. Comparison of the network QoS parameters between the two directions.

	CERN to Cracow	Cracow to CERN
with allocated channel	average latency almost constant zero packet loss (for loads smaller than 90 Mbps)	higher fluctuations in average latency small packet loss (greater for 64 bytes) (for loads smaller than 90 Mbps)
"best effort"	average latency almost constant very small packet loss (for all rates)	not reproducible

The measurements allowed us to observe the asymmetry in the network from the point of view of QoS parameters. The routes from CERN to Cracow and back pass through the same routers, but the transfer latency fluctuates more and the packet loss is higher in the direction from Cracow to CERN. This asymmetry is visible in the measurements with test traffic treated by the network on "best effort" basis, as well as in the tests with the dedicated 100 Mbps channel. We do not present quantitative results for test traffic sent from Cracow to CERN

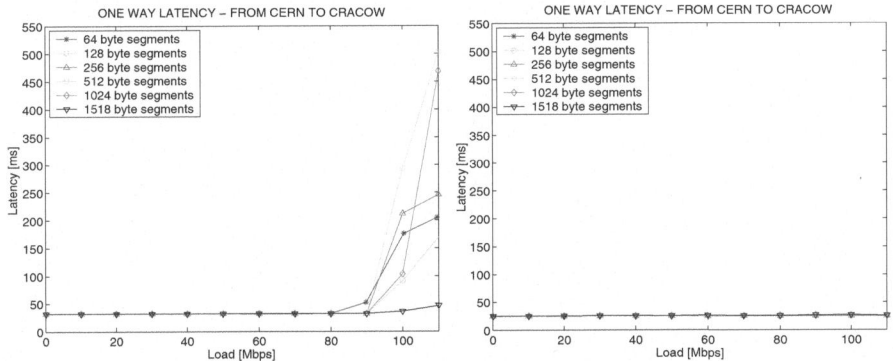

Fig. 2. Average latency as a function of load for packets transmitted from CERN to Cracow. The plot on the left shows results from measurements collected with the test traffic sent over the 100 Mbps allocated channel; the plot on the right is for traffic treated in the network on "best effort" basis.

on "best effort" basis as they were not reproducible. During our tests there was no IP packet re-ordering detected.

The plots with average latency as a function of load for the traffic sent from CERN to Cracow in the "best effort" case and with the dedicated channel are presented in Fig. 2. The transfer latency for the "best effort" case is almost constant. The latency plot for the case with the dedicated channel shows that when approaching the 100 Mbps limit, the latency increases. A similar degradation in performance when approaching the 100 Mbps limit is observed for the packet loss as a function of load, see Fig. 3 (packet loss is expressed as a percentage of the amount of sent traffic). The rate of lost packets is zero up to 80 Mbps even for the smallest packets, but reaching the allocation limit causes a large increase of the number of lost packets. According to the channel allocation contract, any load in excess of the 100 Mbps limit should be dropped. However, we observe a much more severe degradation, close to 100% of the sent traffic, which it hasn't been yet explained. The traffic sent from CERN to Cracow shows very small packet loss in the entire range of loads we used.

The transfer latency and the packet loss plots for traffic sent from Cracow to CERN with the dedicated channel are presented in Fig. 4. The average latency plot shows higher fluctuations comparing with the average latency of packets sent in the opposite direction. Packet loss is small, except for the case of 64 byte packets, when the loss increases for loads larger than 50 Mbps. Note that, even with the allocated channel, we were observing packet loss for the traffic sent from Cracow to CERN. However, there was no loss for the traffic sent in the opposite direction.

Following network evaluation in terms of QoS parameters, we began tests with a higher level communication protocol: TCP/IP. The tests were performed under the Linux operating system, with default values for the TCP/IP parameters. The preliminary results are summarized in Table 2.

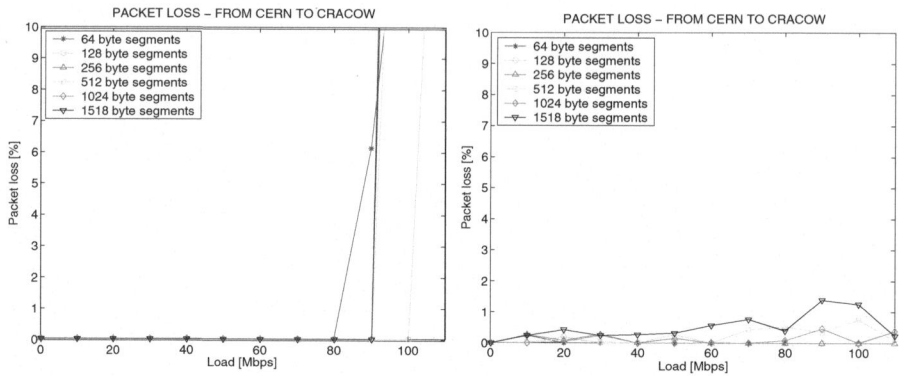

Fig. 3. Packet loss as a function of load for packets transmitted from CERN to Cracow. The plot on the left shows results from measurements collected with the test traffic sent over the 100 Mbps allocated channel; the plot on the right is for traffic treated in the network on "best effort" basis.

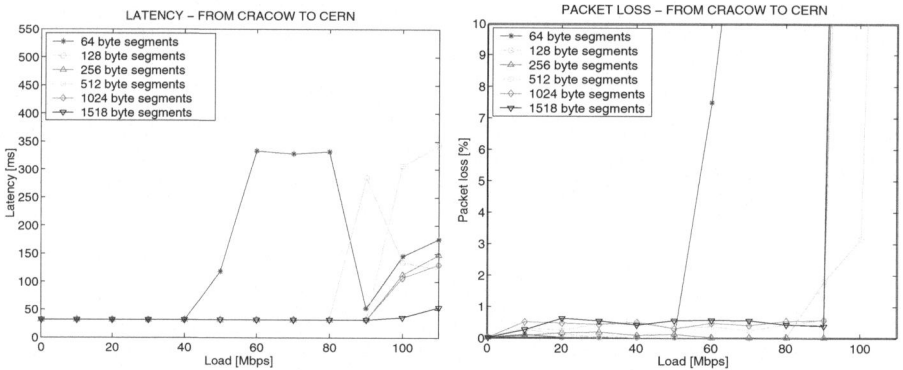

Fig. 4. The plot on the left shows results from the latency measurements as a function of load with the test traffic sent over the 100 Mbps allocated channel from Cracow to CERN. The plot on the right shows packet loss ratio as a function of load for traffic sent over the 100 Mbps allocated channel from Cracow to CERN.

Table 2. Streaming tests with default TCP/IP parameters: 1 Gbyte of data was transferred from CERN to Cracow using a custom application.

	with allocated channel	without allocated channel
average transfer duration	579.66 s	567.18 s
std. dev. of the test duration	12.34 s	28.37 s
average transfer rate	13.8 Mbps	14.1 Mbps

One can notice a larger transfer duration and a smaller transfer rate in the case when an allocated channel is used. This can be attributed to the additional processing time needed for the routers to perform the selection of priviledged packets and counting whether the amount of prioritized traffic doesn't exceed the allocated limit. Note however that the standard deviation of the results is smaller when the channel is allocated. Basically this means that using an allocated channel guarantees certain bounds for the transfer time and rate, whereas not having an allocated channel implies a large variation of these transfer parameters depending on the global network load at that moment.

5   Conclusions

The first set of tests showed the importance of measuring one-way packet behavior as a function of load. We are in the process of obtaining detailed information on the network architecture in order to improve our understanding of the results.

We plan to continue streaming tests in both directions and tune the TCP/IP parameters to make better use of the allocated bandwidth. In the next step we will install the Event Filter software in Cracow and send real, experimental data from CERN to Cracow for processing. In parallel we will install similar systems in several other institutes. Measurements between CERN and the Niels Bohr Institute in Copenhagen will commence shortly.

References

1. GPS167PCI GPS Clock User's manual / Meinberg Funkuhren
2. Alteon WebSystems, Tigon/PCI Ethernet Controller rev 1.4, Aug 1997. Available: www.alteonwebsystems.com
3. "Testing and Modeling Ethernet Switches and Networks for use in ATLAS High-Level Triggers";
   Dobinson, R W; Haas, S; Korcyl K; Le Vine, M J; Lokier, J; Martin, B; Meirosu, C; Saka, F; Vella, K;
   in: IEEE Trans Nucl Sci.: 48 (2001) no. 3 pt. 1 pp607-12
4. "Testing Ethernet networks for the ATLAS data collection system";
   Barnes, F R M; Beuran, R; Dobinson, R W; Le Vine, M J; Martin, B; Lokier, J; Meirosu, C
   in: IEEE Trans Nucl. Sci.: 49 (2002) no. 1 pp.516-20

A Flexible Multi-level
Grid Monitoring Architecture

Gábor Gombás and Zoltán Balaton

MTA SZTAKI Computer and Automation Research Institute
P.O. Box 63., H-1518 Hungary
{gombasg,balaton}@sztaki.hu

Abstract. As part of the GridLab project we have designed and implemented a flexible grid monitoring system that can be used to monitor grid entities like jobs and resources. In addition to basic information retrieval found in many other monitoring systems our design also offers advanced features: persistent connections, guaranteed data delivery for critical data and support for actuators that influence the state of either the monitored entity or the monitoring system itself. The multi-level layout of the various components makes it possible to generate compound metrics from raw measurements, create arbitrary routing networks or get over firewalls.

1 Introduction

Grids [2] are complex systems and therefore, monitoring is essential for understanding their operation, debugging, failure detection and for performance optimisation. Monitoring must be able to provide information about the current state of various grid entities, such as resources and running jobs, as well as to provide notification when certain events (e.g., system failures, performance problems, etc.) occur.

Grids are very large-scale and diverse systems so gathering all information in a central location is out of question, only a distributed solution can be considered. Monitoring also has to be specific, i.e., only data that is actually needed has to be collected. It is also important that data should only be sent where it is needed and only when requested.

The amount of required information can change over time: for example, if a problem is suspected in a service, the granularity of debugging information has to be increased while such level of information is not needed when the service is operating normally. This requires the ability to dynamically modify the range and granularity of monitored information which in turn might require interaction with the monitored entity (job, service, hardware element, etc.) itself.

Storing data is not the task of the monitoring system. Thus, in most cases if the consumer fails to process some data due to a software or hardware failure, the information may be lost. There are cases however (e.g., critical event notifications) when this behaviour is not acceptable, so support for guaranteed delivery of information is also needed.

F. Fernández Rivera et al. (Eds.): Across Grids 2003, LNCS 2970, pp. 214–221, 2004.

Some applications are interested in getting a high volume of raw data they intend to process themselves. Other applications are only interested in preprocessed (converted, filtered, averaged, summed etc.) data. Both needs can be satisfied by building multi-level monitoring systems. Higher levels can collect information from lower levels and can process it before forwarding it to the consumer.

A monitoring architecture with all the above capabilities is designed and implemented as part of the GridLab project [4]. This flexible monitoring system is described in the following sections.

2   Architecture

The architecture of the monitoring system is based on the Grid Monitoring Architecture (GMA, [9]) proposed by the Global Grid Forum (GGF). The input of the monitoring system consists of measurements generated by *sensors*. Measurements taken by sensors are gathered by *producers* that transfer this data to *consumers* when requested. Producers allow consumers to either access measurements via queries or to subscribe to them.

Sensors implement the measurement of one or more measurable quantities called *metrics*. Every metric is defined by a unique name, a list of formal parameters and a data type. The entity to be monitored is determined by providing actual values for the formal parameters. A metric can be either event-like meaning an external event is needed to produce a measurement, or continuously measurable meaning that a measurement is possible whenever a consumer asks for it. Continuously measurable metrics can be made event-like by requesting automatic periodic measurement however.

In addition to the features described in the GMA proposal, *actuators* (similar to actuators in [8] or manipulation services in [6]) are also part of the monitoring system. Actuators implement *controls* that represent interactions with either the monitored entities or the monitoring system itself. Just like metrics a control has a unique name, a list of formal parameters and a data type. In contrast to metrics that can generate multiple results, controls are always single-shot, i.e., every invocation of a control produces exactly one result.

Definitions of metrics and controls can be retrieved by two means: either asking the producer or consulting a registry (like a local file or a grid information system).

2.1   Resource Monitoring

As a grid consists of several layers, the monitoring system should also have multiple levels. Figure 1 shows resource monitoring.

A grid resource consists of one or more nodes. A Local Monitor (LM) service is running on each node and collects information about the processes (P) running on the node as well as the node itself. The collected information is then sent to a Main Monitor (MM) service. The MM is the access point for local users (mainly site administrators and non-grid users).

A grid is a heterogeneous environment so different grid resources (or even different nodes of the same resource) may provide different kinds of information. In order to be able to interpret and analyse data from different sources, the raw data should be converted to some well-defined form. This conversion is done at the Monitoring Service (MS). The MS takes raw data from the MM and converts it to *grid metrics* that are independent of the physical characteristics of the resource itself. Also the MS is the place to enforce grid security rules and map them to local rules.

The MS is also the entity that can interact with other local monitoring systems. If a site uses a different monitoring system (like Ganglia [7] or Nagios [3]), a conversion sensor can be created that extracts data from the local monitoring system and makes it available to grid users through the MS.

The LM – MM – MS triplet demonstrates how *multi-level* monitoring systems can be built using compound producer–consumer entities described in [9]. Every level acts as a consumer for the lower level and as a producer for the higher level. This multi-level architecture allows easy introduction of complex compound metrics. Service discovery is also easier since consumers only need to know where the MS is without knowing the machines (local monitors) behind it. This technique can be extended to create arbitrary routing networks. For example, one can implement a single concentrator element for jobs that run on multiple resources. This way information about the job can be requested at one well-known point, even if the job is constantly moving from one resource to another.

Another good example for using multiple levels when there is no direct network connection (e.g., because of a firewall) between the consumer and a target host. In this case, a producer can be installed on a host that has connectivity with both sides and this producer can act as a proxy between the consumer and the target host. Using proper authentication and authorisation policies at this proxy this setup is more secure and more manageable than simply opening the firewall. In the generic LM – MM – MS resource monitoring setup mentioned above, both the MM or the MS can play the role of the proxy depending on the actual configuration.

2.2   Job Monitoring

Monitoring of jobs is a complicated task and requires interoperation between the monitoring system and other grid services. First, it requires a grid service (called Submitter in Fig. 1) that keeps track where the job is actually running. Next, the grid jobmanager and the Local Resource Management System (LRMS) has to provide a mapping between different job IDs (process ID, local job ID, grid job ID). The multi-level hierarchy of the monitoring system can be used to make this mapping transparent. When a grid user connects to the MS and requests monitoring of a grid job, the MS converts the grid job ID to a local job ID and passes it to the MM. The MM then converts the local job ID to host/process ID pair and passes it to the appropriate LM that takes the actual measurement.

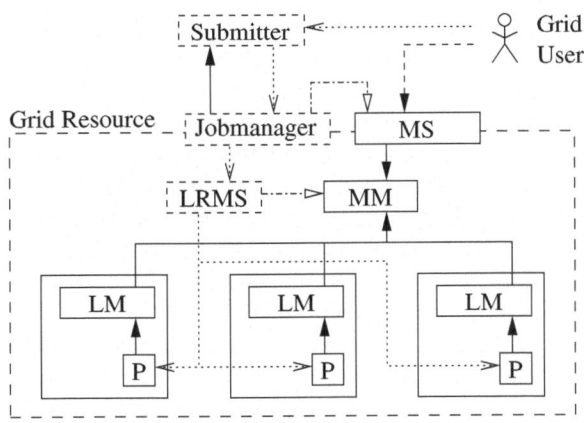

Fig. 1. Resource and job monitoring.

2.3   Consumer–Producer Interaction

Communication between consumers and producers takes place on channels. A channel is a logical connection which has at most one real network connection associated with it. Channels can be either consumer-initiated or producer-initiated, but producer-initiated channels must be explicitly requested previously by a consumer. Consumer-initiated channels are used mainly for interactive monitoring or control execution while producer-initiated channels are good for event reporting and data archiving. The two possible channel directions can also be used to help getting through firewalls.

A channel can be either regular or persistent. A regular channel is always associated with a network connection - if the connection is broken, the channel is destroyed. A persistent channel however can survive if the network connection is lost, and a new connection can be assigned to the same channel. This feature is useful for low-volume notification channels to avoid holding a network connection open unnecessarily when there is no traffic.

Channels are automatically destroyed when they are no longer referenced. Every metric instance (see below) associated with a channel counts as a reference. Since producer-initiated channels has to be explicitly defined by the consumer, the existence of the defining channel counts as a reference too.

Every channel has an identifier assigned by the producer, which is unique per authenticated user. The identifier 0 is reserved to mean the current channel.

After a channel has been established the consumer may send any number of commands to the producer. Every command has a consumer-assigned identifier that will be used by the producer in the response message. The consumer does not have to wait for the completion of the previous command before sending a new one. There is no logical limit for the maximum number of simultaneously running commands, however implementations are allowed to restrict it to some reasonable value.

As described in section 2, measurable quantities are represented by metrics. When a consumer requests some data, it provides a metric name and its actual parameters to the producer, which in turn creates a *metric instance* based on these parameters. Every metric instance is associated with one or more channels where it can send measurements to. Event-like metric instances send their data to every channel they are associated with while instances of continuous metrics generally only send data on the channel where the measurement was requested.

Data sent by the producer is represented by metric values. Every metric value contains the identifier of the metric instance it belongs to. There is a small number of predefined metric instances called "special metrics" which are always available. The first and most important special metric is the `CAPABILITIES` metric that is automatically sent by the producer on every newly created channel. This metric contains (among other things) the protocol version and the list of supported authentication methods.

The producer responds to every command with a message containing the command's identifier, a status code, and an optional identifier for further data. This response message must precede every other data that might be sent as an effect of the command. In the case of parallel commands it is not guaranteed that the order of response messages will match the order of the commands. Response messages are sent on the same channel where the original command was received.

A command might request the producer to send more data to the consumer. Such data can be sent at any time after the successful execution of the command has been reported. There is no limitation of the time period between the command response message and the actual sending of the data. If not explicitly stated otherwise, the producer is allowed not to send any data at all (e.g., event notifications when the watched event never happens). Consumers are advised to implement a timeout mechanism to avoid waiting forever.

2.4   Supported Operations

The following commands are defined between the consumer and the producer:

The *AUTH* command is used to authenticate the user to the monitoring system. It must be the first command issued by the consumer after a new channel has been established. If the AUTH command is successful, the identifier of the created channel will be returned in the command response message. If the authentication fails the channel will be destroyed after the error response has been sent. It is possible to use authentication mechanisms requiring multiple message exchanges; in this case the AUTH command should be issued multiple times. The AUTH command should not be used again after a successful authentication however. If the consumer wishes the producer to also authenticate itself, it should choose an authentication mechanism that supports mutual authentication.

The *COLLECT* command takes a metric name and parameters and instructs the monitoring system to create a new instance of the metric. The newly created metric instance is associated with the current channel. If the command is successful an identifier for the metric instance will be returned. This command in itself does not request any actual data to be sent.

The *STOP* command takes a metric identifier and a channel identifier and instructs the monitoring system that no more metric values for the metric instance should be sent to the specified channel. All metric values of this metric instance that were queued on this channel will be disposed. If the metric identifier is not associated with any other channel the STOP command also destroys the metric instance.

The *SUBSCRIBE* command associates a metric identifier with a channel (which might be different from the one the command was sent on) and instructs the monitoring system that subsequent measurements should automatically be sent to the consumer. If the destination channel is not the current channel, any metric values already queued on the current channel will also be sent to the destination channel.

The *BUFFER* command associates a metric identifier with a channel and instructs the monitoring system that subsequent measurements should be queued. This is the default behaviour of newly created metric instances after a successful COLLECT command. It is possible that the same metric identifier is BUFFERed on some channels while SUBSCRIBEd to others. Buffering large amounts of data in the monitoring system is not desirable as it can cause excessive resource usage and security concerns as well. Thus, the producer may implement limits on the amount of data that can be buffered. If such limits are exceeded information will be lost. It is not specified however that in this case the old information gets overwritten with the new one or the new information will be disposed.

The *GET* command takes a metric identifier and and a channel identifier and performs the following tasks:

- If there are metric values queued for the metric identifier on the destination channel, the monitoring system will send them to the consumer.
- For continuous metrics, a new measurement is requested from the appropriate sensor. When the measurement is completed, the measured metric value will be sent to the consumer on the destination channel. But, as mentioned in the previous section, there is no guarantee when it will happen.

It is possible for the consumer to use wildcard identifiers for either the metric identifier meaning every queued metric values should be sent, and/or for the channel identifier meaning information should be sent to every channel owned by the current user that the metric instance is associated with. These wildcards are useful for consumers that continuously poll the producer for new data.

The *QUERY* command is an optimisation for fast information retrieval. It is equivalent to issuing a COLLECT command with the same arguments, followed by a GET command for the returned metric identifier on the default channel, followed by a STOP command after the resulting data has been received. The QUERY command is only useful for continuously available metrics, it has no effect for event-like metrics.

The *DEF_CHANNEL* command creates a producer-initiated channel. The command takes a destination URL, an authentication method and credentials specific to the requested authentication method.

When the producer opens the actual network connection to the address specified in the DEF_CHANNEL command, it advertises only the single authentication method specified in the command's argument. When the consumer issues the AUTH command, the producer's responses are based on the credentials specified in the DEF_CHANNEL command.

The *SET_CHANNEL* takes a destination channel identifier and reassigns the current network connection to the destination channel while destroying the current channel. The destination channel then becomes the current channel. If the destination channel already had an open network connection, it will be closed.

The *CLOSE_CHANNEL* command destroys a channel. Any metric values that were queued on the channel are disposed. Any metric instances that are not associated with other channels will be destroyed.

The *CONTROL* command takes a control name and parameters and executes the control. The command response contains an identifier for the control's result. The result has the same format as a metric value.

The *COMMIT* command is used by the consumer to notify the producer that it has successfully processed a metric value. This command is used to implement *guaranteed data delivery*. Generally if either the producer or the consumer terminates, queued but not yet processed data will be lost. By executing a control the consumer can request guaranteed delivery for a metric instance. In this case every metric value sent by the producer is tagged with a unique identifier. After receiving and processing the data the consumer must issue the COMMIT command with this unique identifier to notify the monitoring system that the data has safely arrived and therefore can be removed from the producer's buffer.

Sometimes the sensor itself has to know when the data it produced has safely arrived to the consumer. This is needed when the sensor has to forward the acknowledgement to some external entity it gathered the data from. For example, in multi-level setups a sensor at a middle level has to forward the acknowledgement to the lower levels. The producer provides two models for notifying the sensor. In the weak model, the sensor is notified about success when at least one consumer acknowledged the data whereas, the strong model requires acknowledgement from every affected consumers.

Handling of guaranteed data delivery is expensive as it consumes resources of the producer. Therefore the producer might impose resource limits of the number of transactions being active at any given time. If a metric instance produces data exceeding this limit the sensor implementing that metric instance will immediately notified as if the data transfer had been failed.

2.5   Protocol Encoding

The monitoring system prototype implements the protocol encoding as a dynamically loadable module, so it is possible to define multiple encodings. Currently there exists a binary encoding (see [5] for details).

3   Implementation

An alpha version with the basic features implemented was released to the Grid-Lab [4] community in August 2002, and the first official prototype is released in January 2003 for the general public. The prototype contains the implementation of the producer and consumer API, implementation of the LM and the MM. It also contains example sensors for host monitoring and GRM [1] application instrumentation, and several test clients. The current development version (to be released by the end of 2003) contains generic support for actuators and supports secure authentication and detailed access control. It also implements some application-related actuators.

Acknowledgements

This work was sponsored by the European Commission under contract number IST-2001-32133, the Hungarian Scientific Research Fund (OTKA) under grant number T042459 and the Research and Development Division of the Hungarian Ministry of Education under contract number OMFB-01549/2001.

References

1. Z. Balaton, P. Kacsuk, N. Podhorszki, F. Vajda: From Cluster monitoring to Grid Monitoring Based on GRM. Parallel Processing: proceedings / Euro-Par 2001.
2. I. Foster and C. Kesselman, editors: The Grid: Blueprint for a Future Computing Infrastructure, 1999.
3. E. Galstad et al.: Nagios.
   http://www.nagios.org
4. The GridLab Project.
   http://www.gridlab.org
5. GridLab Deliverable D11.4: Extended Architecture Specification.
   http://www.gridlab.org/Resources/Deliverables/D11.4.pdf
6. T. Ludwig, R. Wismüller: OMIS 2.0 – A Universal Interface for Monitoring Systems. Proceedings of the 4th European PVM/MPI Users' Group Meeting, Crakow, Poland, November 1997.
7. M. Massie et al.: Ganglia cluster monitoring toolkit.
   http://ganglia.sourceforge.net
8. R. Ribler, J. Vetter, H. Simitci, D. Reed: Autopilot: Adaptive Control of Distributed Applications. Proceedings of the 7th IEEE Symposium on High-Performance Distributed Computing, Chicago, July 1998.
9. B. Tierney, R. Aydt, D. Gunter, W. Smith, M. Swany, V. Taylor, R. Wolski: A Grid Monitoring Architecture.
   http://www.gridforum.org/Documents/GFD/GFD-I.7.pdf

Automatic Services Discovery, Monitoring and Visualization of Grid Environments: The MapCenter Approach

Franck Bonnassieux[1], Robert Harakaly[1], and Pascale Primet[2]

[1] CNRS UREC
ENS-Lyon 46, Allee d'Italie
69364 LYON Cedex 07, France
{Franck.Bonnassieux,Robert.Harakaly}@ens-lyon.fr
[2] LIP RESO
ENS-Lyon, France
Pascale.Primet@ens-lyon.fr

Abstract. The complexity of grid environments is growing as more projects and applications appear in this quick-evolving domain. Widespread applications are distributed over thousands of computing elements, various communities of users are aggregated into virtual organizations so resources availability is more and more dynamic and final locations of jobs cannot be foreseen. In such contexts, new paradigms and constraints which deeply impact monitoring and visualization possibilities must be addressed. As nodes and even sites appear and disappear quickly in grids, automated resource and service discovery must be performed and launched at a frequency compatible with the dynamic of grid elements. The numerous production sites involved in a grid have their own security policies and system administration principles and procedures, which can eventually be outsourced. A global grid monitoring system must be efficient and not intrusive with respect to security policies and should not interfere with site local rules like logging and auditing. In addition, to nodes and sites the large number of applications and virtual organizations generates multiple, different, abstract views of the grid environments. A grid visualization tool has to be opened and flexible to represent all corresponding virtual views needed. The tool MapCenter has been designed to cope with these new grid monitoring challenges

1 Introduction

Grid middleware and applications are designed to run over a huge number of heterogonous systems, spread in large, different computer centres across several countries. As more grid projects enter into production modes, specification, development, integration and deployment of monitoring tools are more and more complexes.

F. Fernández Rivera et al. (Eds.): Across Grids 2003, LNCS 2970, pp. 222–229, 2004.
© Springer-Verlag Berlin Heidelberg 2004

An adequate grid monitoring system has to fulfil the following paradigms:

- **transparency:** each grid site follows its own security policies and rules. A grid monitoring system must be non intrusive and should not require system administrators to open specific channels or ports. Above all, end systems must not be disrupted by monitoring.
- **dynamic:** grid resources are entering and leaving the grid very often. The grid monitoring system must perform automatic discovery of resources to follow grid daily evolutions
- **manageability:** A grid monitoring system should be easy to integrate and overall to deploy over a large number of sites and resources
- **scalability:** A grid monitoring system must be efficient in order to achieve high rate polling over thousands of grid elements
- **flexibility:** visualization techniques and presentation models must provide users and system administrators with all logical views and dashboards they need.

Most current monitoring architectures and systems (Nagios [4], Ganglia[5], MonaLisa [6], ...) require the deployment of agents on all sites and often on all end nodes, which is very difficult to achieve in the context of large grid systems.

The tool MapCenter has been designed to cope with these new grid monitoring challenges In order to obtain a manageable and really easy to deploy system, MapCenter performs all monitoring features from a central point, even if several MapCenter servers can be distributed for fault tolerance issue. No specific node or agent needs to be deployed on grid sites, and a complete MapCenter monitoring solution can be set up in a few hours.

Our approach has been to structure the architecture into three main layers:

- a **visualization layer**, based on a new presentation model,
- a **monitoring layer**, implemented by an efficient multi-threaded polling framework,
- an **independent resource discovery and modelling layer**, based on various back-ends.

The general MapCenter architecture and the open and flexible presentation model has been described in [7]. This model can match any logical approach of the grid computed from monitoring layers underneath. Logical and graphical views can be created to visualize all dashboards needed by end users (scientist, industrial, system administrator, organization manager ...). In parallel with status visualization features, MapCenter is designed to aggregate all available pieces of grid information and represent logical views to access it. Various grid information system technologies are available and several back-ends have been developed using PHP to grant access to end users. In particular a LDAP Browser and a SQL Query interface are available, and R-GMA [8] back-ends are also being developed. Many dashboards can be created using these back-ends, which enable users to access all kinds of grid information from central points without any knowledge of the collecting and storage technologies used underneath.

This paper emphasises specific monitoring techniques used to achieve more efficient and transparent grid services availability checking. It also underscores automatic discovery and modelling capabilities that allow quick deployement on lots of large scale grid environments and to keep numerous grid topologies and statuses up to date.

2   Advanced Monitoring Techniques

2.1   Transparent Services Checking

A key point for a grid monitoring framework is to use standard protocols to cope with heterogeneity and to keep real grid resources unaware of any polling, without any interfering side-effect on grid end systems.

More precisely all current daemon implementing services are using the socket interface to accept queries (TCP or UDP) from users or other services. Stealth TCP port checking [3] has been implemented to simulate such queries without waking up the daemon. This technique is often referred to as "half-open" check, because you don't open a full TCP connection. You send a SYN packet, as if you were going to open a real connection and wait for a response. A SYN/ACK indicates that the port is listening. A RST is indicative of a non-listener. If a SYN/ACK is received, you immediately send a RST to tear down. This technique decreases the number of packets exchanged and the processor load on the server, and overall remote services are not informed by the kernel of the port checking and hence do not generate unwanted entries in log files.

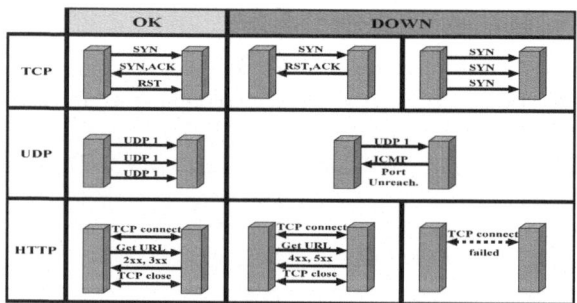

Fig. 1. Monitoring techniques.

UDP port checking capabilities have also been added to check specific grid UDP services. While UDP is simpler than TCP, checking it is actually significantly more difficult. This is because open ports don't have to send an acknowledgement in response to probing, and closed ports aren't even required to send an error packet. Fortunately, most hosts do send an ICMP PORT UNREACHABLE error when you send a packet to a closed UDP port. Thus you can find out if a port is not open, and adversely determine if a port is opened and if the corresponding service is running. Neither UDP packets, nor the ICMP errors are guaranteed to arrive, so retransmission of packets that appear to be lost has been implemented, and we consider that a port is opened after several UDP packet are sent without receiving any reply.

All these advanced monitoring techniques are summarized in figure 1. WWW URL checking has also been implemented by simulating an HTTP request on the URL. This technique is useful to check all grid WWW resources (web sites, repositories, directories, other monitoring info ...) and will be used to check future grid "web services" and OGSA [12] compliant implementations.

2.2 Multithreading and Timeouts

As our monitoring architecture is fully centralized, performance and efficiency of the monitoring layer is a key point. This layer relies on a multi-threaded scheduling architecture optimised for parallel checking of ICMP, TCP, UDP and HTTP services. Normal timeout for a TCP connection is three minutes, which is actually too long to check thousands of ports, even in parallel. In order to assure higher polling efficiency, timeouts of all types of sensors (ICMP, TCP, UDP, HTTP ...) must be tuned. Table 1 shows optimal timeouts and number of retries for all protocols concerning adequate balancing between performance and strong accuracy of results.

Table 1. Timeouts and retries per protocol.

Protocol	Timeout	Retry	Socket
ICMP	5	3	raw
TCP	5	3	raw
UDP	5	3	UDP
HTTP	10	1	TCP

3 Grid Resources Discovery

3.1 Discovery Back-End

To cope with the dynamicity of grids, automatic discovery and logical views creation are mandatory. Resources information is stored in various types of grid information systems and specific stubs must be developed for each of them (e.g. LDAP queries for Globus MDS [9], IBP client [10] for L-BONE [19] , or CGI scripts browsing for PlanetLab [18] ...). Resources discovery and modelling has been implemented and is widely used in MapCenter. Figure 2 presents the general design of the discovery mechanism: the generators use a specific stub to access the grid information system, and finally a data file is generated which contains all objects, symbols, maps and links. This data file also contains logical and graphical views that represent any abstract level of grid representation. Such a data file is then used by MapCenter daemon itself to perform the polling of all objects and the dynamic generation of all html pages.

As an example, a MapCenter site has been created for RLS [13], and logical views for replication services which show all dependencies existing between these elements are generated each day (which master copy can update which replica, which replica can be updated by which one, etc ...)

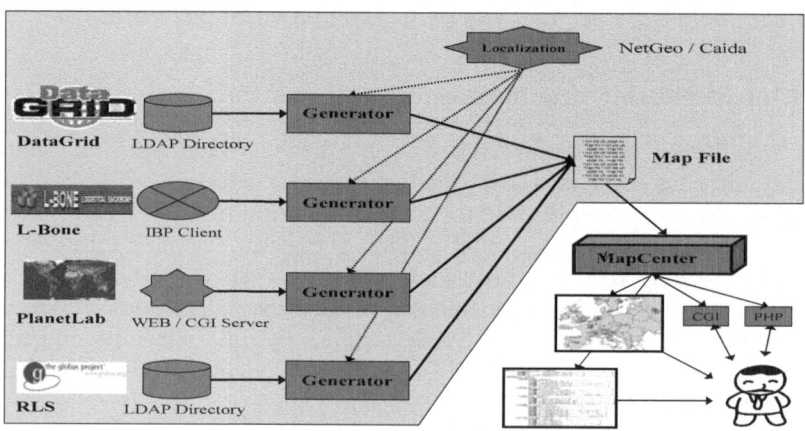

Fig. 2. Discovery Processings.

3.2 Localization Technique

Graphical maps are in general geographic maps with animated grid sites displayed (figure 3). This requires the physical location of each resource discovered. From an IP address or a DNS name, WHOIS databases can be queried and town name or airport code or at least state can be easily found. From this location name, latitude and longitude can be retrieved from geographic databases. In MapCenter discovery backends implementation, all objects discovered are geographically localized using NetGeo [11] tool from Caida. All physical locations are cached locally to achieve higher efficiency and to allow the MapCenter administrator to modify some physical locations, if NetGeo fails or gives erroneous results for some sites.

4   Experiments and Results

4.1   Deployment

MapCenter [14] is now used by several major grid environments: DataGrid [15], DataTag [16], CrossGrid [17], PlanetLab [18], L-Bone [19], RLS [13], and AtlasGrid [20]. Advanced automatic discovery feature is used on most of the grid projects monitored. Figure 3 gives an example of a graphical view of L-BONE USA grid sites, which are monitored in real-time and completely regenerated each night. Table 2 summarized numbers of objects maps and services checked by major MapCenter site deployed.

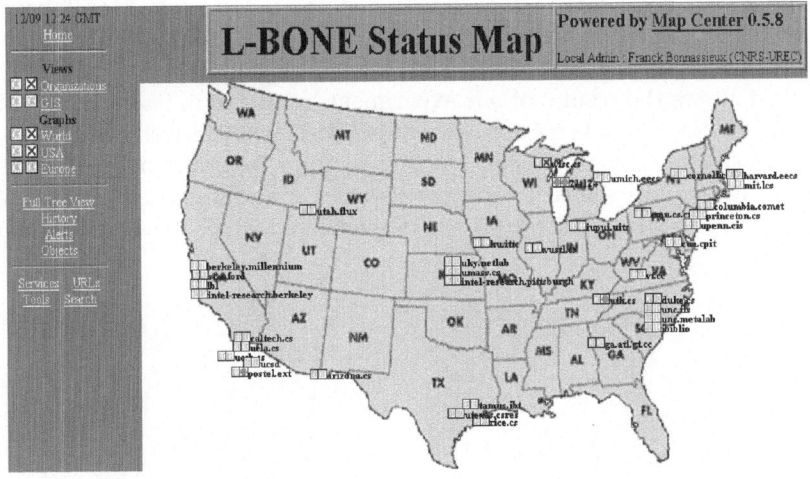

Fig. 3. Graphical view example: USA map for L-BONE.

Table 2. MapCenter sites deployed.

Project	Objects	Maps	Symbols	Links	ICMP	TCP	UDP	URL
DataGrid Static	189	126	235	135	182	428	14	46
DataGrid Dynamic	51	123	302	57	51	133	0	0
DataTAG	51	123	302	57	51	133	0	0
CrossGrid	39	48	46	38	39	111	0	18
PlanetLab	101	107	101	80	101	101	0	0
LBONE	136	154	136	114	136	134	0	0
RLS	105	190	105	135	105	125	0	0
AtlasGrid	19	25	19	28	12	40	0	0
e-Toile	8	9	8	0	8	10	0	0
GRIDIS	7	14	7	10	7	0	0	0
Total	**720**	**851**	**1024**	**643**	**706**	**1181**	**14**	**64**

4.2 Performance

On the performance side, the DataGrid static version is currently monitoring nearly 200 objects (computing or storage elements front-ends, each of them managing worker nodes farms), and the total time for polling various services running on all these objects is less than one minute.

To achieve enhanced performance tests, we have set up various data files containing one hundred objects that we have duplicated to represent up to 50 000 objects with more than 100 000 services (TCP, UDP and HTTP) running. At the moment of out stress tests, 10% of the objects were unreachable, 20% of TCP services and 30% of UDP and HTTP services were down. This situation obviously represents a very bad status which overloaded our monitoring. MapCenter has been installed on a small configuration: Pentium III 900 Mhz, with RAM 128 MB and Linux RedHat 6.2 Kernel 2.2.19.

Figure 4 shows the results of our experiment, with two different scales. With 500 parallel polling threads we were able to poll the 50 000 objects within 10 minutes. In principle, MapCenter is designed to monitor front end node of grid sites (head of farm manager, head to storage element...) and in such a context, even a very large world wide grid can be easily monitored which accurate frequency.

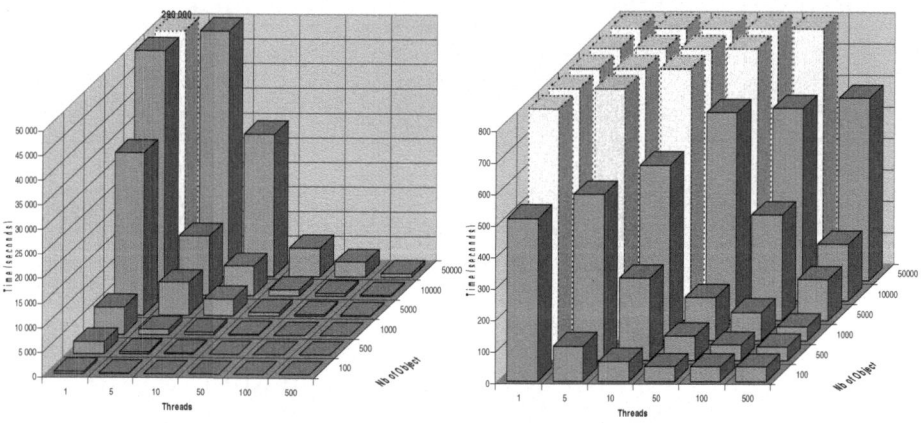

Fig. 4. Performances evaluation.

5   Conclusion

MapCenter does not contain all the advanced features of other monitoring tools like Nagios or Ganglia and is obviously not the ultimate solution for a system administrator in a Grid Operation Centre. MapCenter is more focussed on all potential end-users needs and its flexible presentation model is able to provide a huge variety of logical dashboards. The dynamic resource discovery mechanisms, the transparency of monitoring techniques and the efficiency of its internal engine has permitted us to deploy it very quickly on numerous large grid environments. Based on monitoring and discovery back-ends, MapCenter has been designed to be easily integrated with future technologies arising in grid community, and especially with OGSA [12]. New functionalities development and deployment on current and future grid environments will continue over the next few years.

References

1. Tierney, B., Aydt, R., Gunter, D., Smith, W., Taylor, V., Wolski, R., Swany, M.: "A Grid Monitoring Service Architecture" Global Grid Forum Performance Working Group, 2001.
2. Tierney, B., Crowley, B., Gunter, D., Holding, M., Lee, J., Thompson, M.: "A Monitoring Sensor Management System for Grid Environments" Proceedings of the IEEE High Performance Distributed Computing conference (HPDC-9), August 2000.
3. Fyodor: "The Art of Port Scanning" Phrack Magazine Volume 7, Issue 51 September 01, 1997, article 11 of 17
4. Nagios http://www.nagios.org/
5. Ganglia http://ganglia.sourceforge.net/
6. MONA LISA http://cil.cern.ch:8080/MONALISA/
7. Bonnassieux, F., Chanussot, F., Harakaly, R., Primet, P.: "MapCenter: An Open Grid Status Visualization Tool" PDCS Conference , Louiville, Kentucky 2002.
8. Fisher, W. S.: "Relational Model for Information and Monitoring" Grid Forum Informational Draft GWD-GP-7-1.
9. Czajkowski, K., Fitzgerald, S., Foster, I., Kesselman, C.: "Grid Information Services for Distributed Resource Sharing" Proceedings of the Tenth IEEE International Symposium on High-Performance Distributed Computing (HPDC-10), IEEE Press, August 2001.
10. Bassi, A., Beck, M., Moore, T. and Plank, J.: "The Logistical Backbone: Scalable Infrastructure for Global Data Grids" Asian Computing Science Conference 2002, Hanoi, Vietnam, December, 2002.
11. CAIDA NetGeo, the Internet Geographic Database http://www.caida.org/tools/utilities/netgeo/
12. Foster, I., Kesselman, C., Nick, J., Tuecke, S.: "The Physiology of the Grid: An Open Grid Services Architecture for Distributed Systems Integration" Open Grid Service Infrastructure WG, Global Grid Forum, June 22, 2002.
13. Chervenak, A., Deelman, E., Foster, I., Guy, L., Hoschek, W., Iamnitchi, A., Kesselman, C., Kunst, P., Ripeanu, M., Schwartzkopf, B., Stockinger, H., Stockinger, K., Tierney; B.: "Giggle: A Framework for Constructing Scalable Replica Location Services" Proceedings of Supercomputing 2002 (SC2002),November 2002.
14. MapCenter Web Site for DataGrid http://ccwp7.in2p3.fr/MapCenter
15. European DataGrid projet http://web.datagrid.cnr.it
16. DataTAG Project http://datatag.web.cern.ch/datatag
17. CrossGrid Project http://www.eu-crossgrid.org/
18. PlanetLab http://www.planet-lab.org/
19. Logistical Backbone http://loci.cs.utk.edu/lbone/
20. Atlas Grid http://atlas.web.cern.ch/Atlas/GROUPS/SOFTWARE/OO/grid/

Monitoring Grid Applications
with Grid-Enabled OMIS Monitor*

Bartosz Baliś[1,2], Marian Bubak[1,2], Włodzimierz Funika[1,2], Tomasz Szepieniec[2],
Roland Wismüller[3], and Marcin Radecki[2]

[1] Institute of Computer Science, AGH, al. Mickiewicza 30, 30-059 Kraków, Poland
{balis,bubak,funika}@uci.agh.edu.pl
phone: (+48 12) 617 39 64, fax: (+48 12) 633 80 54
[2] Academic Computer Centre – CYFRONET, Nawojki 11, 30-950 Kraków, Poland
{t.szepieniec,m.radecki}@cyf-kr.edu.pl
[3] LRR-TUM – Technische Universität München, D-80290 München, Germany
wismuell@in.tum.de
phone: (+49 89) 289-28243

Abstract. In this paper, we present our approach to monitoring Grid
applications with a Grid-enabled OMIS Monitor – the OCM-G. The
OCM-G is a monitoring infrastructure for tools supporting application
development, and it provides various monitoring services to obtain information about, manipulate, as well as detect events in an executing
application. The services are accessible via the standarized interface –
OMIS (On-line Monitoring Interface Specification). We describe the architecture of the system and present some design details important for
the monitoring system to fit well the Grid environment, and support
monitoring of interactive applications.

Keywords: Grid, monitoring, services, interactive applications, OMIS

1   Introduction

Monitoring services are indispensable part of each Grid environment. These services may be focused both on the Grid infrastructure and the activity of running
applications. In our view, these two different types of monitoring can be characterized as follows.

- *infrastructure monitoring* collects information about Grid components, such
  as hosts or network connections; this information is indispensable for basic
  Grid activities as resource allocation or load balancing; often this type of
  information has historic value, thus it is stored in a database for a later
  analysis (e.g., statistical, forecasting, etc.),
- *application monitoring* aims at observing a particular execution of an application; the collected data is useful for tools for application development

---

* This work was partly funded by the European Commission, Project IST-2001-32243,
CrossGrid [7]

F. Fernández Rivera et al. (Eds.): Across Grids 2003, LNCS 2970, pp. 230–239, 2004.
© Springer-Verlag Berlin Heidelberg 2004

support, which are used to detect bugs, bottlenecks or just visualize the application's behaviour; this kind of information in principle does not have historic value – it is meaningful only in the context of a particular execution.

A few efforts exist to address application monitoring in the Grid: GrADS / Autopilot, DataGrid / GRM, GridLab / GRM.

The Autopilot toolkit [17] in the GrADS project [10] is oriented towards automatic performance tuning based on behavior patterns. This is a view rather different than ours, since we are interested in providing feedback to the user who is intersted in a particular performance loss.

The application monitoring system developed within the GridLab project [1] implements on-line steering guided by performance prediction routines deriving results from low level, infrastructure-related sensors (CPU, network load). The system is different to ours in the following respects. First, the manipulations on the target application are not supported. Second, the system seems to rely only on full traces, at least at the current state of development. Finally, the predefined semantics of all metrics requires all Grid users to agree on this, which is rather restrictive [12].

The DataGrid project [8] introduces the GRM monitor [14]. The system collects information semi-on-line and delivers it to the R-GMA, a relational information infrastructure for the Grid [15]. Monitoring in GRM/PROVE is mainly based on event tracing. While the GRM/PROVE environment is well suited for the DataGrid project, where only batch processing is supported, it is less usable for the monitoring of interactive applications. First, due the high communication latency introduced by the R-GMA. Second, since it is not possible to achieve low latency and low intrusion at the same time when monitoring is based on trace data. If the traces are buffered, the latency increases, if not, the overhead for transmitting the events is too high.

In this paper, we describe the OCM-G – Grid-enabled OMIS Monitor, a versatile infrastructure for on-line application monitoring designed to support interactive applications.

2   Monitoring of (Interactive) Applications in the Grid

In Fig. 1, layers of a monitoring environment are presented. The bottom layer represents objects to be monitored, e.g., application processes, but also Grid infrastructure, e.g., CPU and network. In the top layer there are various tools, interactive, e.g. for performance analysis or debugging, as well as automatic, for example for automatic load balancing via process migration. Between tools and the monitored objects there is a monitoring infrastructure.

The Grid environemnt poses new requirements for an application monitoring infrastucture. Even more requirements are important when we consider interactive applications. Below we assemble a list of the most important requirements for a Grid application monitoring system, especially to support interactive applications.

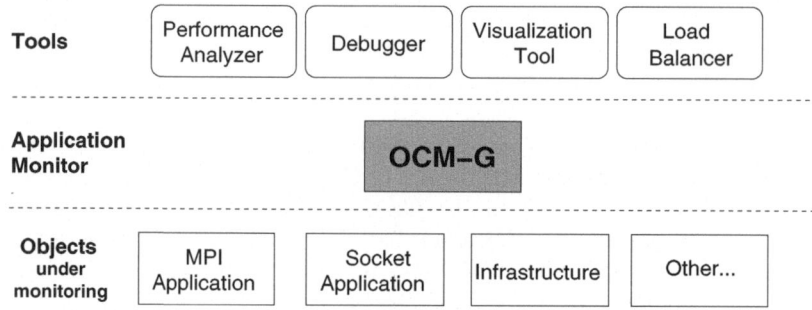

Fig. 1. Layered structure of application monitoring environment.

- **On-Line Mode.** On-line monitoring greatly reduces the data rate, since it allows to specify the information of interest at run-time. In contrast, in off-line monitoring, the measurements and corresponding monitoring information must be specified in advance. In addition, in case of tracing, the off-line approach involves huge trace files. Moreover, for some monitoring activities, such as manipulations (debuggers), on-line operation is essential. For interactive applications on-line monitoring is important for one more reason: the user wants to relate the performance to his interactions, i.e., immediately see the impact of his activities.
- **Efficiency and Scalability.** The Grid may be a highly distributed system, and the running applications may be composed of a large number of proceses spread across multiple sites. Consequently, the monitoring infrastructure should be designed to handle high data rates and scale to large number of monitored objects.
- **Low Intrusiveness.** Each monitoring activity introduces a probe effect which may distort the normal execution of the application. Especially in case of interactive applications, the overhead due to monitoring should be kept as low as possible so that, e.g., low latency is sustained.
- **Transparency for the User.** This requirement includes several aspects:
  - The user should not need to know the architecture or details of the operation of the monitoring system. All he is supposed to do is to send monitoring requests and collect replies.
  - The instrumentation of the code, essential e.g. for performance metrics, should be as much automatic as possible.
  - The compilation of the application to enable monitoring should be as easy as to add some additional parameters to the usual compilation command.
  - The submission of the application (via portal, script, etc.) should not change due to monitoring with the exception, perhaps, of additional command-line parameters.
  - Tools should be able to attach to an application and monitor it at any point of its execution.

- **Grid Service.** In a grid evironment, the application monitoring should be available as a kind of grid service. This means the monitoring system should run permanently, there should be a possiblity to discover it and request some monitoring services.
- **Security.** The monitoring system should ensure the desired level of security, i.e., user authentication and authorization, integrity and confidentiality of monitoring information (if desired), etc.

3   OMIS – A Universal Monitoring Interface

As an intermediate layer, the monitoring system has two interfaces: one towards the tools, the other one towards the running application. While the monitor/application interface is strongly system-dependant, since typically OS services are involved, the tool/monitor interface may be standardized. An example of such a standardized tool/monitor interface is OMIS (On-line Monitoring Interface Specification) [13].

The target system, from OMIS point of view, forms a hierarchy of objects. In the Grid these are *sites*, *nodes* and *processes*. The objects are uniquely identified by so called *tokens*.

OMIS defines a variety of monitoring services which are divided into three classes: *information* services – to obtain descriptive data about objects, *manipulation* services – to change objects' state, and *event* services – to detect events in the target system (especially inside applications). The information and manipulation services are also called *actions*.

By combining these services one obtains a *monitoring request* to perform some monitoring activities. The monitoring request can belong to one of two types: *unconditional* and *conditional*.

- The unconditional service requests are composed of one or more information and/or manipulation services (referred to as actions). They result in an immediate action in the target system, for example *stop process p*; in OMIS syntax: `thread_stop([p])`.
- The conditional service requests (CSR) are composed of an event service and a list of actions. Their semantics is as follows: whenever the event occurs, execute the actions, for example *whenever process p starts a new process, get information about that process*; in OMIS syntax:
  `thread_creates_proc([p]): proc_get_info([$newproc], 0x1)`.

4   Grid-Enabled OMIS Monitor – OCM-G

In this section, we present the OCM-G – a Grid-enabled application monitoring system based on OMIS. First we describe the architecture of the system, then we provide some design details. Finally, we outline the monitoring functionality provided by the OCM-G.

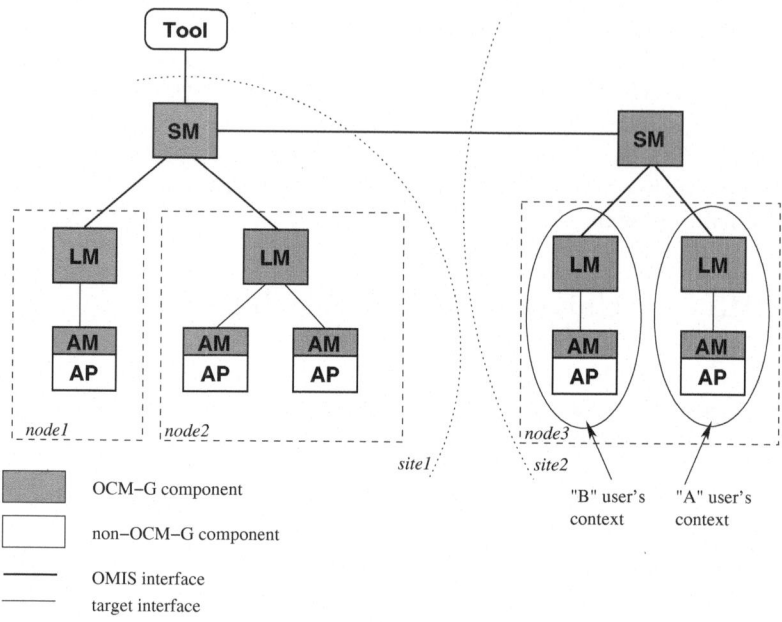

Fig. 2. OCM-G components distributed in a Grid environment.

4.1   Architecture

The OCM-G is a decentralized, distributed system, which is a collection of two types of components: *Service Managers* and *Local Monitors*.

Service Managers (SM) reside permanently, one on each site of the Grid. They are the part of the OCM-G which exposes the monitoring services to tools. Since the SMs are permanent they can be well known and thus the OCM-G can work as a Grid service. The SMs distribute OMIS requests to appropriate Local Monitors on the same site.

Local Monitors (LM) are created on each host of the Grid where there are application processes to be monitored. LMs execute OMIS requests accepted from SMs and send the results back. LMs handle only objects which are on the same host. Because of security issues we decided create on LM per each (host, grid user) pair.

Some parts of the monitoring system are also embedded in the application; these are referred to as Application Module (AM). The AM is necessary to perform monitoring activities in the context of the application, it is essential for reducing data rate (buffering of monitoring information), etc.

Protocol for SM-SM and LM-SM communication is based on OMIS, while LMs and AMs share a common memory segment to communicate. The LMs use OS mechanisms (ptrace or the proc file system) to control the application processes.

Fig. 2 shows how the components of OCM-G are distributed in the Grid.

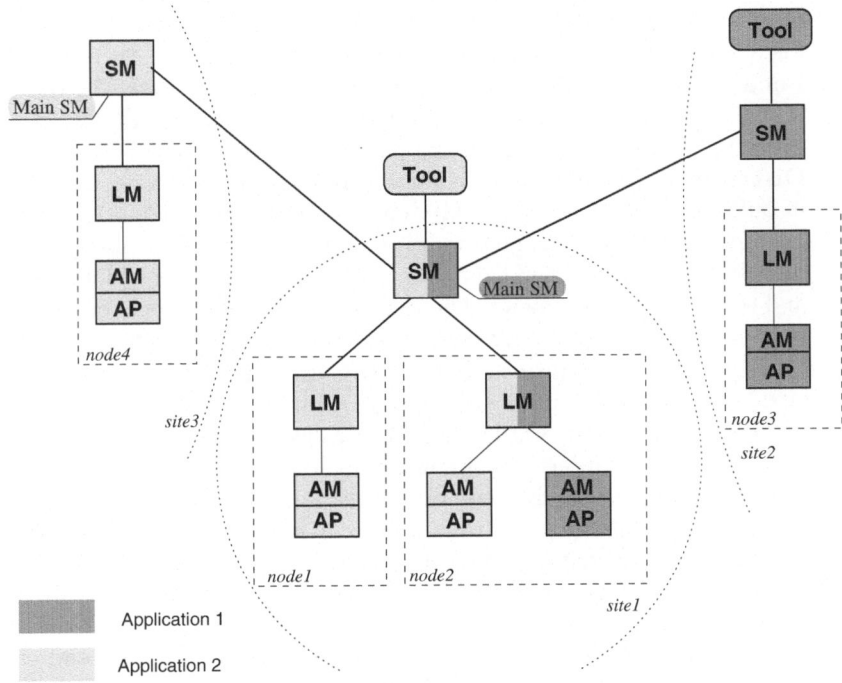

Fig. 3. Two Virtual Monitoring Systems sharing the same OCM-G components.

Beside this physical distribution, the OCM-G has also a logical structure – it is divided into so called Virtual Monitoring Systems (VMS). One VMS is created for each monitored application and is composed of all OCM-G components involved in this application. This concept is introduced to improve the scalability of the OCM-G. The information about the application is only spread across the VMS, which is usually a small part of the whole OCM-G. Moreover, the connections between the SMs are created only if they are parts of the same VMS. Obviously, each LM, SM or a connection between them may belong to more than one VMS. To handle information management in a VMS, one of its SMs is assigned a special role, a so called MainSM. The MainSM plays a role of a central information service for this VMS. Fig. 3 shows an example of two VMSs sharing physical OCM-G components. Note that in the case shown in the figure, the two VMSs belong to the same user, thus not only the SM, but also the LM is shared between them.

4.2   Design Details

In this section, we describe some design details in the OCM-G important to fit the requirements of the Grid environment and interactive applications, described in section 2.

- **Efficiency.** To ensure efficient monitoring, we try to minimize the data rate. This is done in principle with two techniques:
  - **Local Buffering.** The monitoring information is buffered in the context of the application. Only on an explicit demand (pull model), it is extracted by the LM, and sent to be obtained by a tool.
  - **Distributed Evaluation.** To further reduce the data rate, not only is it buffered, but also processed locally and stored in counters or integrating timers. Additionally, we provide the counters and integrators as distributed data structures, i.e. they may be composed of a global object, and some local components. The information stored in local components is on demand collected and combined in the global object.
- **Scalability.** The scalability in the OCM-G is in principle ensured by its decentralized and distributed architecture. However, to avoid problems in sharing information in such a highly decentralized system, and to avoid the necessity for each component to know about each other (which would make the system unscalable again), we introduced the concept of Virtual Monitoring Systems which are centralized logical monitoring systems for each application. This concept was described in the previous subsection.
- **Controllable Intrusiveness.** To minimize the monitoring intrusiveness, we gather the information via **selective run-time instrumentation**. This approach to instrumentation combines the benefits of dynamic and static instrumentation. In general, the *hooks* are inserted statically in the application, while the actual instrumentation code is "hooked up" (hence the name) dynamically. This may be viewed as dynamic activation and deactivation of instrumentation on demand. Our tests showed that the overhead of inactive instrumentation is "in the noise". Moreover, due to the on-line approach to monitoring, the number of active instrumentation may be kept minimal at a given moment.
- **Transparency for the User.** This has several aspects in the OCM-G:
  - The instrumentation is based on binary wrapping, i.e., the user is provided with pre-instrumented versions of communication libraries (e.g., MPI). Thus, only relinking of the application is necessary to enable monitoring of communication subroutines. While this is enough for most performance metrics, the user can also define events in an arbitrary place of the code. This is the only case in which the user has to insert the appropriate code manually. However, even this is greatly simplified, since the code to be inserted is just a single function call.
  - The compilation of the application is handled automatically by a tool provided with the OCM-G. The user issues the normal command to compile the application, only preceded by the name of the tool.
  - The application is submitted to the Grid in the usual way, only a few additional command line parameters are necessary.
  - Tools may be connected to a running application at any time of its execution.
  - It should be mentioned that we require each process of the application to invoke a special function to register in the OCM-G. However, in case

of MPI even this is transparent to the user, as the call to the function is hidden in the instrumentation of MPI_Init().

- **Security.** The OCM-G incorporates security at three levels:
  - users are authenticated using Grid certificates, while communicating with SMs,
  - OCM-G allows to monitor an application to its user only,
  - Local Monitors run as user processes, thus they are limited by the OS protection mechanisms.
- **Operation as a Grid Service.** The Service Managers are designed to run permanently on the Grid and are well-known. This gives good prerequisites to run the OCM-G as a Grid service.
- **Versatility and Flexibility.** It should also be noted that the OMIS/OCM-G approach enables high versatility and flexibility in monitoring.
  - The monitoring services in the OCM-G are various and support different kinds of tools. Moreover, the set of services is extendible by dynamically loaded extensions. Currently available monitoring services are described in section 4.3.
  - The services are relatively low-level, i.e., instead of high-level metrics they return a low level information. Different pieces of such information can be then combined into metrics. For example, instead of a high level request to obtain communication delay for MPI_Send(), one would issue a sequence of simple and lower-level requests: two requests returning time stamps for two events – beginning and end of invocation of MPI_Send(), and some requests to create an integrator and evaluate the delay properly from the time stamps. All this would be done in the context of the application, so there would be no overhead related to multiple requests. This approach allows to construct the metrics by the user with the semantics he needs, it is very easy and much more flexible than providing a set of metrics with a fixed semantics.

4.3   Monitoring Services

To make the description complete, in this section we overview the available monitoring services in the OCM-G. The OCM-G provides all monitoring services defined by the OMIS 2.0 specification, except for those which were undesirable in a Grid environment (e.g. creation of a new process). Additionally, new services are provided, specific for the Grid, or extending monitoring capabilities. Among others, the following functionality is provided by the OCM-G:

1. Debugging services. This includes services for suspending/continuing processes, reading/writing processes' memory, etc.
2. Performance analysis services, for example:
   - services for detecting beginnings and ends of function calls,
   - services for handling probes, which are used by the user to define and detect arbitrary events in an application,

- services for creation and management of counters and integrators – efficient data structures which allow to buffer and preprocess monitoring information in the context of the application.
3. Services for infrastructure monitoring. Some services return information about the current state of infrastructure elements, e.g., examine the status of a network connection. This information may be useful, e.g. in performance analysis – when a user notices a performance loss, he might be interested whether it is caused by the network load or a problem with the algorithm.

5   Previous Experience

Our experience in monitoring and tools goes back to 1995 when the OMIS specification was defined at the Technical University in Munich. In 1997 the OCM – an OMIS-Compliant Monitor [18] for clusters was implemented as well as a few OCM-based tools were developed (such as performance analyzer PATOP and debugger DETOP). Since 1997, there is a collaboration between LRR-TUM and Institute of Computer Science AGH, Cracow. The result of this cooperation is the continuous development and improvement of the monitoring system and tools, among others, towards monitoring and performance analysis of Java applications, threaded applications on shared memory machines, and Grid applications.

6   Summary and Status

In this paper we presented the OCM-G – a universal and flexible monitoring infrastructure for Grid applications. We have shown that the OCM-G is well suited to work in the Grid environment and supports well interactive applications.

Currently the first prototype of the OCM-G is completed and has an operational status. The implementation of this prototype is based on the OCM. The first prototype works on one site only, and supports only one user. It provides all services defined by the OMIS 2.0 document, except for those which were unnecessary or undiserable in the Grid (e.g., for creation of a new process). Some of the new Grid-specific services were also impelmented. The first prototype of the OCM-G implements the new Grid-enabled start-up scheme.

References

1. Allen, G., Davis, K., Dolkas, K., Doulamis, N., Goodale, T., Kielmann, T., Merzky, A., Nabrzyski, J., Pukacki, J., Radke, T., Michael, M., Seidel, E., Shalf, J. , and Taylor, I.: Enabling Applications on the Grid: A GridLab Overview. International Journal of High Performance Computing Applications: Special issue on Grid Computing: Infrastructure and Applications, August 2003.
2. Balaton, Z., Kacsuk, P., Podhorszki, N., and Vajda, F.: Comparison of Representative Grid Monitoring Tools.
   http://www.lpds.sztaki.hu/publications/reports/lpds-2-2000.pdf

3. Balis, B., Bubak, M., Funika, W., Szepieniec, T., and Wismuüller, R.: An Infrastructure for Grid Application Monitoring. In Proc. 9th European PVM/MPI Users' Group Meeting, Linz, Austria, September/October 2002, LNCS 2474, pp. 41-49, 2002.

4. Bubak, M., Funika, W., Baliś, B., and Wismüller, R.: On-line OCM-based Tool Support for Parallel Applications. In: Yuen Chung Kwong (ed.): Annual Review of Scalable Computing, 3, Chapter 3, 2001, Singapore.

5. Bubak, M., Funika, W., and Wismüller, R.: The CrossGrid Performance Analysis Tool for Interactive Grid Applications. In Proc. 9th European PVM/MPI Users' Group Meeting, Linz, Austria, September/October 2002, LNCS 2474, pp. 50-60, 2002

6. GrossGrid – Development of Grid Environment for Interactive Applications. Annex 1 – description of Work, available at: http://www.eu-crossgrid.org

7. The CrossGrid Project: http://www.eu-crossgrid.org

8. The DataGrid Project: http://www.eu-datagrid.org

9. Foster, I., Kesselman, C. (eds.): The Grid: Blueprint for a New Computing Infrastructure. Morgan Kaufmann, 1999

10. The GrADS Project: http://hipersoft.cs.rice.edu/grads

11. The GridLab Project: http://www.gridlab.org

12. GridLab deliverable 11.3: Grid Monitoring Architecture Prototype.
    http://www.gridlab.org/Resources/Deliverables/D11.3.pdf

13. Ludwig, T., Wismüller, R., Sunderam, V., and Bode, A.: OMIS – On-line Monitoring Interface Specification (Version 2.0). Shaker Verlag, Aachen, vol. 9, LRR-TUM Research Report Series, 1997. http://wwwbode.in.tum.de/~omis.

14. Podhorski, N., Kacsuk, P.: Design and Implementation of a Distributed Monitor for Semi-on-line Monitoring of VisualMP Applications. Proc. DAPSYS 2000, Balatonfured, Hungary, 23-32, 2000

15. R-GMA: A Grid Information and Monitoring System.
    http://www.gridpp.ac.uk/abstracts/AllHands_RGMA.pdf

16. Tierney, B., Aydt, R., Gunter, D., Smith, W., Taylor, V., Wolski, R., Swany, M., et al.: White Paper: A Grid Monitoring Service Architecture (DRAFT), Global Grid Forum. 2001. http://www-didc.lbl.gov/GridPerf

17. Vetter, J.S., and Reed, D.A.: Real-time Monitoring, Adaptive Control and Interactive Steering of Computational Grids. The International Journal of High Performance Computing Applications, 14 357-366, 2000.

18. Wismueller, R., Trinitis, J., Ludwig, T.: OCM – A Monitoring System for Interoperable Tools. In: Proc. 2nd SIGMETRICS Symposium on Parallel and Distributed Tools SPDT 98, Welches, OR, USA, August 1998.

The G-PM Tool
for Grid-Oriented Performance Analysis*

Marian Bubak[1,2], Włodzimierz Funika[1,2], Roland Wismüller[3,4],
Tomasz Arodź[1,2], and Marcin Kurdziel[1,2]

[1] Institute of Computer Science, AGH, al. Mickiewicza 30, 30-059 Kraków, Poland
{bubak,funika}@uci.agh.edu.pl
phone: (+48 12) 617 39 64, fax: (+48 12) 633 80 54
[2] Academic Computer Centre – CYFRONET, Nawojki 11, 30-950 Kraków, Poland
[3] LRR-TUM, Institut für Informatik, Technische Universität München,
D-85747 Garching, Germany
wismuell@in.tum.de
phone: (+49 89) 289-17676
[4] Department of Software Science, University of Vienna, A-1090 Vienna, Austria

Abstract. The paper presents the functionality and software design of
G-PM, a tool for evaluation of Grid applications performance. Due to
the highly distributed and dynamic nature of the Grid, the issues of
run-time measurement definition, selective instrumentation, and efficient
data collection mechanisms need to be addressed. Providing data on the
interaction of distributed application components which is meaningful
in the context of an application is essential. The tool offers standard
and user-defined measurements as well as means for performance visualization. It gathers information about a selected application via the well
defined interface to the OCM-G monitoring system. High-level performance properties are defined by the user via a consistent user interface,
allowing for extendible insight into the performance of the application.

Keywords: Grid, performance, tools, monitoring, interactive applications

1 Introduction

The performance analysis and tuning of distributed applications is an essential step in the application development cycle. With the introduction of cross-
organization computing, the inefficiency in the application behaviour leading
to waste of resources becomes a problem of all parties involved in the Grid.
This is particularly important within the CrossGrid project [5], which aims at
extending the Grid architecture to *interactive applications*. Due to the involvement of humans into the computation loop, these applications are often strongly
time-constrained, e.g. the simulation of vascular blood flow and flooding crisis

* This work was partly funded by the European Commission, project IST-2001-32243,
CrossGrid.

F. Fernández Rivera et al. (Eds.): Across Grids 2003, LNCS 2970, pp. 240–248, 2004.

support applications developed within the CrossGrid project. Therefore, performance analysis is one of the key issues in the project. It is addressed by G-PM, a dedicated performance analysis tool.

Compared to existing tools, discussed briefly below, the G-PM features on one hand a rather unique combination of on-line measurement, Grid awareness, and automatic instrumentation for standard application-related metrics, and on the other hand a support for manual instrumentation and user-definable metrics. The G-PM is designed to meet the specific requirements and constraints introduced by the Grid and by the nature of interactive applications. It allows to extend the standard performance metrics, providing the user with a way to specify some higher-level, more abstract metrics suitable in the application context. Contrary to some previously developed tools, the gathered performance data includes the characteristics of the application environment and the Grid infrastructure.

The paper is arranged as follows. Section 2 presents a concise analysis of the existing Grid performance analysis tools. In Section 3, the functionality of the tool is presented. Then, in Section 4, the architecture and design of the tool, as well as the interaction with other parts of the CrossGrid infrastructure are studied. Section 5 presents some details on the idea of user defined metrics based on the probe concept. Finally, Section 6 informs on the development schedule of the tool and on the features included in the first prototype.

2   Related Work

Currently, a number of performance tools already adapted to the Grid [1] exist. Most of those supporting the monitoring of applications are based on an off-line analysis of event traces. This is not suitable for interactive applications, since here the opportunity to relate on-line the performance data with the user's interactions is essential. However, on-line Grid tools are available mainly for infrastructure monitoring. An example is the Network Weather Service [11] that measures and forecasts network and node performance. An exception is the monitoring system GRM [2], adapted to the Grid within the Datagrid project[1]. It offers on-line performance data of Grid applications. However, GRM is mainly based on event traces, does not allow for user-defined metrics, and does not provide infrastructure-related performance data. A number of performance tools implement some ideas close to the ones presented in this paper, but none of them covers all of them. Autopilot [9] exploits a concept called *sensors* corresponding to our probes. User-defined instrumentation is used in the TAU performance analysis environment [7]. In all of these systems, however, the metrics connected with the user-defined instrumentation is already fixed by the instrumentation itself and cannot be configured at run-time. Paradyn [8] belongs to the few tools that strictly exploit the on-line approach, including the instrumentation procedure, but it does not support user-defined metrics.

---

[1] www.eu-datagrid.org

3   Tool Functionality vs. Grid

In this section we relate the functionality of performance tools to the features of
Grid computing and show the designed functionality of G-PM.

Specifics of Interactive Grid Computing. The orientation of CrossGrid towards interactive applications, as well as the nature of the Grid itself, poses new
requirements and constraints on performance analysis. First, within CrossGrid
the application user is allowed to control the application during its execution.
Thus, the information meaningful in the application steering process, such as
performance data, have to be available on-line. Next, the interpretation of the
performance data in a heterogeneous, open Grid system, can only be done in the
context of the application's environment. Thus, the performance characteristics
of the Grid infrastructure itself are required. Finally, the user of the application may be a specialist other than a computer scientist. Hence, the information
provided to the user must not be limited to low-level data (e.g. data volume exchanged between two processes), but rather be more high-level and application
specific. The tools have to be configurable, extendible and application-oriented.

Basic Performance Metrics. The G-PM tool aims at satisfying the outlined
requirements and constraints. It operates in the on-line mode, displaying current
performance data in form of various visualization graphs. Some basic standard
metrics, or measurable quantities, have been specified, both application and Grid
infrastructure related. The first allow for a low-level analysis of the application
behaviour (e.g. data volume of MPI or file operations). Drilling down is allowed
by restricting the analysis to a subset of the application processes, hosts, or to
specific regions in the source code. The Grid infrastructure metrics specify both
dynamic (e.g. CPU or network load) and static (e.g. host memory size) information on the application environment.

User-Defined Metrics. The standard metrics may not carry information related to the environment the application is running in, vital in the application
context, or may not summarize the information in the most suitable form. Thus,
the application developer is enabled to specify his own metrics. The *first* way is
to add some specific events to the application code. These events, called *probes*,
then allow to limit any measurement to the specific, relevant program phases.
Probes may also carry some additional, application-specific information to the
G-PM, which can then be presented by the tool using the standard visualizations.
The *second* way, which aims at customizing the performance data presented to
the user, is to use a metrics specification language. The user can build some
higher-level metrics by combining and transforming the standard metrics, the
metrics based on probes as well as other previously specified higher-level metrics. It should be noted, that for both standard and user-defined metrics, the
object code of the application has to be linked against instrumented versions of
the programming libraries.

4   The G-PM Tool Design

The architecture of G-PM is designed as part of the programming tools environment communicating to the monitoring and other Grid services via the OCM-G monitoring system (see Fig. 1) only. Below we discuss particular aspects of the tool's design.

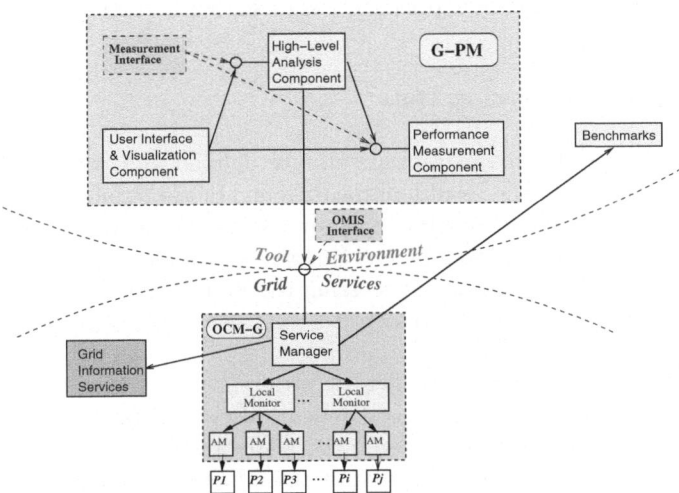

Fig. 1. Structure of G-PM.

4.1   Monitoring System

To provide performance measurements in the on-line mode, G-PM is built on top of the OCM-G [3] monitoring system, an implementation of the On-line Monitoring Interface Specification OMIS 2.0 [6]. OCM-G, which is part of the Grid services, is responsible for supplying low-level monitoring data. This includes the communication with instrumented libraries linked to the application, and the gathering of information supplied by these libraries and other monitoring data sources. Also, the results of micro-benchmarks are accessible through OCM-G.

OCM-G comprises two types of components: Service Managers and Local Monitors (see the lower part of Fig. 1). Service Managers (SM) are the permanent part of OCM-G and there is one SM per site of the Grid. An SM distributes requests to Local Monitors, if the target object is located on the same site, and/or to the other SMs in order to reach objects located outside the site. Local Monitors (LMs) are transient components in OCM-G responsible for execution of OMIS requests; these are created on each host of the Grid where application processes to be monitored exist.

The G-PM tool is implemented as a process running on a user's local workstation. It connects to the nearest Service Manager, to which it submits monitoring requests and from which it receives the corresponding replies (see the upper part of Fig. 1). Once the tool is connected to OCM-G, it may get information about all running applications. Then an application can be chosen to which the tool should *attach*. The application can be monitored only upon the tool have attached to it. The tool can attach to a running application and begin monitoring at any time, provided that the application is linked with an instrumented library.

4.2   Supply of Monitoring Data

Within G-PM performance measurements are defined and presented while the application is running. The results of measurements are numerical values evolving over time. G-PM either displays the current values as e.g. bar graphs or pie charts, or their temporal development in form of a curve at regular intervals. There are principally two kinds of accessing the monitoring data to enable measurements: automatically and user-defined.

Instrumentation.   The G-PM offers a wide variety of standard metrics for performance analysis. These include application-related metrics, like e.g. time elapsed, or volume of interprocess communication and I/O. In addition, the tool allows to measure infrastructure-related metrics, like e.g. node load or link bandwidth. This information is provided and forwarded from proper Grid services. To access the data on standard metrics, e.g. `send data volume`, at a preparatory step the application has to be re-linked with instrumented versions of some run-time libraries. The instrumentation consist of wrappers around the original routines (e.g. communication or I/O) that acquire the necessary performance information. In order to enable the instrumentation, the user has to start the application with a special command line argument handled by the instrumentation code. Additional command line argument can be used to prevent the program from running until there is an explicit request. This allows to define measurements before the application starts executing.

As a rule, measurements are based on counters and integrating timers [3], which are updated by the instrumentation code within the context of the local application process. Consequently, for a typical measurement only a limited number of values has to be read, which results in a low overhead. In cases where very detailed information is required and the higher overhead is acceptable, events can be logged, too.

Probes vs. User Defined Metrics.   As mentioned in Section 3, a performance tool must also be able to provide high-level performance data which is more meaningful in the application's domain. The application-specific data can be classified into three categories: (1) particular, relevant events, meaningful for the application user/developer, e.g. the start/end of a user interaction, (2) correlated events, e.g. start/end events in different processes that indicate the entry into/exit from the same computational phase, (3) performance data computed within the application itself, e.g. the residuum value in a numerical solver.

To provide the tool with this information, the user inserts a set of *probes* into the application's source code. A probe is a special function call, that signals the event connected with the particular position in the source code. This call can receive user-provided parameters that contain application-specific data. If the G-PM does not need the data provided by the particular probe the underlying instrumentation is disabled. Consequently the introduced overhead is low.

Using a probe does not yet imply a specific user-defined metrics. In fact, the same probe can be used to define many different metrics. Based on the concept of probes, G-PM allows the user to define his/her own metrics, which can be built on already existing metrics (standard ones and user-defined ones) and/or any available probes and probe data in the application.

4.3   Component Structure of G-PM

The tool is composed of three main modules, the *Performance Measurement Component* (PMC), the *High-Level Analysis Component* (HLAC) and the *User Interface and Visualization Component* (UIVC), see Fig. 1.

Performance Measurement Component. The PMC implements all standard metrics. This is done by properly programming the monitoring system when a measurement is defined. See [4] for a more detailed description.

High Level Analysis Component. Since the HLAC handles the user-defined metrics it is involved in parsing the metrics specifications and translating the high-level metrics into requests to PMC for the underlying standard metrics. Also, it is responsible for handling the events generated by *probes* and for processing the information passed by these probes from the application to the G-PM tool. While the HLAC reuses the PMC for performing standard measurements, it also communicates directly with OCM-G through the OMIS interface in order to efficiently implement probe-based metrics. For optimization reasons, the implementation of the high-level measurements may require that the evaluation of the measurement based on the metric specification is performed within OCM-G in an distributed way, instead of within the G-PM tool. For more details on the issue please refer to [10].

User Interface and Visualization Component. The User Interface comprises the program's *main window*, which presents a list of defined measurements and visualizations. Another important part is the *measurement definition window* that allows to choose a metrics and to specify its parameters e.g. restrictions on the hosts/code regions where the measurement should be performed. Once the measurement is defined, the user can specify the type and parameters of the measurement's *visualization window* using the *visualization definition window*. The tool provides, a set of *visualization windows*, ranging from bar graphs and pie charts to value versus time function plots.

5   User-Defined Metrics

As mentioned in Section 4, the HLAC allows to measure application-specific
metrics based on user-defined instrumentation of the application's source code.
Among others, the following kinds of user-defined metrics are possible: (1) a
metrics which is defined by an existing metrics (e.g. standard metrics provided
by the PMC), measured only during an execution phase delimited by any two
probe executions; (2) a metrics which can be defined by any parameter of any
probe; (3) a metrics which can be derived from any existing set of metrics by
aggregating or comparing their values.

```
IO_volume_for_interaction(Process[] processes, File[] files,
                          Region[] regions, TimeInterval currTime)
{
  Process p; VirtualTime vt;
  Value volume[][]; Value globalVol[];
  PROBE begin(Process, VirtualTime); PROBE end(Process, VirtualTime);
  volume[p][vt] = IO_volume(p, files, regions) AT end(p, vt)
                - IO_volume(p, files, regions) AT begin(p, vt);
  globalVol[vt] = SUM(volume[p][vt] WHERE p IN processes);
  RETURN SUM(globalVol[vt] WHERE globalVol[vt].time IN currTime);
}
```

Fig. 2. Example of a user-defined metrics.

An example of a metrics specification of the first kind is shown in Fig. 2. In
this example the programmer inserted two probes – *begin* and *end* – into the
application, to mark the beginning and end of an end-user interaction. Based on
these probes and the standard metrics IO_volume for the total volume of disk
I/O, the user has defined a new metrics for the disk I/O during a single end-
user interaction. For each process p, the value of this metrics is defined as the
difference of IO_volume at the *end* event and IO_volume at the corresponding
begin event, where IO_volume is the accumulated volume since the start of the
measurement. The following two assignments in the metrics specification define
how the result is accumulated over space (i.e. the processes) and time.

Since the HLAC is aimed at the optimised implementation of measurements
based on user-defined metrics, the processing of probe events should happen as
locally as possible, i.e. in the best case within the context of the appropriate
process. This implies that the evaluation suggested by the metrics specification
should be performed in a distributed way, as discussed in [10].

6   Concluding Remarks

The first prototype of G-PM is available since February 2003. Due to the limitations of the OCM-G, this prototype it is restricted to a single cluster of worksta-

tions. Also, only a subset of standard metrics is available (send/receive volume, delay time, application CPU time). Two visualization types are implemented: the bar graph and a multi-curve value-versus-time plot. The HLAC component of the tool currently supports two specialized types of high-level metrics, which are configurable to a limited extent. The fully functional version of the G-PM tool is currently being implemented and will be available by the end of 2004. Like all other system software developed in the CrossGrid project, it will then be freely available via a public software license.

Acknowledgements

We are very grateful to Bartosz Baliś, Tomasz Szepieniec, Marcin Radecki from AGH, Kraków as well as to Hamza Mehammed from TUM, Munich for their valuable remarks.

References

1. Balaton, Z., Kacsuk, P., Podhorszki, N., and Vajda, F.: Comparison of Representative Grid Monitoring Tools. Laboratory of Parallel and Distributed Systems (SZTAKI), LPDS-2/2000, 2000
   ftp://ftp.lpds.sztaki.hu/pub/lpds/publications/reports/lpds-2-2000.pdf
2. Balaton, Z., Kacsuk, P., Podhorszki, N., and Vajda, F.: From Cluster Monitoring to Grid Monitoring Based on GRM. In: Sakellariou, R., Keane, J., Gurd, J., and Freeman, L. (eds.), Euro-Par 2001 Parallel Processing, 7th International Euro-Par Conference, August 2001, Manchester, UK, pp. 874-881, vol. 2150, Lecture Notes in Computer Science,Springer-Verlag, 2001.
   http://link.springer.de/link/service/series/0558/papers/2150/
   21500874.pdf
3. Baliś, B., Bubak, M., Funika, W., Szepieniec, T., and Wismüller, R.: An Infrastructure for Grid Application Monitoring. In: Kranzlmüller, D. and Kacsuk, P. and Dongarra, J. and Volkert, J. (Eds.), Recent Advances in Parallel Virtual Machine and Message Passing Interface, 9th European PVM/MPI Users' Group Meeting, September - October 2002, Linz, Austria, 2474, Lecture Notes in Computer Science, 41-49, Springer-Verlag, 2002
4. Bubak, M., Funika, W., and Wismüller, R.: The CrossGrid Performance Analysis Tool for Interactive Grid Applications. In: Kranzlmüller, D. and Kacsuk, P. and Dongarra, J. and Volkert, J. (Eds.), Recent Advances in Parallel Virtual Machine and Message Passing Interface, 9th European PVM/MPI Users' Group Meeting, September - October 2002, Linz, Austria, 2474, Lecture Notes in Computer Science, 50-60, Springer-Verlag, 2002
5. CrossGrid - Development of Grid Environment for interactive Applications, EU Project, IST-2001-32243, Technical Annex.
   http://www.eu-crossgrid.org
6. Ludwig, T., Wismüller, R., Sunderam, V., and Bode, A.: OMIS — On-line Monitoring Interface Specification (Version 2.0). Shaker-Verlag, 1997, Aachen, Germany, vol. 9, ISBN 3-8265-3035-7.
   http://wwwbode.in.tum.de/~omis/OMIS/Version-2.0/version-2.0.ps.gz

7. Malony, A., and Shende, S.: Performance Technology for Complex Parallel and Distributed Systems. In: Kotsis, G., and Kacsuk, P. (eds.), Proc. Third Austrian-Hungarian Workshop on Distributed and Parallel Systems, DAPSYS 2000, 37-46, Kluwer, 2000.
    http://www.cs.uoregon.edu/research/paracomp/papers/dapsys2k.ps.gz
8. Miller, B.P., et al.: The Paradyn Parallel Performance Measurement Tools. In: IEEE Computer, vol. 28(11): 37-46, Nov. 1995.
    http://www.cs.wisc.edu/paradyn/papers/overview.ps.gz
9. Vetter, J.S., and Reed, D.A.: Real-time Monitoring, Adaptive Control and Interactive Steering of Computational Grids. In: The International Journal of High Performance Computing Applications, vol. 14, pp. 357-366, 2000
10. Wismüller, R., Bubak, M., Funika, W., and Baliś, B.: A Performance Analysis Tool for Interactive Applications on the Grid. Workshop on Clusters and Computational Grids for Scientific Computing, September 2002, Le Chateau de Faberges de la Tour, France. To appear.
11. Wolski, R., Spring, N., and Hayes, J.: The Network Weather Service: A Distributed Resource Performance Forecasting Service for Metacomputing. In: Future Generation Computer Systems, vol. 15, pp. 757-768, 1999

Jiro Based Grid Infrastructure Monitoring System – State of Development Report

Bartosz Ławniczek, Grzegorz Majka, Krzysztof Zieliński, and Sławomir Zieliński

Academic Computer Centre "Cyfronet",
Department of Computer Science , AGH-UST
Kraków, Poland
bartek@spruce.jp, mikej@ds5.agh.edu.pl,
{kz,slawek}@cs.agh.edu.pl

1 Introduction

The article presents the current state of grid infrastructure monitoring system and prospect of its further evolution. The system is developed as a part of ACK Cyfronet's contribution to the Crossgrid project. The system's first prototype functionality is mainly concerned with the instrumentation of resources and dynamic deployment issues, which are crucial for usability of the software. The functionality of the monitoring agents, the first prototype consists of, was provided by using Java Management Extension (JMX) and Jiro technologies. This functionality has been described in more detail in [1].

The process of deploying the monitoring software and collection and distribution of monitored information is very much dependent on the underlying software technology. The questions about the future of and maturity of Jiro technology induce consideration about alternatives. In that context, the mechanisms offered by the JMX framework should are discussed.

The structure of the paper is as follows. Section 2 presents the monitoring system deployment and configuration scenario. Next section contains analysis and comparison of Jiro and JMX based dynamic deployment mechanisms. The more detailed description of JMX services supporting dynamic configuration is presented in Section 4. The differences between freely available JMX reference implementation and a commercial product have been elaborated in Section 5. Jiro and JMX services supporting construction of events distribution layer has been described in Section 6. Interoperability aspects that are crucial for integration of the monitoring system with other components are covered by Section 7. The paper is ended with conclusions.

2 Monitoring System Startup Scenario

Detailed functional description of the Jiro and Java Management Extension based grid infrastructure monitoring system is described in [1]. This section will address only the system deployment and configuration process requirements.

The system is constructed according to a five layers architecture, that defines instrumentation, agent, management, database and user interface layers.

F. Fernández Rivera et al. (Eds.): Across Grids 2003, LNCS 2970, pp. 249–256, 2004.

The tasks of the layers are as follows:

- **instrumentation layer** is expected to expose devices' parameters' values to the outside world,
- **agent layer** provides means for upper layers to communicate with the instrumentation layer,
- **management logic layer** is responsible for filtering notifications passed by the lower ones as well as performing pre-programmed administrative actions in cases of typical failures,
- **database layer** stores data about current state of the system as well as about its history,
- **user interface layer** is responsible for presenting the state of the system to the user.

Because grid systems are built of many computer nodes connected with each other via computer network, the remote instantiation of monitoring software seems to be a necessary functionality of grid management infrastructure. Saying more precisely, the components of instrumentation and agent layer should be launched on each monitored computational, storage or communication resource. An important aspect is that grid system's configuration usually changes dynamically as new nodes are attached to the system or switched off. That means that the grid monitoring software should be able to adapt dynamically to the changing configurations.

The monitoring system first prototype setup procedure consists of the following basic steps:

1. installation of the core Jiro services on a selected node,
2. installation of Jiro Deployment Station service and necessary native libraries on the monitored nodes,
3. startup of the Jiro Lookup Service,
4. deployment of the monitoring agents on selected nodes,
5. startup of the monitoring agents.

Figure 1 depicts a sample installation of JIMS.

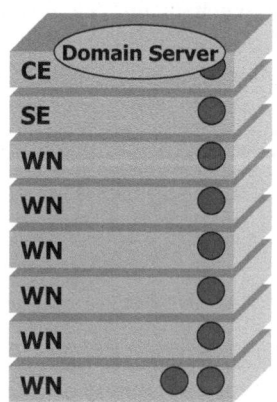

Legend:
CE – computing element
SE – storage element
WN – worker node
    – MBean

Domain Server runs core Jiro services; other hosts run only the Jiro Deployment Station.

Fig. 1. An example JIMS startup configuration.

The installation procedure assumes that it is possible to use multicast communication between the host running the Jiro Lookup Service and the hosts running monitoring agents. The availability of multicast is needed for the monitoring agents to discover the lookup service with which they are to register. Although there is a possibility to pre-configure the lookup service location, making the user do so would make the system practically unusable for two reasons:

- it would not be able to use replicas of the lookup service,
- it is not feasible to keep track of configuration of all monitoring agents in grid systems.

Therefore, automatic configuration seems to be the only option for such a system. Detailed installation procedure can be found in [2].

3   System Startup

The requirement of system flexibility results in the need for implementing at least two features: dynamic deployment and discovery of running system entities. Dynamic deployment is a very important feature because it makes easier both version management and system configuration. Since the system entities are expected to run on many host machines, it is desirable for an administrator to reduce the number of software packages to be installed on each individual node prior to running services. Therefore, an ideal solution would be to make the administrators install only the core packages that are not expected to change for a relatively long period of time and leave installation of the other parts of a distributed system to its users. On the other hand, the services providing for dynamic deployment should not introduce significant overhead from the users' point of view.

The deployment of a new service is typically composed of three stages: sending the code implementing the service, matching the code's privileges against the security policy in place on the target machine and running the service (possibly in an environment with limited access to the hosting machine resources). There are a number of possible solutions for enabling dynamic deployment in distributed systems. In the technological context of JIMS, there are at least two worth consideration, i.e. Jiro Deployment Station and Java Management Extension's M-let service.

Both the solutions do not require much programmer's effort to. implement an interface for running the deployed service. In Jiro's case no additional coding is needed; the JMX based solution only requires providing a descriptor containing an URL for the Management Bean (MBean) implementing the service to be loaded. Since the MBean interface is basic for most of objects implemented in distributed systems based on the JMX environment, fulfilling such requirement is not an issue for the programmer.

The first prototype of JIMS uses the Jiro-based mechanism for deploying the host monitoring services. The monitoring code is organized in two parts: one to be installed on machines to be monitored prior to setting up the system and second – to be deployed, run and revoked at runtime. The pre-installed part consists of an implementation of the deployment station service and a native monitoring library, which is loaded by the deployed service at launch time. The functionality of the deployment station with no deployed services is restricted to keeping its registration with the Jiro Lookup Service up to date, which results in sending a few packets to the network. From the hosting station's point of view, that introduces practically no overhead.

JIMS provides a couple of tools to make the deployment easier: ExtFinder (which is an extended version of OKI Lab's Jini Service Finder) and Installer. Both of them can be used to deploy monitoring agents to the target machines. However, since the ExtFinder is equipped only with a BeanShell-based command line tool, the drag-and-drop oriented Installer seems to be more convenient.

Since the low-level system entities can be deployed and started any time, it is necessary to provide means of finding other system services for them. There are two commonly used approaches to this topic: registration and discovery. Jiro platform provides a replicable registry of system objects, called Lookup Service. Each system entity is required to register in it at startup and keep its registration valid (re-register after lease timer expiration). Since there can be more than one Lookup Service in a Jiro domain (which in JIMS approach typically covers one computing cluster), a fair level of failure safety is provided. The Lookup Service acts also as a repository of proxies used to communicate with registered objects. By downloading such a proxy from the repository, a client does not even have to know the communication protocol it is using (the proxy hides the protocol details). Such functionality, although convenient, is not always needed, especially in homogenous and low-level environments, i.e. environments with many objects that are speaking the same protocol and are of little use to an end user. Therefore, although Jiro Lookup Service is used by the first prototype of JIMS, it is possible, that future releases will switch to active discovery mechanisms.

The active discovery mechanisms rely heavily on network multicast/broadcast capabilities. Typically, an object that wants to discover other entities sends a query on a network's multicast/broadcast address and then waits for responses sent by the services that match the query. In order to keep track of entities in place, the query is re-sent periodically. One drawback of such an approach is the requirement for the network to support multicast or broadcast communication[1]. That requirement is easily fulfilled by clusters (they form a single local network). That is enough for JIMS's agent layer, because its database will connect directly only to the agents on the local network.

Mechanisms of active discovery are available in the Java Dynamic Management Kit (JDMK™) – a commercial implementation of JMX, but the freely available reference implementation of Java Management Extensions does not provide them [3]. That means that switching to active discovery would require implementing discovery from scratch or adopting it from some other technology.

---

[1] That requirement is also present when using Jiro-based approach, since the instances of Lookup Service are found by sending a query to a well-known multicast address. The workaround is to preconfigure the system entities with address of a Lookup Service instance compromises the system's failure safety.

4   JMX Based Configuration Mechanisms

JMX based environments offer JMX M-let Service, which allows the agent, other MBeans, as well as management applications to create MBeans by downloading class files from remote locations. This service could be exploited to achieve easy configuration of the grid infrastructure monitoring system. In addition, the M-let Service lets agents expand their code base at runtime. Therefore, it could be considered as an attractive alternative to Jiro Deployment Station functionality.

Since the M-let Service is a core JMX component, it must reside in every JMX-compliant server. In order to load new MBeans, users point the service to a remote descriptor (M-let). The descriptor is an XML-like text file that contains information about loading classes and creating MBeans. The M-let service loads this file, processes the information it contains and downloads the named classes in order to create one or more MBeans. Figure 2 illustrates how the M-let service works. The M-let service downloads an M-Let File, which contains mandatory attribute specifying class name that contains MBean implementation. The only other mandatory attribute contains a single JAR file or a list of JAR files that contain the classes, objects and resources needed to support a specified MBean class or serialized object file.

M-let service is also an MBean registered in the agent, and it can be used by the agent itself, other MBeans, or remote management applications. It supports loading of MBean classes and their resources from remote locations by using M-let files and acts as a class loader, providing the ability to expand an agent's codebase.

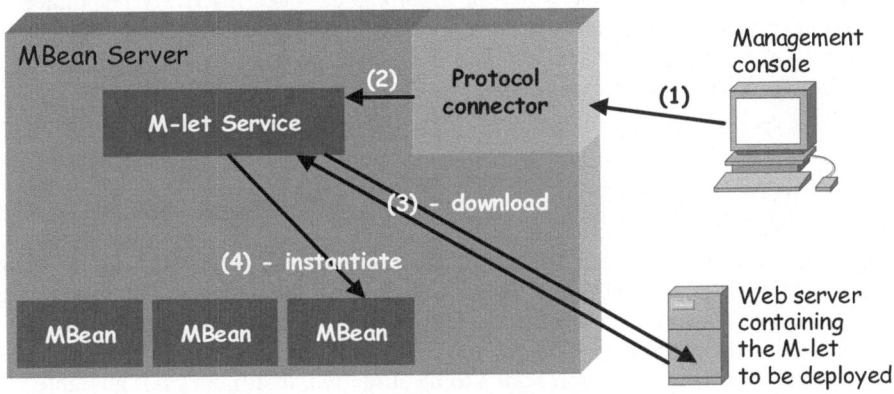

Fig. 2. The M-let service operation.

5   Support for Dynamic Configuration

JMX specification [4] does not define any service supporting dynamic resource discovery. Such a service is offered by commercial implementation of JMX available from SUN Microsystems, called Java Dynamic Management Kit (JDMK). Because this functionality has been considered crucial for the grid monitoring system, the first prototype of JIMS has been implemented using JDMK classes implementing it.

The discovery service provides for discovering management agents in a network. That service relies on a discovery client object which sends out multicast requests to find agents. In order to be discovered an agent must have a registered discovery responder in its MBean server. Applications may also use a discovery monitor, which detects activation or deactivation of discovery responders.

The combination of these functionalities allows interested applications to establish a list of active agents and keep it current. In addition to knowing about the existence of an agent, the discovery service provides the version information from an MBean server's delegate and the list of communication MBeans that are currently registered.

The application containing the discovery client can initiate a search at any time. For example, it might do a search when it is first launched, and search again periodically for information about the communicators which may have changed. For each search, the discovery client broadcasts a request and waits for return information from any responders. There are two types of response mode:

- *unicast response mode* - the responder creates a datagram socket for sending the response only to the discovery client,
- *multicast response mode* - the discovery responder uses the existing multicast socket to send response, broadcasting it to the same multicast group as the request. Every member of the multicast group receives the message, but only the discovery client can make use of its contents.

In passive discovery, the entity seeking knowledge about agents listens for their discovery responders being activated or deactivated. When discovery responders are started or stopped, they send out a proprietary message that contains all discovery response information. A *discovery monitor* object waits to receive any of these messages from the multicast group[2].

6   System Operation

The communication between the agent layer and the upper layers of the system depends heavily on the user requirements and can be quite intensive. Therefore, either a low-overhead communication mechanism must be used or the MBeans should be able to reduce the communication volume by e.g. filtering redundant messages.

Although the second solution seems to be attractive, it still does not guarantee that the rest of the system will not be flooded with messages while introducing an additional processing overhead on each monitored node and making the functionality of the MBeans more complex. That would be in contrast with the assumption of simplicity of MBeans. Because of that, although message filters cannot be omitted, JIMS does not implement their functionality inside agent layer. If the message filtering and aggregation functionality would be integrated into other system layer, it is more likely that the database layer would serve for this purpose.

---

[2] A discovery monitor is often associated with a discovery client. By relying on the information from both, it can keep an up-to-date list of all agents in a given multicast group.

In either case, a communication scheme best suiting the needs of communication should be chosen. The two possible alternatives for the first prototype of JIMS were Jiro Event Service or JMX RMI-based communication. The Event Service is a standard service for Jiro environment. Being topic-based, the service provides basic means for event filtering by structuring the event types in a hierarchy. Moreover, one instance of the service provide means for communication to the whole Jiro domain, so there is no need to install it on every single machine in the monitored cluster. On the other hand, JMX messaging with its filtering capabilities provides enough functionality for the agent layer entities. It is worth to say that the JMX filters can actually block sending a message to the network, which saves bandwidth and CPU power on the listener's host [5].

7   Interoperability Aspects

The investigated monitoring system is based on Java technology and exploits RMI for remote communication between system components and reporting monitored events. The interoperability with systems implemented in other technologies is provided via SOAP Gateway. The concept of this component follows OGSA guidelines which proposes Web Services as "glue" technology for future generation grids.

The SOAP Gateway is designed and implemented under Crossgrid Project. It exposes a functionality of monitoring system as Web Services and allows access to interfaces of MBean Server Agent services and monitoring MBeans via standard SOAP protocol. An important feature of SOAP Gateway is its auto-configuration mechanism. The Gateway actively or passively discovers all MBean Servers available in monitoring domain. This procedure exploits the discovery services described in Section 5. Such a solution makes the monitored resources list accessible from the Gateway consistent, even when grid nodes are temporarily switched off.

The Gateway translates SOAP RCP invocations on monitoring system MBeans to RMI invocations. Inside the Gateway each MBean server is represented by a proxy RMI connector. This solution guarantees that full functionality of each MBean Server could be accessed via SOAP Protocol.

Under Crossgrid Project the SOAP Gateway will be used for integration of JIMS with R-GMA at the first stage. However, the proposed solution is far more general and could be used by any WS-enabled application.

8   Conclusions

The presented comparison study of Jiro Services and Java Management Extension lead to the conclusion that both environments pose very similar or at least replaceable functionality. Jiro environment seems to be more sophisticated and rather centralized as relaying on Jini Lookup Service. JMX is less centralized and lightweight what better satisfies scalability requirement of grid monitoring system.

Jiro Deployment Station and Lookup Service based system startup is more difficult in configuration and management in comparison to the JMX M-Let Service. The important point is that JMX implementation works reliably.

Jiro has more powerful and well designed Event Service implementing most of CORBA Event and Notification Service functionality. It provides rather general filtering capabilities in contrast to rather simple filtering and notification mechanisms available in JMX. This is not going to be a problem as event distribution layer represents separate well defined functionality which could be implemented with support of many existing open source events distribution tools.

Jiro environment has still many drawbacks and seems not to be supported in the future. Thus, structuring JIMS around JMX would guarantee easy migration of the system from Jiro services to JMX services without compromising any functionality of the monitoring system developed in the first phase of Crossgrid Project.

References

[1] Crossgrid Project Deliverable 3.2, www.crossgrid.org/Deliverables/M12pdf/CG3.3.3-D3.2-v1.0-TCD100-JiroMonitoring.pdf
[2] Crossgrid Project Deliverable 3.3, http://www.crossgrid.org/Deliverables/M12pdf/CG3.3.3-CYF-D3.3-v1.1-Jiro.pdf
[3] Java Dynamic Management Kit Technical Overview, http://www.sun.com/products-n-solutions/telecom/software/ javadynamic/tech_overview.html
[4] Java Management Extensions Specification, http://jcp.org/aboutJava/communityprocess/final/jsr003/index3.html
[5] H. Kreger, W. Harold, L. Williamson, Java and JMX. Building Manageable Systems, Addison-Wesley, 2002, pp. 120-122.

Performance Prediction in a Grid Environment

Rosa M. Badia[2], Francesc Escalé[2], Edgar Gabriel[1,3], Judit Gimenez[2],
Rainer Keller[1], Jesús Labarta[2], and Matthias S. Müller[1]

[1] High Performance Computing Center Stuttgart,
Allmandring 30, D-70550 Stuttgart, Germany
{keller,gabriel,mueller}@hlrs.de
[2] European Center for Parallelism of Barcelona (CEPBA),
Technical University of Catalonia (UPC),
Campus Nord, Mòdul D6, Jordi Girona, 1-3, 08034 Barcelona, Spain
{rosab,fescale,jesus,judit}@cepba.upc.es
[3] Innovative Computing Laboratories,
Computer Science Department,
University of Tennessee, Knoxville, TN, USA

Abstract. Knowing the performance of an application in a Grid environment is an important issue in application development and for scheduling decisions. In this paper we describe the analysis and optimisation of a computation- and communication-intensive application from the field of bioinformatics, which was demonstrated at the HPC-Challenge of Supercomputing 2002 at Baltimore. This application has been adapted to be run on an heterogeneous computational Grid by means of PACX-MPI. The analysis and optimisation is based on trace driven tools, mainly Dimemas and Vampir. All these methodologies and tools are being extended in the frame of the DAMIEN IST project.

1 Introduction

The efficient execution of a complex scientific application in a distributed, heterogeneous environment where resources are shared with others is a challenge for the developer and user. The DAMIEN [4,7] project (Distributed Applications and Middleware for Industrial Use of European Networks) aims to produce a tool-chain to support developers and scientific users of Grid-applications. To achieve this goal, new tools are created as well as existing and widely accepted tools are extended to work in a distributed and heterogeneous Grid-environment.

For the HPC-Challenge at Supercomputing 2002 in Baltimore, we demonstrated a computationally and communication-intensive application of the area of bioinformatics, RNAfold [6], running on a computational Grid, successfully employing the DAMIEN tool-chain. This computational Grid consisted of 22 high-performance computers installed at the sites of our partners, constituting a distributed, heterogeneous Metacomputer. Regarding the heterogeneous setup of the machines used, we validated the prediction of the run-time of the application on a computational Grid.

F. Fernández Rivera et al. (Eds.): Across Grids 2003, LNCS 2970, pp. 257–264, 2004.
© Springer-Verlag Berlin Heidelberg 2004

In this paper we focus on two of the DAMIEN-tools, namely PACX-MPI, which will be introduced in the next section, and Dimemas, described in section 3. Section 4 then describes experiments done with these two tools in conjunction with the application RNAfold.

2   PACX-MPI

The middleware PACX-MPI [5] is an optimized MPI implementation and enables MPI-conforming applications to be run on a heterogeneous computational Grid without requiring the programmer to change the source code.

The hosts making up the computational Grid are coupled through an interconnecting network, e. g. the Internet. Communication between MPI-processes within the host is done with the optimized vendor MPI, while communication between MPI-processes on different hosts is carried out over the interconnecting network. For this communication to run efficiently, two MPI-processes on each host, the so called daemons, are employed. Any communication between two remote MPI-processes has to be passed to these daemons, who then transfer the message to the other host. While the internal connections provide very high bandwidth in the range of several hundred MB per second with latencies as low as 4 μs, the external connection between hosts sometimes offer a connection of poor quality, depending on various factors, e. g. distance between hosts, network provider and even time of day. The main interest is therefore to speed up communication over the external connections, either within the scope of PACX-MPI or the application. In order to speed up the interconnection between hosts, methods are being examined within the scope of the DAMIEN project.

Within this paper, however we focus on the application-level optimizations applied for Grid Computing.

3   Performance Prediction: Dimemas

Dimemas is a performance prediction simulator for message passing applications. It reconstructs the time behavior of a parallel application on a target architecture. The inputs to Dimemas are: a tracefile of an execution of the application on a source machine that captures the CPU bursts versus the communication pattern information; and a configuration file that contains a set of parameters that model the target architecture. Complemented with a visualization tool [3,10,8], it allows the user to gain insight into the application behavior.

The initial Dimemas architecture model considered networks of Shared Memory Processors (SMP). In this architecture, each node is composed of a set of processors and local memory. The interconnection of these nodes is modeled with input/output links and a set of buses. In the IST project DAMIEN [4], Dimemas had been extended to predict for Grid architectures. Therefore, the target architecture is now a set of machines, each of them can be a network of SMPs. Different machines are connected through an external Wide Area Network (WAN) or through dedicated connections.

Dimemas has different models for point to point communications and collective operations, with user-configurable parameters to fit different communication library implementations and networks characteristics.

For point to point communications a very simple model expressed in Fig. 1 is considered [1]. This figure illustrates how a point to point communication between two processes (i and j) is simulated by Dimemas. The model takes into account some user defined parameters, as the latency or the network bandwidth. The latency is considered as a resource consuming delay (the CPU of process i cannot continue its calculations), but the *flight* time, a latency considered for remote calculations, is non resource consuming. The transfer time, which is calculated as the division of the message size by the network traffic, is also a non resource consuming time, therefore, the sending process i eventually would be able to continue with other calculations. Additionally, Dimemas simulates the resource contention (the simulation waits till the necessary links and busses required for the communication are available) and also takes into account the influence of the traffic in the network for remote communication ($f(traffic)$).

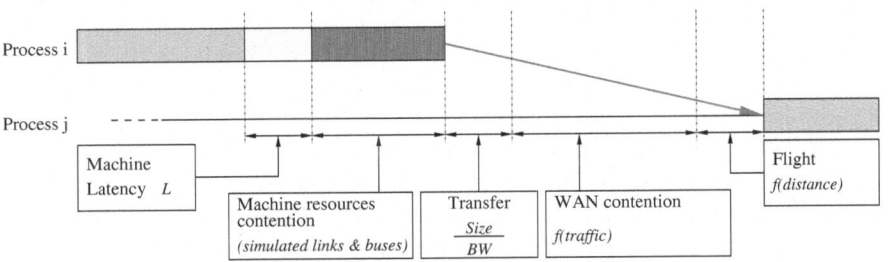

Fig. 1. Point to point Dimemas communication model.

This general model can be applied to any type of communication, no matter if it is local or remote. What will vary depending on the case are the values (for example, a local latency will often be shorter than a remote latency) or the existence itself of some of the parameters (the function of traffic and the flight time only are considered for remote communications).

For collective operations, the two phase schema of these kind of operations is taken into account: a first phase where all processes send data to the root processor and a second phase where the root processor sends data to all other processors. Eventually, a collective operation will only have one of those phases. Also, each of those phases can follow different behaviors: logarithmic, linear ...

When considering collective operations through a computational Grid, each of the previous phases is decomposed into two more: the part which takes places inside each server and the part the takes places in the network. Dimemas takes into account all these possibilities by means of a user configurable table of parameters for each machine in the Grid and one for the network. Further details can be found in [1].

4 Experiments

Every organism's code of live, the genes, are stored in deoxyribonucleic acid (DNA), which is available in every cell of the organism. Still the ribonucleic acid (RNA) plays an even more important role in gene expression and protein synthesis.

The single-stranded RNA is subject to a process called folding, where the RNA's bases start pairing in a semi-chaotic fashion, increasing the order of the RNA-structure into a tertiary (3-dimensional) structure, resulting in a state of minimal energy. This tertiary structure determines the RNA-sequence's function. The *ab-initio* computation of such a tertiary structures is infeasible to achieve with contemporary computers, but may be predicted with the help of the corresponding secondary structure [2].

The application RNAfold calculates the secondary structure of RNA. It was developed as part of the ViennaRNA package at the University of Vienna [6] and MPI-parallelized. For iGrid2002 and the HPC-Challenge at SC2002, this application was enhanced by Sandia National Labs and HLRS, namely the energy parameters were updated, the application was integrated into the framework of a virtual reality environment and the communication pattern was improved in several consecutive steps to make it more efficient. Particularly the last optimization made it viable to run on a Metacomputer using PACX-MPI. Still it's computationally expensive in the order of $O(n^3)$, and also communication intensive: $O(n^2)$, n being the number of bases in the sequence.

At first, the communication was analyzed, using Vampir [10]. Here, it showed, that the computation is split in two parts: the first main communication follows a regular pattern: each process is communicating with each predecessor and its successor. In addition, process zero, which collects the intermediate results, distributes them onto a single, distinguished node storing it for the second step. In the second step, the secondary structure of minimal energy is reconstructed by collecting the data onto process zero again. The former communication step used five MPI_Isends to/from it's predecessor and successor, which were integrated into one MPI_Isend.

The second communication pattern was specifically inefficient for high-latency Metacomputing connections: process zero requests the data necessary for reconstruction from the process storing the particular data (sending three integers: matrix id, x,y-coordinates), which then delivers the data (returning one integer). The data requested consists of the F^M-matrix, F_{ij}^M storing the minimum free energy of substructure $[i, j]$ of the sequence, if i and j are part of a so-called multi-loop and the F^B-matrix, F_{ij}^B being the minimum free energy of substructure $[i, j]$ of the sequence, with bases i and j forming a pair. Since it was recognized, that process zero requests all values twice (some values over 700 times), a caching mechanism was implemented. Through the help of counters recorded from within the application into a file, it was recognized that values are requested following a regular pattern (see Fig. 2 for access pattern of the F^B-matrix and the F^M-matrix; colors encode the ordering of accesses, blue to red). One notes, that for the F^M-matrix values are accessed in a linear fashion,

i. e. process zero requests consecutive values of this matrix starting in this case from the diagonal center upwards (and downwards) and from the upper center to the rightmost corner (and backwards). For the F^B-matrix values requested from process zero are also clustered together.

To improve the efficiency of the communication, prefetching was introduced. While for F^B-matrix a square-sized area of the matrix was prefetched and transmitted, for the F^M-matrix a heuristic was integrated guessing the future values of the matrix being asked for: either a horizontal or a vertical line, both either incrementing or decrementing. This improved the computation time even for single HPC calculations of large sequences.

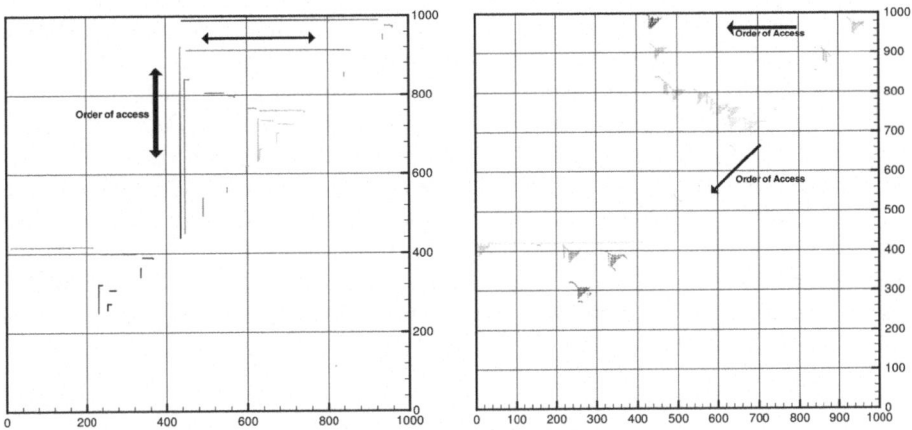

Fig. 2. Access pattern of the F^M-matrix (left) and the F^B-matrix (right).

4.1 Experiments at CEPBA-UPC

A first set of experiments was performed at the European Center for Parallelism of Barcelona(CEPBA) at the Technical University of Catalonia (UPC). The heterogeneous Metacomputer used in this case was composed of two machines: an SGI Origin O2000 server with 64 processors (Karnak) and an IBM RS-6000 SP with 8 by 16 Nighthawk Power3 processors (Kadesh).

Dimemas tracefiles of local executions on the SP3 were extracted with mpidtrace, the Dimemas tracefile generator. These tracefiles were then used to feed Dimemas simulator with different input configurations. To estimate the characteristics of the connection between the two machines the ping program was used. Depending on the network situation at each moment, the nominal values of the WAN parameters can vary at each moment. Afterwards, measurements of distributed executions between these two machines were performed to validate Dimemas predictions. The prediction for these cases was obtained by setting the network bandwidth to 0.5 MB/s and the flight time (network latency) to 4.9 ms.

We compared the results on the predicted values versus the measured values on, and the differences ranged between the 8% and the 17%, which we consider to be very good results.

4.2 Parametric Studies with Dimemas

Rather than predicting for a given configuration, Dimemas is also very useful for performing parametric studies of applications. In this sense, one can study which will be the best configuration in terms of machines, nodes and processors to run the application or which will be the threshold on the network parameters that will degrade the behavior of the application communications.

As an example the yeast DNA sequence has been used as data input, run with eight processors. The input configuration was set to two machines, with four processors each. A set of two hundred simulations were performed, randomly varying the values of two parameters: the network bandwidth and the flight time (latency of the network due to the distance). For each value of the flight time and network bandwidth a prediction was calculated. Each point of Fig. 3 shows the value predicted by Dimemas for the execution time against the network bandwidth and the flight time. Since this is a three-dimensional plot only projections are shown. We can observe that this application is sensitive both to the network bandwidth and to the flight time. However, for values of network bandwidth above 1MB/s, the performance of the application will be mainly sensitive to the flight time parameter. This experiment was performed using the Metacomputing tool ST-ORM [9].

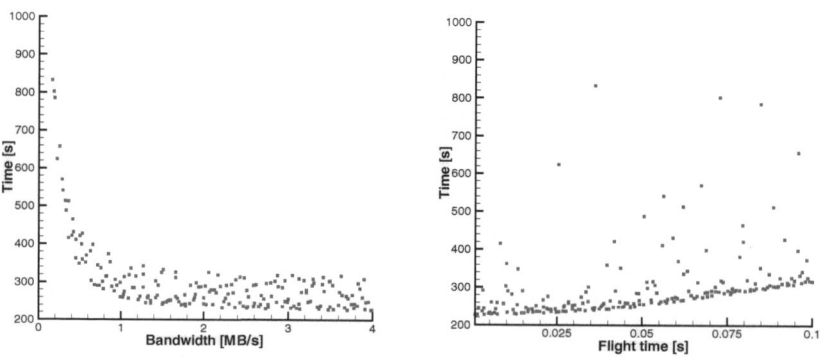

Fig. 3. Results of parametric study using Dimemas and ST-ORM.

4.3 Experiments between Both Sites

Testing the prediction of Dimemas on links with high-latency was performed on a distributed heterogeneous Metacomputer consisting of a 512 processor Cray

T3e900 (Hwwt3e) installed at HLRS and the IBM-SP3, as well as the Origin-2000 installed at CEPBA. Figure 4 summarizes the results of the tests performed. In the x-axis there are the different benchmarks and configurations that we have used for these experiments. The benchmarks are `Test_1000` to `Test_6000`, with 1000 and 6000 bases respectively, which are synthetic data sets to RNAfold. The configurations that have been considered are 4+4, with 4 processors on the O2000 and 4 on the T3E; and 6+6 and 14+14, with 6 and 14 processors on the IBM-SP and on the T3E respectively. For all these cases, some of the measurements were done more than one time (Measure 1 and Measure 2) showing how influent the network state can be on the achieved performance.

To estimate the latency and bandwidth of the network between Barcelona and Stuttgart, a combination of ping and traceroute tools were used. From the values obtained with those tools, a range of flight times and bandwidths were identified. These range of values were then used to feed Dimemas and obtain different prediction lines: for first line (in solid), the bandwidth was set to 70kB/s and the flight time to 10ms; for second line (in dashed), to 100kB/s and 10ms and for third line (in dotted) to 200kB/s and 1ms respectively. One may observe how Dimemas is able to capture the behavior of the application under this range of values, since all measured values (except one for the 4+4 configuration with `Test_4000`, which is slightly above the prediction) fall between the Dimemas predictions.

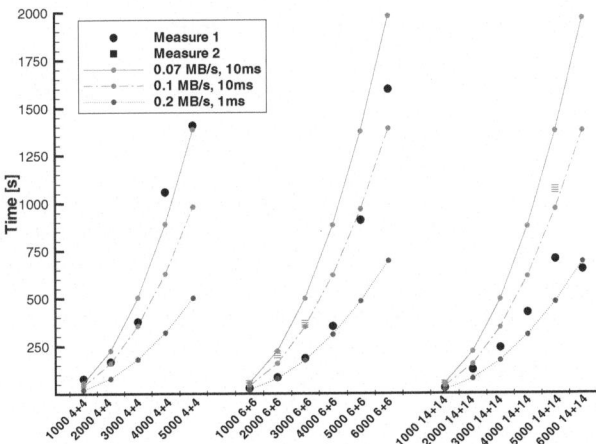

Fig. 4. Results obtained with a distributed Metacomputer.

5   Conclusion

The use of performance analysis and prediction tools for parallel codes is a must on computational Grids due to the complexity of the environment and of the codes themselves. The DAMIEN project aims at the development of tools for message passing applications on heterogeneous computational Grids. This paper presented some of the work performed in this project.

We demonstrated that the tools work for real applications, especially that Dimemas is not only able to analyze the sensitivity to network parameters like latency and bandwidth, but also to predict the behavior of the application in the extreme environment of the Grid. In addition, we introduced some application optimizations, like caching and prefetching, to reduce the sensitivity to latency and thus improve the performance.

Acknowledgments

This work was supported by the European Commission under contract number DAMIEN IST-2000-25406.

References

1. R. M. Badia, J. Labarta, J. Gimenez, and F. Escalé. DIMEMAS: Predicting MPI applications behavior in Grid environments. In *Workshop on Grid Applications and Programming Tools (GGF8)*, June 2003.
2. R. L. Baldwin and G. D. Rose. Is protein folding hierarchic? II – Local structure and peptide folding. *Tibs 24*, pages 77–83, February 1999.
3. H. Brunst, W. E. Nagel, and H.-C. Hoppe. Group-Based Performance Analysis of Multithreaded SMP Cluster Applications. In R. Sakellariou, J. Keane, J. Gurd, and L. Freeman, editors, *Euro-Par 2001 Parallel Processing*, pages 148–153. Springer, 2001.
4. E. Gabriel, R. Keller, P. Lindner, M. S. Müller, and M. Resch. Software Development in the Grid: The DAMIEN tool-set. In P. M. A. Sloot, D. Abramson, A. V. Bogdano, J. J. Dongarra, A. Y. Zomaya, and Y. E. Gorbachev, editors, *Computational Science - ICCS 2003*, volume 2659, pages 235–244. Springer, 2003.
5. E. Gabriel, M. Resch, T. Beisel, and R. Keller. Distributed Computing in a Heterogeneous Computing Environment. In *PVM/MPI*, pages 180–187, 1998.
6. I. L. Hofacker, W. Fontana, L. S. Bonhoeffer, M. Tacker, and P. Schuster. Vienna RNA Package. Internet, December 2003. http://www.tbi.univie.ac.at/~ivo/RNA.
7. M. S. Müller, E. Gabriel, and M. Resch. A Software Development Environment for Grid-Computing. In *Concurrency and Computers – Practice and Experience*, 2003. Special issue on Grid computing environments.
8. Paraver. Internet, December 2003. http://www.cepba.upc.es/paraver.
9. ST-ORM. Internet, December 2003. http://www.easi.de/storm.
10. Vampir. Internet, December 2003.
    http://www.pallas.com/e/products/vampir/index.htm.

ULabGrid, an Infrastructure to Develop Distant Laboratories for Undergrad Students over a Grid

O. Ardaiz, P. Artigas, L. Díaz de Cerio, F. Freitag, A. Gallardo, R. Messeguer,
L. Navarro, D. Royo, and K. Sanjeevan *

Computer Architecture Department,
Polytechnic University of Catalonia
Avda. del Canal Olimpic, s/n
Castelldefels 08860, Barcelona, Spain
{oardaiz,partigas,ldiaz,felix,agallard,
meseguer,leandro,dolors,sanji}@ac.upc.es

Abstract. There has been a lot of discussion and study in the recent past about how distance learning could be improved using emerging technologies. Collaborative tools based on the web/internet infrastructure such as e-mail, discussion groups, video/audio conferencing and virtual campuses have been proposed and implemented in many areas of distance learning. We had proposed [3] ULabGrid as a new architecture that enables educators to design collaborative, distant laboratories for undergraduate students using the Grid infrastructure. We describe here some of the changes we have made to the proposed architecture and the prototype that is being developed and present the results of our efforts to date.

1 Introduction

Many collaborative laboratory systems proposed in the literature that target individual tools tend to be unreusable, in spite of the fact they involve a significant amount of duplicated effort. For example, systems such as the Exploratarium [1] and JSPICE [17] are based on scripts that need to be modified in order to add new applications to the system. Other designs are more flexible, for example, the MOL [15] prototype employs static web interfaces that can be adapted for individual tools. However these static interfaces are not adequate for any tool. Solutions that address individual issues are generally reusable, but the tasks of adapting them for a production environment and integrating them into a complete computing infrastructure are non-trivial (VNC [16]).

As far as we know, PUNCH (Purdue University Network Computing Hubs) is the first and, to date, the only web-based computing system that is designed to support arbitrary tools and is utilized on a regular basis in a university environment [10],[11],[12]. However, the PUNCH system is not built over a GRID.

In this study, we design and implement a collaborative distance learning application that uses the ULabGrid infrastructure [3]. The users we target are

---

* Authors listed in alphabetic order.

F. Fernández Rivera et al. (Eds.): Across Grids 2003, LNCS 2970, pp. 265–272, 2004.
© Springer-Verlag Berlin Heidelberg 2004

undergraduate students. The system will allow users to run the tools needed to develop the labs through the net and will provide operating system services for networked resources (provides user-transparent file, process, and resource management functions, handles security and access control across multiple administrative domains, and manages state information - session management). Users will be capable to run tools remotely from everywhere at any time using their own computers.

2   Advantages of Using a Grid for Collaborative Laboratories

According to a definition, "A grid is a large-scale geographically distributed hardware and software infrastructure composed of heterogeneous networked resources owned and shared by multiple administrative organizations which are coordinated to provide transparent, dependable, pervasive and consistent computing support to a wide range of applications" [4]. Some of the more common problems that emerge when using educational software in a distant laboratory at the present time could be solved using a Grid infrastructure.

- *Software installation and maintenance.* Under a Grid infrastructure, software will be installed and maintained by an expert (system administrator) and the students need not spend time downloading, installing and configuring their own machines.
- *Licensing.* Often, the software used in educational labs is not a free distribution and the educational center has only a limited number of licenses. A Grid infrastructure could manage the number of licenses that are running in the global system and allow the students to work with the software from home.
- *Lack of hardware resources.* Sometimes, the software can only run on very powerful or specific machines so the students can't work at home with this software. In a Grid these specific machines belong to the Grid and the students only need to access it remotely.
- *High cost in changing the lab contents (hardware and software).* Changes and updates to the software are once again handled by the administrator - freeing the student from the burden of doing it at home.
- *Non homogeneous results.* Another problem solved if the software lab resides on a Grid is the fact that the results of the exercises for all students are guaranteed to be from a unique environment. It will make the detection of errors easier for both students and teachers.
- *Large-scale geographically distributed hardware and software infrastructure shared by multiple administrative organizations.* Using a Grid infrastructure, we could communicate with more than one learning laboratory - thereby, the students could collaborate with others that are working with the same tools in different universities. At the same time, a university with various campuses geographically distributed could share all their software in a global way.

- *Transparent computing.* The students don't have to spend time knowing how to use a particular software and could concentrate all their efforts on the learning process. For example, they could program in C - independent of the programming tool. This will improve the student's learning curve.

At present, there are toolkits for programming in a Grid infrastructure that have been designed to provide additional support for industry standardization based on the Grid protocols, for example, the Globus Project [8]. Using a Grid for Collaborative Laboratories could not be possible without a parallel research effort. In one hand, development and promotion of standard Grid protocols (e.g. OGSA) to enable interoperability and shared infrastructure. On the other hand, development and promotion of standard Grid software APIs and SDKs to enable portability and code sharing. The above point "Large-scale geoghaphically distributed hardware and software infrastructure shared by multiple administrative organizations" is hard to complete without standards and probably has no sense without them.

Some of the challenging aspects of collaborative applications built on a grid architecture are the real-time requirements imposed by human perceptual capabilities and the rich variety of interactions that can take place. Using a Grid for Collaborative Laboratories could not be possible without the improvement of network speed (computer speed doubles every 18 months and network speed doubles every 9 months, difference = order of magnitude per 5 years) (Globus-World 2003).

2.1   Educational Applications of Grid Tecnology

From previous charateristics of grid tecnology we can distinguish three main educational applications of grid technology. First ,it might permit students to access remote instruments and data for laboratory experiments using real instrumentation and real data sources. Second it should permit collaboration and knowledge sharing among students in different institutions; and third it should permit creation of virtual courses and classes among different organizations.

3   Framework for Collaborative Learning Applications over Grids

The ULabGrid infrastructure is being developed using the de-facto standard provided by the Globus toolkit 3 (GT3) [7]. The resource management pillar known as the Master Management Job Factory (MMJFS) provides support for: resource allocation, job submission and the management of job status and progress. The information services pillar known as the Index service provides support for discovery. The information provided by these services with regard to estimated execution time and queue delays will be used to schedule lab exercises on the available resources. The data management services of GridFTP will be used to manage the transfer of data between nodes, while the Grid Security Infrastructure (GSI) will help to ensure secure access to resources.

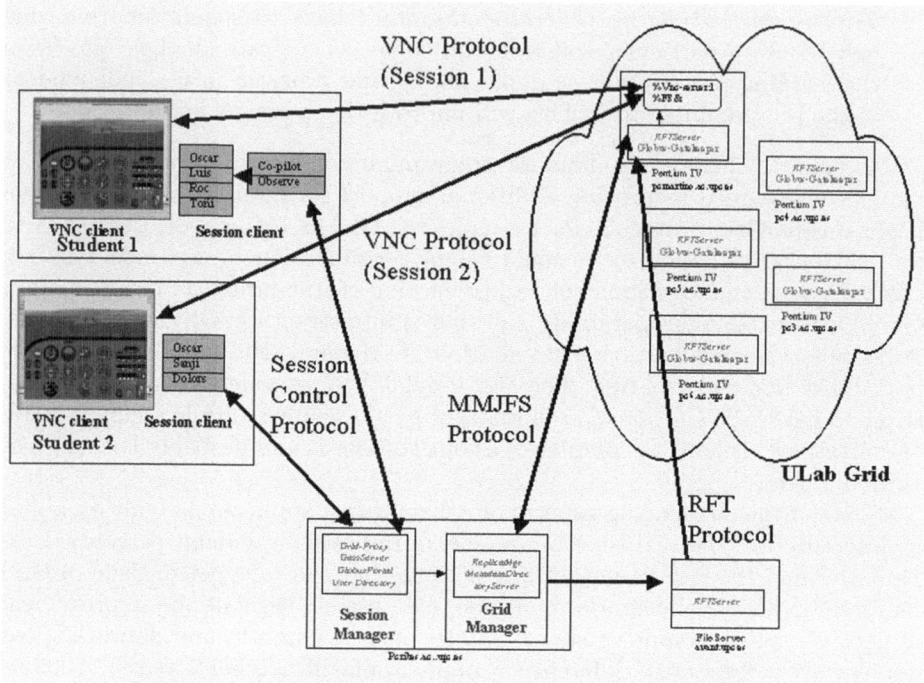

Fig. 1. Functional Working of the Session and Grid Managers.

The infrastructure being developed essentially consists of four main components:

– *User:* end/user, basically the client for the system
– *Collection of resources:* collection of computing/storage nodes that comprise the Grid
– *Session manager:* part that manages every on-going client session(including setup and client requests for session status changes).
– *Grid manager:* to manage the resources (including resource discovery, file transfer, job status etc.). This component must provide an efficient way to organize all networked resources and will be responsible for choosing the best available resources given static demands(user requirements) and dynamic data (network load, machine load etc.)

We expand upon the functionality of the two, last-mentioned components in the following section.

3.1   Functional Working of the Session and Grid Managers

As shown in Figure 1 the functional working of the session and grid managers can be described in five steps:

1. User connect to the server where the session manager is running, asking for a new connection and providing information regarding him/her self, name of the application they want to run, identification of the group they belong to(if any) and the identification of the terminal at which they are working.
2. The session manager, after authenticating the user, queries the Grid manager for the computational resource requested and passes this identifier to the user
3. Before starting the remote execution, the Grid manager transfers all the user's files via globus RDT services to the selected remote machine. With the application name, the remote machine name the Grid manager starts a VNC server process and the application on the remote machine via the services offered by MMJFS.
4. The user now starts the VNC client on his/her machine to begin the session with the remote machine on the grid.
5. During the session, the user can request the Session manager to:
   a) Let her know about other users of the same group who are working on the application.
   b) Allow him to be just a passive student (without ability to control).
   c) Allow him to be an active student (be allowed to take control of the application and collaborate).

4   Case Study. Collaborative Learning in a Flight Simulator

We have researched different learning environments that might take advantage of grid properties. Simple collaborative learning applications such as chats, or shared blackboards can be executed on a grid, however they do not take advantage of fundamental characteristics of grids. We were looking for a learning software application that required a large amount of computing resources, processing power, memory and network bandwidth. In our nearby school of aeronautics we found that flight simulators was such an application. Though they currently use a commercial simulator, they pointed us to a free simulator whose source code was available, which will allow us to add new functionality in the future. FightGear [6] is a flight simulator that allows one to pilot different kinds of airplanes, in many topographic scenarios that are computer generated, and require large amounts of processing power. We need to measure which resources this application needs from a grid, so that a resource management technique is designed to assign simulation sessions to grid resources.

4.1   Group Flight Lessons

Learning to fly is a complex and responsible task. An instructor will always be required so that no error is committed since security is of paramount importance. Collaborative learning will be an effective method for learning to fly. We are investigating how students can benefit from collaborative learning by techniques such as sharing navigation controls, or annotating flight directions, etc.

5   Early Technical Results

Our initial experience with the Flight Simulator program over the ULabGrid system gave us the opportunity to extract some important concluding results.

5.1   Resource Requirements and Resource Scheduling

Initial trials with the Flight Simulator program show that it has high computational requirements. A single simulator session consumes 100Pentium III processor running Linux (RedHat). Flight Simulator has very high computational demands because it generates 3 dimensional scenarios on-the-fly using the OpenGL library [14]. It also has high demands on network bandwidth. We have found that there are different implementations of VNC with different compression ratios, and protocol complexity, one of such implementation is specially suited for OpenGL applications. In fact this implementation was the only one with acceptable screen refresh rates. We are currently working on obtaining network bandwidth requirements figures.

We are investigating resource-scheduling algorithm for such an application. Work by Bote et. Al. [4] shows it is an interesting area of research. Also interactive applications resource scheduling is a novel research area [13]

5.2   Shared Cursor Control

Another interesting result from initial trials is to do with the shared control of the navigation panel. The VNC protocol permits sharing screens and input devices. An initial test we conducted allowed both students to share control of the mouse cursor. Though of course this will not be a possibility in a real plane, for educational purposes it might be a nice feature, we have to investigate this.

5.3   Overlays for Scalability and Intra Group Communication

Overlays [9], are a software infrastructure for many-to-many communications. So that if large groups of students collaborate, they might be required. Instead of initiating one VNC session per student, a multicast overlay will permit one single VNC session per group. Also, overlays might allow intra group communications.

6   Related Work

To our knowledge there are very few works trying to use the grid for educational purposes. There are some proyects implementing a Grid to permit students to access remote instruments and data for laboratory experiments using real instrumentation and real data sources. With that goal in mind it has been design the World-Wide Telescope [18], it is an educational tool that allows students worldwide to access data gathered by a telescope for studying astronomy, though it has not been implemented with grid technology. Datagrid [5], a grid to provide high energy physicist with PetaBytes of data from the Large Hadron Collider, has been said to permit students to access same data and tools that scientist. There is even less work on using a grid to permit collaboration and knowledge sharing among students in different institutions; or to permit creation of virtual courses and classes among different organizations. Globus Toolkit is being extended to provide a collaborative framework by Amir et al. [2].

Acknowledgments

This work has been supported by the Ministry of Science and Technology of Spain and the European Union (CICYT TIC2001/0995-C02-01 and TIC2002/ 04258-C03-01).

References

1. Adasiewicz, C.: Exploratorium: User friendly science and engineering. NCSA Access 9, 2, 10-11.
2. Amin, K., Nijsure, S., Laszewski, G. von.: A Grid Services Framework for Collaborative Applications. IEEE/ACM SC2002: SuperComputing 2002, November 2002, Baltimore, USA.
3. Ardaiz, O., Artigas, P., Díaz de Cerio, L., Freitag, F., Messeger, R., Navarro, L., Royo, D.: ULabGrid, an infrastructure to develop distant laboratories for undergrad students over a Grid. In Proceedings of the First European Across Grids Conference, 2003.
4. Bote, M., Dimitriadis, Y., Gómez-Sánchez, E.: Grid uses and characteristics: a grid definition. In Proceedings of the First European Across Grids Conference, 2003.
5. Data Grid Project. http://eu-datagrid.web.cern.ch/eu-datagrid. 2001.
6. Flightgear. www.flightgear.org. 2003.
7. Foster I., Kesselman C.: The Globus Project: A status report. In Proceedings of the 1998 Heterogeneous Computing Workshop (HCW'98), pp 4-18, 1998.
8. The Globus Project. www.globus.org. 2003.
9. Jannotti, J., Gifford, D. K., Johnson, K. L., Kaashoek, M. F., O'Toole, J. W.: Overcast: Reliable multicasting with an overlay network. In Proceedings of the Fourth Symposium on Operating System Design and Implementation (OSDI), October 2000.
10. Kapadia N.H., Figueiredo R.J., Fortes J.A.B.: PUNCH: Web Portal for Running Tools. IEEE Micro. May-June 2000.
11. Kapadia, N. H., Fortes, J. A. B., Lundstrom, M. S., Royo D.: PUNCH: A Computing Portal for the Virtual University. Forthcoming in a special issue on Virtual Universities and Engineering Education.
12. Kapadia, N. H., Robertson, J. P., and Fortes, J. A. B.: Interface issues in running computer architecture tools via the world-wide web. In Proceedings of the Workshop on Computer Architecture Education at the 25th Annual International Symposium on Computer Architecture (ISCA'98) June 1998.
13. Kumar, R., Talwar, V., Basu, S.: A Resource Management Framework For Interactive Grids. Middleware Workshops 2003: 238-244.
14. OpenGl High Performance 2D 3D Graphics. www.opengl.org. 2003.

15. Reinefeld, A., Baraglia, R., Decker, T., Gehring, J., Laforenza, D., Ramme, F., Romke, T., and Simon, J.: The MOL project: An open, extensible metacomputer.
16. Richardson T., Sta ord-Fraser T., Wood K.R., Hopper A.: Virtual network computing. IEEE Internet Computing, 2(1):33-38, January-February 1998.
17. Souder, D., Herrington, M., Garg, R. P., and DeRyke, D.: JSPICE: A component-based distributed Java front-end for SPICE. In Proceedings of the 1998 Workshop on Java for High-Performance Network Computing (1998).
18. Szalay, A., Gray, J.: The World-Wide Telescope. Volume 293, Number 5537, pp. 2037-2040. Issue of 14 Sep 2001.

Wireless Java-Enabled MIDP Devices as Peers in a Grid Infrastructure

Miika Tuisku

Helsinki Institute of Physics, CERN
Miika.Tuisku@cern.ch

Abstract. Combining Mobile Internet and Grid technologies could mean the ability to command the power of supercomputers with a mobile device. The computing and data transfer capacities of mobile devices are expanding and Grid-related technologies are already being employed in them. In this paper, we survey the current technologies and standards, mainly concentrating on MIDP (Mobile Information Device Profile) devices and Java (J2ME) interfaces. The technology has a potential for many new interesting applications. This paper outlines a feasibility study, a technological review and examples of applications.

1 Introduction

While wireless devices such as high-end Personal Digital Assistants (PDA) and Mobile Communicators have become as powerful as some Personal Computers (PC), the fact that they can be constantly connected to the Internet opens doors for new types of networked applications. Although Microsoft Windows has dominated the desktop computer, eventually the mobile phone will be dominated by Java [19]: All major mobile phone manufacturers have introduced handsets based on the Java 2 Micro Edition [20] language in order to provide a homogeneous application platform for 3rd party developers. The market tendency is that soon every new phone is Java-enabled which will steadily propagate to cover the current one billion subscriber base by year 2006, as the ARC Group researchers estimate [12].

Besides the Mobile Internet traditional Internet computing is experiencing a conceptual shift from a Client-Server model to Grid and Peer-to-Peer (P2P) Computing models. In these models, computing and information resources as well as the meta-data about them are scattered throughout the Internet. The precursors of Grid technology are used e.g. to find extra-terrestrial intelligence from outer space (Seti@Home) [24] or to find cure for AIDS (fightAIDS@Home) [15] by donating unused computing cycles or to share digital music files with peer groups (Napster) [13] by extending searches to every computer in the P2P network.

As these two key trends: Mobile Internet and the Grid, are likely to find each other, the resource constraints that wireless devices pose today affect the level of interoperability between them. The goal of this research is to investigate how

F. Fernández Rivera et al. (Eds.): Across Grids 2003, LNCS 2970, pp. 273–281, 2004.

well the most limited wireless Java devices (MIDP) [20] can make use of Grid technologies.

2   Motivation and Background

Grid is the umbrella that covers many of today's distributed computing technologies. Grid technology attempts to support flexible, secure, coordinated information sharing among dynamic collections of individuals, institutions, and resources. This includes data sharing but also access to computers, software and devices required by computation and data-rich collaborative problem solving [11]. As a scientific example the Grid will help European Organization for Nuclear Research (CERN) to effectively share and manage the collision data from the new Large Hadron Collider (LHC) with rate of 100-1000 Mb/s. The difference between Computational Grids and P2P networks is roughly that they are currently targeted for different audiences. The vision of Computational Grids is to provide tools for power users and usually scientists to harness the power of the grid in the same way as plugging into a socket on the wall for electricity. Today P2P networks are used to create virtual communities to access commodity resources such as MP3 files.

A Computational Grid is a collection of computers, on-line instruments, data archives and networks all tied together by a shared set of services that, when taken together, provides users with transparent access through interface devices to the entire set of resources [9].

A P2P network is a collection of users, interface devices, computers, on-line instruments, data archives and networks all tied together by a shared set of services that, when taken together, provides all the elements transparent access to each other [9].

So far the use of Grid services has required a modern workstation, specialized software installed locally and expert intervention. In the future these requirements should diminish considerably. One reason is the emergence of Grid Portals as gateways to the Grid. Another reason is the Web Service boom in the industry. The use of XML as a network protocol and an integration tool will ensure that a future Grid peer could be a simple wireless device. The main argument for XML is that it separates applications from the network and developers will be able to create applications to run on different platforms and networks.

The special resource constraints that today's wireless devices pose are numerous [20]:

- Persistent storage is limited and shared by all applications. Modern low-end PDAs are pre-equipped with maximum of 8 Mb memory. Simple mobile phones have only 256 kb of memory.
- Runtime heap is small, 128-256 kbs.
- Network bandwidth is very limited and latency is high: GSM 9.6 kb/s, HSCD 43.2 kb/s, GPRS 144 kb/s, WLAN 11Mb/s.
- Processor performance is modest RISC/CISC 16-50 Mhz.

- Electrical power is confined to that available from small batteries.
- Screen size for building a user interface is minimal. Mobile phones may only have space for 3-6 lines of text on screen.

We will concentrate on the most limited category of wireless Java 2, Micro Edition (J2ME[tm]) devices that use the Mobile Information Device Profile (MIDP). The MIDP specification contains Java packages (see Figure 1.) that have to suffice for applications limited with 128 kilobytes of Java runtime and 8 kilobytes of persistent memory. The MIDP implementation itself has to fit into 256 kilobytes of non-volatile memory [20]. The Applications that these devices understand are Midlets (analogues to Applets, Servlets etc). Typically the maximum size of a midlet varies from 30-50 kbs and a user can download four to six applications to their mobile phone. J2ME is a set of technologies and specifications developed for small devices like smart cards, pagers, mobile phones, and set-top boxes. J2ME uses subset of Java 2, Standard Edition (J2SE[tm]) components, like smaller virtual machines and leaner APIs. J2ME has categorized wireless devices and their capabilities into profiles: MIDP, PDA and Personal. The MIDP and PDA profiles are targeted for handhelds and Personal profile for networked consumer electronic and embedded devices.

As the technology progresses in quantum leaps any strict categorization is under threat to become obsolete. It can already be seen that J2ME Personal profile (a.k.a. PersonalJava) are being used in high-end PDAs such as PocketPCs and Mobile Communicators. These device profiles are likely to grow after new releases. Despite the physical limitations of wireless devices that may remain constant, memory and processing power is increasing all the time. For example Samsung has recently introduced an integrated chip that contains most functionality of a mobile phone, with support for multiple operating systems (Windows CE, Palm OS, Symbian and Linux), 356 Mb of Flash ROM and 256 Mb of RAM memory together with a 203 Mhz Arm processor [2].

3   Mobile Devices and Grid

3.1   Feasibility

A Wireless PDA/Mobile phone can be envisioned in the following roles in a Grid Infrastructure:

- Data consumer: Provide an intelligent user interface for remote analysis and control.
- Data producer: Ability to register physical phenomena by functioning as a sensor or captor.
- Storage element: Provide a persistent storage for data produced or configuration information used in the Grid.
- Computing element: The capability of running small computational tasks or jobs on demand.

Planned further research will provide a detailed analysis of how feasible each role is for Java-enabled wireless MIDP device by means of literature study and prototype construction.

Special attention will be given to application of industry standard protocols and their derivatives for facilitating the devices' possibilities to act in these roles. Nevertheless the biggest factor remains the extent that the Grid Security Infrastructure (GSI) model can be applied.

3.2   Emerging Technologies and Related Work

Comparison with Wireless Application Protocol

One of the advantages that MIDP has over browser-based technologies such as WAP is that it is universal and it provides the same application programming interface (API) to various devices whether they are mobile phones, two-way pagers, or low end PDAs. Furthermore MIDP includes facilities for persistent storage of data which are kept intact throughout the normal use of the platform, including reboots and battery changes. As in the J2SE Java development environment, MIDP provides an enhanced user experience by providing tools for building richer and responsive graphical user interfaces (GUI) for applications that load the server and the network more optimally. MIDP applications are able to process small tasks in the background while transferring data. This fact will alleviate the higher response times resulting from wireless networks. According to Nokia's internal studies and informal tests [1] the average latency for a HTTP based round trip accross GSM based network is 5-10 seconds for first round and 2-4 seconds for following round trips. These figures are much larger than from those of accessing Web pages with modern personal computers connected to wireline network.

Wireless Clients with Enterprise Java

Java 2 Micro Edition (J2ME), as part of the overall Java framework, is designed to interoperate with Java 2 Enterprise Edition (J2EE), which includes tools for developing Internet-aware distributed multi-tier applications. This specification not only enables Object Oriented Web application development but also stand-alone Java applications. Sun has published blueprints for 'Designing Wireless Clients for Enterprise Applications with Java Technology' [14], which takes advantage of various J2EE specification methologies. Technologies that are particularly of interest for wireless application development are XML-based protocols, Java Messaging Service (JMS) and Java Servlets.

Open Mobile Alliance

MIDP-enabled mobile phones have the potential to become de facto the mobile payment and personal access medium by incorporating X.509 certicates as digital fingerprints inside the WIM/SWIM [7] card. Open Mobile Alliance (OMA) has

java.io	MIDP subset of system input and output through data streams
java.lang	MIDP subset of the core Java programming language
java.util	A small subset of utility classes
javax.microedition.io	Networking support using the Generic Connection Framework; MIDP 2.0 includes new socket, UDP, serial, and secure connection types, and push functionality
javax.microedition.lcdui	MIDP user interface classes
javax.microedition.lcdui.game	Gaming classes such as sprites, game canvas, and layer manager
javax.microedition.media	The interfaces for controlling (Control) and rendering (Player) audio - sound classes compatible with the Mobile Media API (JSR 135) specification
javax.microedition.media.control	Sound -control classes (ToneControl and VolumeControl) - compatible with the Mobile Media API (JSR 135) specification
javax.microedition.midlet	The application (MIDlet) interface, its life-cycle classes and its interactions with the runtime environment, and the application manager
javax.microedition.pki	Public key class for certificates used to authenticate information for secure connections
javax.microedition.rms	Persistence classes for storage and retrieval of data

Fig. 1. The J2ME MIDP 2.0 API package structure [20].

published specifications for such a WAP Public Key Infrastructure (WPKI). In addition to hardware based smart card storage, X.509 certificates can be stored from MIDP applications into the Record Medium Storage (RMS) on the phone. A prominent software for building PKI-aware wireless applications is the Bouncy Castle Crypto package [21], which is an Open Source implementation of popular cryptographic algorithms including a lightweight cryptographic API for J2ME.

Project JXTA

Another technology that has potential for J2ME devices is JXTA, a P2P protocol framework, that contains an implementation for J2ME. JXTA for J2ME is a lightweight edge peer that operates through JXTA relays. JXTA relays act as proxies for completing more complex tasks for wireless devices and collecting and trimming incoming data for forwarding through a low-bandwith connection. Meanwhile wireless peers have to poll the relay periodically to acquire the collected responses. JXTA for J2ME implements basic JXTA features such as User, Group and Peer discovery, creating pipes and groups and communicating with other peers. JXTA is based on simple a XML message-passing technique and JXTA for J2ME is primarily targeted for online gaming, financial services and instant messaging. JXTA has also been studied as a large framework for a distributed computing platform [17] and as a development platform for a large economics-based Grid computing marketplace [23].

Open Grid Services Architecture and XML Protocols

The XML protocol-based Web Services interfaces were initially promising as a communication method between wireless devices and back-end servers. A prime candidate for wireless Grid applications is the new Open Grid Services Architecture (OGSA) model used in the Globus Toolkit 3 [10]. Wrapping the existing Grid middleware with XML interfaces holds the promise of providing a universal solution also to wireless devices. As it happens the XML multipurpose protocol stack can be reused over and over again, while the protocol implementation and payload can be described with Web Service Description Language (WSDL) in plain text. However given account to the limited memory constraints, Web Services technology is likely too heavy for first generation MIDP devices. The fact remains, that Web Service protocol implementations such as kSOAP [3] weigh 41 kilobytes i.e. over 30 percent of standard application memory of low-end MIDP device whereas more lightweight protocols such as kXML-RPC [3] requires only 24 kilobytes. The overhead of Simple Object Access Protocol message parsing in light J2ME-based wireless devices has also been studied and the results show 2-3 times slower response times compared to a proprietary protocol that communicates with a proxy client that utilizes Web Services on behalf of the wireless client [26]. The upper scale of MIDP devices is quickly changing and highend mobile phones will provide as large memory footprints as 16Mb (eg. Nokia 6600, the first MIDP2 implementation available Q4/2003). Mobile Web Services is a future technology trend addressed by Microsoft, Open Mobile Alliance and the Parlay Group.

Software Agents for Wireless Devices

The Foundation for Intelligent Physical Agents (FIPA) [4] was formed in 1996 to produce software standards for heterogeneous and interacting agents and agent-based systems. The FIPA lists publicly available Agent platforms [5], some of which are built with wireless devices in mind such as Agent Development Kit, Fipa OS and LEAP. According to the Wireless World Research Forum (WWRF), Agents are one of the key enabling technologies for future wireless devices especially combined with web services and instant messaging capabilities [8]. The Helsinki Institute of Physics has also studied GSI enabled Agent platforms in development of the Mobile Analyzer concept [16]. The Java Community Process (JCP-87) is also currently specifying a new Application Programming Interface (API) for Java Agent Services (JAS) [22].

3.3 Example Applications

The most natural way for small wireless devices to function on the grid is to provide ubiquitous access to timely information as data consumers. As such they provide a handy alternative and extension to traditional access media such as stand-alone networked applications or Web browsers. While the capabilities of acting as a Computing Element or a Storage Element is very limited, wireless devices such as mobile phones can be used as sensors or captors in novel ways:

- By default, base stations report locations of mobile phones into the central database of Mobile Switching Center. Individual phones can be tracked anonymously and timed as they move from point A to point B. This mobile phone location and related data can be used in e.g. traffic planning and monitoring [25]. When mapping velocities of mobile phone users on public highways, it is possible to measure traffic flow and indicate possible traffic jams and thus provide valuable, accurate and cost efficient information via radio, Internet and Short Message Service.
- The movement of lungs and heartbeats cause interference with mobile phone connections and can be detected by an active phone close to the human body. This data can be used to produce valuable information of pulse and breathing rate for realtime healthcare applications [18]. It can be used as an inexpensive way of monitoring vital signs of victims of earth quakes or avalanches or as a remote diagnostic tool for doctors and their patients.

These two examples were presented because they require few or no modifications to standard mobile phones. This is an important factor for maximum deployment potential. Currently sensors like cameras, global positioning systems (GPS) and thermometers are being introduced into wireless devices. Especially cameras and the digital images they produce will catalyze novel applications e.g. in computer vision and pattern recognition area that would require increasing amounts of computing power in the future:

- Although the resolution of today's camera phones are limited (Nokia 7650, 300k pixels), Optical Character Recognition (OCR) techniques developed by IBM are able to interprete 4000 chinese characters in 6 fonts. Combining this with a translation service (An IBM Zurich research laboratory showcase) would be useful for western tourists with camera phones in China.

While today's mobile phones are able to download new ringtones, logos, and new games from the wireless network, the Software Defined Radio (SDR) Forum [6] defines an open architecture for reconfigurable wireless technology. This technology plays key role in seamless network convergence for multi-mode wireless devices that are capable of roaming into heterogenous access environments and to utilize applications specific to these environments.

- The Software inside mobile phones is becoming complex and such software can already be referred as an operating system in the same way as in personal computers and workstations. Many of the problems or bugs that users face in daily operation are not hardware based and can be fixed with software updates called patches. A scenario where constantly connected wireless devices could update themselves automatically would need a security infrastructure similar to one used in the Grid, where users and service entitities trust each other.

4 Summary and Discussion

In this paper, the role of mobile devices in a Computing Grid environment was outlined. We presented the current state of mobile devices, their feasibility for different roles in a Grid, and presented some example applications.

The P2P and Grid concepts represent two ends of the same problem. P2P has already viable tools to connect most limited wireless devices in a Grid-like fashion. Academic Grid tools like Globus, Condor or Legion on the other hand are suitable for creating global grids connecting computing centers. The missing link between these high and low end Grid computing concepts could be filled with emerging technologies to create end-to-end distributed computing applications with mobile control.

The research work will rely on the capabilities of the GridBlocks framework (http://gridblocks.sourceforge.net) being developed by the Helsinki Institute of Physics. The framework will be extended to provide the required functionality to connect a Wireless Java device to the Grid. The outcome is also dependent of the maturity of J2ME specification implementations. MIDP profile has been chosen for this reason. The current release of MIDP specification is version 2.0, but at the time of writing there is no supported hardware available. MIDP specification version 2.0 includes many important new features such as Secure Socket Layer and Wireless Transport Layer Security support, signed midlets, over-the-air provisioning and push architecture.

The future activities will be as follows:

- Creating a wireless test environment. Studying the development environment and the limits of chosen wireless devices (a recent low-end PDA and a mobile phone). Designing and implementing a P2P network for these devices.
- Designing and implementing wireless Grid applications (in Data Consumer and Data Producer roles). Study the possibilities to make the applications secure (Grid Security model). Designing and implementing security features where possible.

Acknowledgements

I wish to thank Marko Niinimäki and Matti Heikkurinen for inspiring ideas, Vesa Sivunen for the great help in preparing the poster and John White for proofreading.

References

1. Nokia Corporation. Efficient midp programming. Available on:
   http://www.forum.nokia.com, 2002.
2. Digitoday. Samsung kutisti matkapuhelimen sirulle. Available on:
   http://www.digitoday.fi/digi98fi.nsf/pub/dd20030204092832_kni_44873884, 2003.
3. Open Source Initiative Enhydra. ksoap, kxml, kuddi for j2me. Available on:
   http://me.enhydra.org.

4. Foundation for Intelligent Physical Agents. Fipa. Available on: http://www.fipa.org, 2002.
5. Foundation for Intelligent Physical Agents. Publicly available agent platform implementations. Available on: http://www.fipa.org/resources/livesystems.html, 2002.
6. Software Defined Radio Forum. Software defined radio. Available on: http://www.sdrforum.org, 2002.
7. Wireless Application Protocol Forum.Wireless application protocol public key infrastructure definition. Technical report, 2001.
8. Wireless World Research Forum. Book of visions. Available on: http://ist-wsi.org, 2001.
9. I. Foster. The industrial grid conference, paris; conference slides. 2001.
10. I. Foster and C. Kesselman. Globus: A metacomputing infrastructure toolkit. *International Journal of Supercomputer Applications*, 11(2), 1997.
11. I. Foster, C. Kesselman, and S. Tuecke. The anatomy of the Grid: Enabling scalable virtual organizations. *International Journal of Supercomputer Applications*, 15(3), 2001.
12. ARC group. Future mobile handsets - 2002 edition:Worldwide market analysis and strategic outlook 2002-2007. Available on: http://www.arcgroup.com, 2002.
13. Roxio Inc. Napster. Available on: http://napster.com.
14. Sun Microsystems Inc. Blueprints for designing wireless clients for enterprise applications. Available on: http://java.sun.com/blueprints/wireless, 2002.
15. Scripps Research Institute. Fightaids@home. Available on: http://www.fightaidsathome.org.
16. M. Niinimäki J. Karppinen, T. Niemi. Mobile analyzer - new concept for next generation of distributed computing. Submitted to The 3rd IEEE/ACM International Symposium on Cluster Computing and the Grid, (CCGrid 2003), Japan 2003., 2003.
17. G. Ruetsch J. Verbeke, N. Nadgir and I. Shaparov. Framework for peer-to-peer distributed computing in a heterogeneous, decentralized environment. Technical report, 2002.
18. Nicola Jones. Mobile monitor. Available on: http://www.newscientist.com/news/news.jsp?id=ns9999398, 2001.
19. Seamus McAteer. Java will be the dominant handset platform. Available on: http://www.microjava.com/articles/perspective/zelos, 2002.
20. Sun microsystems Inc. J2me. Available on: http://wireless.java.sun.com.
21. Legion of Bouncy Castle. Bouncy castle crypto package. Available on: http://www.bouncycastle.org, 2002.
22. Java Community Process. Java agent services. Available on: http://jcp.org/en/jsr/detail?id=87, 2002.
23. GridBus project. Compute power market. Available on: http://compute-powermarket.jxta.org, 2002.
24. Seti@Home. Seti@home. Available on: http://setiathome.ssl.berkeley.edu.
25. Tiehallinto. Matkapuhelimet kertovat maanteiden ruuhkapaikat. Available on: http://www.tiehallinto.fi/tied/2002/matkapuhelimet.htm, 2002.
26. V.Bansal and A.Dalton. A performance analysis of web services on wireless pdas. Technical report, 2002.

TCP Behavior on Transatlantic Lambda's

Wim Sjouw[1], Antony Antony[2], Johan Blom[1], Cees de Laat[1], and Jason Lee[1]

[1] Universteit van Amsterdam, 403 Kruislaan,
1098 SJ Amsterdam, The Netherlands
{jblom,delaat,wsjouw}@science.uva.nl, jrlee@lbl.gov
[2] NIKHEF, 409 Kruislaan,
1098 SJ Amsterdam, The Netherlands
antony@nikhef.nl

Abstract. Recent research in the area of high speed TCP has revealed that the protocol can misbehave in cases of high bandwidth long delay networks. Here we present work that clearly demonstrates this behavior of TCP flows in detail. This examination has led us to study the influence of the underlying network as well as the end user system using bursty a protocol such as TCP under such conditions. We describe briefly what the requirements are for such an extreme network environment to support high speed TCP flows.

1 Introduction

In general, Grid applications can be very demanding on bandwidth requirements. Provisioning (very) high speed optical paths (called lambdas) could provide a solution to this problem. However, the question remains, do these kinds of paths behave normally in respect to user applications if they are extended over long ($>$ 5000 km) distances? To test this SURFnet [7] provisioned a 2.5 Gbps Lambda [5] between Amsterdam and Chicago. Initial tests on this link were conducted to understand how transport protocols, such as TCP, behave and what additional requirements high speed flows impose on the environment, including end user systems. Initial throughput measurements of a single TCP stream over such an extreme network infrastructure showed surprisingly poor results. Later in 2002 the same set of experiments was repeated on the DataTAG [3] infrastructure with similarly poor results. The reasons are examined in the following paragraphs.

2 Properties of the Network Infrastructure

The initial network configuration using the SURFnet Lambda (2.5 Gbps) is shown in Figure 1. Two high-end Personal Computers (PCs) were connected to each other, using Gigabit Ethernet via two Time Division Multiplexer (TDM) switches and one router. One TDM was located in Amsterdam, the other one in Chicago. The switches encapsulate Ethernet packets in SONET frames up to the rate of the specific SONET channel (622 Mbps initially, later 1.25 Gbps). The

F. Fernández Rivera et al. (Eds.): Across Grids 2003, LNCS 2970, pp. 282–290, 2004.

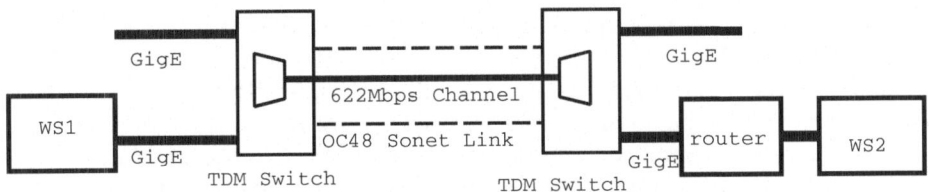

Fig. 1. Initial network setup. Two hosts connected back via two TDM switches interconnected at OC48 Link (96 msec RTT), sub channeled into an OC12.

Round Trip Time (RTT) was about 100 ms and thus had a high bandwidth-delay product. The link was exclusively used for research so there was no background traffic to influence the results. Initial tests were done in a back to back configuration which showed a throughput close to the speed of the SONET channel speed between the switches. Tests done with the same switches placed in Amsterdam and in Chicago, using a single stream TCP session, yielded a throughput (80 Mbps) an order of magnitude less than the bottleneck (SONET channel) capacity. This difference led us to the conclusion that the problem lay in the large RTT. Traces of TCP flows showed the burstiness of TCP during the slow start phase. This lead to the idea that the TDM switch could not cope with the amount of data being bursted and thus was dropping packets. Flow control was not operational. The DataTAG configuration was essentially the same with the TDM's replaced by routers (Cisco 760x's). In order to estimate the maximum possible burst-size which would not cause packet loss in the switch, we used a tunable UDP stream. This enabled us to mimic the bursty nature of TCP's slow start phase. Using UDPmon [9], 5000 numbered UDP packets, each with a length of 1000 Bytes, were sent with no inter packet delay from the sender to the receiver. The first loss occurs after about 1500 packets. Thereafter every one in three packets is dropped. The bottleneck mentioned is probably the cause of this since the ratio of dropped packets agree with the bandwidth ratio. Furtheron, after about 2400 packets, a continuous block of about 150 packets is lost. We assume that these are dropped at the receiver. Reading out of the (SNMP) counters at the switches in the path supported this assumption. The receiving PC is overwhelmed and it drops a series of packets. Assumedly they are dropped while being copied from the memory of the Network Interface Card (NIC) to the memory of the receiving process. In section 3.2 this receiver limitation is discussed more extensively. Here we focus on the intrinsic bottleneck on the sender side of the TDM switch.

The number of packets dropped by the switch, N_d, during a burst is related to the number of packets in the burst, N_b. The speed of the incoming interface, f (fast), the speed of the outgoing interface, s (slow), and the buffer memory available at the output port of the bottleneck link, M. For simplicity we assume an average packet length of size l. The loss can then be expressed as:

$$N_d = N_b \frac{f-s}{f} - \frac{M}{l} \tag{1}$$

Using equation 1, setting $N_d = 0$, $N_b = 1500$ as that is the maximum burst which got through, and $l = 1000$ Bytes it is possible to compute the available memory on the TDM switch to be approximately 0.5 MBytes. This was later confirmed by the manufacturer. Once we know the memory at the bottleneck and thus the size of the burst in packets that can pass through the TDM switch, we can calculate the maximum possible bandwidth a TCP flow can achieve during slow start without packet loss. We assume there are no other bottlenecks in the end-to-end path and that no congestion events have occurred.

To first order, the throughput TCP can obtain is approximated by:

$$B = \frac{f}{f - s} \frac{M}{R} \tag{2}$$

where B is the throughput that a TCP flow can achieve and R is the round trip time. Assuming that TCP will try to reach a stable state with a throughput equal to the speed of the slowest interface, we can then substitute $B = s$ into equation 2. This leads to a memory requirement to support a high-bandwidth-delay product TCP flow as:

$$M = \frac{f - s}{f} sR \tag{3}$$

For the network shown in Figure 1 to support a 622 Mbps end-to-end TCP flow the minimum memory required should be about 3 MBytes ($f = 1$ Gbps, $s = 622$ Mbps, $R = 100$ msec). This is far more than is actually implemented. From preliminary discussions with a few vendors, we understand that Ethernet to TDM encapsulation devices are primarily designed for high-speed Local Area Networks (LAN) and Metropolitan Area Networks (MAN), where the RTT is small (< 20 ms), thus accommodating the bursty nature of TCP flows during the bandwidth discovery phase. The problem arises when these LAN's and MAN's are interconnected via other high-speed long-latency networks. The buffer requirements for any device which has traffic flows over it that are high-bandwidth high-latency, and has disproportional interface speeds, should have enough buffer space to handle the difference in input and output speed of the interfaces for the RTT of those flows. Equation 3 applies for those situations.

If we solve the quadratic equation 3 for s we can compute the TCP through-put for various values of RTT and given values of M and f under the assumption there are no other bottlenecks present and the TCP flow does not encounter a congestion event during the slow start phase.

$$s = \frac{f}{2} \left(1 \pm \sqrt{1 - \frac{4M}{fR}} \right) \tag{4}$$

The result is plotted in Figure 2. The black area is a *forbidden* area for TCP flows as packet loss may occur. This leads, for example, to an end-to-end throughput of about 44 Mbps, using the TDM switch and a 100 ms RTT link (Amsterdam to Chicago). Values we get using this formula matched the throughput (80 Mbps) obtained in TCP tests using iperf. As real hosts always have some shaping

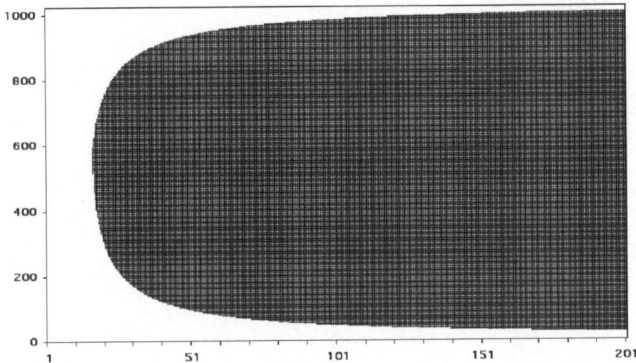

Fig. 2. Forbidden (shaded) area shows where packet loss may occur in single stream TCP flows for a given memory size of 0.5 MByte and an incoming speed of 1 Gbps. Horizontally is the round trip time of the desired destination and vertically the provisioned "slow" speed at a TDM switch.

capacities it is not unrealistic that the calculated number is smaller than the experimental obtained values.

3 TCP

TCP is a sender-controlled sliding *window* protocol [2]. New data up to "window size" is sent when old data has been acknowledged by the receiver. The sending host limits the window size through application parameters such as socket buffer size and "congestion window" *Cwnd* [1]. TCP adjusts the *Cwnd* dynamically using different algorithms depending on which phase the flow is currently in. We will concentrate here on the slow start phase because of indications that this phase does not properly develop into the next phase, steady state.

3.1 Bandwidth Discovery Phase (Slow Start)

This is the start up phase of a TCP flow. After the protocol handshake [6] the sender will try to discover what the available bandwidth is so that it can compute the correct value for *Cwnd*. This discovery is done by injecting data into the network until a congestion event occurs. Fast convergence and accuracy of bandwidth discovery have a large influence on the overall performance of TCP. The *Cwnd* size determines how fast a flow can reach a steady state and the stability of the flow once it has reached that state. The *Cwnd* effectively doubles every RTT, as long as no congestion event is generated. Thus a flow should only be limited by an intrinsic bottleneck (i.e. packet loss). If the limiting bandwidth between two hosts is the speed of the sending host (i.e. slow NIC, slow CPU) then the bandwidth discovery phase will always work correctly. However, if the

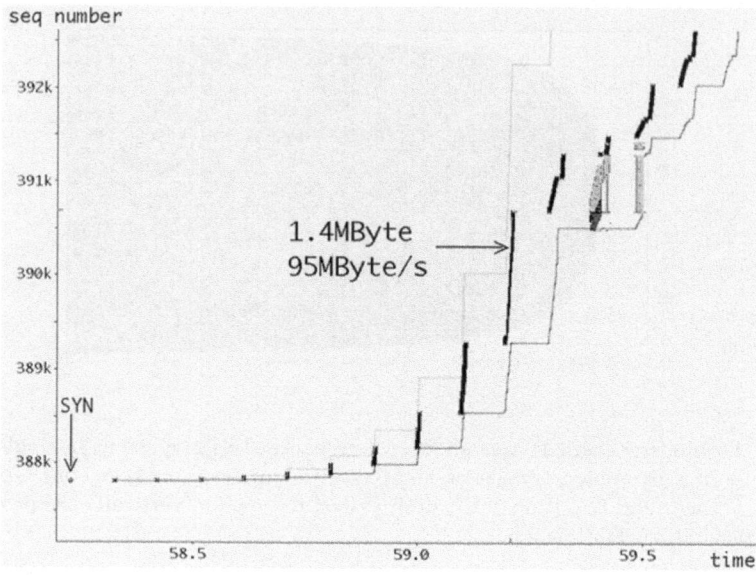

Fig. 3. Time sequence graph showing initial phase and congestion event after 10 RTTs.

capacity of the network connection between the two hosts is the limiting factor (i.e. router/switch buffer) then the bandwidth discovery phase will fail. At a certain point the doubling of the congestion window will overrun the bottleneck by a large number of packets causing loss [4]. In Figure 3 using a Time Sequence Graph (TSG), we show our observation of large packet loss caused by a bottleneck. After 9 RTT's a burst of 512 packets leaves the PC; at 10 RTT's this is doubled to 1024 and this amount overruns the buffer in the switch, causing retransmissions.

In a later stage of the project the bottleneck was removed: the SONET link between the TDM switches was upgraded to 1.25 Gbps. This upgrade made it possible to map a 1 Gbps Ethernet connection completely into the SONET link. The end to end performance showed some improvement. In fact traces show a similar behavior as in the bottleneck case but at higher speed during the slow start phase TCP decides to go into collision avoidance mode even without any packet loss. The reason for this strange behavior is assumed to be a receiving workstation dependent behaviour and is the subject of the next paragraph.

3.2   Receiver Limitations

Identically configured machines exhibit the property that the receiver capacity is less than the sender capacity. This is due to the difference in overhead of sending a packet versus receiving a packet. If the sender is able to send data with a speed close to 1 Gbps, the receiver may not be able to keep up. The receiver becomes overloaded and will start to drop packets, which in turn will

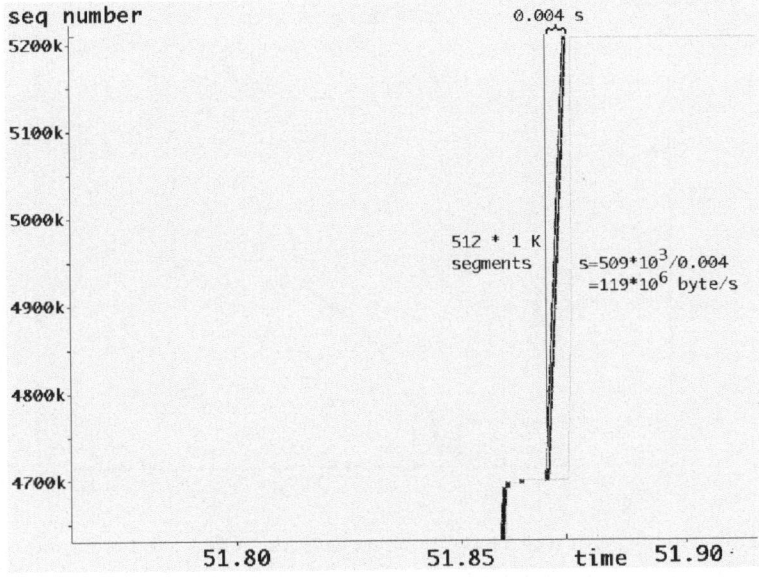

Fig. 4. Time sequence graph showing instantaneous speed of flow.

cause a TCP congestion event. Figure 4 shows the instantaneous speed of a flow during slow start. Notice that after 9 RTT's 512 packets leave the host. The sending host sends this data as IP packets as fast as it can. In this case the 512 packets are sent in about 4 ms, yielding an instantaneous speed close to 1 Gbps, which is line-speed. This burst then overruns the receiver buffer and causes the flow to fall out of the slow start phase into the congestion avoidance phase. Therefore, this case is similar to that of a buffer overflow at the TDM switch as discussed in the previous subsection.

4   Host Parameters

Implementations of the TCP algorithm vary between operating systems. The implementation governs the behavior of TCP as does the architecture of the PC. There are several system parameters that can greatly influence host performance. They are: host bus width, bus speed, number of devices that share the bus, the efficiency of the Network Interface Card (NIC), interrupt coalescence, [9], etc. Thus using the same parameters [8] on two different configurations can still produce varying results, especially during the slow start phase. We refer to values specific to a configuration of a PC as *the host parameters*. This also includes the TCP implementation. If we average performance over longer periods of time these differences may become less noticeable. From our experience it has been observed that some seemingly slower hosts, in terms of CPU and bus speed, are not necessarily the slowest for TCP transfers. This is due to the fact that

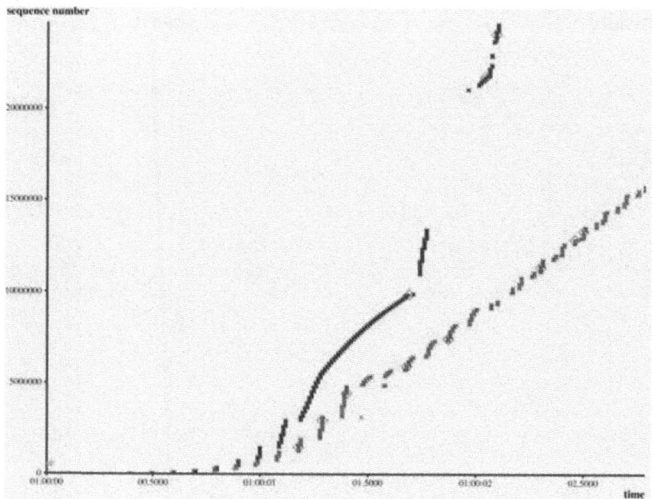

Fig. 5. TSG comparing initial phase of Linux and Mac OS X (red is Linux, and blue is Mac OS X).

slower hosts pace out the packets better than a faster PC (i.e. shorter bursts), hence there is less chance for overflowing bottleneck queues in the path or the receiving host. The TSG in Figure 5 shows a comparison between Mac OS X and Linux 2.4.19, both are the sender. The data was captured at the receiver side, Linux 2.4.19, using tcpdump. It clearly shows that the Mac paces out the packets better then Linux. Therefore, one solution could be to pace out the packets such that the average speed will not be higher than that of the bottleneck in the path, should it be either the network or the receiver. The influence of shaping the packet stream can be seen in Figure 6. Here we show what the effect is of introducing a delay between packets sent by UDPmon in the identical experiment to the one in section 2. The only difference being that the network bottleneck was removed here: the path was 1 Gbps end to end. This means that only end system effects remain. What clearly shows up in the graphs is that with an inter packet delay of 15 μsec no more packets are lost and a throughput of 500 Mbps is obtained.

5   Conclusion

From the results we conclude that the sender should not burst packets, but try to shape the flow i.e. using a leaky bucket type of algorithm. Though this may be hard to implement in the OS since it requires that the OS maintain a timer per TCP flow with μsec resolution, which could incur lots of overhead. Our initial suggestion is that future OS kernels should delegate the task of pacing the packets to NICs and allow the NIC to implement this feature at the hardware level. In the network some measures can be taken to avoid packet loss which destroys

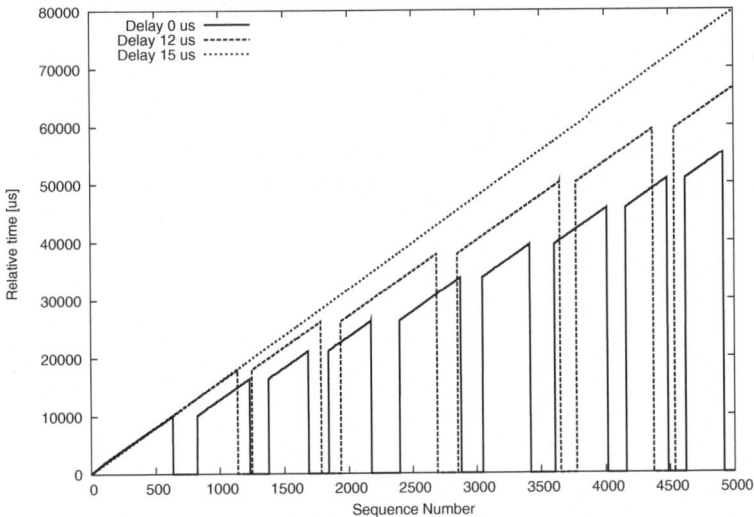

Fig. 6. UDPmon arrival time results obtained with varying inter packet delay: 0, 12, 15 μsec as a function of the packet sequence number. Dropped packets are marked with zero arrival time.

TCP performance, such as hardware flow control, bursting up to the size of the memory (super packets), traffic shaping and (Weighted) Random Early Discard ((W)RED) a layer 3 option. It is also clearly shown that the end systems dictate the overall performance. Their combination of hard and software is crucial.

Acknowledgments

The transatlantic links used for conducting this research are provided to us by SURFnet, TYCO and LEVEL3: Antony Antony and Hans Blom are funded by the IST Program of the European Union (grant IST-2001-32459) via the DataTAG project [3]. Jason Lee was supported in part by the Director, Office of Science, Office of Advanced Scientific Computing Research and Mathematical, Information and Computational Sciences Division under U.S. Department of Energy Contract No. DE-AC03-76SF00098 and NIKHEF.

References

1. Mark Allman, *et al.*, "TCP Congestion Control", RFC2581
2. Tom Dunigan, Matt Mathis, Brian Tierney, A TCP Tuning Daemon http://www.sc2002.org/
   paperpdfs/pap.pap151.pdf
3. EU DataTAG, http://www.datatag.org
4. Sally Floyd, "Limited Slow-Start for TCP with Large Congestion Windows", http://www.icir.org/floyd/hstcp.html

5. Cees de Laat, Erik Radius, Steven Wallace, "The Rationale of Optical Networking Initiatives", iGrid2002 special issue, Future Generation Computer Systems, volume 19 issue 6 (2003).
6. RFC 793, "Transmission Control Protocol", Editor Jon Postel.
7. SURFnet 2.5 Gbps Lambda to Chicago, Press release http://www.surfnet.nl
8. TCP Tuning Guide, http://www-didc.lbl.gov/TCP-tuning/
9. UDPMon, http://www.hep.man.ac.uk/~rich/net/

Grid Characteristics and Uses: A Grid Definition*

Miguel L. Bote-Lorenzo, Yannis A. Dimitriadis, and Eduardo Gómez-Sánchez

School of Telecommunications Engineering, University of Valladolid
Camino Viejo del Cementerio s/n, 47011 Valladolid, Spain
{migbot,yannis,edugom}@tel.uva.es

Abstract. This paper discusses the concept of grid towards achieving
a complete definition using main grid characteristics and uses found in
literature. Ten definitions extracted from main literature sources have
been studied allowing the extraction of grid characteristics while grid
uses are defined in terms of the different types of application support
provided by grids. A grid definition is proposed using these characteristics
and uses. This definition may be very useful to determine the limits
of the grid concept as well as to explore new application fields in grid
computing. In this sense, the extracted characteristics are employed to
determine the potential benefits a grid infrastructure may provide to
Computer Supported Collaborative Learning applications.

1 Introduction

The origin of the grid concept may be established in the early 90's when great
efforts were made to deploy several gigabit testbeds such as CASA [19] that
linked super-computing sites across the USA. However, the term grid still did
not exist a that time, and the terms metasystem and metacomputer where used
instead referring to "the computing resources transparently available to the user
via a networked environment" [21].

The successes of these testbeds inspired the 1995 I-WAY experiment [4] which
provided a large-scale testbed (multiple supercomputers, advanced visualization
de-vices and mass storage systems at 17 different places within North America
connected through ATM networks) in order to allow mainly high-performance
applications to be studied in a controlled environment. The I-WAY experiment in
turn motivated some very important projects such as the National Technology
Grid, which coined in 1997 the term grid, "a name derived from the notion
of the electrical power grid", to call the "truly U.S. national-scale advanced
computational infrastructure" they envisioned [22].

It was not until 1998 that grid computing entered the mainstream of research
with both the establishment of the Global Grid Forum (www.gridforum.org) by
early grid developers and practitioners, and the publication of the book [10]
that laid the groundwork of the field and defined the term computational grid as

---

* This work has been partially funded by Spanish Ministry of Science and Technology projects TIC2002-04258-C03-02, TIC2000-1054 and Castilla y León Regional
Government project VA 117/01.

F. Fernández Rivera et al. (Eds.): Across Grids 2003, LNCS 2970, pp. 291–298, 2004.

"a hardware and software infrastructure that provides dependable, consistent, pervasive, and inexpensive access to high-end computational capabilities" [6]. But this entrance turned into not only the intensification of the research on the field but also the conflation of the term grid that does not seem to have a clear and complete definition, i.e. a definition highlighting all main characteristics and uses of a grid. Instead, definitions found in literature usually highlight them only partially (and sometimes poorly).

Having a complete grid definition built using all main characteristics and uses may be considered important for several reasons. First, it is indispensable to exactly determine whether a given technology can be considered to be a grid or not [7]. In this sense, a grid definition can show how grid technologies can be found in application fields other than supercomputing. In addition, it allows studying the potential benefits that the use of a grid can report to application fields still unexplored by grid researchers. For example, the main project supporting this research is devoted to the use of grid infrastructure in Computer Supported Collaborative Learning (CSCL) applications.

The lack of a complete grid definition has already been detected in literature [7,11]. Significantly, very recent works [14] challenge the already existing definitions of grid. However, such a complete definition has not been given yet.

Thus, the aim of this paper is to advance towards a complete grid definition made up of all main grid characteristics and uses found in grid literature. Hence, grid characteristics have been extracted from grid definitions provided in main literature sources while grid uses are defined in terms of the types of application support supplied by grids according to literature. Also, we perform an initial step towards the definition of the grid concept within the field of CSCL, in order to evaluate its suitability, limitations and potential benefits.

This paper is organized as follows. Section 2 examines ten literature definitions in order to find out the main characteristics that a grid is supposed to have. Section 3 categorizes the different types of support that grids can provide to applications. Both the list of grid characteristics and uses are employed in section 4 to build grid definition. Section 5 explores the field of CSCL within the context of grid, as it was de-fined in the previous sections and based on our research work in this domain. Conclusions may be found in section 6.

2   Main Grid Characteristics

Ten definitions extracted from main grid literature sources have been examined to find out the essential characteristics that a grid is supposed to have in order to be considered as such. As a result, a total number of ten characteristics has been identified. Both the definitions and the characteristics found in them, either explicitly or implicitly are shown in Table 1 together with their references. These characteristics may be described as follows:

- *Large scale*: a grid must be able to deal with a number of resources ranging from just a few to millions. This raises the very serious problem of avoiding potential performance degradation as the grid size increases.

- *Geographical distribution*: grid's resources may be located at distant places.
- *Heterogeneity*: a grid hosts both software and hardware resources that can be very varied ranging from data, files, software components or programs to sensors, scientific instruments, display devices, personal digital organizers, computers, super-computers and networks.
- *Resource sharing*: resources in a grid belong to many different organizations that allow other organizations (i.e. users) to access them. Nonlocal resources can thus be used by applications, promoting efficiency and reducing costs.
- *Multiple administrations*: each organization may establish different security and administrative policies under which their owned resources can be accessed and used. As a result, the already challenging network security problem is complicated even more with the need of taking into account all different policies.
- *Resource coordination*: resources in a grid must be coordinated in order to provide aggregated computing capabilities.
- *Transparent access*: a grid should be seen as a single virtual computer.
- *Dependable access*: a grid must assure the delivery of services under established Quality of Service (QoS) requirements. The need for dependable service is fundamental since users require assurances that they will receive predictable, sustained and often high levels of performance.
- *Consistent access*: a grid must be built with standard services, protocols and inter-faces thus hiding the heterogeneity of the resources while allowing its scalability. Without such standards, application development and pervasive use would not be possible.
- *Pervasive access*: the grid must grant access to available resources by adapting to a dynamic environment in which resource failure is commonplace. This does not imply that resources are everywhere or universally available but that the grid must tailor its behavior as to extract the maximum performance from the available re-sources.

3   Main Grid Uses

Opposite to what is often believed, the grid is not only a computing paradigm for providing computational resources for grand-challenge applications. Instead, it is an infrastructure that bonds and unifies globally remote and diverse resources in order *to provide computing support* for a wide range of applications. It is important to notice that grid uses are thus not defined in terms of applications (as usually found in the literature) but rather of the support the grid provides.

The different types of computing support offered by grids can be categorized according to the main challenges that they present from the grid architecture point of view. This categorization is the following:

- *Distributed supercomputing support* allows applications to use grids to couple computational resources in order to reduce the completion time of a job [18] or to tackle problems that cannot be solved on a single system [6]. The

Table 1. Grid definitions from the literature listed in chronological order, and features they mention among **(1)** large scale, **(2)** geographical distribution, **(3)** heterogeneity, **(4)** resource sharing, **(5)** multiple administration, **(6)** resource coordination, **(7)** transparent access, **(8)**, dependable access, **(9)** consistent access, and **(10)** pervasive access. Features marked with * are implicit rather than explicit. The definition that coined the term grid is highlighted in bold letters.

Definition	Features
"The computing resources transparently available to the user via this networked environment have been called a metacomputer" [21]	7
"A metasystem is a system composed of heterogeneous hosts (both parallel processors and conventional architectures), possibly controlled by separate organizational entities, and connected by an irregular interconnection network" [16]	3,4*,5
"Metasystem is a wide-area environment in which users operate transparently, consisting in workstations, PCs, graphics-rendering engines, supercomputers and nontraditional computing devices such as televisions" [15]	2,3*,7
"Networked virtual supercomputers, or metacomputers, are execution environments in which high-speed networks are used to connect supercomputers, databases, scientific instruments, and advanced display devices, perhaps located at geographically distributed sites" [8]	2,3*
"The National Computational Science Alliance calls its prototype infrastructure the National Technology Grid, a name derived from the notion of the electrical power grid that transformed the U.S., and indeed the world, during the past century" [22]	
"Computational grids are large-scale high-performance distributed computing environments that provide dependable, consistent, and pervasive access to high-end computational resources" [9]	1,8,9,10
"A computational grid is a hardware and software infrastructure that provides dependable, consistent, pervasive, and inexpensive access to high-end computational capabilities" [6]	8,9,10
"The real and specific problem that underlies the Grid concept is coordinated resource sharing and problem solving in dynamic, multi-institutional virtual organizations" [11]	4,6,10
"A distributed network computing (NC) system is a virtual computer formed by a networked set of heterogeneous machines that agree to share their local resources with each other. A Grid is a very large scale, generalized distributed NC system that can scale to Internet-size environments with machines distributed across multiple organizations and administrative domains" [18]	1,2*,3,4,5,7*
"Grid technologies and infrastructure support the sharing and coordinated use of diverse resources in dynamic, distributed virtual organizations - that is, the creation, from geographically distributed components operated by distinct organizations with differing policies, of virtual computing systems that are sufficiently integrated to deliver the desired QoS" [12]	2,3,4,5,6,7*,8,10
"A Grid is a system that coordinates resources that are not subject to a centralized control using standard, open, general-purpose protocols and interfaces to deliver nontrivial qualities of service" [14]	5,6,8,9

main problems raised by applications requiring this support are the need to co-schedule the use of scarce and highly expensive resources, the scalability of protocols and algorithms to a large number of nodes, latency-tolerant algorithms as well as achieving high levels of performance [6]. Typical applications that require distributed supercomputing are weather forecasting and military scenario simulations.

– *High-throughput computing support* allows applications to use grids to put unused processor cycles to work in generally loosely coupled or independent tasks [6]. 'Parameter sweep' applications such as Monte Carlo simulations are well suited for high-throughput computing.

– *On-demand computing support* allows applications to use grids to retrieve re-sources that cannot be cost-effectively or conveniently located locally [6]. Challenging issues in order to provide on-demand computing support are resource lo-cation, scheduling, code management, configuration, fault tolerance, security, and payment mechanisms [6]. A financial application allowing users to perform accurate stock market analysis and price prediction employing their home desktop computer is a representative example of application requiring on-demand computing.

– *Data-intensive computing support* allows applications to use grids to synthesize new information from distributed data repositories, digital libraries and databases [6]. Challenges for the data-intensive computing support include the scheduling and configuration of complex, high-volume data flows [6]. The creation of a new database using data mined from a number of online databases would be an example of data-intensive computing application.

– *Collaborative computing support* allows applications to use the grid to enable and enhance human-to-human interactions [6] in a synchronous or asynchronous way [11] via a virtual space. The real-time requirements imposed by human perceptual capabilities as well as the wide range of many different interactions that can take place are one of the most challenging issues of collaborative computing support [6]. Typical examples of applications that may use a collaborative computing infrastructure provided by grids are groupware applications and multiconferencing applications.

– *Multimedia computing support* allows applications to use grids to deliver contents assuring end-to-end QoS [18]. Main challenges for the multimedia computing sup-port derive from the need to provide QoS across multiple different machines. Videoconference applications is a typical example of application requiring multimedia computing support.

4 A Grid Definition

According to the list of grid characteristics extracted from literature and to the different categories of support provided by grids that have been identified in this paper, a grid can be defined as *a large-scale geographically distributed hardware and software infra-structure composed of heterogeneous networked resources owned and shared by multiple administrative organizations which are* coordinated to provide transparent, dependable, pervasive and consistent computing support to a wide range of applications. These applications can perform either distributed computing, high throughput computing, on-demand computing, data-intensive computing, collaborative computing or multimedia computing.

5 CSCL as an Application Field within the Grid Context

The definition just presented can help to determine the suitability, limitations and potential benefits of the grid within a certain domain. One relevant field is Computer Supported Collaborative Learning (CSCL). CSCL is a discipline devoted to research in educational technologies that focus on the use of information and communications technology (ICT) as a mediational tool within collaborative methods (e.g. peer learning and tutoring, reciprocal teaching, project or problem-based learning, simulations, games) of learning [5,23]. Therefore, it seems appropriate to explore and apply grid technology, as defined above, to this multidisciplinary and complex field. Though CSCL is closely related to groupware or CSCW (Computer Supported Collaborative Work), there are substantial differences in the context and objectives of each field. Thus, works published in CSCW literature, such as [1], focus much more on the technological support instead of a deep analysis of the domain.

CSCL applications are inherently distributed, since students have to collaborate through networked computers, though we may distinguish cases in which students are collocated (and collaboration also happens face to face) and those in which collaboration is strictly carried through the computer [3]. Besides, CSCL applications may involve synchronous or asynchronous interactions, or a mixture of them [5]. In addition, Component Based Software Engineering (CBSE) offers a flexible paradigm for distributed applications development that is being exploited for CSCL [2]. For applications with these characteristics, the computational grid can offer a suitable infra-structure that facilitates their deployment and enhances their performance. Particularly, the analysis of grid pints out several benefits for the use of grid technologies to deploy CSCL applications.

The *large scale* of the grid may allow the of a high number of single/group participants collaborating within the CSCL application. Though in purely synchronous collaboration the number of participants is usually low, in applications involving only asynchronous interactions, or a mixture, a large number of participants may be involved. For example, applications allowing children from different schools to collaborate asynchronously in order to publish and consult an electronic magazine using CSCL tools may involve a large number of users at different locations in a wide area. Moreover, the wide *geographical distribution* of grid resources should enhance the participation of users from very distant places. Again, many CSCL applications have their users co-located, but others such as distance universities tools may have users spread along one country or even a larger area. Besides, the *heterogeneous nature* of grid *shared resources* may allow users to participate employing heterogeneous devices such as computers, PDAs or electronic black-boards, as well as data or software resources such as simulators or other domain packages. This allows the use of locally un-available computational resources for processing data (such as in Punch [17]), for visualization (like in CoViS [20]) or for content delivery (a secondary but necessary service in CSCL). Therefore, an efficient use of grid resources may benefit such needs of the CSCL domain. Concerning performance, *dependable access* provided by the grid infrastructure that offers either guaranteed or best effort service can improve application performance over *ad hoc* deployment decisions, which becomes specially important when the application is run over a wide area network, such as an synchronous brainstorming. Finally, one grid feature that will appeal CSCL application developers is *transparent access*, since it eases some serious problems such as automatic application deployment and configuration, that can be passed onto the grid scheduler and per-formed with some optimality criteria. This is especially valid either for component or web services based implementations of CSCL applications, towards which the grid seems to be shifting, as promoted by the Open Grid Services Architecture (OGSA) [13].

In summary, the complex, dynamic and contextualized nature of the CSCL field is especially motivating with respect to the use of grid. CSCL applications call for some infrastructure that allows the use of heterogeneous distributed resources in a scalable manner, and that facilitates the deployment in order to improve performance. The computational grid, as defined above, offers this support and can then be used satisfactorily for the CSCL domain. However, further study is necessary in order to precisely determine how CSCL applications can benefit from the grid, especially by providing a clear correspondence between components (or web services) present in a formal architectural framework and the corresponding grid services, eventually within the OGSA.

6   Conclusions and Future Work

Grids are mainstream technology that do not have a clear and complete definition in the literature. Establishing a complete grid definition is considered an important goal in order to allow determining the limits of the grid research field as well as exploring new fields of application in grid computing.

To tackle this problem, ten definitions extracted from main literature sources have been studied allowing the extraction of the ten main characteristics of grids. In addition, grid uses have been defined in terms of the different types of application support provided by grids according to the literature. Both grid characteristics and uses have been used to build a grid definition.

The establishment of a grid definition in this paper is not an isolated effort. On the contrary, this definition is currently being used within the framework of the main project supporting this work in order to explore the possibility of using CSCL applications within grid computational environments. In this sense, the analysis of the characteristics extracted in section 3 shows that the support provided by grid technologies may offer a number of benefits to CSCL applications, although a formal study is still necessary together with an analysis of experimental data within real systems.

References

1. Amin, K., Nijsure, S., and von Laszewski, G. Open Collaborative Grid Services Architecture (OCGSA). In *Proc. Euroweb'02*, Oxford, UK, pp. 101–107, 2002.
2. Asensio, J.I., Dimitriadis, Y.A., Heredia, M., Martínez, A., Álvarez, F.J., Blasco, M.T. and Osuna, C. From collaborative learning patterns to component-based CSCL application. In *Proc. ECSCW'03 workshop "From Good Practices to Patterns"*, Helsinki, Finland, 2003.
3. Crook, C. *Computers and the Collaborative Experience of Learning*. Routeledge, London, UK, 1994.
4. DeFanti, T., Foster, I., Papka, M., Stevens, R., Kuhfuss, T. Overview of the I-WAY: Wide Area Visual Supercomputing. *Int. J. Supercomp. App.*, **10**(2):123–130, 1996.
5. Dillenbourg, P. *Collaborative Learning: Cognitive and Computational Approaches*. Elsevier Science, Oxford, UK, 1999.
6. Foster, I. *Computational Grids*, pp. 15–52. In [10], 1998.
7. Foster, I. What Is the Grid? A Three Point Checklist. *Grid Today*, **1**(6), 2002.
8. Foster, I. and Kesselman, C. Globus: a Metacomputing Infrastructure Toolkit. *Int. J. Supercomp. App.*, **11**(2):115–128, 1997.
9. Foster, I. and Kesselman, C. The Globus Project: a Status Report. In *Proc. IPPS/SPDP'98 Workshop on Heterogeneous Computing*, pp. 4–18, 1998.
10. Foster, I. and Kesselman, C. *The Grid: Blueprint for a Future Computing Infrastructure*. Morgan Kaufmann, San Francisco, CA, 1998.
11. Foster, I., Kesselman, C., and Tuecke, S. The Anatomy of the Grid: Enabling Scalable Virtual Organizations. *Int. J. Supercomp. App.*, **15**(3):200–222, 2001.
12. Foster, I., Kesselman, C., Nick, J., and Tuecke, S. Grid Services for Distributed System Integration. *Computer*, **35**(6):37–46, 2002.
13. Foster, I., Kesselman, C., Nick, J., and Tuecke, S.. The Physiology of the Grid: an Open Grid Services Architecture for Distributed Systems Integration. Global Grid Forum technical report, 2002.
14. Grimshaw, A. What is a Grid? *Grid Today*, **1**(26), 2002.
15. Grimshaw, A. and Wulf, W. The Legion Vision of a Worldwide Virtual Computer. *Comm. of the ACM*, **40**(1):39–47, 1997.
16. Grimshaw, A., Weissman, J., West, E., and Loyot Jr., E. Metasystems: an Approach Combining Parallel Processing and Distributed Heterogeneous Computing System. *Parallel and Distributed Computing*, **21**(3):257–270, 1994.
17. Kapadia, N., Figueiredo, R., and Fortes, J. PUNCH: Web portal for running tools. *IEEE Micro*, **20**(3):38–47, 2000.
18. Krauter, K., Buyya, R., and Maheswaran, M. A taxonomy and survey of grid resource management systems for distributed computing. *Int. J. of Software Practice and Experience*, **32**(2):135–164, 2002.
19. Lyster, P., Bergman, L., Li, P., Stanfill, D., Crippe, B., Blom, R., and Okaya, D. CASA Gigabit Supercomputing Network: CALCRUST Three-Dimensional Real-Time Multi-Dataset Rendering. In *Proc. Supercomputing'92*, Minneapolis, 1992.
20. Ramamurthy, M., Wilhelmson, R., Pea, R., Louis, M., and Edelson, D. CoVis: A National Science Education Collaboratory. In *Proc. American Meteorological Society 4th Conference on Education*, Dallas, TX, 1995.
21. Smarr, L. and Catlett, C. Metacomputing. *Comm. of the ACM*, **35**(6):44–52, 1992.
22. Stevens, R., Woodward, P., DeFanti, T., and Catlett, C. From the I-WAY to the National Technology Grid. *Comm. of the ACM*, **40**(11):50–60, 1997.
23. Wasson, B. Computer Supported Collaborative Learning: an Overview. Lecture notes IVP 482, University of Bergen, Norway, 1998.

An Overview of European Grid Projects

Marian Bubak[1,2], Piotr Nowakowski[2], and Robert Pajak[2]

[1] Institute of Computer Science, AGH, al. Mickiewicza 30, 30-059 Kraków, Poland
bubak@uci.agh.edu.pl
phone: (+48 12) 617 39 64, fax: (+48 12) 633 80 54
[2] Academic Computer Center CYFRONET, Nawojki 11, 30-950 Kraków, Poland
{ymnowako,ympajak}@cyf-kr.edu.pl
phone: (+48 12) 632 33 55, fax: (+48 12) 634 10 84

Abstract. This document summarizes the various Grid research projects currently funded by the European Union. The authors present brief description of each project, along with their chronological breakdown, geographical distribution, the middleware being used and project foci: from middleware- and infrastructure-oriented undertakings to applications, which build on existing Grid infrastructures.

Keywords: Grid, Projects, Gridstart.

1 Introduction

Grid research is currently on an upswing in Europe and elsewhere. In response to this new trend in information sciences, the European Union has taken an active role in encouraging and sponsoring European Grid-related activities, mostly under the auspices of the Information Society Technologies Programme (IST). This document is an attempt at summarizing numerous European Grid undertakings, their plans for the future and their present state.

This review was initially developed for internal usage within the CrossGrid project, but with time it became clear that its usage could spread beyond the CrossGrid team and to the Grid community as a whole, as well as the general public. Therefore, this document contains general information alongside technical issues. References are provided where applicable.

2 Research Focus

This document summarizes a total of 19 EU Grid projects, organized in three waves:

- First wave, for projects starting in late 2000 / early 2001: three projects, funded on the order of 15M.
- Second wave, for projects starting in late 2001 / early 2002: six projects, funded on the order of 20M.
- Third wave, for projects starting in late 2002: nine projects, funded on the order of 14M.

F. Fernández Rivera et al. (Eds.): Across Grids 2003, LNCS 2970, pp. 299–308, 2004.

All these projects are part of the European Union's 5th Framework Programme, and most of them fall under the Information Society Technologies programme, which constitutes a part of the 5th FP and encompasses research initiatives related to the development of the "Information Society" concept currently advanced by the EU. As the 6th Framework Programme nears its commencement date, more Grid projects can be expected to appear.

Figure 1 provides a graphical overview of the three waves.

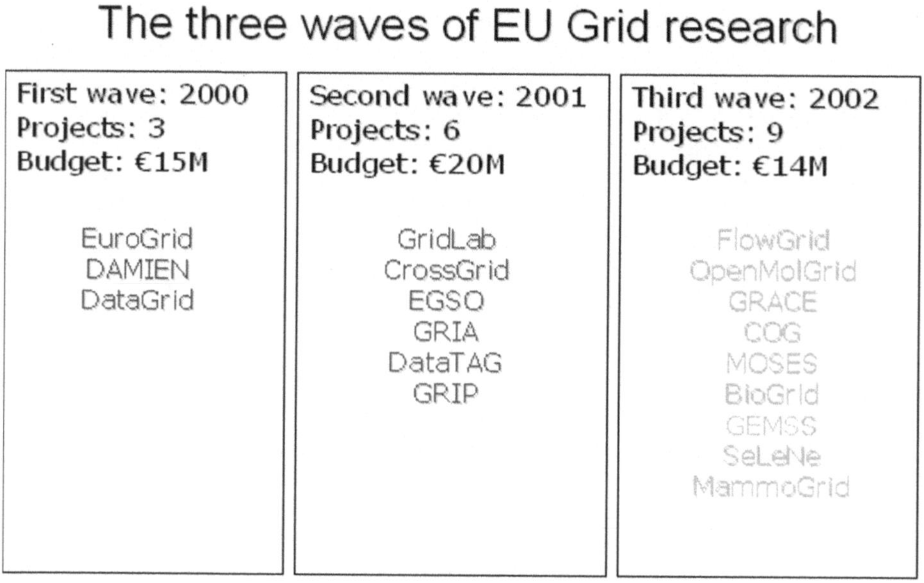

The three waves of EU Grid research

First wave: 2000 Projects: 3 Budget: €15M	Second wave: 2001 Projects: 6 Budget: €20M	Third wave: 2002 Projects: 9 Budget: €14M
EuroGrid DAMIEN DataGrid	GridLab CrossGrid EGSO GRIA DataTAG GRIP	FlowGrid OpenMolGrid GRACE COG MOSES BioGrid GEMSS SeLeNe MammoGrid

Fig. 1. The three waves of EU Grid research.

2.1   First Research Wave

This wave includes three projects, namely: EuroGrid, DataGrid and Damien. These early undertakings are mostly middleware- and infrastructure-oriented. While each of them supports several applications, their most important achievements are in defining common standards, testing and developing middleware, exploring the issues of Grid deployment in a geographically-distributed environment, setting up international testbeds, encouraging international cooperation and generating publicity for computing Grids in general. The most notable difference between all three projects is that DataGrid bases on the Globus middleware developed at the Argonne National Laboratory in the U.S., EuroGrid makes use of the European Unicore package and Damien develops its own proprietary middleware.

2.2   Second Research Wave

This wave includes six major projects, namely: GridLab, CrossGrid, EGSO, GRIA, DataTAG, GRIP. Most of these build on the earlier achievements of first wave projects (most notably DataGrid) and try to extend their functionality to cover new areas of interest (such as interactive applications or heterogenous Grid environments). The GRIP project delves in introducing compatibility between Globus and Unicore packages, while DataTAG extends the outreach of DataGrid by creating a transatlantic testbed linking DataGrid test sites with those of their American partners (iDVGL and GriPhyN).

2.3   Third Research Wave

The third research wave, starting in late 2002 encompasses nine projects: Flow-Grid, OpenMolGrid, GRACE, COG, MOSES, BioGrid, GEMSS, SeLeNe and MammoGrid. Most of these are dedicated to specific application areas and do not concern themselves much with middleware issues, as they generally inherit ready-to-use solutions from earlier projects. As these projects have just recently taken off and are still in a conceptual phase, little in the way of concrete results is available so far.

2.4   The GridStart Initiative

The Gridstart initiative is a special-case scenario in that it is not a research project, but instead a joint undertaking aimed at fostering international cooperation and exchange of ideas. Gridstart brings together representatives of various EU-funded Grid undertaking, aids in dissemination of project results, encourages interaction amongst similar activities both in Europe and the rest of the world and stimulates the early take-up by industry and research of Grid-enabled applications.

The GridStart initiative unites 10 separate research projects including all those belonging to the first two waves listed above.

3   Individual Project Descriptions

This section contains brief descriptions of each individual Grid-related undertaking funded by the EU as of December 2002. The projects are listed in an alphabetical order.

3.1   AVO

The Astrophysical Virtual Observatory (AVO) Project is a Phase-A, three year study for the design and implementation of a virtual observatory for European astronomy. A virtual observatory is a collection of interoperating data archives and software tools which utilize the internet to form a scientific research environment in which astronomical research programs can be conducted. In much the same way as a real observatory consists of telescopes, each with a collection of unique astronomical instruments, the VO consists of a collection of data centres each with unique collections of astronomical data, software systems and processing capabilities. The need for the development of a Virtual Observatory is driven by two key factors. Firstly, there is an explosion in the size of astronomical data sets delivered by new large facilities like the ESO VLT, the VLT Survey Telescope (VST), and VISTA. The processing and storage capabilities necessary for astronomers to analyse and explore these data sets will greatly exceed the capabilities of the types of desktop systems astronomers currently have available to them. Secondly, there is a great scientific gold mine going unexplored and underexploited because large data sets in astronomy are unconnected. If large surveys and catalogues could be joined into a uniform and interoperating "digital universe", entire new areas of astronomical research would become feasible.

3.2   BioGrid

The purpose of the BioGrid project is to conduct a trial for the introduction of a Grid approach in the biotechnology industry. This trial consists of two major steps: the integration of three existing technologies and the production of a working prototype. The existing technologies to be integrated are: (i) PSIMAP agent technology (ii) classification server: Automatic model classification (iii) space explorer: knowledge visualization technology. BioGrid will change the perspective of biologists from a partial view of biological data towards a holistic view of documented data seamlessly integrated with expression and interaction data. This constitutes the basis of a next generation research infrastructure for large proteomics and genomics databases.

3.3   COG

The Corporate Ontology Grid project will utilize the power of Grid technology to solve real data integration problems in a large enterprise. The consortium will use ontological software to unify the information that currently lies in multiple data formats on the corporate Grid. This unification will be achieved by creating a central modeling environment that is mapped to the data source Grid and provides common meaning to the disparate formats.

3.4   CrossGrid

The CrossGrid initiative aims to address issues, which relate to applications requiring the presence of a person in a computing loop. These types of applications have not heretofore been considered for deployment in a Grid environment, and hence require the creation and integration of new software components into existing Grid software suites (such as Globus).

3.5   DAMIEN

DAMIEN is a project that started out in early 2001 to continue the successful work of the European pilot project for GRID-Computing METODIS. METODIS had successfully shown the feasibility of the GRID-approach in industry. The objective of DAMIEN is to develop further building blocks for a middleware environment for distributed industrial simulation and visualization in the GRID.

3.6   DataGrid

DataGrid is a project funded by the European Union that aims at enabling access to geographically distributed computing power and storage facilities belonging to different institutions. This will provide the necessary resources to process huge amounts of data coming from experiments in three different disciplines: High Energy Physics, Biology and Earth Observation.

Next generation scientific exploration requires computing power and storage that no single institution alone is able to afford. Besides, easy access to distributed data is required to improve results sharing. The proposed solution is that different institutions working in the same scientific field put their computing, storage and data resources together in order to achieve the required performance levels.

3.7   DataTAG

The DataTAG project will create a large-scale intercontinental Grid testbed that will focus upon advanced networking issues and interoperability between these intercontinental Grid domains, hence extending the capabilities of each and enhancing the worldwide program of Grid development. The project will address the issues which arise in the sector of high performance inter-Grid networking, including sustained and reliable high performance data replication, end-to-end advanced network services, and novel monitoring techniques. The project will also directly address the issues which arise in the sector of interoperability between the Grid middleware layers such as information and security services. The advance made will be disseminated into each of the associated Grid projects.

The fundamental objective of the DataTAG project is to create a large-scale intercontinental Grid testbed involving the European DataTAG project, several national projects in Europe, and related Grid projects in the USA. The project will explore some forefront research topics like the design and implementation of advanced network services for guaranteed traffic delivery, transport protocol optimization, efficiency and reliability of network resource utilization, user-perceived application performance, middleware interoperability in multi domain scenarios, etc.

3.8   EGSO

EGSO, the European Grid of Solar Observations, is a Grid testbed that will lay the foundations of a virtual solar observatory. The EGSO project addresses the problem of combining heterogeneous data from scattered archives of space- and ground-based observations into a single "virtual" dataset. The heterogeneous nature of the solar data will be mitigated using a set of Unified Observing Catalogues, and new Solar Feature Catalogues and Solar Event Catalogues will allow the user to search for observations on the basis of events and phenomena, rather than just time and location. EGSO will provide a friendly User Interface that can be used to select, process and retrieve data from the archives that are part of the project. Follow this link for a summary of some of the objectives of EGSO.

EGSO will be of great benefit to the solar community, but it will also act as the interface to solar data for the Space Weather, Climate Physics and Astrophysics communities. In addition, since many of the problems that the EGSO applications address exist in other fields, the technology developed for the project could be used on other Grid projects. As with other EC funded projects, EGSO supports the Open Source policy.

3.9   EuroGrid

The EuroGrid project is a Research and Technology Development project funded as part of the IST Program by the European Commission with a project term from November 1, 2000 through October 31, 2003. EuroGrid demonstrates the use of Grids in important scientific and industrial communities, addresses the specific requirements of these communities in a European Grid middleware, and highlights the benefits of using trans-European Grids.

The objectives of the EUROGRID project are:

- to establish a trans-European Grid of leading High Performance Computing centers.
- to operate and support the EuroGrid software infrastructure.
- to develop important GRID software components and integrate them into EuroGrid (dynamic resource broker, accounting and billing, interface for coupled applications and interactive access).
- to demonstrate distributed simulation code from significant application areas (biomolecular simulations, meteorology, coupled CAE simulations).
- to make the EuroGrid middleware available to other Grid projects.

3.10   FlowGrid

The objective of the FlowGrid project is to establish a Virtual Organization for conducting on-demand flow simulations (CFD) by setting up a Grid infrastructure and by developing, deploying and sharing software, computing resources and knowledge. The specific measurable objectives of the FlowGrid project are:

- to establish a network of Grid-enabled CFD centers from different European countries
- to develop and implement novel client software for accessing CFD solutions on the grid

- to develop scalable and generic middleware to support the deployment of CFD solvers on the Grid
- to assess the performance of the parallel version of the CFD solvers, by running real industrial applications on parallel distributed computers

3.11   GEMSS

The central objective of the GEMSS project is to demonstrate that the Grid can be used to provide medical practitioners and researchers with access to advanced simulation and image processing services for improved pre-operative planning and near real-time surgical support for specific time-critical applications. The GEMSS will build on existing Grid technologies, maintaining compliance with standards thereby ensuring future extensibility and interoperability, to provide support for sophisticated authorization, workflow, security, error detection and recovery.

3.12   GRACE

Today's search engines are extremely centralized. In order to index a document it must be downloaded, processed and its index stored - all in one central location. However the centralized approach may not always be applicable. GRACE specifically addresses the situations where centralized indexes are unfeasible and proposes the development of a decentralized search and categorization engine built on-top of Grid-technology.

The idea is to develop a distributed search and categorization engine that will enable just-in-time, flexible allocation of data and computational resources. GRACE aims at making petabytes of information, distributed on vast amounts of geographically distant locations, highly accessible. GRACE handles unstructured textual information, (text files, documents, Web pages, text stored in databases), typically handled by meta search engines.

3.13   GRIA

The GRIA project will take Grid technology into the real world, enabling industrial users to trade computational resources on a commercial basis to meet their needs more cost effectively. The GRIA consortium is developing business models, processes and semantics to allow resource owners and users to discover each other and negotiate terms for access to high-value resources. GRIA will implement an overall business process to find, procure and utilize resources capable of carrying out these high-value, expert-assisted computations. The project will focus on two application sectors: structural and hydrological engineering, and digital TV and Movie post-production. These have very different technological requirements, but share a need for large amounts of computational power to meet peak loads. By focusing on business processes and the associated semantics, GRIA will enable users to provision for their computational needs more cost effectively, and develop new business models for some of their services.

3.14   GridLab

The GridLab project will develop a easy-to-use, flexible, generic and modular Grid Application Toolkit (GAT), enabling todays applications to make innovative use of global computing resources. The project is grounded by two principles: simultaneous development of infrastructure, applications and user communities, leading to working scenarios, and dynamic use of grids, with self-aware simulations adapting to their changing environment.

3.15   GRIP

The GRIP project aims to make two major Grid systems, UNICORE and Globus interoperate and as part of this to establish standards in the Global Grid Forum that take account of middleware technology developed in Europe, e.g. UNICORE. GRIP is working on unifying the two packages through developing a special layer of middleware, separating both Globus and Unicore from higher layers of Grid services and applications.

3.16   MammoGrid

The MammoGrid project aims to develop and utilize a European distributed database of mammograms to investigate effective methods of co-working between European healthcare professionals in the field of breast cancer screening. It will develop Grid-based methods for sharing and managing mammographic images and related data between countries.

3.17   OpenMolGrid

The main objective of the OpenMolGRID project is to provide a unified and extensible information-rich environment for solving molecular design/engineering tasks relevant to chemistry, pharmacy and life sciences. This will be achieved by extending the currently used local approach to the global dimension by building the OpenMolGRID environment on top of the Grid infrastructure provided by the EuroGrid project. The system will provide seamless integration of existing, widely accepted, relevant computing tools and data sources. The OpenMolGRID system will comprise a set of application-oriented tools that are built on core Grid services and functions provided by the EuroGrid infrastructure. The system will target both academic and commercial end-users (especially chemical and pharmaceutical industry).

3.18   SeLeNe

SeLeNe is a one-year research project funded by the EU outside of the IST priority. The project is conducting a study into the technical feasibility of using Semantic Web technology for dynamically integrating metadata from heterogeneous and autonomous educational resources, and for creating personalized views over this Knowledge Grid.

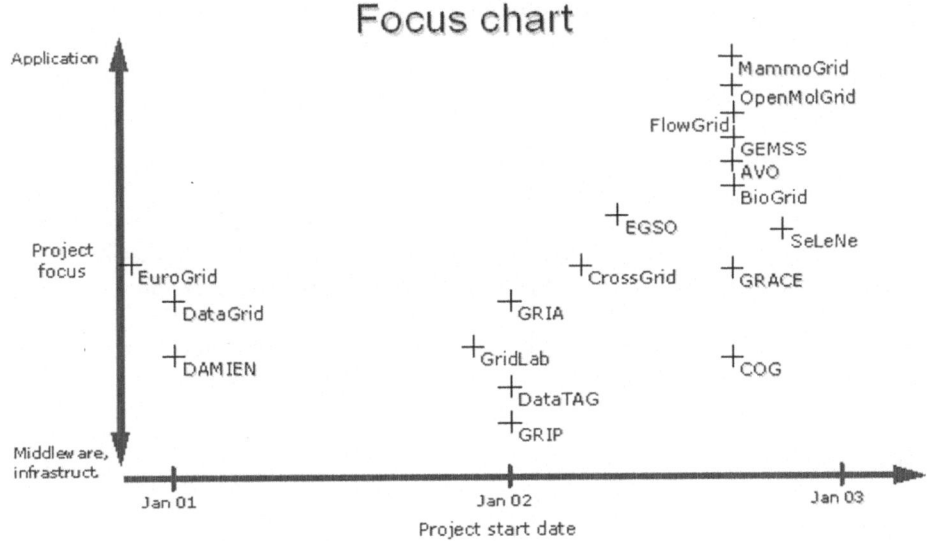

Fig. 2. Grid project focus.

4 Application Areas and Trends

The projects mentioned in the previous section cover a wide range of interests and research areas - from purely scientific problems to societally important challenges, such as weather forecasting and flood prediction. Over time several key trends can be discerned:

- Grid research in general is moving from middleware- and testbed-oriented issues to purely applicational areas. The initial "trailblazing" projects, such as EuroGrid or DataGrid focus heavily on developing common standards and testing various middle-ware packages/components, while the latter undertakings try to build on what is already available and extend Grid functionality to deal with new problems and challenges (see Fig. 2).
- We are also witnessing a shift from computationally-intensive applications, such as high energy physics analyses and weather forecasting to knowledge discovery and categorization.
- As far as middleware is concerned, the Globus Toolkit is emerging as a common standard for Grid development and deployment. Most current Grid research projects use version 2.x of the toolkit, but since the Grid Services (OGSA) compatible version 3.0 was released, projects have started shifting to that version. The European alternative to Globus - the Unicore suite - is used as well, but does not appear to be gaining popularity.
- When observing some of the newer projects, one can discern a shift from all-encompassing long-term research initiatives (such as Eurogrid, DataGrid, CrossGrid or GRIP) to smaller, focused projects. These projects typically take less time to complete and require fewer resources.

- Industry representatives are starting to actively participate in Grid research. This is especially true of newer projects, which have attracted substantial industrial and commercial involvement (i.e. COG, GEMSS or FlowGrid).

Acknowledgements

The authors would like to thank John Brooke (University of Manchester) Edgar Gabriel (High Performance Computing Center, Stuttgart) Hans Christian Hoppe (Pallas GmbH) Daniel Mallmann (Forschungszentrum Julich) Michael M. Resch (High Performance Computing Center, Stuttgart) Florian Schintke (Zuse-Institute Berlin) and Mike Surridge (IT Innovation) for providing input to this compilation.

References

1. Grid Today: http://gridtoday.com/
2. EnterTheGrid (Primeur weekly): http://EnterTheGrid.com
3. ISTWeb project database: http://www.cordis.lu/ist/projects.htm
4. Eurogrid website: http://www.eurogrid.org/
5. DataGrid website: http://www.eu-datagrid.org/
6. Damien website: http://www.hlrs.de/organization/pds/projects/damien/
7. GRIA website: http://www.gria.org/
8. GridLab website: http://www.gridlab.org
9. GRIP website: http://www.grid-interoperability.org/
10. DataTAG website: http://datatag.web.cern.ch/datatag/
11. CrossGrid website: http://www.eu-crossgrid.org/
12. EGSO website: http://www.mssl.ucl.ac.uk/grid/egso/
13. Biogrid website: http://bio.cc/Biogrid/
14. GEMSS website: http://www.ccrl-nece.de/gemss/
15. GRACE website: http://pertinax.cms.shu.ac.uk/projects/cmslb2/
16. GridStart website: http://www.gridstart.org/
17. Globus Toolkit 3: http://www.globus.org/about/news/gt3/

The CrossGrid Architecture:
Applications, Tools, and Grid Services*

Marian Bubak[1,2], Maciej Malawski[1,2], and Katarzyna Zając[1,2]

[1] Institute of Computer Science, AGH, al. Mickiewicza 30, 30-059 Kraków, Poland
{bubak,malawski,kzajac}@uci.agh.edu.pl
phone: (+48 12) 617 39 64, fax: (+48 12) 633 80 54
[2] Academic Computer Centre – CYFRONET, Nawojki 11, 30-950 Kraków, Poland

Abstract. This paper describes the current status of the CrossGrid Project architecture. The architecture is divided into six layers. The relations between main components are presented in UML notation. A flexible concept of plugins that enable creation of uniform user-friendly interface is shown. A brief discussion of OGSA technology and its possible application to CrossGrid services is given as an interesting area of future work.

Keywords: Grid, architecture, services, interactive applications.

1 Introduction

The CrossGrid Project development is driven by applications which are characterized by interaction with a person in a processing loop [5,2]: simulation and visualization for surgical procedures, a flooding crisis team decision support system, distributed data analysis in high-energy physics, air pollution modeling combined with weather forecasting. Each application requires a response from the Grid to an action by that person in different time scales: from real time through intermediate delays to long waiting periods. These applications are simultaneously compute- and data-intensive.

The medical application requires an environment enabling simulation, visualization and interaction which will allow a medical doctor to change simulation parameters through a graphical interface in near-real time. For the flood prediction and protection application an interactive Grid system should allow experts to steer a cascade of meteorological, hydrological and hydraulic simulations. Data analysis in high-energy physics needs on-line access to large distributed databases and data mining services. Air pollution and weather modeling requires on-line progress monitoring of simulation results in order to decide about further job execution. A new programming environment is necessary to support application development and on-line monitoring and performance analysis [5].

* This work was partly funded by the European Commission, project IST-2001-32243, CrossGrid [6]

F. Fernández Rivera et al. (Eds.): Across Grids 2003, LNCS 2970, pp. 309–316, 2004.
© Springer-Verlag Berlin Heidelberg 2004

The first objective of this paper is to present the current status of the software architecture, and the second one is the analysis of CrossGrid services in order to find a way of integrating them into the OGSA model.

2 Definition of the CrossGrid Architecture

This paper presents the second version of the architecture of the CrossGrid Project, i.e. the general overview of software components and their relationships. The components are applications, tools that support application development and new Grid services that are being elaborated within the Project. Dependencies on external components, such as Data-Grid [7] and Globus software [10] are presented as well.

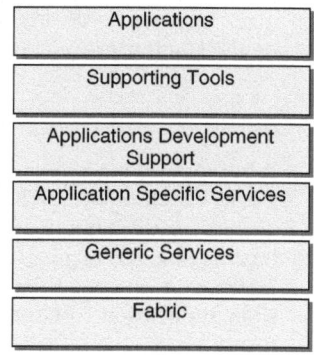

Fig. 1. Architecture layers.

In the first description of the CrossGrid architecture [4] we followed the layer structure proposed in [8]. We distinguished six layers that are shown in Fig. 1. Below the applications and tools we placed applications development support layer, consisting of programming libraries and environments. The grid services were divided into generic and application specific, whereas the lowest layer constitutes the fabric of Grid-enabled resources.

Current approach results from the first software requirements, design documents and use cases of applications, services and tools [6] and it is presented using UML component diagrams (see Fig. 2). It is oriented toward dependencies between the software components.

2.1 Services

The CrossGrid software is built upon the existing Globus and EDG [7] software. The Resource Broker from the DataGrid is extended by adding the functionality of handling MPI parallel jobs. The Data Access package of CrossGrid allows estimation of data access time to files located on various forms of storage - from tapes to disks and databases. This functionality is used by the EDG Replica Manager for finding best replicas of datasets located on the grid.

To enable user-friendly access to the CrossGrid services, the specialized environment is prepared. It consists of the Roaming Access Server that enables uniform access from all different places. The graphical Migrating Desktop can be invoked in a Java-enabled browser and it gives the user the same personalized environment. The applications producing visual output can be incorporated into the desktop by the flexible mechanism of plugins 3.

In CrossGrid, there is a lot of effort put in development of various monitoring services. They are divided into application and infrastructure monitoring and are

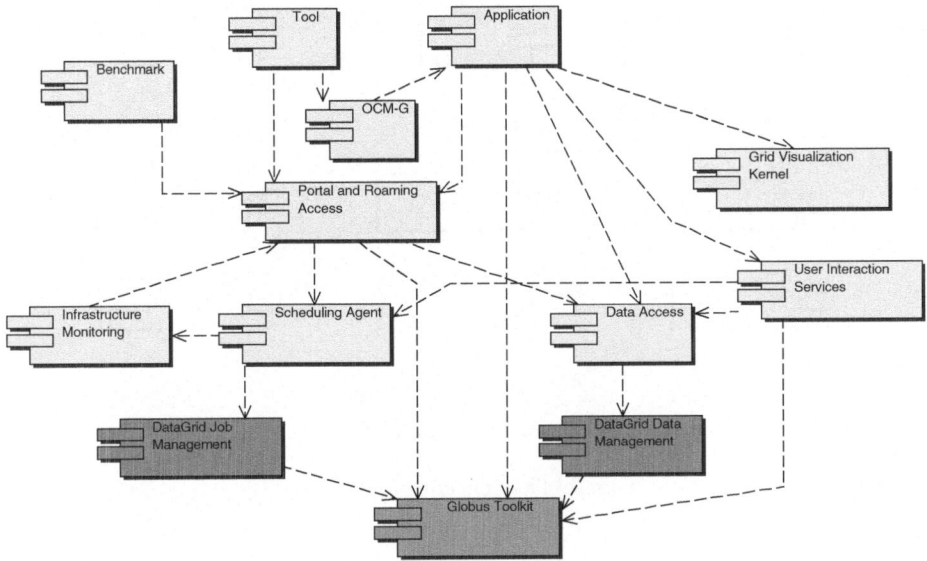

Fig. 2. Overview of the architecture.

accompanied by the post-processing mechanisms. The application monitoring system OCM-G [1] gives the output to the on-line performance measurement tool [3]. The Jiro-based infrastructure monitoring system can be used to gather information about clusters and network devices, like routers and switches and can produce performance alerts. Also the possibility of tracking network traffic on the level of IP packets is provided by the SANTA-G monitoring tool.

2.2   Tools

The important amount of work in CrossGrid is devoted to design and implementation of the tools that are intended to facilitate development of grid applications. These tools include MPI code verification, performance analysis and grid benchmarks.

In Fig. 2 there is a dependency between applications and tools. Current application kernels are used for development and testing of the tools, and eventually the tools will be used to facilitate the application development process. Benchmarks and performance analysis tool have also their place in CrossGrid portal and can be used within the same user interface as the applications.

The performance analysis tool is not directly connected to the application process, but uses the OCM-G monitoring system. OCM-G and the tool communicate using OMIS interface [1]. The possibility to measure the performance of one of the High Energy Physics application that is using MPI, was shown. As the tools become more stable, more applications can benefit from using the tools for the development.

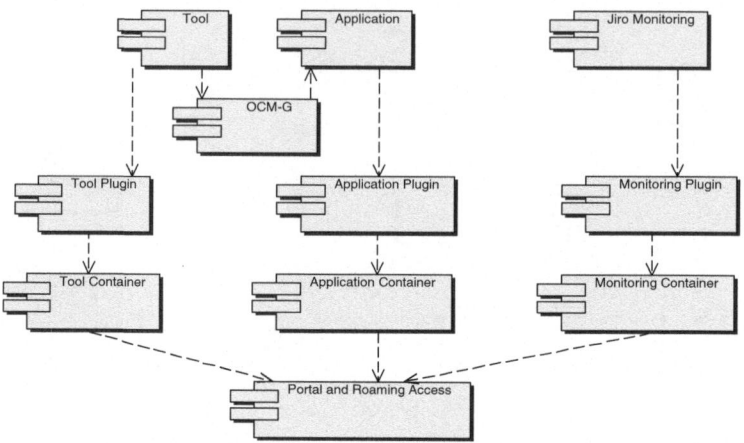

Fig. 3. The concept of plugins.

This definition of the CrossGrid architecture is driving the implementation of the prototypes.

3   CrossGrid Services and OGSA

The second objective of the paper is the analysis of the CrossGrid services and, as a result, a proposal of the way they could be integrated into the OGSA service model. It is inspired and based on the schedule of the development of Globus 3.0 and OGSA technology [9].

OGSA which was recently proposed and is actively being developed by the Globus Project, is intended to be a basic technology for building Grid systems. Through Web services, actual interoperability and implementation independence may be achieved. The basic service semantics included in the Open Grid Services Infrastructure (OGSI) are used as building blocks of Globus Toolkit 3.0 (GT3). The Global Grid Forum OGSA Working Group is discussing the higher level set of services that are used in Grids and that can be integrated into the OGSA framework [10].

The objective of OGSA activity is to make it the standard for all Grid services. Every service that wants to be a part of the Grid should be OGSI-compliant. It will give the standard way for discovery, inspection and interoperability with service. It is not required that all external communication with a service has to be done by means of XML/SOAP. The service may use any other communication protocols when e.g. high performance is necessary. It may however use OGSA mechanisms only for advertising itself to enable discovery by other services or use Service Data model to expose and publish some information for external consumers.

In our opinion, those Grid services that are being developed in CrossGrid may also be designed and implemented as OGSA-compliant giving significant contribution to the Grid community. In the following subsections we give the short overview of CrossGrid new services and the discussion of the possible application of OGSA mechanisms in their development.

3.1   Portals and Roaming Access

These services in CrossGrid are giving user the simple and transparent access to grid services, independently from user location. The central point is the Roaming Access Server (RAS), which acts as an interface between users desktop and the underlying Grid middleware from CrossGrid, DataGrid and Globus services. It also stores information about user profile, settings and current session. In addition to standard grid services, like batch job submission, data transfer, etc. the user has also access to control application-specific input with validation of parameters and output. Handling of these specific interaction is done by extensible concept of plugins that are provided by application developers. We believe that this approach may be general enough to make it useful not only to CrossGrid applications. With the help of OGSA the standard interfaces to user profile and session data can be defined.

3.2   Job Scheduling

The task of scheduling user jobs and submitting them to grid resources in Cross-Grid is done by the services called the Scheduling Agents. In current design their role is to accept requests in the form of Job Description Language (JDL) and based on their optimization strategies that use the information from monitoring systems they decide where to submit the job. For actual job submission and management, the DataGrid software is used. Taking into account the possible usage of this service by others, it would be valuable to have Grid Service interfaces to this scheduling service. This however requires collaboration with other grid projects that are also working on scheduling problem.

3.3   Grid Monitoring

There are three kinds of monitoring systems in CrossGrid: one for application monitoring [1] and the two for infrastructure that are based on Jiro and the specific hardware. As there is the need for exporting this monitoring data to some external consumers, like schedulers and archivers, it would be helpful to have some standard way of accessing and storing this monitoring information. It is agreed to have Web Service interfaces for infrastructure monitoring systems. As OGSA introduces a new, XML based model of Service Data that is used for information propagation and discovery, it seems natural that all monitoring systems can expose a OGSI-compliant interface to publish the information they provide.

3.4 Data Access

Data Access package in CrossGrid provides middleware for accessing large data residing on tape libraries. It uses techniques to optimize access time and is going to be integrated within the DataGrid framework for Replica Management and optimization. The middleware is designed to use Web Services technology for communicating between its components. As it is designed to be interoperable with other software, it would be possible to integrate it with the Replica Location Framework [12], that is a part of higher level services delivered with GT3.

3.5 User Interaction Services

User Interaction Services comprise a set of Grid Services which allow the setup and interactive steering of complex Grid applications consisting of modules for simulation and visualization. The services focus on discovery of HLA [11] Runtime Infrastructure (RTI) processes that coordinate distributed application components and on efficient Grid-based data transfer protocols as an alternative for current RTI communication. As a proof-of-concept example, they use the Cross-Grid biomedical simulation application, which requires near real time steering of simulation parameters during runtime of the simulation running on the Grid. User Interaction Services take advantage of service discovery mechanisms that are present in OGSA and in their future development will be integrated into OGSA model.

3.6 Proposed Steps toward OGSA

The first step toward OGSA can be the usage of the Web services technology to expose external interfaces of individual services. This can be applied to Roaming Access, Scheduling and Data Access services in CrossGrid. This step is independent of the changes in the evolving Grid Service framework and may be considered even for the first prototype.

The second step may consist of using specific extensions to web services that are present in the OGSA model. These are mechanisms for dynamic service creation, lifetime management, introspection and information (service data) management based on XML. Dynamic service creation and lifetime management mechanisms can be used when it is required to control the state of some process, e.g. user session in a portal, data transfer or a running simulation. The service data model can be applied to monitoring systems that can be used as information providers to other services.

Finally, after the implementation of CrossGrid services with compliance to OGSA standards, there is a possibility of integration of them into the broader framework of high level services, that are based on Globus Toolkit. It can be a contribution to the the effort of Global Grid Forum to standardize the higher level services based on OGSA architecture.

During the second year of the project it was decided to continue development basing on GT2.x in order to preserve the compatibility with EDG software.

However, the development of the services is proceeding in such a way that the software will be OGSA-ready. It means that the effort required to adapt existing components to OGSA will be minimized.

4   Summary

The definition of the CrossGrid architecture presented here, along with its components, their functionality and relations between them as well as with components from Globus and DataGrid projects is verified by the successive prototypes. The software was integrated during two successful project meetings in Santiago and Poznan. It is compatible with the releases of EDG [7] software and is running on the same testbed. The code is available publicly from the project CVS repository and the developers portal [13].

Acknowledgments

The authors would like to thank M. Turała, M. Garbacz, P.M.A. Sloot, D. van Albada, L. Hluchy, W. Funika, R. Wismüller, J. Kitowski, N. Meyer, and J. Marco for discussions and suggestions, as well as P. Nowakowski for his comments. This research is partly funded by the European Commission the IST-2001-32243 Project CrossGrid.

References

1. Balis, B., Bubak, M., Funika, W., Szepieniec, T., and Wismuüller, R.: An Infrastructure for Grid Application Monitoring In: Kranzlmueller, D., Kacsuk, P., Dongarra, J., Volker, J. (Eds.): Recent Advances in Parallel Virtual Machine and Message Passing Interface, Proc. 9th European PVM/MPI Users' Group Meeting, Linz, Austria, September/October 2002, LNCS 2474, pp. 41-49, 2002
2. Bubak, M., Marco, J., Marten, H., Meyer, N., Noga, N., Sloot, P.M.A., and Turała, M.: CrossGrid - Development of Grid Environment for Interactive Presented at PIONIER 2002, Poznan, April 23-24, 2002, Proceeding, pp. 97-112, Poznan, 2002
3. Bubak, M., Funika, W., and Wismüller, R.: The CrossGrid Performance Analysis Tool for Interactive Grid Applications. In: Kranzlmueller, D., Kacsuk, P., Dongarra, J., Volker, J. (Eds.): Recent Advances in Parallel Virtual Machine and Message Passing Interface, Proc. 9th European PVM/MPI Users' Group Meeting, Linz, Austria, September/October 2002, LNCS 2474, pp.50-60, 2002
4. Bubak, M., Malawski, M., Zając, K.: Towards the CrossGrid Architecture. In: Kranzlmueller, D., Kacsuk, P., Dongarra, J., Volker, J. (Eds.): Recent Advances in Parallel Virtual Machine and Message Passing Interface, Proc. 9th European PVM/MPI Users' Group Meeting, Linz, Austria, September/October 2002, LNCS 2474, pp. 16-24, 2002
5. CrossGrid - Development of Grid Environment for Interactive Applications. Annex 1 - description of Work. http://www.eu-crossgrid.org
6. CrossGrid Project: Deliverables of M3 and M6 of the project: http://www.eu-crossgrid.org

7. DataGrid Project: http://www.eu-datagrid.org
8. Foster, I., Kesselman, C., Tuecke, S. The Anatomy of the Grid. Enabling Scalable Virtual Organizations. International Journal of High Performance Computing Applications **15** (3) 200-222 (2001);
   http://www.globus.org/research/papers/anatomy.pdf
9. Foster, I., Kesselman, C., Nick, J.M., and Tuecke, S.: The Physiology of the Grid. An Open Grid Services Architecture for Distributed Systems Integration, January 2002, http://www.globus.org
10. Global Grid Forum: http://www.ggf.org
11. High Level Architecture Specification http://www.sisostds.org/stdsdev/hla/
12. Replica Location Service http://grid-data-management.web.cern.ch/grid-data-management/replica-location-service/RLS.html
13. CrossGrid Software Repository http://gridportal.fzk.de

Comparison of Grid Middleware
in European Grid Projects

Ariel Oleksiak and Jarek Nabrzyski

Poznań Supercomputing and Networking Center, Poznań, Poland
{ariel,naber}@man.poznan.pl

Abstract. This paper presents early results of the work on the report containing an analysis of EU funded grid projects. The goals of this research, undertaken with the support of the GRIDSTART project, include study of various solutions, discovery of overlapping efforts, stimulating the reuse of grid components developed within the scope of European projects and identification of open issues in particular areas of grid development. The paper focuses mainly on ten initiatives clustered by GRIDSTART. We present here a brief survey of grid projects, a taxonomy used to categorise projects' efforts, an analysis of applications, and a summary of research and development performed within the scope of particular projects.

1   Introduction

Grid technology is being developed within the framework of many research and development projects. These efforts, undertaken in Europe as well as in the US and Asia-Pacific region, are to provide various communities of users with grid-aware and efficient applications, to prepare the needed grid infrastructure and to develop middleware enabling application developers, scientists and researchers to fully exploit the functionality of grids. Particular projects focus on various aspects of grids, however, they often have many common aspects and interests as well. As the directions proposed by the European Commission in the 6th Framework Programme include stronger coordination of European research activities and their targeting, the need for consolidation of technical approaches of grid projects in Europe has arisen. In order to achieve this goal, ten EU funded projects have been clustered in the framework of the GRIDSTART project [1].

2   Grid Projects

Basically, the aforementioned report focuses on European grid projects clustered in the framework of GRIDSTART activity. However, recent projects funded by the European Commision through the Framework Programme (FP5) are taken into consideration as well in order to show how they evolve when compared to previous projects. Generally there are more than 20 projects in Europe. The following of them have been taken under the umbrella of the GRIDSTART project:

F. Fernández Rivera et al. (Eds.): Across Grids 2003, LNCS 2970, pp. 317–325, 2004.

- **AVO (Astrophysical Virtual Observatory)** [2].The main goal of the AVO is to provide a collection of diverse data archives and software tools to establish a Virtual Observatory.
- **CrossGrid (Large-Scale Grid-Enabled Simulations)** [3]. CrossGrid develops grid services and programming tools for interactive simulation and visualization applications in areas such as medicine, physics and earth sciences.
- **DAMIEN (Distributed Applications and Middleware for Industrial Use of European Networks)** [4]. The goal of the DAMIEN project is to develop essential software supporting the grid infrastructure especially providing a solid MPI-based metacomputing layer and tools for performance analysis and optimization. These results are applied in the CAE industrial application.
- **DataGrid (Next Generation Scientific Exploration)** [5]. DataGrid aims to enable access to geographically distributed computing power and storage facilities belonging to different institutions. This will provide the necessary resources to process huge amounts of data coming from scientific experiments in three different disciplines: High Energy Physics, Biology and Earth Observation.
- **DataTAG (Research & Technological Development for a TransAtlantic Grid)** [6]. DataTAG aims to construct a transatlantic grid testbed providing interoperability between European and US projects.
- **EGSO (European Grid of Solar Observations)** [7]. The main objective of EGSO is to lay the foundations of a virtual solar observatory combining heterogeneous data from scattered archives of space- and ground-based observations into a single "virtual" dataset.
- **EUROGRID (European Testbed for Grid Applications)** [8]. EUROGRID develops core grid software components, which will be tested using biology, meteorology, and industrial applications.
- **GRIA (Grid Resources for Industrial Applications)** [9]. GRIA devises business models and processes that make it feasible and cost-effective to offer and use computational services securely in an open grid marketplace.
- **GridLab (Grid Application Toolkit and Testbed)** [10]. The aim of GridLab is to enable software to fully exploit dynamic resources through the development of a Grid Application Toolkit and a set of necessary grid services, and testing them on the real testbed using application frameworks.
- **GRIP (GRid Interoperability Project)** [11]. GRIP realizes the interoperability of Globus and UNICORE, two leading software packages central to the operation of the grid.

The remaining EU funded grid initiatives (being informal partners of GRID-START) are the following:

- BioGrid (Bio-technology Information & Knowledge Grid),
- COG (Corporate Ontology Grid),
- FLOWGRID (Flow-Simulations on-demand using Grid-computing),

- GEMSS (Grid-enabled Medical Simulation Services),
- GRACE (Grid Search & Categorization Engine),
- GRASP (GRid based Application Service Provision),
- MammoGrid (European federated mammogram database implemented on Grids),
- MOSES (Modular & Scalable Environment for Semantic Web),
- OpenMolGrid (Open Computing Grid for Molecular Science & Engineering),
- SeLeNe (Self e-Learning Networks).

Focus of European grid projects is summarized in Figure 1, taking their start-up times and funds into consideration.

FP5 IST Grid Projects

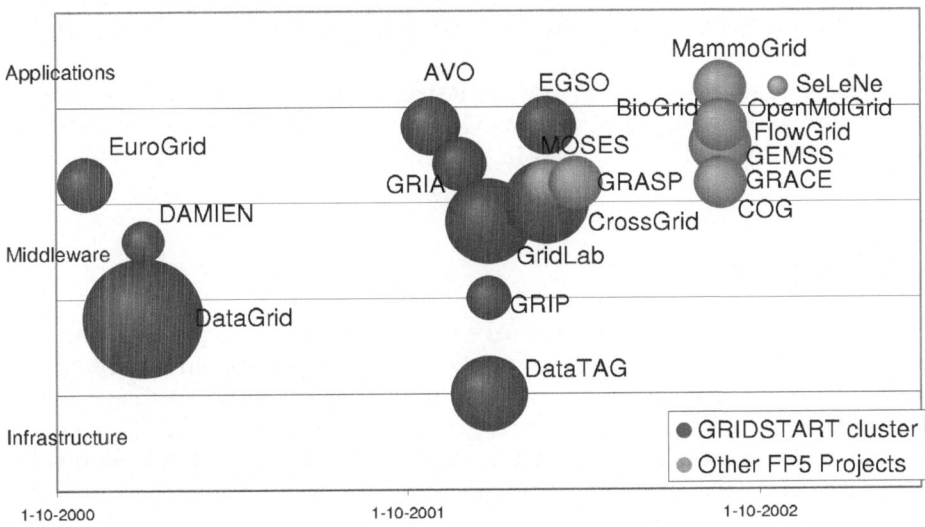

Fig. 1. Focus, start-up date and funds of FP5 grid projects (the size of the "bubbles" denotes the funding level of the corresponding project).

The size of points presented in the figure corresponds to the funding of projects. For example, the largest project's (DataGrid) funds correspond to 9.8 million Euros, and the smallest one's (SeLeNe) are less than 300 thousands Euros. The horizontal axis indicates start-up dates, and the vertical one the focus of projects. The focus is ordered from the lowest level grid components, at the bottom of the figure, to the highest level, at the top. For example, projects with their focus situated in lower parts of the figure may work mainly on fabric or connectivity layers. If focus is placed between Middleware and Applications on the vertical axis it means that the project's activities concern high level (collective or application specific) services or application environments and tools.

Figure 1 allows us to draw certain general conclusions. First of all, one can see how the number of grid projects has increased in the years since 2000. The first group of projects contained only three initiatives. Furthermore, instead of a few large projects, many smaller activities focused on more specific goals have appeared. Most of the new initiatives are application oriented. Generally, the objectives of European grid projects are quite differentiated and cover all three aspects of grid development we have considered. Initially, larger funds were targeted at middleware and smaller for infrastructure and applications. These first grid initiatives should provide a solid basis for the next, more application-oriented projects. Finally, we would like to emphasize that the projects oriented towards applications or middleware do not necessarily ignore grid components located in other layers. Some details concerning project activities in various grid areas are presented in Section 5 and will be a topic for further research.

A large effort on a national level has also been made to develop grid environments. The UK e-Science program is a good example of such an effort supporting many grid projects including GridPP, AstroGrid, GEODISE, OGSA-DAI and many others.

Of course, there are many grid initiatives outside Europe: US projects involved into grid development such as GrADS, GriPhyN, IPG, iVDGL, PPDG, and TeraGrid as well as activities in, for example, Southern Korea, Japan and Australia.

3   Taxonomy

Grid development may be categorised according to various separate areas such as security, resource management, application development environments and many others listed below in this section. Grid projects activities focus usually on a subset of these areas. Moreover, grid environments often have a common general architecture divided into layers. Thus, the comparison has been divided into three main parts according to the taxonomy we've prepared. The first - general - contains a comparison of the focus and goals of projects. The focus denotes whether the project is application, middleware or infrastructure oriented. The second part includes architecture and analysis of components in particular layers. The following layers are considered (based on [13]):

- Applications and Portals,
- Application Development Environment and Tools,
- Middleware (Generic and Application Specific Services),
- Fabric.

The main part of the comparison contains areas of grid computing. We hope they cover all (or at least all of the most important) aspects of grid environments. They are as follows:

- Portals and Mobile Access,
- Applications,

- Application Development Environment and Tools,
- Resource Management and Scheduling,
- Information,
- Monitoring and Performance Analysis,
- Logging,
- Data Management,
- Security,
- Accounting,
- Testbeds and Networks,
- Dissemination Plans.

In order to compare all activities in a credible and exhaustive way, a set of *templates* corresponding to particular areas listed above was prepared. These templates were then circulated to all projects from the GRIDSTART cluster to gather information concerning considered projects. Each template contains important issues related to a given area. Basically, they have been divided into three groups. The first group includes general issues such as the main requirements and functionality of the project's component. The second group, called external, defines connections (e.g. interfaces) of mechanisms developed in the scope of a given area with other components and users. The "details" group, in turn, deals with all specific issues related to a particular area.

4   Applications

A comparison of domains and classes of applications used and developed in European grid projects may serve as an example of the analysis. These issues are rather general, but very important since particular applications and their users stimulate the development of grid technology.

There are several interesting aspects of applications that can influence the structure and the scope of the projects. These aspects include application domains, classes (types), requirements and user communities. Here we confine our analysis to application domains and classes.

The numbers of projects belonging to the GRIDSTART cluster developing applications from particular domains are presented in Table 1. We have distinguished the following general domains: Earth and Environmental Sciences, Biology and Medicine, Physics and Astronomy, Engineering, and Multimedia.

As shown in the table, scientific domains such as life sciences, earth observations, weather prediction and physics are the main forces stimulating development of grid environments. For instance, such stimulating factors, in the case of the DataGrid project, were based on requirements coming from the high energy physics field including demands of experiments which require processing huge amounts of data. On the other hand, several projects deal with industrial applications including CAE or multimedia. This trend is quite common for the development of new technologies. They are often used at first in scientific communities and afterwards become widely accepted and used for commercial purpose.

Table 1. Application Domains in FP5 IST Grid Projects.

Application Domain	Number of Projects
Earth and Environmental Sciences	4
Biology and Medicine	4
Physics and Astronomy	5
Engineering	3
Multimedia	1

We have also tried to classify these applications according to the categorisation presented in [13]. The following major classes of applications (for details see [12]) have been presented in Table 2 along with a number of projects dealing with applications belonging to these classes:

Table 2. Application Classes in FP5 IST Grid Projects.

Application Class	Number of Projects
Distributed supercomputing	5
High throughput	1
On demand	5
Data intensive	4
Collaborative	1

As one can see, various classes of applications are being developed by projects in the cluster. However, the majority of applications deal with large amounts of data (data intensive) or require huge computing power (distributed supercomputing) often in a bounded amount of time (on demand).

5   Research and Development in FP5 IST Grid Projects

EU-funded projects are exploring and developing various aspects of grid environments. These aspects have been presented in Figure 2. One can distinguish areas of grid development explored by the majority of projects as well as specific for a few of them. However, this figure does not correspond exactly with the extent of developments in given areas, since some projects place different emphasis on them. Furthermore, some technologies belonging to a specific area may be developed to a greater extent than in others. More detailed analysis of these issues is a topic for further research.

Projects belonging to the **GRIDSTART** cluster explore many interesting problems, which are very relevant for further development of grid technology. For instance, the interoperability issue is addressed by the DataTAG and GRIP projects. The former attempts to provide a transatlantic testbed including US

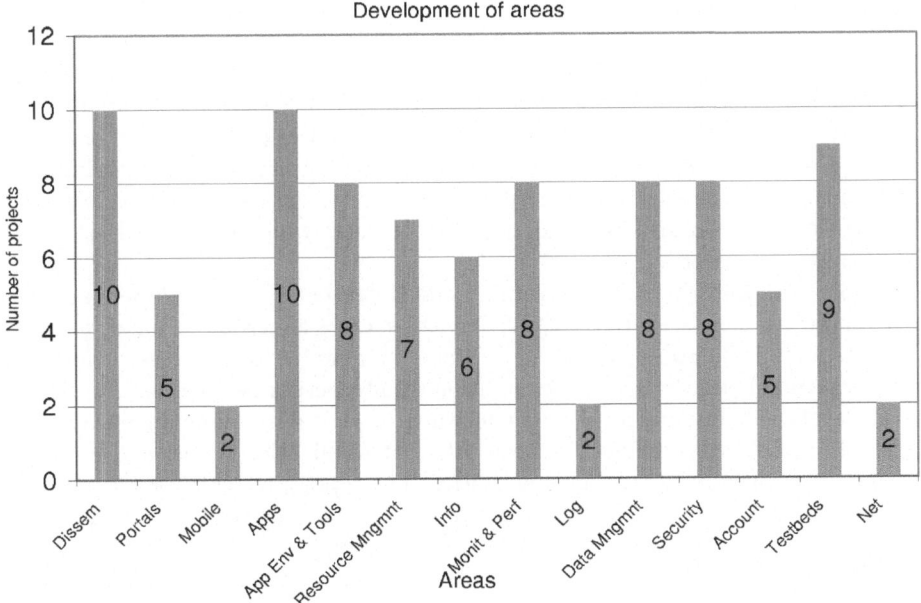

Fig. 2. Development of particular grid areas in the scope of the GRIDSTART cluster.

projects and DataGrid testbed taking advantage of the GLUE schema (a common schema for information systems). The latter realizes the interoperability of Globus and UNICORE, two leading software packages central to the operation of the grid. Network infrastructure is being developed mainly by DataTAG including the design of new network protocols for fast data transfer and the aforementioned transatlantic testbed. Other projects (e.g DataGrid, GridLab, CrossGrid) create their own testbeds as well. Grid projects work also on various applications and assemble many user communities as stated in Section 4. For example, AVO and EGSO develop application specific solutions in the astrophysics domain. Industrial applications are addressed by GRIA and DAMIEN. Applications in DataGrid, EUROGRID and CrossGrid projects concern several domains. The GridLab project adapts two application frameworks (used mainly by astrophysicists) to grid environments. Programming tools such as APIs, SDKs and toolkits are also being developed. The main goal of GridLab is to develop the Grid Application Toolkit which will enable applications to adapt dynamically to grid environments. Tools for MPI applications and performance optimisation are the objective of the DAMIEN and CrossGrid projects. We can also distinguish between projects dealing with compute-intensive and data-intensive applications. GridLab and EUROGRID belong to the former group. DataGrid, CrossGrid and EGSO are typical "data oriented" projects.

In view of the limited size of this paper a brief overview of develement in areas of grid technology has been presented. Further details will be available in the report which is being compiled in the scope of the GRIDSTART project.

6 Summary

This paper summarizes the first steps and early results of the work on the analysis and comparison of European IST grid projects. Results presented in the paper contain a brief survey of projects, a proposed taxonomy, an overview of applications and a summary of efforts in particular areas of grid technology. This research forms the basis for further analyses such as comparison of more detailed information and including another projects which do not belong to the GRIDSTART cluster.

The work, whose initial results have been presented in the paper, also addresses the needs of the GRIDSTART project such as a consolidation of technical developments in Europe, a focused and active contribution to the development of international standards, the stimulation of interaction between grid activities at all levels within Europe, driving forward of grid developments by identifying and amplifying synergies between different application areas, and a central repository of information for grid activities. The report, which is being compiled on the basis of projects' analysis, will constitute a background for the above issues and the design of a roadmap for grid development.

Grid users and developers will be able, using this report, to take advantage of the following information:

- Overlapping issues, i.e. identification of problems that are solved in an identical way by different projects,
- Status of software components and solutions developed by the IST grid projects,
- Recommendations for possible collaboration between particular projects,
- Open issues and challenges concerning areas, methods and problems which need to be studied and solved,
- An attempt to answer the question: what we can expect within the next few years in the grid technology area.

Acknowledgements

This work was partially funded by the European Commission programme through the EU GRIDSTART Project (IST-2001-34808).

Special thanks to Heinz Stockinger from CERN for help in collecting information concerning projects clustered by GRIDSTART.

References

1. GRIDSTART project website: http://www.gridstart.org
2. AVO project website: http://www.eso.org/projects/avo
3. CrossGrid project website: http://www.eu-crossgrid.org/project.htm
4. DAMIEN project website: http://www.hlrs.de/organization/pds/projects/damien
5. DataGrid project website: http://www.edg.org

6. DataTAG project website: http://datatag.web.cern.ch/datatag
7. EGSO project website: http://www.mssl.ucl.ac.uk/grid/egso/egso_top.html
8. EUROGRID project website: http://www.eurogrid.org
9. GRIA project website: http://www.gria.org
10. GridLab project website: http://www.gridlab.org
11. GRIP project website: http://www.grid-interoperability.org
12. Foster, I., Kesselman, C. eds.: The Grid: Blueprint for a New Computing Infrastructure, Morgan Kaufmann (1998)
13. Desplat J.C., Hardy J., Antonioletti M., Nabrzyski J., Stroinski M., Meyer N: Grid Service Requirements. ENACTS report (2002)

Author Index

Lecture Notes in Computer Science

For information about Vols. 1–2837

please contact your bookseller or Springer-Verlag

Vol. 2892: F. Dau, The Logic System of Concept Graphs with Negation. XI, 213 pages. 2003. (Subseries LNAI).

Vol. 2891: J. Lee, M. Barley (Eds.), Intelligent Agents and Multi-Agent Systems. X, 215 pages. 2003. (Subseries LNAI).

Vol. 2890: M. Broy, A.V. Zamulin (Eds.), Perspectives of System Informatics. XV, 572 pages. 2003.

Vol. 2889: R. Meersman, Z. Tari (Eds.), On The Move to Meaningful Internet Systems 2003: OTM 2003 Workshops. XIX, 1071 pages. 2003.

Vol. 2888: R. Meersman, Z. Tari, D.C. Schmidt (Eds.), On The Move to Meaningful Internet Systems 2003: CoopIS, DOA, and ODBASE. XXI, 1546 pages. 2003.

Vol. 2887: T. Johansson (Ed.), Fast Software Encryption. IX, 397 pages. 2003.

Vol. 2886: I. Nyström, G. Sanniti di Baja, S. Svensson (Eds.), Discrete Geometry for Computer Imagery. XII, 556 pages. 2003.

Vol. 2885: J.S. Dong, J. Woodcock (Eds.), Formal Methods and Software Engineering. XI, 683 pages. 2003.

Vol. 2884: E. Najm, U. Nestmann, P. Stevens (Eds.), Formal Methods for Open Object-Based Distributed Systems. X, 293 pages. 2003.

Vol. 2883: J. Schaeffer, M. Müller, Y. Björnsson (Eds.), Computers and Games. XI, 431 pages. 2003.

Vol. 2882: D. Veit, Matchmaking in Electronic Markets. XV, 180 pages. 2003. (Subseries LNAI).

Vol. 2881: E. Horlait, T. Magedanz, R.H. Glitho (Eds.), Mobile Agents for Telecommunication Applications. IX, 297 pages. 2003.

Vol. 2880: H.L. Bodlaender (Ed.), Graph-Theoretic Concepts in Computer Science. XI, 386 pages. 2003.

Vol. 2879: R.E. Ellis, T.M. Peters (Eds.), Medical Image Computing and Computer-Assisted Intervention - MICCAI 2003. XXXIV, 1003 pages. 2003.

Vol. 2878: R.E. Ellis, T.M. Peters (Eds.), Medical Image Computing and Computer-Assisted Intervention - MICCAI 2003. XXXIII, 819 pages. 2003.

Vol. 2877: T. Böhme, G. Heyer, H. Unger (Eds.), Innovative Internet Community Systems. VIII, 263 pages. 2003.

Vol. 2876: M. Schroeder, G. Wagner (Eds.), Rules and Rule Markup Languages for the Semantic Web. VII, 173 pages. 2003.

Vol. 2875: E. Aarts, R. Collier, E.v. Loenen, B.d. Ruyter (Eds.), Ambient Intelligence. XI, 432 pages. 2003.

Vol. 2874: C. Priami (Ed.), Global Computing. XIX, 255 pages. 2003.

Vol. 2871: N. Zhong, Z.W. Raś, S. Tsumoto, E. Suzuki (Eds.), Foundations of Intelligent Systems. XV, 697 pages. 2003. (Subseries LNAI).

Vol. 2870: D. Fensel, K.P. Sycara, J. Mylopoulos (Eds.), The Semantic Web - ISWC 2003. XV, 931 pages. 2003.

Vol. 2869: A. Yazici, C. Şener (Eds.), Computer and Information Sciences - ISCIS 2003. XIX, 1110 pages. 2003.

Vol. 2868: P. Perner, R. Brause, H.-G. Holzhütter (Eds.), Medical Data Analysis. VIII, 127 pages. 2003.

Vol. 2866: J. Akiyama, M. Kano (Eds.), Discrete and Computational Geometry. VIII, 285 pages. 2003.

Vol. 2865: S. Pierre, M. Barbeau, E. Kranakis (Eds.), Ad-Hoc, Mobile, and Wireless Networks. X, 293 pages. 2003.

Vol. 2864: A.K. Dey, A. Schmidt, J.F. McCarthy (Eds.), UbiComp 2003: Ubiquitous Computing. XVII, 368 pages. 2003.

Vol. 2863: P. Stevens, J. Whittle, G. Booch (Eds.), "UML" 2003 - The Unified Modeling Language. XIV, 415 pages. 2003.

Vol. 2860: D. Geist, E. Tronci (Eds.), Correct Hardware Design and Verification Methods. XII, 426 pages. 2003.

Vol. 2859: B. Apolloni, M. Marinaro, R. Tagliaferri (Eds.), Neural Nets. X, 376 pages. 2003.

Vol. 2857: M.A. Nascimento, E.S. de Moura, A.L. Oliveira (Eds.), String Processing and Information Retrieval. XI, 379 pages. 2003.

Vol. 2856: M. Smirnov (Ed.), Quality of Future Internet Services. IX, 293 pages. 2003.

Vol. 2855: R. Alur, I. Lee (Eds.), Embedded Software. X, 373 pages. 2003.

Vol. 2854: J. Hoffmann, Utilizing Problem Structure in Planing. XIII, 251 pages. 2003. (Subseries LNAI).

Vol. 2853: M. Jeckle, L.-J. Zhang (Eds.), Web Services - ICWS-Europe 2003. VIII, 227 pages. 2003.

Vol. 2852: F.S. de Boer, M.M. Bonsangue, S. Graf, W.-P. de Roever (Eds.), Formal Methods for Components and Objects. VIII, 509 pages. 2003.

Vol. 2851: C. Boyd, W. Mao (Eds.), Information Security. XI, 453 pages. 2003.

Vol. 2849: N. García, L. Salgado, J.M. Martínez (Eds.), Visual Content Processing and Representation. XII, 352 pages. 2003.

Vol. 2848: F.E. Fich (Ed.), Distributed Computing. X, 367 pages. 2003.

Vol. 2847: R.d. Lemos, T.S. Weber, J.B. Camargo Jr. (Eds.), Dependable Computing. XIV, 371 pages. 2003.

Vol. 2846: J. Zhou, M. Yung, Y. Han (Eds.), Applied Cryptography and Network Security. XI, 436 pages. 2003.

Vol. 2845: B. Christianson, B. Crispo, J.A. Malcolm, M. Roe (Eds.), Security Protocols. VIII, 243 pages. 2004.

Vol. 2844: J.A. Jorge, N. Jardim Nunes, J. Falcão e Cunha (Eds.), Interactive Systems. Design, Specification, and Verification. XIII, 429 pages. 2003.

Vol. 2843: G. Grieser, Y. Tanaka, A. Yamamoto (Eds.), Discovery Science. XII, 504 pages. 2003. (Subseries LNAI).

Vol. 2842: R. Gavaldá, K.P. Jantke, E. Takimoto (Eds.), Algorithmic Learning Theory. XI, 313 pages. 2003. (Subseries LNAI).

Vol. 2841: C. Blundo, C. Laneve (Eds.), Theoretical Computer Science. XI, 397 pages. 2003.

Vol. 2840: J. Dongarra, D. Laforenza, S. Orlando (Eds.), Recent Advances in Parallel Virtual Machine and Message Passing Interface. XVIII, 693 pages. 2003.

Vol. 2839: A. Marshall, N. Agoulmine (Eds.), Management of Multimedia Networks and Services. XIV, 532 pages. 2003.

Vol. 2838: N. Lavrač, D. Gamberger, L. Todorovski, H. Blockeel (Eds.), Knowledge Discovery in Databases: PKDD 2003. XVI, 508 pages. 2003. (Subseries LNAI).